JACK QUARTER, LAURIE MOOK,
AND ANN ARMSTRONG

Understanding the Social Economy

A Canadian Perspective

UNIVERSITY OF TORONTO PRESS
Toronto Buffalo London

Toronto Buffalo London
www.utppublishing.com
Printed in Canada

ISBN 978-0-8020-9695-1 (cloth)
ISBN 978-0-8020-9645-6 (paper)

Printed on acid-free, 100% post-consumer recycled paper with vegetable-based inks.

Library and Archives Canada Cataloguing in Publication

Quarter, Jack, 1941–
Understanding the social economy : a Canadian perspective / Jack Quarter, Laurie Mook, Ann Armstrong.

Includes bibliographical references and index.
ISBN 978-0-8020-9695-1 (bound) ISBN 978-0-8020-9645-6 (pbk.)

1. Community development – Canada. 2. Cooperative societies – Canada. 3. Nonprofit organizations – Canada. 4. Canada – Social policy. 5. Economics – Canada – Sociological aspects. I. Mook, Laurie II. Armstrong, Ann, 1951– III. Title

HD2769.2.C3Q37 2009 306.30971 C2009-904054-9

University of Toronto Press acknowledges the financial assistance to its publishing program of the Canada Council for the Arts and the Ontario Arts Council.

University of Toronto Press acknowledges the financial support for its publishing activities of the Government of Canada through the Book Publishing Industry Development Program (BPIDP).

UNDERSTANDING THE SOCIAL ECONOMY: A CANADIAN PERSPECTIVE

In *Understanding the Social Economy*, Jack Quarter, Laurie Mook, and Ann Armstrong examine a wide array of organizations founded upon a social mission – social enterprises, nonprofits, co-operatives, credit unions, and community development associations. Organized under the framework of the 'social economy,' this comprehensive study addresses an area often overlooked in the business curricula despite its important role in Canada's economy.

Suitable for courses addressing community economic development, co-operatives, and nonprofit organizations, the volume presents a unique set of case studies as well as chapters on organizational design and governance, social finance and social accounting, and accountability. The examples provide useful context and allow for an in-depth examination of the relationships between Canada's social infrastructure and the public and private sectors. A much-needed work on an important but neglected facet of business studies, *Understanding the Social Economy* is an invaluable resource for the classroom and for participants working in the social sector.

JACK QUARTER is a professor and co-director of the Social Economy Centre at the Ontario Institute for Studies in Education, University of Toronto.

LAURIE MOOK is the co-director of the Social Economy Centre at the Ontario Institute for Studies in Education, University of Toronto.

ANN ARMSTRONG is the director of the Social Enterprise Initiative at the Rotman School of Management, University of Toronto.

Contents

Foreword

The social economy has always been with us; for as long as there have been government and for-profit enterprise, there have been people who have sought to advance the broad prosperity of our society from the peripheries of these two economic behemoths. These people, by and large, recognized a pressing social need and worked diligently – whether as part of a non-profit, co-operative, community organization, or social enterprise – to address it outside the standard strictures of business and government. They were typically driven not, as some have conjectured, by a hatred of profits or by bleeding-heart liberalism, but by a recognition that there is some necessary work government and business are not equipped or inclined to do effectively. In embracing this work, the social sector created a third way. This is the heart of the social economy and it is, as I say, nothing new.

What is new is our collective understanding and categorization of this social sector, and our explicit acknowledgment that it is worthy of study and analysis on its own merits. Until relatively recently, the social sector, and thus its true impact on our society, was largely hidden. The myriad participants in what has now come to be recognized as the social sector were heretofore lumped into awkward subcategories of the public and private sectors, treated as an insignificant afterthought or ignored entirely by academia, industry, and policymakers. But in the past decade, we have finally come to see the sector in its collective strength; it is finally being recognized for its size, its economic importance, its social impact, and its unique contribution to society.

A text like *Understanding the Social Economy: A Canadian Perspective*, which takes a comprehensive view of the sector as a whole, is an important next step in deepening our understanding of the social economy. I am particularly pleased that my University of Toronto colleagues, Ann Armstrong from the Rotman School of Management along with Laurie Mook and Jack Quarter from the Ontario Institute for Studies in Education (OISE), have emerged at the forefront of this burgeoning field. In this text, they have created a usable and effective guidebook to understanding the Canadian social economy in the broad, global context. By thoughtfully combining commentary, sector analysis, and case studies, they have usefully blended the 30,000 foot overview of the mountain with a detailed examination of what is happening at the rock face. In doing so, they have devised a helpful classification scheme and identified critical issues that will lay the foundation for further research in the field. This text therefore represents a vital step to increasing the reach and effectiveness of the sector, as its participants continue to shape our society for the better.

Roger Martin
Dean, Rotman School of Management

Preface

The primary business of business is to make money, and not surprisingly business schools focus on the market as that is where businesses make money. While this focus is understandable, it does exclude important components of our society that can also involve money, but not as its primary focus. The purpose of this book is to bring to the fore Canada's social economy, an umbrella concept for the many types of organizations created to meet a social need but also involving economic aspects such as the payment of wages and benefits to employees, the purchase of supplies, and in some cases, the exchange of services in the market. As is noted in chapter 1, Statistics Canada (2006a) estimates that non-profits alone contributed $80.3 billion to Canada's Gross Domestic Product (GDP), or 7.1 per cent. This figure does not include the contributions of co-operatives and credit unions, other major players in the social economy. In brief, organizations that are started for social reasons do make significant economic contributions. Even if the social dimension is perceived as being part of another domain, or an externality as economists may refer to it, there is an economic component to organizations established for social purposes that should be acknowledged.

There is another equally important point to this argument: it is naive to view businesses whose focus is making money apart from their social responsibilities. Within business schools, this issue is labelled in many ways, as is discussed in chapter 2. However, the common denominator of the differing labels is that businesses are embedded within a society and have responsibilities that go beyond simply making money. The movement for corporate social responsibility (CSR) differs from the focus of this book in so far as the goal of CSR is to make businesses more conscious of society and the environment and of how these dimensions are not simply externalities but can be part of good business practice. This point bears mentioning because it underscores an underlying theme of this book: it is not possible to segregate the economic from the social. Our focus on the social economy differs from corporate social responsibility, but the difference is one of degree rather than one of dichotomy.

Within society, the social economy is a bridging concept for a vast array of organizations that form a social infrastructure. A society without social service agencies, social clubs, religious congregations, non-profit theatrical groups, trade unions, and professional associations is unimaginable – it is not a society. The organizations in the social economy may also be viewed as a laboratory through which ideas that have significance for business are experimented with. Among the cases presented in *Understanding the Social Economy* are examples of worker co-operatives, businesses that are owned in common and democratically operated by the people that work in them. Such organizations stretch the notion of employee participation that has been embraced by forward-thinking managers. Is the democratic workplace an idea with legs that can be adopted more generally? This same question can be asked about the social economy – is it far-fetched to think of businesses that balance their commercial and social objectives?

The book is organized in three parts:

- Part 1 consists of chapter 1, and provides an overview to the social economy. This chapter defines the social economy, sets out its underlying characteristics, presents some basic data, and discusses the components of the social economy. The chapter emphasizes that organizations in the social economy, while having distinct characteristics, interact with the private and public sectors in many ways. The different forms of interaction are illustrated in Part 2.
- Part 2 is a typology of the major components of the social economy and how they interact with the private and public sectors. It consists of five chapters, one devoted to each major component: social economy businesses that earn their revenues from the market; community economic development (CED), or organizations in the nexus between the market, state, and social economy; social enterprises, that is, businesses serving groups with disabilities and other social disadvantages; public sector non-profits or organizations that overlap between the social economy and the state; and civil

society organizations, or the vast array of associations that serve the needs of a membership and the public.
- Part 3 consists of three chapters that each address critical issues related to organizations in the social economy: organizational design and governance, financing, and social accounting and accountability. These chapters are somewhat different than those in the first two parts in that they raise problems that are of common concern to organizations in the social economy and consider ways that these may be resolved.

Understanding the Social Economy is designed to create an appreciation of the many contributions of the vast array of social economy organizations and to understand the challenges that they face. We discuss basic concepts that apply to this topic and utilize many cases studies – both mini-cases that are embedded within each chapter and major case studies at the end of the chapter – to help illustrate the concepts that are discussed in the chapters. While there are other books on the social economy, the unique feature of *Understanding the Social Economy* is that it attempts to relate this field to business schools and thereby hopes to overcome its neglect. This text comes with additional materials available at www.utppublishing.com to assist course instructors, as well as a bibliography and index. At the end of each chapter there are discussion questions, and we suggest that readers review the end-of-chapter questions prior to reading each chapter.

Acknowledgments

We would like to thank the many people who have worked with us on *Understanding the Social Economy: A Canadian Perspective*. Jennifer DiDomenico, editor of Business and Economics at University of Toronto Press, has been an invaluable support from the beginning in helping us see through this project, always available and always generous with her time and her thoughtful suggestions. We would also like to thank other staff at the University of Toronto Press who have assisted us – Patricia Simoes, editorial assistant; Anne Laughlin, managing editor; and our copyeditor, Kate Baltais, whose attention to detail was extraordinarily beneficial. Thanks to Greg Devitt of Greg Devitt Designs for the creative cover, and our gratitude to Monica Kronfli for her work on the index.

We extend our appreciation to Roger Martin, dean of the Rotman School of Management, for taking time to write the foreword for this book. We also thank Peter Pauly, vice-dean at the Rotman School, for his support of scholarship on the social economy.

In order to write the book, we had to collect information from organizations in the social economy. Many people were forthcoming with information and ideas that helped us with this book. We lack sufficient space to do justice to the entire group, but we single out in particular the primary contacts for the end-of-chapter case studies and some of the shorter cases: Patricia Barclay, president of The Big Carrot; Andy Morrison, CEO of Arctic Co-operatives Ltd.; Terri Proulx, community business counsellor, Winnipeg Social Purchasing Portal; Andrew Macdonald, manager of Social Enterprise, the Print Shop at Eva's Phoenix; Reg Winsor, executive director, Newfoundland and Labrador Arts Council; Ben Hudson, internal communications specialist, Mountain Equipment Co-op; Michel Labbé, president, Options for Homes; Geoff

Cape, executive director, Evergreen; Marty Donkervoort, general manager, Inner City Renovation; Carolyn Lemon, founder and board member of Common Ground Co-operative; Nancy Neamtan, president and CEO of Le Chantier de l'économie sociale; Jolene MacNeil, administrator, Cape Breton Labourers' Benevolent Fund; Eric Plato, director of finance, Frontier College; Paul Wilkinson, organizer, Quint Community Development Corporation; and Jorge Sousa, University of Alberta, for his assistance with the Atkinson Housing Co-operative mini-case.

The research that went into this book was generously supported by funds from the Social Sciences and Humanities Research Council of Canada (SSHRC) through the Social Economy Suite, and in particular the Community-University Research Alliance for Southern Ontario's Social Economy, housed at the Social Economy Centre of the University of Toronto.

We also want to recognize the personal support of our families and friends.

We dedicate this book to the tens of thousands of organizations that form Canada's social economy.

Jack Quarter
Laurie Mook
Ann Armstrong

Cases for Analysis

A Closer Look (Mini Case Studies)

Chapter 7

Chapter 8

Chapter 9

Tables and Figures

Tables

Figures

PART 1

An Overview of the Social Economy

1 An Introduction to Canada's Social Economy

A Closer Look: Inner City Renovation Inc.

Inner City Renovation Inc. is a business with a social mission (a social enterprise in the classification system used in this book), that creates quality jobs in the construction industry in Winnipeg for persons on the margins of the labour force, about half of Aboriginal origin (Donkervoort, 2007a). Inner City Renovation Inc., set up in 2002, is currently the only operating unit of Inner City Development Inc., which in turn is owned by two non-profit organizations: Community Ownership Solutions and Social Capital Partners. The mission of Inner City Development is to create quality jobs for low-income Manitobans. Among the company's goals are: good quality wages; benefits with supplemental health care; education and training (both on the job and in the classroom); opportunity for advancement; and the opportunity for employees to take part in workplace decision-making and ownership of the enterprise. By 2008, Inner City had twenty-five full-time year-round employees and annual revenue approaching $2 million.

In order for Inner City Development to achieve its goals, it has had to build a broad coalition of support from business, labour, community organizations, Aboriginal organizations, and educational institutions. Inner City Development identified what were many old, boarded-up homes in the inner city of Winnipeg, and set up Inner City Renovation in response to this opportunity. The organizational support arrangements have varied over the years, but an important one was initial financing and technical assistance from Social Capital Partners in Toronto, led by Bill Young, an investor and philanthropist (Donkervoort, 2007b). In addition, there is a part-time social worker who is available to assist the employees. Inner City Development is relatively self-sustaining in that in 2006 and 2007 it broke even. However, it does receives subsidies: one from the province for education and training, which is available to any business that provides training to its employees; and a second in that Marty Donkervoort, the general manager and the visionary who planned the business, has his salary paid from a separate organization, Community Ownership Solutions, a related non-profit with a charitable registration. If the cost of these supports was transferred to Inner City, it would be in the red. Nevertheless, this company represents a good example of combining business and social mission, in this case creating gainful employment in inner city Winnipeg for low income residents who have had a history of chronic unemployment.

Inner City Renovation Inc. is but one of a vast social infrastructure in Canada that we label as the social economy. In our view, the social economy is broad and embraces an immense array of organizations with a social mission including market-based organizations, those overlapping substantially with the public sector, and civil society organizations serving members and in some cases the public. It can also include organizations that engage in non-monetary exchange or what is commonly referred to as the informal or gift economy (Cheal, 1988; Klamer, 2003). Our definition of the social economy casts a broad net:

> *Social economy* is a bridging concept for organizations that have social objectives central to their mission and their practice, and either have explicit economic objectives or generate some economic value through the services they provide and purchases that they undertake.

There are two central concepts in this definition: social mission and economic value. Our conception of social mission includes environmental goals since these are an expression of members of a society, and therefore one form of social objective. Other definitions of the social economy are more focused, for example, some privilege market activities and focus on what we label as social enterprises (see, e.g., see Borzaga and Defourny, 2001; Defourny, 1999; Defourny and Monzon Campos, 1992). For instance, in Belgium, the concept of *social market economy* focuses on organizations that earn most of their revenues from the sale of goods and services (Walloon Council of the Social Market Economy, 2008). In this text, we refer to such organizations as social economy businesses (chapter 2). However, we argue in this and subsequent chapters that it is inappropriate to privilege market activities in reference to the social economy, as there are many examples of organizations that do not exchange their services on the market yet generate economic value, either explicitly as through the purchase of supplies or implicitly in the imputed value of their services. Indeed, much of our research has involved illustrating the economic value of volunteers (Mook, Quarter, and Richmond, 2007). Even though they are unpaid labour, they are central to the workforce of the social economy and of critical importance to the broader society. The early twentieth century economist, Arthur Pigou, pointed out the flawed logic of emphasizing market exchange when he mused that if bachelors en masse married their housekeepers, and assuming that they did the same work but no longer received wages, it would have a negative effect on the gross domestic product. This is known as Pigou's Paradox.

There are differing interpretations of the social economy, and in general they can be grouped into those that focus on distinct organizational forms (non-profit, co-operatives, credit unions, mutual associations) and those that focus on distinct criteria or norms that differentiate organizations in the social economy from society as a whole (Borzaga and Defourny, 2001; Spear, forthcoming).

In francophone parts of Europe, the social economy is seen to include co-operatives (including credit unions), mutual societies, associations, and social enterprises (CIRIEC, 2007). Other forms of non-profits such as those without earned revenues and other organizations relying heavily on government funding and influenced in part by government policies are excluded; as will be seen, later in this book, this group of organizations is labelled as public sector non-*profits* in our framework. The francophone European tradition has also been picked up in Quebec, where le Chantier de l'économie sociale is the apex organization for the social economy (Mendell and Neamtan, forthcoming). Le Chantier's characterization of social organizations was set out as follows at the Economic and Employment Summit in Quebec in 1996: 'The mission is services to members and community and not profit-oriented; management is independent of government; workers and/or users use a democratic process for decision-making; people have priority over capital; and participation, empowerment, individual and collective responsibility are key values' (Chantier de l'économie sociale, 2005).

Some argue that the social economy in Quebec has the characteristics of a social movement in that it is based on a broad coalition of organizations and it is impacting government policies (Mendell and Neamtan, forthcoming; Mendell and Rouzier, 2006). A social movement perspective is reflected in the statement adopted at the Social and Solidarity Economy Summit in Montreal in 2006: 'We, actors of the social economy from the community, co-operative and mutual benefit movements and associations, from cultural, environmental and social movements, unions, international cooperation and local and regional development organizations, affirm with pride and determination our commitment to building a social and solidarity economy locally, regionally, nationally and internationally' (Chantier, 2008).

The vision is not simply to strengthen organizations in Quebec's social economy but to build a new society 'locally, regionally, nationally and internationally.' This vision is also expressed by Quebecers Shragge and Fontan (2002: 9) who argue that 'a social economy implies a basic reorientation of the whole economy and related institutions.' In this book, we do not treat the social economy as a social movement, but as a unique set of institutions that are part of a broader society. Nevertheless, we recognize that the social economy could evolve into a social movement.

The European Commission (2008) takes a broader view than the francophone tradition and does not impose the same restrictions on the inclusion of some forms of non-profits as in francophone Europe and Quebec as set out by CIRIEC (also known as the Centre International de Recherches et d'Information sur l'Économie Publique, Sociale et Coopérative) and le Chantier. As will become apparent, this broader view is embraced in this book. The differences of opinion have to do in part with the fact that some forms of non-profits have a closed membership that can be self-perpetuating rather than representative of a broader membership. From our perspective, as is argued subsequently in this chapter, democracy is part of a broader concept, *civic engage-*

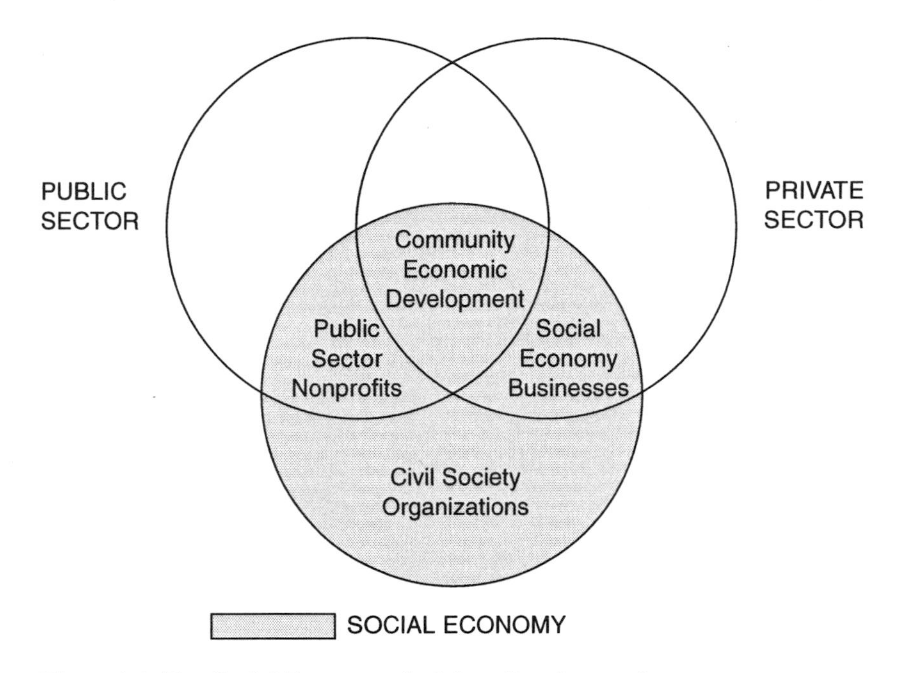

Figure 1.1 The Social Economy: An Interactive Approach

ment, and many organizations that might not fit the criteria for democracy still serve as important points for members of a community to engage in socially constructive projects.

Similar to other theorists (e.g., Bouchard, Ferreton, and Michaud, 2006; Pestoff, 1998), we situate the social economy in relation to other parts of the economy. However, our framework has one additional feature that makes it unique: it also focuses on how organizations in the social economy interact with other parts of society. For that reason, we use a Venn diagram to illustrate the relationship and refer to our framework as *an interactive approach* (see Figure 1.1).

The Venn diagram emphasizes the dynamic interaction between the social economy and the private and public sectors. The boundaries, as shall be illustrated subsequently, are fluid; rather than viewing the social economy as an entity unto itself, it is presented in its relationship with the rest of society, for the organizations in the social economy receive support from government, from private sector businesses, and from individuals who work in other parts of the economy, many of them being members of organizations within the social economy. More importantly, organizations in the social economy are an infrastructure for society as a whole. It is unimaginable to think of society without the tens of thousands of mutual associations through which people interact and without the many public service organizations that assist those with special challenges or marginalized groups.

Our emphasis in the chapters that follow is on how the various players in the social economy interact with the rest of society. The argument to be made is that organizations of the social economy interact in differing ways and serve many functions in relation to government and the private sector. In other words, the social economy is by no means uniform.

As will become evident in the chapters that follow, the organizations in the social economy tend to associate with each other around common purposes. Often there is an apex or umbrella organization that becomes the voice of member organizations with a common bond of association, for example, the Canadian Environmental Network serves that function for environmental organizations across Canada; the Canadian Labour Congress (CLC) for unions; the Canadian Ethnocultural Council for ethnocultural groups; and the Canadian Conference of the Arts for arts groups. The list is extensive. As will be illustrated, one organization's bonds of association can extend into many networks, or put differently, the organization may find many commonalities with many other organizations. A religious organization may also be an ethnocultural organization and be part of networks related to reducing poverty (e.g., Kairos Canada). However, organizations do not necessarily associate with each other because they are part of a common sector called the social economy or the non-profit or voluntary sector. The one notable exception, the social economy in Quebec, as will be discussed in greater detail in chapter 3, appears to have a common cause, perhaps even a social movement (Favreau, 2006; Mendell and Rouzier, 2006; Mendell and Neamtan, forthcoming). Among co-operatives too, as will be discussed in chapter 2, there are linkages that suggest that there is a co-operative sector, although any semblance to a social movement (e.g., the 'co-operative commonwealth') could be argued to be an artefact of history. However, throughout the social economy, the primary bonds among organizations are related to their functions, and that is how they coalesce. The approach taken in this text is to characterize the social economy as a classification system or taxonomy, with a broad range of organizations, and to understand the richness of this mosaic and the varying functions that these organizations serve in interacting with other parts of society.

Even though we shall argue in the discussion that follows that there are some normative characteristics of the social economy, and that some organizations fit within it and others do not, the boundaries, as will be discussed in subsequent chapters, are fluid. Through attempting to understand these boundaries, greater clarity can be achieved about which organizations are viewed as fitting in.

Although different in their services, size, location, sources of funding, and in many other ways, all of the organizations in the social economy have a *social mission* that guides their program and policies. They may operate in the market but in all cases their market orientation combines a social mission.

Components of the Social Economy

In the overlap between the social economy and the private sector, as shown in Figure 1.1, we find social economy businesses, or organizations with a social mission that earn either all or a sizable portion of their revenues from the marketplace. These organizations (discussed in detail in chapter 2) function effectively in the private market, and without external supports such as government funding. The bulk of social economy businesses are co-operatives with shares that earn their revenues from the market, for example, credit unions, marketing co-operatives (largely in farming, but in other endeavours as well), and food retailing co-operatives. Some are commercial non-profits such as automobile associations, Blue Cross, and recreational organizations such as YM-YWCAs. There is a debate in the literature about whether to use non-profit or not-for-profit; the same is true for legislation, as some jurisdictions use not-for-profit. In this text, we use non-profit throughout, and it should be viewed as synonymous with not-for-profit. It should be noted that other terminology is used in reference to non-profit organizations including non-government organization (or NGO), a trust, a society.

The section in Figure 1.1 showing the overlap between the social economy and the private and public sectors involves organizations engaged in community economic development (CED). This is an amorphous category of organizations that function within the market, but do so according to different values, a central one being *community service*. Chapter 3 discusses community economic development, which is defined by the Canadian CED Network as, 'a community-based and community-directed process that explicitly combines social and economic development and fosters the economic, social, ecological and cultural well being of communities' (CCEDNet, 2007). In Canada, CED groups are increasingly in so-called underdeveloped areas, and they tend to rely on government funding (either grants or contracts), in particular in the formative period, but they do also attempt to achieve independence by exchanging their services in the market. We have separated this group from social economy businesses, as discussed in chapter 2, because of their reliance on government funding and other forms of social support.

Like CED organizations, social enterprises earn revenues from the market, but they also rely on government and foundation programs. As discussed in chapter 4, social enterprises (sometimes referred to as social purpose businesses) employ people with extraordinary challenges, for example, psychiatric and intellectual disabilities, racial groups who have experienced discrimination historically, or very recent immigrants who have difficulty finding employment. Other social enterprises have the appearance of a conventional business, but are owned by a non-profit. Their surplus income may either help to subsidize the non-profit to fulfil its social mission or alternatively it may receive subsidies from the non-profit, one example being Inner City Renovation (referred to above). Businesses owned by Aboriginal communities also appear here.

In Figure 1.1, organizations shown in the overlapping area between the social economy and the public sector are labelled as public sector non-profits (see chapter 5). Public sector non-profits interact with government in differing ways, some being very closely aligned and others being relatively independent. These are not to be confused with those labelled as community economic development, organizations that also involve some overlap with the public sector but in combination with the private sector. Although some public sector non-profits may earn revenues from the market, government is a major stakeholder and provides substantial funding, in the form of either grants or contracts, and in some cases, substantial policy guidance. Public sector non-profits also typically have a charitable status to facilitate the receipt of donations. Unlike CED organizations, public sector non-profits are not attempting to become completely independent of government, and given the nature of their services (e.g., higher education and health care), it is unlikely that they could. As government has moved away from the direct provision of services, it has entered into agreements with non-profits that involve a transfer of funds and some policy direction, the assumption being that the non-profits are closer to the community and in a better position to deliver the service(s). This relationship is referred to as a partnership by Salamon (1987, 1995) in that it takes advantage of the strengths of both government and non-profits. Others view the relationship more critically, and emphasize government's intent to save money (Smith and Lipsky, 1993).

Organizations in the section *civil society* in Figure 1.1 are the most numerous of the social economy sub-groupings (see chapter 6). They include two types: non-profit mutual associations and civil society organizations. Non-profit mutual associations serve a defined membership, the members having a mutual interest that they seek to satisfy through the organization. Mutual associations can be professional groups, non-certified workplace associations, social clubs, burial societies, religious congregations, ethnocultural groups, business associations, unions, and so on. Their members often work in the private and public sectors, and sometimes these organizations define themselves around functions that relate to the private or public sectors, for example, the members of a union. Often members of these mutual societies intersect with each other on more than one dimension, for example, as in the Association of Polish Engineers in Canada (2007). Also, many mutual associations are unincorporated, though they still may have a formal structure with a constitution, for example, union locals, tenant associations, neighbourhood groups, and home and school associations. Increasingly, mutual associations are being formed online, a point that we will discuss in chapter 6.

Non-profit mutual associations are similar to co-operatives in their membership structure, voting arrangements (one member/one vote), and their general orientation of serving the interests of members. However, unlike most co-operatives these organizations tend not to have explicit economic objectives, excepting business associations representing private sector interests. Non-profit mutual associations exist to meet the social needs of their members, and by providing a context in which people sharing a common interest can engage with each other, they contribute to their members' needs and to the broader society.

The second grouping within the category civil society is non-profit member-based associations serving the public. These organizations are funded entirely by donors, membership fees, and fundraising events, and volunteers are a substantial portion of their workforce. While these are not mutual associations in that their orientation is to the public rather than to their membership, they are also neither public sector nor market based. For want of a better label, this group is referred to as *civil society organizations*. There are some striking examples in human rights such as Amnesty International, in basic service provision such as Habitat for Humanity, and in the many health care foundations that raise funds for medical research into, for example, breast cancer and heart disease. These health care organizations (like the Canadian Cancer Society) combine a public interest with member self-interest. Many advocacy groups fit into this category. Even though they are funded by members who may also serve as volunteers, their orientation is to the public and to changing public policy. Groups associated with the environment, feminist issues, human rights, and peace are common examples. Such groups might be better classified as sociopolitical, but unlike political parties that contest elections, they are primarily associated with broader social movements that lobby for social change outside of the electoral process.

Underlying Characteristics

Organizations of the social economy share some common characteristics that will be discussed under four criteria: (1) social objectives in their mission; (2) social ownership; (3) volunteer/social participation; and (4) civic engagement. These criteria represent an effort to define the social component in the social economy and differentiate organizations in the social economy from those in the private and public sectors. However, in reality, the line between social economy organizations and the private and public sectors is not always clear and is subject to debate, as discussed in Part 2 of this book.

Social Objectives

As stated, organizations in the social economy are set up to meet social objectives that, as a rule, are written into the charter of the organization. The social objectives are not add-ons, as when a conventional business decides to embrace *corporate social responsibility*, but central to the organization's mission from its inception. Among organizations in the social economy, these social objectives take on different forms, depending on whether the organization is pursuing charitable objectives, meeting the needs of a membership (mutual aid), or competing in the market for its revenues.

CHARITABLE OBJECTIVES

Charitable objectives are one expression of an organization's social mission. Since their religious origins in the Middle Ages in England, charitable organizations have had a lengthy tradition of social giving (Hopkins, 1987). Members of religious organizations believed that they were furthering the purpose of their religion by assisting those in need. As charitable activities broadened from their narrow religious base, English society attempted to spell out what was permissible, as reflected in the Statute of Charitable Uses (or Statute of Elizabeth) of 1601: 'Relief of aged, impotent and poor people; the maintenance of sick and maimed soldiers and mariners, schools of learning, free schools and scholars in universities; the repair of bridges, ports, havens, causeways, churches, sea banks and highways; the education and preferment of orphans; the relief, stock or maintenance of houses of correction; marriages of poor maids; supportation, aid and help of young tradesmen, handicraftsmen, and persons decayed; the relief or redemption of prisoners or captives; and the aid or ease of any poor inhabitants covering payments of fifteens, setting out of soldiers, and other taxes' (cited in Monahan and Roth, 2000: 28).

That statute reflects the beginnings of the secularization of charity from its religious roots and, to a degree, from a strict focus on the relief of poverty. The growth of social work as a profession reflects this secularization of services with a charitable purpose.

The concept of charity has been broadened from its original notion of relieving poverty and now includes such social objectives as the advancement of education, the advancement of religion, and other purposes beneficial to the community. These objectives have permitted organizations with such functions as international aid, education, youth programs, health care, family services, culture and the arts, and heritage and environmental protection to be classified as having a charitable status. Therefore, a distinction can be made between charity as a community's response to those in dire need and organizations with broader charitable objectives (meeting the criteria required for charitable status under the taxation laws that permit donors to achieve a tax benefit). Although modern charities are of both types, organizations meeting the broader criteria are more commonplace. This change can be called the universalization of charity.

MUTUAL AID

While charitable organizations often involve the delivery of assistance by the more fortunate to the less fortunate, non-profits serving a membership (mutual associations) and co-operatives are based on the principle of self-help or mutual aid (Craig, 1993). The members of these organizations share a common bond of association (e.g., a common heritage, occupation, or location) and a need that they attempt to meet through a service to themselves. The organizations have their roots among exploited groups in society (MacPherson, 1979) but, unlike the recipients of charity, they have sufficient strength to help themselves. Some of the oldest associations in the New World were mutual benefit societies in which people, often of common religion, ethnocultural heritage, or geographical origin (a city from which they emigrated), arranged services like insurance and burials for members. In rural areas, farmers formed mutual property-and-casualty insurance organizations because of difficulties in obtaining affordable services. Similarly, credit unions were started in the latter part of the nineteenth century in Germany and, at the beginning of the twentieth century, through Catholic parishes in Quebec, because of either the unavailability of consumer loans or usurious interest rates (Kenyon, 1976). About the same time, farm-marketing co-operatives were started to enable members to obtain a fair price for their products and to make the basic purchases (MacPherson, 1979).

Over the years, people with common bonds such as a place of work, profession, business, religion, or ethnic identity have formed non-profit mutual associations and co-operatives. While some of these adhere to the tradition of being organized around exploited groups (a union local or workplace association), others simply involve a common social interest (a historical society), a shared experience (the members of a Legion club who have fought in a war), a profession, or some other commonality, including a privileged status such as the members of a golf club or a business association. The bonds of association might differ, but such organizations are set up to meet social and cultural objectives.

SOCIAL VERSUS COMMERCIAL OBJECTIVES

It could be argued that by satisfying their customers, a profit-oriented business also meets social objectives. While this argument has some validity, particularly in the service sector, capital invested in profit-oriented businesses, and especially in mature companies (as opposed to small owner-operated firms), has a very weak social commitment. With the exception of small owner-operated enterprises that are tied to a neighbourhood or some larger firms that depend on a particular location for their products (e.g., resource extraction), profit-oriented businesses remain loyal to a community only as long as they obtain a competitive rate of return. When a greater return is possible from other investments or from manufacturing products elsewhere, profit-oriented businesses will shift their loyalties. By comparison, social economy organizations not only regard the service as their priority but also they have loyalties to either a defined community or a defined membership. An apparel manufacturer, for example, may move production to countries where labour rates are cheap, whereas social objectives and the community's location will guide the decisions of a religious body (or any social organization for that matter). In that respect, social organizations differ from the rootless, impersonal structures of mature profit-oriented businesses.

There are profit-oriented businesses with social investment criteria that more closely resemble the practices of organizations in the social economy. For example, a handful of profit-oriented businesses mirror the ownership arrangements of non-profits in that their shares are held in trust and, like non-profits, are owned by no one (Quarter, 2000). Similarly, there are other businesses that are created to carry out a social mission; Newman's Own, which donates to charitable causes all of its after-tax profits ($125 million in twenty years), is one such example (Newman's Own, 2007), as is the British firm, Traidcraft, that assists co-operatives and small producers in poorer countries in gaining a fair price for their products (Evans, 1997). These unusual businesses are discussed in chapter 2.

Even for social organizations, there is a tension between social and commercial objectives that has been heightened by the neoliberal agenda of cutbacks in public funding. For organizations earning their revenues in the market, it is necessary to be competitive, and this may involve matching the standards of profit-oriented businesses. For organizations relying on government funding, there is increasing pressure to compete for contracts and to earn a greater portion of their revenues from other sources (Akingbola, 2002; Smith and Lipsky, 1993). The term *social entrepreneurship* has found its way into the non-profit culture and has influenced how these organizations operate (Dees,

1998). For a social organization to achieve the spirit of its mission, commercial goals should be subsumed within its social objectives. But if these objectives are being sacrificed for commercial success, then the organization is drifting and moving away from the social economy.

Vancity Credit Union is an outstanding example of how an organization can combine a social mission and economic objectives.

A Closer Look: Vancity Credit Union

Vancity (2007), formed in 1946, is Canada's largest credit union with $12.3 billion in assets, more than 381,000 members, and 57 branches throughout Greater Vancouver, the Fraser Valley, and Victoria. Vancity is part of a network of credit unions in communities across Canada that is affiliated with the Credit Union Central of Canada. Another large group is affiliated with le Mouvement des caisses Desjardins, the umbrella organization for credit unions/caisses populaires in francophone Canada. Desjardins (2008) is the largest employer in Quebec, and the sixth largest financial institution in Canada, with assets of $144 billion in 2007. Vancity is very much a business, indeed a highly successful business. However, it is a business with a difference, first because as a co-operative, Vancity's board of directors is elected by its members or users of the service according to the principle of one member/one vote. Vancity applies the co-operative principles of the International Co-operative Alliance, to be discussed in chapter 2. The second factor that makes Vancity distinct is it has strong commitments to the broader community. Perhaps this differentiation between membership and the broader community is artificial because the members live in the broader community and reflect its aspirations. Vancity has emphasized the so-called triple bottom line: financial, social, and environmental. It is the developer for an environmentally leading-edge community in Victoria and the sponsor of a set of investment funds that emphasize socially responsible criteria, the Vancity Circadian Funds. For these reasons, we refer to businesses such as Vancity as *social economy businesses* (see Figure 1.1). As a measure of Vancity's social commitments, the organization has produced a social report since 1997 that carefully audits its social and environmental performance.

Social Ownership

Profit-oriented businesses are pieces of property that belong to their owners, shareholders in the case of publicly traded corporations, and therefore can be bought or sold for personal gain. The shareholders are the primary beneficiaries of profits paid out as dividends and also the beneficiaries of profits that are reinvested in the firm – because retained earnings are likely to enhance the value of the property. The context of private ownership is important for understanding the significance of the distinct ownership arrangements in the social economy. All forms of non-profits, including those with a charitable status, are organizations without shareholders. It is common in the United States to refer to non-profits as *private* (Independent Sector, 1997; Salamon and Anheier, 1997), signifying their independence from government. That descriptor can also be misleading because it implies that non-profits are like private sector businesses. In this book, non-profits are labelled as social to emphasize their distinctiveness from the private and public sectors. Although their assets are a form of property, they belong to no one unless the organization's dissolution clause specifies otherwise. For the dissolution of organizations with charitable status, the usual practice is to pass the assets on to another charity with similar objectives. For example, if a religious congregation closes, the assets normally would go to the umbrella organization. For other non-profits, including co-operatives without shares (e.g., housing, child care, and health care), the normal practice is similar. Co-operatives with shares (e.g., food retail and farm marketing organizations, credit unions) might specify that, in the event of dissolution, the net assets would be divided among the members. When a co-operative or club can be demutualized, and the assets divided among the members, that organization loses some of its distinctiveness from a profit-oriented business. Normally, co-operatives have an indivisible reserve that represents social property available for use by future members, and if they are demutualized, the members receive less than full value for their shares.

However, for social organizations, dissolution for reasons other than financial insolvency is highly unusual. Although such organizations have assets, they do not exist to enhance their members' personal wealth. Whereas personal gain is the hallmark of ownership in the private sector, and share value is a primary consideration in its future disposition, social benefit is the defining characteristic for organizations in the social economy. The purpose of such organizations is service either to members or to the public, and organizational arrangements are undertaken with that objective in mind, not personal gain.

Members of non-profit mutual associations do gain personally from the services of their organization. However, a distinction should be made between financial gain, as when a business is the property of its owners, and social benefit, as in a mutual association. Often the membership of mutual associations could be viewed as a subsection of the public, and just as publicly oriented non-profits focus on a clientele, not all of the public, the same could be said of non-profit mutual associations.

Even where social organizations have shares, as in most co-operatives, they do not serve the same purpose as in a profit-oriented business. Such shares do not reflect the value of the organization or what investors are prepared to pay on the stock market; rather they have a relatively constant value and are comparable to a membership fee (Ellerman, 1990). They can go down in value if a co-operative has financial difficulties, but in general they stay at a constant level (or at an initial value adjusted for inflation). When members leave, the reimbursement normally is the original contribution plus a modest interest rate agreed to by the organization.

Similarly, when a social organization has a year-end surplus, the use of that income is guided by its primary objective, improving and broadening the availability of the service. For co-operatives with shares, surplus earnings may result in a patronage dividend, not based on shareholdings as in the private sector, but either on the use of the service by members or on an egalitarian basis. When organizations in the social economy lose money (i.e., have a year-end deficit), unless the loss can be absorbed through reserves, their service is usually reduced or the cost to patrons is increased. If the losses become too great, the organization may have to close.

Therefore, the financial dynamics of a social organization differ from those of a profit-oriented business. Although some social organizations may hold valuable assets, the concept of ownership as in the private sector is not that applicable. Rather the assets of social organizations can be characterized as a *social dividend* passed from generation to generation. These social dividends are the building blocks of society and are property neither of private individuals nor of government. Private individuals may contribute to creating these building blocks through donations of their wealth; in some cases, vast amounts such as the fortunes of Andrew Carnegie, John D. Rockefeller, and Henry Ford in the United States, or more recently George Soros, Bill and Melinda Gates, and Warren Buffett. Foundations of this size are less well established in Canada, but Philanthropic Foundations Canada indicates that in 2005 there were 2,397 active Canadian grant-making foundations with assets of $13.9 billion that made total grants of over $1.2 billion the previous year (Imagine Canada, 2005; Philanthropic Foundations Canada, 2008). Such donations represent the conversion of private wealth into social wealth, or to the building blocks of the social economy. However, the primary creators of social wealth are the public at large through lesser donations, volunteer participation, and taxes, all of which create the basis for government grants to social organizations.

Whereas the ownership arrangements for social organizations are distinct from those of profit-oriented businesses, the difference from the public sector is not as clear-cut. Government assets are also a form of social property intended to serve the public good. These assets may be part of government departments or the civil service, or they may be held at arm's length through Crown corporations. These corporations are set up to supply a service to the public for such reasons as the government wants some influence over policy or because it is difficult for the private sector to earn a profit. In such corporations, a level of government holds the shares and has the same rights as shareholders in a profit-oriented business. The beneficiary of any profit or any increase in the value of the assets is the government representing the public at large. When a government corporation is privatized, the public interest and not personal gain ought to be the primary motivation. Therefore, ownership in the public sector has qualities similar to those in the social economy.

Arguably, the view that no one owns the organizations of the social economy is based on a narrow definition that equates ownership with property rights. As Dahl (1970) suggests, ownership can be conceived as a bundle of rights, and the rights for members of social organizations differ from shareholders in the private sector. In the social economy, members do have the right to control the organizations to which they belong. But unlike owners in the private sector, they are unlikely to benefit financially from the sale of their assets. Members of social organizations, through their representatives on the board of directors, are analogous to trustees or stewards, with the responsibility to see that assets are being utilized in a manner consistent with the organization's objectives. In other words, social organizations are trust arrangements passed through generations so that they may continue to serve society.

Volunteer/Social Participation

The label *voluntary* is often applied to organizations in the social economy because most rely on the contributions of volunteers. For non-profit mutual associations and co-operatives, the volunteer component is oriented to enhancing the services of the organization for its members; for that reason, we refer to this form of uncompensated service as *social labour*. It has the same character as volunteer service, but rather than being oriented to the public or groups outside the organization, it is intra-organizational. This distinction between volunteer service and social labour is not usually made in national surveys, which tend to lump together all forms of volunteer service.

According to the National Survey of Nonprofit and Voluntary Organizations conducted by Statistics Canada for the calendar year 2003: 'Virtually all nonprofit and voluntary organizations rely on volunteers to some degree, and more than half rely solely on volunteers to fulfill their mission' (Hall et al., 2005: 32). For tasks other than serving on the board of directors, Sharpe (1994) found that about 70 per cent of nonprofits with charitable status used volunteers (about 63 per organization). In other words, while all charitable organizations have a volunteer board of directors, most also have volunteers in other types of services, and some rely heavily on volunteers. Nor, as stated earlier, is volunteering limited to non-profits with charitable status; volunteering occurs in all sectors of the economy, and within the social economy among organizations with and without charitable status. The combination of paid labour and volunteers is referred to as co-production (Brudney, 1990). Among organizations engaging in co-production, those with a charitable status are its heaviest beneficiaries.

U.S. data for the year 2000 indicate that 44 per cent of adults over the age of 21 (83.9 million) volunteered with formal organizations, contributing a total of 15.5 billion hours. That amount of service was equivalent to over 9 million full-time positions (Independent Sector, 2001). In the United Kingdom there were 16.3 million volunteers for non-profits in 1995, with full-time equivalents of 1.47 million positions or 6.3 per cent of the paid labour force (Kendall and Almond, 1999). In Canada, the aforementioned Statistics Canada survey for the year 2003 estimated that there were 12 million volunteers (45 per cent of the population aged 15 and over), who contributed 2 billion hours, with a full-time job equivalents of 1 million (Hall et al., 2005). These patterns are similar to those discerned by Salamon et al. (1999) in their study of twenty-two countries, where 28 per cent of the population, or 10.6 million full-time equivalents, volunteered. In those countries, volunteers represented 56 per cent of the paid workforce of non-profits, that is, for every two hours of work by paid employees in non-profits, volunteers contributed more than one hour. These surveys indicate that volunteer contributions are important to religion, education, social services, recreation, sports and social clubs, and health organizations. Informal volunteering (outside a formal organizational framework) is also a major form of service.

In spite of the large amounts of volunteer service, it is misleading to refer to organizations that use volunteers as voluntary because the term implies grassroots groupings without either a permanent administrative structure or paid staff. Such an impression is quite erroneous. Rather, most volunteers fit into bureaucratized, mature social organizations often crossing many locales. These organizations reserve for their volunteers specific positions with expectations that exist apart from the individuals who fill them. These positions are not voluntary in the sense that they are created by volunteers but rather are predefined by staff for the volunteers. The volunteers might give these roles their own personal touch, and some might perform better than others; but in general the expectations associated with each position exist apart from particular volunteers. Moreover, the organizations with which volunteers are associated are sufficiently stable that they do not depend on specific individuals. Volunteers are needed to execute a full complement of services, but turnover among volunteers does not necessarily change the organization's character.

Volunteers can also be differentiated according to their degree of involvement, some having tasks that involve substantial time and a strong organizational identification (e.g., a Scout troop leader) and others having a passive affiliation such as a token membership. Putnam (1995) refers to such a passive role as 'tertiary' in that it involves only a weak link to an organization, for example, a financial donation (often characterized as a membership fee). Nevertheless, these nominal forms of involvement are of importance to organizations because they assist with financing and may be used to enhance their influence. For organizations advocating on behalf of issues, having a large membership may influence the public's perception of their initiatives. Amnesty International has been highly successful in mobilizing supporters, who number about 2.2 million in 150 countries (Amnesty International, 2008). Using the standard of Amnesty International (Canada), about 10 per cent of supporters are active members and have a regular role in organizing Amnesty's campaigns for human rights. However, passive members of an organization can be mobilized for specific campaigns such as letter writing, petitions, and demonstrations. With the advent of the Internet and other forms of modern communication, such mobilizations have become easier (Brunsting and Postmes, 2002; Deibert, 2000), and there are now Internet organization devoted to mobilizations, for example, MoveOn.

Even for those social organizations that have a relatively apolitical role, having large cadres of volunteers – whether they are active or passive – is status-enhancing. In its annual report, the American Red Cross can claim with justification that 'with more than 35,000 paid employees and nearly 825,000 volunteers, we are prepared to respond at a moment's notice' (American Red Cross, 2005: 6). Frontier College is another non-profit that mobilizes large numbers of volunteers – 5,000 across Canada in the past year – for adult literacy programs.

A Closer Look: Frontier College

Frontier College (2007) was founded in 1899 to make education available to labourers in work camps across the country. The Labourer-Teacher program was Frontier's prototype and continues to this day in such settings as farms, processing plants, rail gangs, in lumber and mining camps, in prisons, and in urban factories and in remote communities. However, given the changing nature of society and of literacy challenges, Frontier has oriented itself more to cities where adults with literacy challenges are found in greater numbers. Approximately, one in six Canadians experience challenges with literacy, so there is a need that organizations like Frontier College continue to meet. Although most of Frontier's programs are oriented to adults, they include Reading Circles for children in their neighbourhoods. The adult programs focus on those with limiting disabilities, domestic, migrant, and recent-immigrant workers. One program, Beat the Street, assists adults who did not graduate from high school to earn their GED (general education diploma), and thereby have some credential for access to the job market.

Frontier is but one example of the impressive array of non-profits that mobilize volunteers to assist adults with literacy challenges. Their apex organization, the Movement for Canadian Literacy, has provincial and territorial affiliates across the country (e.g., Literacy Nova Scotia), and it works with government agencies such as the federal National Literacy Secretariat, founded in 1987 in recognition of the seriousness of this social problem. These are organizations that rely heavily on volunteer-supported services, with funding for core staff coming from a combination of government grants and donations from private and corporate sources. With the groups that Frontier serves, earning revenues from services is challenging.

Frontier College, the Red Cross, and Amnesty International are examples of mature social organizations operated by a permanent staff that also mobilize large cadres of volunteers. In addition to mature social organizations, there are also voluntary associations. Smith (1997: 115) describes voluntary associations as 'grassroots' and defines them as 'locally based, significantly autonomous, volunteer-run, formal, non-profit groups that have an official membership of volunteers and that manifest significant voluntary altruism.' Smith's emphasis on grassroots groups would be limited to a subset of non-profits and co-operatives that lack the administrative and bureaucratic arrangements of mature social organizations. This is not an insignificant number, as the Statistics Canada survey of Canada's non-profits in 2003 indicates that 54 per cent are without paid staff (Hall et al., 2005). This survey probably underestimates the numbers that operate with volunteers only because it was of incorporated non-profits and therefore excludes a large number of neighbourhood groups, tenant associations, home and schools, union locals, and social clubs. Voluntary associations rely on volunteers both for their activities and for maintaining a relatively simple organizational framework.

An example of grassroots, voluntary associations in Canada are those that arose from the Grandmothers to Grandmothers campaign initiated by the Stephen Lewis Foundation, an organization that supports grassroots groups in sub-Saharan Africa that are fighting against

HIV/AIDS. Because of the high death rates, grandmothers in sub-Saharan Africa have become the primary caregivers to orphans. The Grandmothers to Grandmothers campaign was launched in March 2006, and about 200 self-organizing groups of Canadian grandmothers (e.g., the Grey Grannies) have sprung up and raised more than $4 million for African grandmothers and the children in their care (Stephen Lewis Foundation, 2008).

The Grandmothers groups, while autonomous and self-organizing, are associated with a larger organization, the Stephen Lewis Foundation. They reflect the pattern of modern organization in which people organize on a specific shared interest and possibly unrelated to a specific geographical location (Wellman and Gulia, 1999). Such organizations are increasingly facilitated by modern forms of communication such as the Internet and include discussion groups, political mobilization organizations, and online self-help groups for concerns related to physical and mental health, and social problems such as addiction (Baym, 1996; Cooper, 2000; Eysenbach et al., 2004; Ferguson, 1997; Ryan, 2007). The Internet is transforming the notion of voluntary association from its original roots in stable neighborhoods to a non-geographic cyberspace. Internet groups represent a form of grassroots voluntary association that is on the rise (Wellman and Gulia, 1999) at a time when geographically based voluntary associations appear to be in decline (Putnam, 2000; Skocpol, 1999).

Civic Engagement

Most analyses of the social economy refer to democracy as one of its defining characteristics (Bouchard et al., 2006; Chantier de l'économie sociale, 2005). Democracy, as it is characterized in the literature on the social economy, refers to organizations that elect their governing body from their membership. The concept is not as good of a fit with organizations such as hospitals, universities, and food banks that have a closed board of directors that are not elected by a broader membership (a point that is developed in chapter 5). While democracy is very important, we view it as a component of the broader concept of civic engagement, that is, providing a space through which people can engage with each other in a constructive manner. Therefore, we use *civic engagement* as one of our defining characteristics of the social economy, but discuss democracy within this context.

In his critique of American society, Robert Putnam (1993, 1995, 1996, 2000) argues that social or civic engagement, a key component of social capital, is on the decline. While his primary focus is analysing the reasons for the decline, he also describes the important role of mutual associations in engaging people with each other. Putnam (2000: 384–5) traces the role of mutual associations historically: 'During the years from 1879 to 1920 civic inventiveness reached a crescendo unmatched in American history, not merely in terms of numbers of clubs, but in the range and durability of the newly founded organizations. From the Red Cross to the NAACP, from the Knights of Columbus to Hadassah, from Boy Scouts to the Rotary club, from the PTA to the Sierra Club, from the Gideon Society to the Audubon Society, from the American Bar Association to the Farm Bureau Federation, from Big Brothers to the League of Women Voters, from the Teamsters Union to the Campfire Girls, it is hard to name a major mainline civic institution in American life today that was not invented in these few decades.'

Putnam argues that during the last three decades of the twentieth century civic engagement dropped; newer associations (e.g., business associations or other interest groups) were more narrowly defined, were less likely to involve their members actively, and were more transient. In spite of changing patterns of social interaction, the organizations of the social economy remain primary locations for civic engagement through which people connect with each other, even if the patterns of association have become more impersonal than they were in the past.

The proponents of civil society also emphasize the value of association, although much of the current interest in civil society has been spurred by the collapse of communism in Eastern Europe and by the powerful role of citizens' movements such as Solidarity in Poland. As such, the current theories of civil society are anti-government or, to borrow the critique of Hall (1995: 2), can be characterized as 'societal self-organizing in opposition to the state.' While that view may be valid in societies with a tyrannical government and where social organizations receive minimal support from the state, it seems unbalanced where state social programs have an important role in some minimal redistribution of wealth and in sustaining social organizations that are necessary supports for members of society. Some of the anti-state perspectives of civil society are unmistakably conservative in their orientation, for example, Green (1993), who argues for a 'civic capitalism' that is reminiscent of Thatcherite conservatism in the United Kingdom.

Primarily, the civil society proponents are searching for a space – distinct from both the state and the market – that offers focal points for constructive forms of civic engagement. In a world in which vast power resides with transnational corporations and, to a lesser extent, with state institutions, dynamic social organizations are reflective of a pluralism that is characteristic of a democratic society. Having a variety of viewpoints and a culture that encourages people to organize around their viewpoints are important features of civil society and reflective of vibrant civic engagement. In addition, by creating a framework through which the members of a society can relate to each other, social organizations present opportunities for reconstructing the ties that occur more spontaneously in a society with strong local communities. This role is vital in a democracy and is an essential aspect of civic engagement. Even though social organizations are capable of being destructive (Barber, 1998; Seligman, 1998), the vast majority are engaged in humanistic services (to borrow Samuel Martin's [1985] label) to improve the quality of social life. These services include education, culture, religion, recreation, labour rights, health care, and political association, to name but a few – services that are basic to humanity.

There are differing expressions of civic engagement within social organizations. In those with an active membership, civic engagement is central to the organizational culture. Such organizations include some forms of co-operatives (in particular, worker, housing, and farm marketing co-operatives) and many types of mutual associations, neighbourhood groups, and social clubs. Such organizations become a sub-community within a broader society in which the members engage with each other around shared services and may participate in the governance to make policy and planning decisions. Members sit on planning committees, and if there is a board of directors, the members elect it from among their group according to the principle of one member/one vote. These organizations might be described as a *social democracy*, not in the sectarian political sense but quite literally democracy within a social institution. Voting rights in such organizations are accorded on the basis of one member/one vote rather than according to property holdings as in profit-oriented businesses (Ellerman, 1990).

Where mutual associations are small and highly personal grassroots associations (often referred to as collectives), civic engagement can become quite intense. Such organizations are usually not incorporated; rather than a board as its legal representative, there is a less formal arrangement involving broader participation in decision-making (Rothschild-Whitt, 1982). This small size often leads to a 'face-to-face' direct form of democracy, as in feminist collectives. Social relations are highly personal, roles are flexible and interchangeable, decisions are arrived at through consensus, and management (to the extent that it exists) is often a shared responsibility. Because decision making can be emotionally charged and conflicted (Mansbridge, 1982), such arrangements are not necessarily a recipe for harmony, but reflect direct civic engagement with a high level of member participation.

Similar forms of intense civic engagement can occur in public sector non-profits with a closed membership (e.g., rape crisis centres and food banks) in which the employees, volunteers, and the board members attempt to achieve consensus on issues. These organizations think of themselves as collectives, and even though membership is closed, they endeavour to practice democracy internally.

At the opposite extreme, there are many civil society organizations (mutual associations and volunteer organizations) with members that are uninvolved or passive. One reason is that the service of the organization is not especially important to the members or, in the terms of Kurt Lewin (1935), is a small part of their life space. A passive membership is typical of such member-based organizations as credit unions, retail food co-operatives, and professional and business associations. Essentially, a small group (such as the director or the board chairperson) runs the organization with the tacit consent or tolerance of the larger group. On occasion, the leaders may resort to proxy voting because they require member participation to satisfy the constitution. This is most likely where the membership is widely dispersed. This pattern of a passive membership, referred to earlier as tertiary membership (Putnam, 1995), is reflective of the decline of civic engagement in the modern world. Nevertheless, while far from the ideal, these organizations still represent a social location with which members can identify, and even in this type of arrangement, members may on occasion choose to become involved, for example, because they have more time available, when they are upset with a particular decision, if they suspect financial mismanagement, or if there is some external threat to the organization. In some respects, there are parallels between these arrangements and a political democracy where the electorate is uninvolved but still cherishes the opportunity to participate when it sees fit.

Even among public sector non-profits such as hospitals and social service agencies with a closed membership consisting of the board of directors only, volunteer board members can make enormous time commitments and engage with each other to achieve consensus in deliberations. Moreover, through such organizations, volunteers participating in service roles connect with each other and become associated with a broader purpose. In these large non-profits, the employees are often unionized, and this represents another form of civic engagement (Akingbola, 2006).

These variations from the ideal type notwithstanding, it appears that organizations in the social economy do afford their members the opportunity for civic engagement. They not only contribute to the pluralism that is a hallmark of a democratic society but also engage in the practice of democracy, acculturating their members with decision-making skills and with knowledge about organizations that can be generalized to the political domain.

The Size of the Social Economy in Canada

While there is not much research about the size of the social economy, some estimates can be put together from government data on non-profits and co-operatives. A Statistics Canada survey for the year 2003 estimated that there were 161,000 non-profits, about half of which have a charitable status (Hall et al., 2005). This figure excludes unincorporated non-profits (e.g., union locals). The number of unincorporated associations is difficult to estimate, but they would add substantially to the numbers of non-profits. In 2003, there were 9,200 co-operatives in Canada, although there is some overlap between the two sets of numbers as some co-operatives are also classified as non-profits, in particular in sectors such as housing, child care, and health care (Co-operatives Secretariat, 2006).

Statistics Canada estimates that non-profits contributed $80.3 billion to Canada's gross domestic product (GDP), or 7.1 per cent (Statistics Canada, 2006a). This amount is a subset of non-profit total revenues that Statistics Canada estimates at $112 billion, but a portion of this amount represents transfers from government (Hall et al., 2005). Co-operatives, by comparison, had revenues in 2003 of $35.8 billion, an amount that was predominantly earned from services and, to a lesser extent, from membership fees, although a small amount would be transfers from government and a portion of this would be from co-operatives also classified as non-profits (Co-operatives Secretariat, 2006). Together, non-profits and co-operatives contributed about 8 per cent to Canada's GDP output in 2003. However, this estimate excludes the imputed value of volunteer work, which Statistics Canada estimated at $14 billion in the year 2000.

The employment contribution of organizations in the social economy is also substantial. According to Statistics Canada, non-profits alone employed just over two million people in 2003 of which 56 per cent were full-time and the estimated full-time equivalent was 1.5 million (Hall et al., 2005). For that same year, co-operatives employed another 155,000, with estimated full-time equivalents of about 115,000 (Co-operatives Secretariat, 2006). Together, these represent about 1.6 million full-time equivalents as the social economy workforce for 2003, or about 10 per cent of Canada's workforce for 2003. This estimate excludes the labour contribution of volunteers, estimated by Statistics Canada's 2003 survey at two billion hours, or the equivalent of one million full-time positions,[1] and it also excludes the workforce of organizations such as farm mutual insurers, who also can be classified as part of the social economy.

Therefore, it can be seen that the social economy represents not an insignificant component of Canada's economy and workforce. Most of the organizations within the social economy are small (for 54% of non-profits, volunteers are their entire workforce); however, the organizations of the social economy also can be quite large. For example, agriculture co-operatives, although having declined in importance due to the demutualization of some of the largest ones, were still marketing and processing a large share of farmers' production, notably in poultry, dairy, and hogs. Two co-operatives are among the top twelve corporations in the food and beverage-manufacturing sector in Canada. Moreover, eight non-financial co-operatives are among the top 500 corporations in Canada; two of these are among the top 100 corporations (Co-operatives Secretariat 2006). Also, as noted, le Mouvement des caisses Desjardins, the umbrella organization for credit unions/caisses populaires in francophone Canada, is the largest employer in Quebec and, with a workforce of more than 39,000, is the sixth largest financial institution in Canada with assets of $144 billion in 2007 (Desjardins, 2008). Similarly, among non-profits, universities and hospitals are major employers in communi-

1 These data originate from the Statistics Canada CANSIM II Data Base. CANSIM is an official mark of Statistics Canada.

ties across Canada, and have a major impact on the economies of those communities.

Farm mutual insurance companies could also be included within this statistical profile. These companies were started by farmers in rural areas to provide protection against fires and natural disasters, and they have the structure of a co-operative in which the policyholders are members. The Canadian Association of Mutual Insurance Companies (CAMIC; the apex organization) has 98 member organizations from across Canada with 3.7 million policyholders and with premiums of $4.2 billion (CAMIC, 2007).

Why Use the Social Economy Framework?

Most researchers in this field work with organization types such as non-profits, co-operatives, credit unions, social enterprises or social purpose businesses, and practices such as community economic development. It is relatively unusual in countries like Canada to use the social economy framework as a bridging concept for all organizations with a social mission. The social economy has a larger following in Western Europe, in particular in the francophone countries such as Belgium and France, but now more generally. In Canada, its greatest strength is in Quebec where le Chantier de l'économie sociale serves as an umbrella organization, fuelled by a $53 million trust fund that it has amassed with support from the federal and provincial governments and labour-sponsored investment funds in Quebec (see chapter 3). In addition, CIRIEC operating in Quebec has been an intellectual force for research on the social economy. The federal government also allocates funding, primarily to universities across Canada, to stimulate research on the social economy, one such grant leading to the Social Economy Centre at the University of Toronto.

In spite of this funding, research utilizing the social economy framework per se remains rare in most parts of Canada, with researchers in the field preferring to apply more familiar concepts such as co-operatives and non-profits. While this is one way of referring to the players, we feel that it is also limiting because there is great overlap between some forms of organization in the social economy, and the commonalities are determined less by the form of incorporation than by the nature of their services and how they generate their revenues. Indeed, it is possible, as the example of Inner City Renovation Inc. (at the beginning of the chapter) illustrates, for a non-profit and business to synthesize their energies towards the same goal. Common Ground, an organization serving the intellectually disabled, goes even further in that it is a co-operative, non-profit with a charitable registration, and it is the owner of four businesses in which the intellectually disabled are business partners. Inner City Renovation and Common Ground are organizations with multiple forms of incorporation oriented to a common social goal. The social economy represents a bridging concept for organizations with a social mission whether they are non-profit, charities, co-operatives, or businesses. The premise we utilize in this book is that social economy is useful in capturing the array of services that form Canada's social infrastructure. All of the organizations that we discuss in this book have a social mission and all make an economic contribution, hence, the social economy.

Conclusion

The social economy is another way of looking at Canada's social infrastructure, and arguably one that enhances its prominence more than a focus on forms of incorporation. More importantly, the social economy highlights similarities among organizations with a social mission rather than exaggerating their differences. Also, the social economy highlights that the social infrastructure has economic value in that it transacts more than $100 billions of revenues, has a workforce of more than one million full-time-equivalents, and also engages armies of volunteers who contribute about two billion hours annually. Although the organizations within the social economy are varied, there are commonalities, as discussed above, namely, that they are organizations with a social mission; that they are owned in the conventional sense by no one; that they mobilize volunteer or unpaid labour; and that they are venues for civic engagement in its many manifestations.

The social economy is a bridging concept that illustrates the breadth of the social infrastructure. It is also a laboratory for testing assumptions about social innovations. In the chapters that follow, we shall look at differing aspects of the social economy. The book is divided into three parts: Part 1, or chapter 1, provides an analysis of the social economy. Part 2 consists of in-depth discussions of the social economy's components and how they interact with other parts of society: chapter 2 discusses organizations that overlap with the private sector, or social economy businesses; chapter 3 focuses on community economic development; chapter 4 reviews social enterprises and social entrepreneurship; chapter 5 covers public sector non-profits; and chapter 6 examines civil society organizations, including mutual associations.

Part 3 of the book consists of three chapters: in chapter 7, we discuss organizational development strategies related to the social economy; chapter 8 looks at innovative forms of financing for the social economy; and in chapter 9, we introduce social accounting and accountability.

Each of these chapters is supplemented by case studies that explore the organizations in greater detail and bring out specific issues, for example, challenges in starting such an organization, raising finances, business planning, and evaluation issues. These cases studies are detachable, and could be used in a variety of courses.

* * *

DISCUSSION QUESTIONS

1. The emphasis in this book is on how organizations of the social economy interact with the rest of society. Discuss these interactions and give examples of each from your local community.
2. What are the main types of social economy organizations identified by the authors, and what are the main differences between them?
3. What are the main characteristics of social economy organizations presented in this chapter? What other characteristics would you consider?
4. Using the Venn diagram, Figure 1.1, classify the following organizations: (1) Free the Children (www.freethechildren.com); (2) ATIRA (www.atira.bc.ca); and (3) Mountain Equipment Co-op (www.mec.ca). Explain your reasoning. Provide additional examples from your own experiences.
5. Some argue that public sector non-profits should be considered as part of the social economy. Others argue that this is inappropriate because they are simply part of the public sector. Similarly, some argue that non-profits and co-operatives that earn their revenues from the market should be considered as part of market-based social organizations. Others argue that they should be viewed as part of the private sector. What are the strengths and weaknesses of each argument?
6. How can an increased understanding of the social economy help you to be a more engaged citizen?

* * *

Case for Analysis: The Big Carrot[2]

The Big Carrot is a democratically structured and worker-owned organic foods retailer. When it was incorporated in 1983, there was not appropriate legislation for a worker co-operative – a business owned and operated democratically by employees (who also serve as the members with one vote each in general meetings) – so The Big Carrot incorporated as a business but with the by-laws of a worker co-operative. As will be seen, the organization has maintained that structure since; therefore, in this case study, we often refer to The Big Carrot either as a co-operative or worker co-operative, and where appropriate, its employees as members.

Since its founding in 1983 as a small store in Toronto's east end that employed nine, The Big Carrot has expanded to a supermarket with a staff of 187 of which 65 are members, and with annual sales in the fiscal year 2007–08 of $27 million. The Big Carrot is also one-third owner of Carrot Common, a small mall in which it is housed. As the business has grown, The Big Carrot has expanded and taken over other stores in the mall creating an organic fresh meat store, a body care shop, a supplement department called The Wholistic Dispensary, and an Organic Juice Bar, and it is now is expanding the supermarket itself. Of the profits that The Big Carrot receives from Carrot Common, one-third goes to an organization called Carrot Cache, which provides loans and grants to organizations related to organic agriculture and other co-operative businesses, both in Canada and internationally.

Background

Six of the founders of The Big Carrot were employees of another organic foods retailer in Toronto, a sole proprietorship which the

---

2 An earlier article by Mary Lou Morgan and Jack Quarter, 'The Problem of a Successful Worker Co-operative: The Case of The Big Carrot,' from the book *Worker Empowerment: The Struggle for Wordplace Democracy*, Jon Wisman, ed. (Toronto: Bootstrap Press, 1990), served as resource material for this case study. We would like to thank Mary Lou Morgan, the first manager of The Big Carrot, and Heather Barclay, the current president of the board of directors, office manager, and twenty-year member, for their insights on the organization and for their assistance with this case study.

employees believed would be sold to them. The owner did sell 46 per cent of the shares and also permitted the employees to manage the operation. It was during this period that the core group of The Big Carrot's founders received their first taste of workplace democracy. The store prospered, sales doubled, and business experience was acquired. However, the majority owner decided to return to the business as 'boss,' and the six employees who were managing the store in his absence determined that their energies could be better used to establish their own enterprise. Well prepared to operate their own store, they nevertheless lacked previous experience in starting a business, particularly one with worker ownership, a matter that required much research on their part.

Financing was a challenge, and is acknowledged as one for worker-owned businesses in general. There should be no mystery as to why this is so: Business financing requires assets and credibility and, in the eyes of the financial community, ordinary working people and the unemployed do not achieve high ratings on either of these. To the members of The Big Carrot without jobs or substantial savings, the $125,000 required for the original market seemed overwhelming. Personal loans totalling $25,000 ($5,000 for five members) were secured from a small credit union. To secure an additional $20,000, four more people were accepted as members. With $45,000 in hand, $25,000 was borrowed from friends and relatives. The most difficult step was a $50,000 bank loan to purchase equipment. The bank manager hesitated, requesting a market survey, collateral, and the name of the persons or entity 'in charge.' Five members of the co-operative were made individually liable, and three members had to use their homes as security.

In all, it took nine discouraging months to arrange the financial package. At times, it seemed doubtful that the business would ever become operational. The financial package placed a lot of pressure on The Big Carrot to achieve sales that would permit it to break even. Interest charges were very high and the arrangements were cumbersome. In order to establish a substantial member investment in the enterprise, The Big Carrot had to take on more members than seemed prudent, given the projected sales at start-up. And instead of the co-operative being collectively responsible for the bank loan, as is usual for a business loan, members were treated individually. However, the business took off and by the first year-end, sales passed $1 million, and by the second year-end, annual sales were $2 million.

The financing required for expansion in 1987 to the supermarket and mall was far greater than for the initial store, but the co-operative had acquired credibility. Its customers purchased $265,000 of non-voting preferred shares at 10 per cent interest. Good fortune was also needed, in this case a benevolent real estate developer, David Walsh, and the availability of a parking lot across the street with the necessary space for an 8,000 square foot supermarket and a fourteen-store mall (Carrot Common). In total, the deal came to $6.5 million, with Walsh arranging the financing. The Big Carrot financed $700,000, which covered the costs of constructing and equipping the supermarket, in addition to making a token investment in the mall. Despite support from its customers and the deal with Walsh, the financial community was resistant. Before a loan was arranged, The Big Carrot was turned down by three banks, two trust companies, and the Credit Union Central of Ontario. Finally, the Federal Business Development Bank (often a small-business lender of last resort) agreed to a five-year $250,000 loan. Unlike the bank loan for the first store, board members who signed limited their liability. The remaining financing was from store revenues ($70,000) and supplier credits ($115,000).

Short-term repayment costs on the loan caused the co-operative to sustain business losses of $250,000 in the two years after the expansion. However, sales continued to increase, expenses were brought under control as the loans were paid down, and the store started turning a profit.

Workers with a Difference

The full-time workers at The Big Carrot are also members, each with one vote in meetings. To become a member, workers must commit to a one-year probation, which permits both the applicant and the co-operative to determine whether the arrangement is mutually beneficial. After acceptance, $5,000 is invested in class B par value shares, which are deposited into a capital account and accumulate interest at 10 per cent per year. This investment entitles the member to a common (class C) share with a nominal value of $1 and bearing one vote (one member/one vote). Although the investment in the co-operative is a prerequisite, members must work at least 24 hours per week, that is, be full-time workers. If members want to take a leave, they cease to have voting rights until they resume working the minimum hours. In this way, The Big Carrot has associated the right to vote with labour, a standard practice in a worker co-operative. In addition to the full-time staff who become members, The Big Carrot has a cadre of part-time employees, on average about 122, who work during peak hours, typically the weekend. This is common practice in grocery retailing.

Like the Mondragon Co-operative Corporation in the Basque region of Spain, which influenced its structure, The Big Carrot has endeavoured to assure that membership remains affordable by holding the initial investment at a constant amount. In that respect, The Big Carrot differs from a worker co-operative that permits its shares to be tied to the market value of the firm like conventional businesses in general. If those companies are successful, then the price of membership can become prohibitive, and the end result is often a sale to private owners.

At The Big Carrot, both the membership fee and the rights of membership are set up to assure continuance of the co-operative. Not only has the membership fee been maintained at a constant amount, and therefore at a discount in constant dollars, but the co-operative also loans new members the $5,000 and permits them to pay off the loan by a small check-off against salary.

One issue that arises in organizations of this sort is what percentage of the current members should have to approve a new member. Originally, The Big Carrot required unanimous approval of existing members, but to facilitate new membership, the requirement has been reduced so that at least 80 per cent of members must vote and of the voters 80 per cent must vote yes. This is still a high proportion, reflecting the importance of having new members who fit well with the existing group. In addition to the technical skills needed for their job, members require a commitment to organic foods and the ability to participate in a democratically governed business. Finding this combination can be challenging.

Pay and Benefits

As a self-governing business, the members of The Big Carrot have had to decide how much to pay for various jobs, that is, to pay themselves. When the co-operative was first formed, pay was egalitarian and very low. As sales increased, members with greater experience wanted this recognized in their compensation. After lengthy discussions, the members agreed to recognize responsibilities and experience in compensation, but enshrined within its by-laws a maximum ratio of 3:1

between the highest and lowest paid, although in practice the differences have been less. The current hourly pay ranges from $10 to $24.25.

One of the challenges in determining pay is that The Big Carrot must be competitive in a low-wage industry. The Big Carrot has deviated from the norms of the industry in trying to avoid traditional gender patterns of employment. Thus, it has limited its use of part-time workers and strived for lower turnover. The end result is a larger number of staff, usually members, in the middle of the pay structure and salaries lower than industry norms for senior management. Nevertheless, industry standards inevitably influence the salary scale at The Big Carrot, as prices must be competitive.

Because each member is a worker as well as an owner, any discussion about earnings is often challenging. Nevertheless, The Big Carrot has attempted to define its earnings' policy around principles based on fairness and the productivity of each worker. Any year-end surplus is generally divided as follows: 10 per cent for the community; 20 per cent for the collective reserve, retained in perpetuity in the business; and 70 per cent as labour dividends to be divided among the members according to hours of work. Labour dividends are allocated to each member's account, not immediately paid out, and in effect become a reinvestment in the business. (The account also contains each member's initial investment of $5,000 and 10 per cent annual interest.) Under current policy, the labour dividends are paid out as cash flow allows. Due to increased profits over the past few years, members have also been paid bonuses prior to the determination of dividends.

The Big Carrot's procedure for allocating surplus earnings is adapted from the Mondragon Co-operative Corporation, the difference being that for Mondragon the total money in the capital account is retained until a member leaves the co-operative. This has the practical advantage of providing the co-operative with a pool of investment capital, but has the disadvantage of creating a large drain of capital if many long-time members retire simultaneously. It also means that members have to forgo access to part of their earnings until retirement. To avoid the problem of a run on its capital, and to give its members better earnings in the short term, The Big Carrot modified the Mondragon by-law to suit its own needs.

Another Mondragon by-law that was adopted had to do with the allocation of losses. The founders of The Big Carrot, assuming quite optimistically that losses were unlikely, agreed that they should be divided according to the same formula as surpluses, that is, 70 per cent would be applied to individual capital accounts. In the period following the expansion, however, there were sizable losses, resulting in an unfair burden on the original members. These same people, who had already experienced very low earnings when the expansion occurred, now were faced with a total loss of the accumulated labour dividends in their capital accounts because they took the risk to expand. Finally, it was agreed that the losses be dealt with through a special 'start-up loss' account that would be amortized over five years and would be shared by all members during that period.

Although The Big Carrot is owned by its members, ownership rights are partial and do not include the right to sell the store for personal gain. In the event of dissolution, members are entitled only to the amount in their capital account. Monies in addition would go to the co-operative movement or to some appropriate organization designated by the members.

Governance

As is evident in the preceding discussion, the members of The Big Carrot are responsible for its policies, that is, for the policies that affect them. Each member has one vote in electing the board of directors (the legal governance) from among its group and in meetings. The seven-person board of directors meets every week with the general manager attending. During its twenty-five years, the co-operative has relied on different management styles, sometimes selecting the general manager from among its group and other times hiring outside. Members attempt to reach consensus on major issues at the long and lively meetings scheduled every other Wednesday.

From the beginning, The Big Carrot experimented with its decision-making processes in an effort to strike a balance between effective decision-making and meaningful participation. When there were only nine members, the firm was a participatory democracy in which all issues were decided collectively. As the operations became more complex, decisions were delegated and there was greater selectivity about group matters. Knowing which issues were appropriate for the board and which were the domain of the total membership required experimentation. Similarly, there were ongoing discussions about the decisions that management could make without consulting the board.

The Big Carrot has had an ongoing tradition for ad hoc committees that take on specific issues and that make recommendations to the governance. To address concerns of individual workers, there are procedures including formal grievances as well as a solid harassment policy.

As owners-in-common, the members of The Big Carrot are highly motivated in their work. There is a strong emphasis on worker self-management, relative to other similar businesses. However, because of the democratic structures, decision-making can be time consuming and change can be challenging. Although the democratic structures of The Big Carrot have created a high degree of worker involvement, democracy can come with a price. The role of management is constantly discussed, and management's powers can be challenged by both the board and the members in general. Traditional business training does not prepare managers properly for this challenge. Heather Barclay, a twenty-year member and the current president of the board of directors and office manager, highlights the challenge for members and management (personal communication): 'There always seems to be a constant "pull" between the necessity for a hierarchical system to run the business and the need for the "equality" of the membership. In members meetings, we are all equal but as soon as we go downstairs our roles shift. This can and often has led to some conflict, especially for those members that do not hold managerial positions.'

* * *

DISCUSSION QUESTIONS

1. What do you feel are the main advantages and disadvantages of the organizational and ownership arrangements of The Big Carrot? If you were creating a business, would you consider this structure? If so, would you want modifications?
2. What qualities are needed to assume a senior management role in The Big Carrot? Does business school training adequately prepare managers for this type of organization? What changes, if any, are needed?

* * *

PART 2

The Components of the Social Economy

2 Social Economy Businesses

As discussed in chapter 1, social economy businesses are organizations that balance their economic and social mission and that earn either all or a sizable portion of their revenues from the marketplace. In Figure 1.1, we located social economy businesses in the overlap between the private sector and the social economy, and in chapter 1 we identified as fitting within this overlap co-operatives, credit unions, and commercial non-profits that exchange their services in the marketplace. However, prior to considering in greater detail the organizations within this overlap, we shall discuss the line between the social economy and the private sector, and how we decide which firms are in the private sector and which are predominantly in the social economy. This is a complex issue because social economy businesses and some private sector businesses that take their social commitments seriously could be viewed as siblings, not organizations that are categorically distinct. Also, social economy businesses are under pressure to be competitive, and increasingly this may mean shifting the balance between their economic and social mission.

For all types of organizations that function in the market, the prerogatives of capital are critical to survival, but for social economy businesses their social objectives are of importance. Therefore, a defining criterion for social economy businesses, as distinct from conventional private sector firms, is that *the prerogatives of capital (e.g., rate of return, capital valuation) do not dominate over the social objectives in the organization's decision-making.*

Social economy businesses may embed what is increasingly referred to as 'social entrepreneurship' (Dees, 1998), a phenomenon discussed in chapter 4 on social enterprises. In this chapter our emphasis is on social

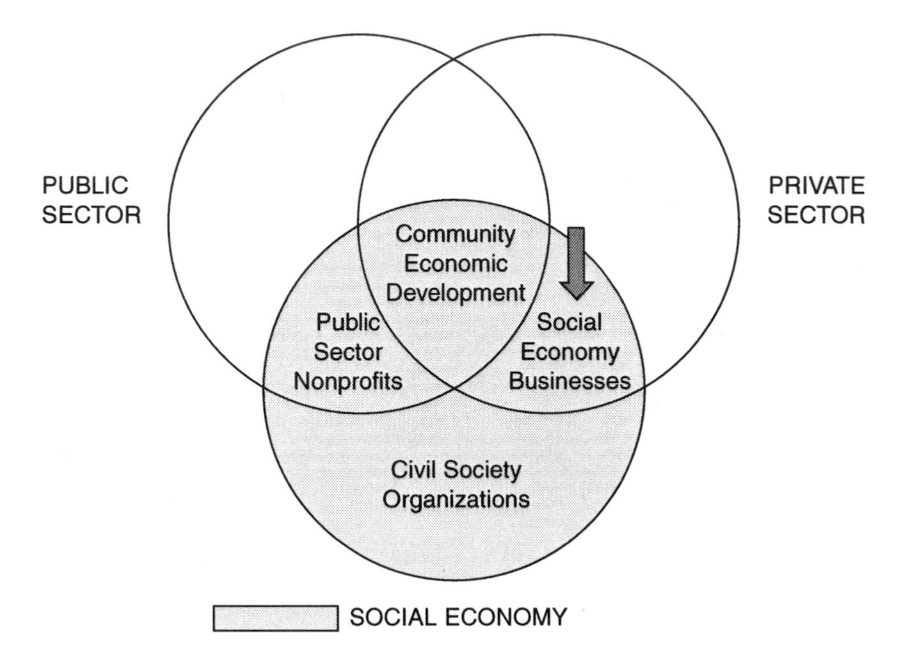

Figure 2.1 The Social Economy: An Interactive Approach

economy businesses, that is, some forms of co-operatives including credit unions and non-profits that earn their revenues from the market. However, we recognize that there are some businesses within the private sector, somewhat anomalous, that are set up to solve a social problem, and that these organizations blur the distinction from the social economy.

We begin the discussion with businesses in the private sector (i.e., property belonging to either shareholders or private owners) that have strong social objectives, not simply as a means to earn profits but as a primary part of their mission. We refer to this group as social businesses, as distinct from social economy businesses. Following that, we proceed to the social economy businesses, first co-operatives and credit unions followed by non-profits.

Defining the Line

On the surface, the distinction between market-based organizations in the social economy and the private sector should be very clear, but as we explore this distinction in greater detail, it will become apparent that the line is open to conjecture. One reason is that among private sector firms, corporate social responsibility (CSR) has become part of corporate consciousness as businesses find that it is in their interests to be perceived as good corporate citizens. This strategy can be construed as social marketing, something which firms such as The Body Shop and Ben and Jerry's have done effectively, but as will be seen, it can also go beyond social marketing into a genuine desire to change business practices and priorities (Quarter, 2000).

Although corporate social responsibility is often viewed as a unique line of scholarship, it is also part of a growing body of knowledge that challenges market autonomy and situates the economy within a social framework that emphasizes the reciprocal relationship between society and the economy. The theoretical roots of this work can be found in Polanyi's concept (1957) of the economy as an 'instituted process', Granovetter's (1985) subsequent elaboration on 'embeddedness', and in the more recent development of the social capital concept (Putnam, 1993, 1995, 1996, 2000). All of these theoreticians make the argument that the economy is not an end unto itself but part of a broader society ('embedded' in Granovetter's terms).

This same issue – the connection between business, economy, and broader society – has been taken up in business schools and economics departments of universities, although the labelling of it varies. First, there is scholarship that explores the social impact of corporate behaviour, including: corporate social responsibility (Carroll, 1979, 1991, 1999; Drucker, 1984); corporate social performance (Asmundson and Foerster, 2001; Roman, Hayibor, and Agle, 1999); virtue theory and other theories of business ethics (Arjoon, 2000; Martin, 2002); multiple bottom-line management (Fiksel, McDaniel, and Mendenhall, 1999; Roberts and Cohen, 2002; Waddock, 2000); and stakeholder theory (Clarkson, 1995; Wheeler and Sillanpää, 2000). Although these lines of inquiry are distinct, they share an effort to broaden the framework for evaluating corporate performance, to embed performance within an explicit value framework, and to create methods of accounting for corporate social performance.

Second, there is the field of socially responsible investment, usually referring to the inclusion of explicit social and environmental criteria in the assessment of investment impacts (Becker and McVeigh, 2001; Bruyn, 1987; Carmichael, 2005; Ellmen, 1989; Hebb, 2001; Quarter, Carmichael, and Ryan, 2008).

Third, there is a related line of inquiry, widely known as alternative economics, that presents a more fundamental critique of conventional economics, particularly its impact on human society, or to quote the book subtitle of Schumacher (1973), 'Economics as if people mattered.' Among the alternative economists are critics of environmental exploitation (Ekins, Hillman, and Hutchinson, 1992; Henderson, 1991; Sachs, Loske, and Lindz, 1998; Schumacher, 1973), the exploitation of women (Mies, 1986; Milani, 2000; Shiva, 1989; Waring, 1996, 1999), the inadequacy of conventional methods of growth and of the need for alternatives (Daly and Cobb, 1994; Ekins, 1986) including new methods of accounting for social value (Gray, Owen, and Adams, 1996; Hopwood, Burchell, and Clubb 1994; Mathews 1997; Mook, Quarter, and Richmond, 2007; Tinker, 1985). This latter field is also labelled as *social and environmental accounting*, and it too attempts to broaden the domain that is normally considered in accounting frameworks (see chapter 9).

While these lines of inquiry have a strong following among social critics, it is not evident to what extent they have influenced business practice. Nevertheless, there are private sector firms whose social commitments are part of their mission, and not simply as a means to earn a profit. These may be viewed as odd firms, but often the exceptions indicate what is possible and for that reason some select examples are presented. The differences between these firms and social economy businesses are often subtle, and might be perceived as 'splitting hairs' in that all embrace a social mission and some appropriate balance between social and commercial objectives.

Muhammad Yunus (2007), the founder of the Grameen Bank, envisions a class of businesses that he labels as 'social businesses.' His conception goes much further than corporate social responsibility, which he readily dismisses, and involves a 'self-sustaining company that sells goods and services and that repays its owners for the money they invest, but whose primary purpose is to serve society and improve the lot of the poor' (2007: 82). Yunus cites the Grameen Bank and the 'Grameen family of 25 companies' set up to serve the poor primarily of Bangladesh as examples of social businesses, as is the partnership between Grameen and the French multinational Danone, referred to as Grameen Danone, in that it brings enriched yogurt at cost to poor Bangladeshi villages. The underpinning of a social business is that the investment is for social benefit, and the expectation is that the investors will receive their investment back, not dividends and capital appreciation, as is the case in a capitalist investment. Yunus allows, however, that a profit-oriented business owned by the poor can also be a social business in that it brings benefits to the poor.

Another class of firms operating in the private sector but with a strong social mission manufactures or deploys green technologies on a wide scale. These are businesses that are attempting to generate profits for investors, but their primary product is sustainable energy. Among manufacturers, the Vancouver-based firm, Ballard Power Systems Inc., is considered a leader in the design and development of hydrogen fuel cells (Ballard, 2007). Ballard is absorbing large financial losses as it struggles to create a market for a product that could revolutionize energy use and have a major impact on carbon emissions.

Nor is Ballard one of a kind; *Clean Energy Canada*, a Government of Canada website, lists hundreds of such firms, not only for fuel cell technologies but also for wind energy, solar thermal, solar water heaters, biomass, ocean energy, and photovoltaic cells. The list is extensive, and wind energy per se includes more than 150 organizations, predominantly private sector firms developing and marketing new technologies and other innovations. In contrast to social economy organizations, the commercial objectives of these firms predominate, but they have a product or service that meets a pressing social need – to improve the quality of the physical environment, for example, Bullfrog Power.

A Closer Look: Bullfrog Power

Bullfrog Power is a privately owned company whose power comes from clean, emission-free sources like wind power and low impact water power. In Alberta, all of Bullfrog's power comes from wind turbines; in Ontario, 20 per cent comes from wind and 80 per cent from certified low impact hydro (Bullfrog, 2008). Bullfrog generates for the grid the equivalent amount of energy from green sources as used by its clients in their homes and businesses. To cover the costs, Bullfrog clients pay a premium that is invested in the production of green energy sources. For clients in Alberta, the premium is 50 cents per day; in Ontario it is $1 per day. Bullfrog does not simply sell power to its clients but works with them to encourage conservation. In addition, it partners with environmental non-profits in mutually beneficial arrangements. With the World Wildlife Foundation Canada, it has engaged in joint communication programs intended to reduce carbon emission; with the Pembina Institute, it promotes renewable energy for Canadian homes. Bullfrog is a member of the Canadian Wind Energy Association (2008), a non-profit organization that promotes the development and application of wind energy, and Canadian Business for Social Responsibility (2008), that embraces the twin objectives to 'improve performance and contribute to a better world.' A tangible indicator of Bullfrog's social commitments is that it donates 10 per cent of its profits 'to organizations that support sustainability.' Bullfrog is a business designed to earn profits for its owners, but it also has very tangible social and environmental objectives, an example of a social business.

Another class of firms with a social mission has negated the prerogatives of shareholders or other forms of ownership by placing the shares within a trust or a similar arrangement, which prevents them from being exchanged on the market. This arrangement creates the structure of a non-profit, that is, a corporation without shares. The first of these was the huge multinational, Carl Zeiss AG, founded in 1846 in Jena, Germany, and a leader in the optical and opto-electronic industries. Zeiss operates in thirty countries with more than 11,000 employees and sales in 2005–06 of 2.4 billion euros, yet curiously it is owned by a foundation, the Carl Zeiss Stiftung (Zeiss, 2007). This arrangement has been in place since 1889, a year after the death of the founder, Carl Zeiss, when his partner Dr Ernst Abbe (to honour the memory of Zeiss) set up the Carl Zeiss Stiftung, a benevolent trust for the benefit of the employees, to which he transferred his entire fortune worth millions of deutschemarks (Oakeshott and Schmid, 1990). The Carl Zeiss Group is an anomaly in that it competes for markets like any other corporation, excepting that its shares are held in the foundation. The company's website is explicit about this point: 'The shares cannot be enlisted for exchange at a stock market.'

Zeiss is unusual, but by no means one of a kind. The John Lewis Partnership (2007), one of the largest retailers in the United Kingdom, is also owned by a trust set up initially in 1929 (and finalized in 1950) by the founder's son, Spedan Lewis, who believed that he was creating 'perhaps the only alternative to communism,' as he stated on the cover of his 1954 book, *Fairer Shares*. The Partnership, as it is called, has 65,000 employees (called partners) at its twenty-six department stores and 183 Waitrose supermarkets and sales of 5.7 billion pounds in 2006, yet it too operates without shareholders in the conventional sense. Lewis's vision, which he presented in his books – *Partnership for All* (1948) and *Fairer Shares* (1954) – involved utilizing the dividends that would normally be paid to shareholders as a bonus for the employees and creating a council to which employees, each with one vote, elected representatives (see Quarter, 2000).

Ernest Bader, the founder of the British firm, Scott Bader, which manufactures and supplies composites and specialty polymer and also operates worldwide, pushed the model further and created a movement of businesses without shares named the Industrial Common Ownership Movement (ICOM), the member businesses using a variation of the worker co-operative model discussed later in this chapter (Blum, 1968; Hoe, 1978; Quarter, 2000). Bader, a Quaker, was part of a small group of Christian Socialist business owners who met in Northampton in the 1950s to discuss how they could create an alternative to the capitalist model. Like Lewis, Bader gave the company's shares to a trust, in this case a charitable trust limited by guarantee called the Scott Bader Commonwealth. The Commonwealth, technically speaking, owns the operating company, but more correctly it provides a shield that protects the company from the machinations of capitalist ownership and has allowed it to preserve its independence and to grow. Bader also promoted the principles of industrial democracy both for Scott Bader and more generally, the employees being granted a vote in electing representatives to the operating company's board of directors. The Industrial Common Ownership Movement that Bader founded merged with Co-operatives U.K. in 2001, its members being mostly small worker co-operatives.

Newman's Own (2007), a business started in 1982 by actor Paul Newman and friend A.E. Hotchner, takes a different approach and donates all of the firm's after tax profits, an impressive $200 million in twenty-five years, to education and charitable causes both in the United States and internationally, thus negating one of the primary prerogatives of capitalist ownership, the right to profit. Newman and Hotchner's memoir of their work is aptly titled, *Shameless Exploitation in Pursuit of the Common Good*.

Another social business is Craigslist (2008), an online advertising network in communities throughout the world for services such as jobs, internships, housing, personals, and forums. Craigslist is a privately held company with three owners, its founder Craig Newmark, its CEO Jim Buckmaster, and eBay. The revenues come from paid job ads in select cities and paid broker apartment listings in New York City. The other listings are free. Unlike Newman's Own, which charges the going rate for services and then channels the net income into worthy causes, Craigslist does not charge users of most services. It is therefore analogous to a public service paid for by some users and by the willingness of its owners to forgo the typical prerogatives of ownership. In addition, the founder of Craigslist created Craigslist Foundation to assist with the education of non-profit leaders.

Social Economy Businesses

Social businesses function within the private sector, but with distinct social objectives. Social economy businesses, by comparison, also operate in the market, but are co-operatives and non-profits. Given the discussion of anomalous cases above, the distinction is subtle, but we emphasize that the cases above are highly atypical.

As noted in chapter 1, we designate the following general groupings of social economy businesses: market-based co-operatives, credit unions, and commercial non-profits. We shall discuss each of these groups in turn, but before doing so return briefly to our definition. The defining feature of social economy businesses, as distinct from the social economy as a whole, is that in addition to balancing their economic and social objectives, social economy businesses earn either all or a sizable portion of their revenues from the marketplace: but how much? On the surface, the question is simple and requires designating an amount, but an additional complexity is considering what is earned revenue and whether the proportion of earned revenue should increase over time.

Regarding earned revenues, do we consider membership fees as a form of payment for service, as is common in many non-profit mutual associations? Union dues, for example, are a payment for services, as are annual fees for a business or professional association, or a membership in a social club. The form of payment differs from a typical market exchange, which tends to be for a product or service at one point in time, but would be analogous to the purchase of insurance, with the premium being paid over a time period, as is commonly the case with dues or membership fees. Therefore, we include membership fees and dues as earned revenues.

Government contracts are more complex because increasingly government agencies have tended to avoid the label of grants and have preferred contracts. Here we would differentiate between a contract for a specific service and with a finite timeframe and a contract for a package of services, as provided by a social service agency. The latter is typically a form of ongoing funding, although without proper reporting it could be terminated. The latter is in effect a renaming of a grant, with more strings attached, as distinct from the archetypical contract that tends to be focused, time limited, and not renewed repeatedly.

Another criterion that might be taken into consideration is whether the organization is attempting to generate an increasing portion of its revenue from the market, as a conventional business typically would, or whether it is content to earn a portion of its revenue from the market without any aspiration to increase that share. This might be the case for a theatre group that requires a percentage of earnings from ticket sales in order to qualify for subsidies from government and supporting foundations. Under these circumstances, it is a stretch to label such an organization as a social economy business. Therefore, it seems important not only to consider what portion of an organization's revenues are earned but also whether the organization aspires to increase the earned portion further, as a social economy business typically would be expected to do. We now turn to the differing classes of social economy businesses.

Co-operatives/Credit Unions

Co-operatives and credit unions are organizations set up to meet their members' needs, in other words a form of mutual association. Credit unions are simply co-operatives engaged in financial services for their members, and are in essence financial co-operatives, although increasingly credit unions attempt to differentiate themselves from other forms of co-operatives. The International Co-operative Alliance (2007), the umbrella organization for co-operatives and credit unions worldwide, uses as a definition: 'A co-operative is an autonomous association of persons united voluntarily to meet their common economic, social, and cultural needs and aspirations through a jointly-owned and democratically-controlled enterprise.' The definition emphasizes *voluntarily* and therefore the ICA does not include state-imposed forms of collectivization, as was common practice in the Soviet Bloc under communism. The definition also refers to three forms of needs – *economic, social, and cultural* – that co-operatives meet through joint or shared ownership and through democratic decision-making by the members. In other words, like our definition of a social economy business, co-operatives attempt to strike a balance between the economic and the social.

This definition is reinforced by a set of principles, originally conceived in 1844 in Rochdale, England, by a group known as the Rochdale Pioneers, who have been credited with founding the world's first co-operative. The Rochdale principles, as they are called, were revised in 1937, 1966, and most recently in 1995 in Manchester, England. The current principles are: voluntary membership; democratic member control; member economic participation; autonomy and independence; education, training, and information; co-operation among co-operatives; and concern for community. These principles reinforce the concept of an association set up to serve member needs and controlled by members according to the principle of one member/one vote.

The principle of *member democratic control* can be misleading because it might create the impression that the members make daily decisions. Co-operatives are corporations with a board of directors, and that body hires management who are responsible for daily operations. Members, if they choose to participate in the governance, cast one vote in electing the board of directors, participate in the annual general meeting, and may get involved in committees that report to either the board or management. Although some co-operatives, typically in services such as housing and child care, have a very active membership, many do not. The members are users of the service, and that is the extent of their involvement.

Nevertheless, having an organization based on one member/one vote is not necessarily attractive to prospective management. Also, the limitation of voting shares to members can create challenges in attracting outside investors because, unlike capitalist corporations, they cannot normally be represented on the board of directors and exert the same degree of control that major investors typically would. These factors as well as the tradition of a limited return on member investment in the organization have created challenges for co-operatives as they attempt to compete in modern markets with capitalist corporations. An indication of this concern is that in 1995 the principle of 'limited rate of interest' on share capital was dropped from the earlier versions of the co-operative principles and included within a more general principle of 'member economic participation.'

The challenges of external investment have led to demutualization of some large agricultural co-operatives, particularly in grain marketing (e.g., the Saskatchewan Wheat Pool). This issue has become such a concern that the home page of the International Co-operative Alliance has a section called 'Demutualization Watch.' Demutualization does raise another issue, however, as one of the principles of the social economy that we presented in chapter 1 is *social ownership*. When a co-operative can be demutualized or converted into a capitalist corporation, it is difficult to argue that its ownership is social. In the explanation for 'member economic participation' in the Rochdale principles, reference is made to an 'indivisible reserve' that is social property rather than belonging to individual members. Italian law obliges co-operatives to set aside 20 per cent of their net income (profits) in an indivisible collective reserve (Zevi, 2007) and the Mondragon co-operatives in the Basque region of Spain do the same (MacLeod, 1997). For organizations that can be demutualized, and this might also include non-profits with significant assets, the line between them and the private sector becomes less visible, and they are like the examples we provided above of corporations operating within the private sector but with organizational arrangements and social objectives that differ from the norm.

Co-operation between co-operatives, one of the principles, speaks in part to co-operatives working together with each other and obtaining the practical benefits of creating apex organizations that serve common interests, a point that we will address in greater detail below. However, this principle also refers to the building of a co-operative movement, not simply in one country but also worldwide, a movement in its original conception referred to as a 'co-operative commonwealth' (Webb and Webb, 1920, 1921). While the numbers of members of co-operatives worldwide continue to grow – 800 million from among the ninety-two member countries, as estimated by the International Co-operative Alliance in 2007 – the dream of a co-operative commonwealth is no longer referred to, or at least is limited to the zealous few. However, the International Co-operative Alliance and national member associations such as the Canadian Co-operative Association and the Conseil Canadien de la Coopération do refer to a *co-operative movement* and believe passionately in it.

Canada has among the highest member saturation per capita, about one in three people belonging to at least one co-operative, although the number of co-operatives and the members per capita have not grown over the past decade due largely to consolidations among financial co-operatives and demutualizations among some large agricultural co-operatives. Other countries with a strong co-operative presence are Norway, Finland, Germany, Belgium, France, Honduras, Singapore, Kenya, and Argentina. India alone has 236 million members of co-operatives and China has 180 million. Together co-operatives worldwide employ 100 million, and they play a significant role in the economy of many countries, although not on the scale envisaged by the Webbs when they referred to the co-operative commonwealth. The International Co-operative Alliance (2006) estimates that the 300 largest co-operatives internationally, including mutual insurers, have annual revenues of $963 billion and assets of between $30 and $40 trillion, with food and agriculture and retail and financial services predominating. Put in perspective, co-operatives internationally would be equivalent to the world's tenth-largest economy. As a proportion of the overall GDP contributed by co-operatives, the largest are: Finland (16.1%), New Zealand (13.9%), Switzerland (11.0%), Netherlands (10.2%), and Norway (9.0%). The Emilia Romagna region of Italy contains one of Europe's most concentrated co-operative sectors, with 15,000 organizations directly accounting for over 40 per cent of the region's GDP through such services as housing, food retailing, and health care.

Different Co-operative Models

Although all co-operatives share the features discussed above, the essence being a mutual association that attempts to meet its members' needs, there are differing co-operative structures. The examples that follow are limited to organizations classified as social economy businesses (typically with member shares) and exclude co-operatives that rely in substantial degree on government funding (typically, non-profit organizations or co-operatives without share capital, as discussed in chapter 5).

Marketing Co-operatives

In this model, the members are independently employed, most often self-employed, and establish a co-operative for a common service, usually marketing. This group is also referred to as *producer co-operatives* to signify that the members are independent producers. We prefer 'marketing' as that label describes the predominant activity of the organization in which producers associate. The roots of *marketing co-operatives* are in farming, but they are also found in other forms of primary production such as fishing, transportation (such as taxi, airport limousine, and trucking services), artisans, and consultants. Both in Canada and internationally, the strength of marketing co-operatives remains predominantly in farming.

Farm marketing co-operatives began forming in Canada in the latter half of the nineteenth and early twentieth centuries, when farmers organized to obtain greater control over the price of their products and the basic purchases that they required, a history captured in Canada by Ian MacPherson's classic account, *Each for All* (1979). The objective was for farmers, who became members of the co-operative, to obtain a fair price for their products. Surplus earnings, not reinvested in the co-operative, were rebated to the members as a 'patronage dividend' based on use of the service.

Canada's farmers were influenced by the Grange (Patrons of Husbandry) and the Patrons of Industry, U.S. agricultural organizations. The first experiments in Canada were creamery co-operatives and mutual insurance arrangements to protect their property against the unexpected. These initiatives were followed by the Prairie grain-marketing co-operatives, starting with the Grain Growers Grain Company in Manitoba in 1907, and subsequently the Saskatchewan Co-operative Elevator Company and the Alberta Co-operative Elevator Company (MacPherson, 1979). Until recently, grain-marketing co-operatives were dominant in Canada, and they were among the largest corporations in the country. However, almost all have demutualized and become publicly traded corporations. Nevertheless, farm marketing co-operatives retain a strong role in Canada's economy, and internationally they are the strongest economic component of the non-financial co-operative sector.

According to the Co-operatives Secretariat (2007a), in Canada 150 farm-marketing co-operatives reported a combined business in 2004 of $9.7 billion[1] with the strongest market share in poultry and eggs (55%), dairy (39%), honey and maple sugar (26%), grains and oilseeds (18%), and livestock (18%). Canadian maple sugar co-operatives have 35 per cent of the world's market (International Co-operative Alliance, 2007). Within British Columbia, 75 per cent of the apple crop is sold through co-operatives (Canadian Co-operative Association, 2007a).

1 The revenue figures for farm marketing co-operatives for 2004 still include the Saskatchewan Wheat Pool and Lilydale, but both demutualized in 2005 and thus ceased to appear in the following years' figures.

In spite of substantially reduced market share in the grain and the dairy marketing sector, farm marketing co-operatives are among the largest co-operative corporations. In dairy marketing, the major co-operatives are: Agropur and Nutrinor (Quebec), Gay Lea (Ontario), and Scotsburn (Nova Scotia). In meat and poultry processing, the major marketing co-operatives are Coopérative Fédérée de Québec and Lilydale (Alberta), although this organization recently demutualized. Many of the farm marketing co-operatives have storied histories, including Scotsburn, a major player in Atlantic Canada's dairy sector.

A Closer Look: Scotsburn Co-operative Services Ltd.

Scotsburn Co-operative Services Ltd., known commercially as Scotsburn Dairy Group, is a large dairy processing and distribution co-operative operating throughout the Atlantic region of Canada. There are 3,150 members consisting of dairy and livestock farmers in the region, and in 2004 the co-operative transacted over $255 million of business (Co-operatives Secretariat, 2007a, b). Scotsburn was formed in 1900 by a group of farmers in the Scotsburn area of Pictou County, Nova Scotia, who decided to build a creamery to manufacture butter from milk produced on local farms. Initially, because of low production, Scotsburn functioned only in the summer months (Scotsburn, 2008). In 1946, a period of expansion, a livestock feed manufacturing and storage plant was built, and Scotsburn changed from a joint stock company to a co-operative.

Scotsburn has expanded over the years through purchases and mergers with other dairy co-operatives, and it now distributes fresh and frozen dairy products throughout the Atlantic region. It operates five processing facilities and eleven distribution centres in Nova Scotia (Canadian Co-operative Association, 2007b). In addition to dairy production, Scotsburn provides farm supplies and services, including livestock feed, bulk petroleum, farm supplies, and hardware, as well as a convenience store and lunch counter in the community of Scotsburn. The co-operative employs 700 full-time and another 250 part-time, and it is the largest Atlantic Canadian-owned processor and distributor of fresh quality dairy products and ice cream.

According to the International Co-operative Alliance (2007), farm-marketing co-operatives also are very strong in other parts of the world, and they are major economic players in the United States where approximately 30 per cent of farmers' products are marketed through 3,400 farmer-owned co-operatives, including some well-known brand names such as Sunkist, Ocean Spray, and Welch's Grape Juice; in Japan, where 91 per cent of all Japanese farmers are members; and such other countries as Finland, Norway, Poland, Korea, Kenya, Brazil, Colombia, and Uruguay.

In other words, the pattern of strong farm marketing co-operatives is not only particular to Canada but also an international phenomenon. In Canada, marketing co-operatives have worked well in farm communities, but they have been much less effective for other forms of produce and services. In 2004, there were fifty-four fishery co-operatives, predominantly in the Atlantic Provinces where the stock of fishing has been in serious decline (Co-operatives Secretariat, 2007a). Most are small and their total revenues were $238 million.

One service, other than farm products, that marketing co-operatives have been successful with is the work of artisans like the Inuit in northwest Arctic regions and the Cree and Inuit of Northern Quebec (see the case study of Arctic Co-operatives Ltd., at the end of chapter 2).

Other services with a significant number of marketing co-operatives are taxis, airport limousines, and the freight business. For such organizations, the communications and administrative aspects of the business are organized as co-operatives, for example, the radio service for a taxi or limousine. There are also a significant number of marketing co-operatives for consulting groups of various sorts. In general, though, marketing co-operatives have had great success with farm produce, but the co-operative marketing model has not moved to a great extent beyond the farm.

User or Consumer Co-operatives

Co-operative Retailers and Wholesalers

Farm marketing co-operatives tend to be the largest co-operative corporations, but the bulk of co-operative memberships are users or consumers of particular services. The historical term applied to this group is *consumer co-operatives,* and it was in reference to co-operative stores in which the members purchased goods and services. However, we prefer the label *user* because it is somewhat broader and captures the range of services that co-operatives of this sort embrace. Like co-operatives in general, *user co-operatives* are mutual associations that meet the needs of their members, but unlike a marketing co-operative in which the members are either independent or semi-independent producers or service providers who associate with each other to market their service, in a user co-operative the members themselves use or purchase the services. The user co-operative is the archetypical model, and the one that is most often associated with co-operatives.

There are many types of user co-operatives in such services as farm supplies and machinery, food retailing and wholesaling, financial services, day care, health care, housing, electrification, water supply, transportation (automobile sharing), and even funeral services. Almost all of the twelve million Canadian who belong to a co-operative are members of a user co-operative, with credit unions most predominant.

The roots of the user co-operative in Canada go back to the nineteenth century to mutual insurance organizations formed by farmers (although technically, these are not considered as co-operatives) and to co-operative stores in mining communities (the first believed to be in Stellarton, Nova Scotia, in 1861 (MacPherson, 1979). Some of these early experiments in co-operative stores were organized through trade unions. However, two primary influences pushed this movement forward: first, the large flow of immigrants from Britain contained people who became leaders of co-operatives in Canada; and second, farmers who organized marketing co-operatives for their products also formed co-operatives from which they purchased supplies and equipment.

The early farm-supply organizations started as buying clubs, but subsequently they burgeoned into major co-operative corporations with a full range of farm products such as animal feed, seeds, fertilizers, chemicals, petroleum, building materials, and machinery, selling to both individual farmers and other co-operatives. In 2004 there were 219 supply co-operatives with revenues of $4.4 billion (Co-operatives Secretariat, 2007a, b). Their strongest markets are for farm petroleum (45%), fertilizers and chemicals (23%), and animal feed (14%). Farm supply co-operatives are predominantly in the Prairies, the heartland of Canada's agriculture, and two of the ten largest co-operatives in Canada – United Farmers of Alberta Co-operative Ltd. (the fourth largest) and Interprovincial Co-operatives Limited, in Saskatchewan (the twelfth largest) – specialize in this market. However, farm supplies are also sold in other retail co-operatives as well.

Farm supplies provided the initial impetus for user co-operative stores, but by the mid-1920s retail co-operatives in Canada developed their own strength. Revenues from the consumer group, excluding farm supplies, were $10.7 billion in 2004, with food products accounting for 39 per cent of the total and petroleum products, dry goods, and home hardware being the other main items sold. Retail co-operatives developed primarily around two systems, one in the West and the other in the Atlantic. In the West, Federated Co-operatives, a powerful Saskatoon-based corporation, serves as the wholesaler for 283 retail outlets, and in 2006, it posted revenues of $5.4 billion and was among the hundred largest non-financial corporations in Canada. Although the retail co-operatives in the Federated system are concentrated in small communities, they are found in some urban centres such as Saskatoon, Regina, and Calgary; the Calgary Co-operative being the largest retail co-operative in North America, with $925 million in revenues and 413,274 members (users) in 2006, giving it nearly 40 per cent of the Calgary market (Co-operatives Secretariat, 2007b). In the Atlantic, ninety-seven retail co-operatives are clustered around Co-op Atlantic in Moncton, which like Federated acts as the wholesaler and organizer of the system. In 2006, Co-op Atlantic had sales of $547 million, making it the sixth largest co-operative in Canada.

By comparison, in Central Canada, where much of the population lives, retail co-operatives have had minimal penetration (Co-operatives Secretariat, 2007a). Among centres of at least 500,000 people, only in Calgary have retail food co-operatives had a significant market penetration. They have tended to serve smaller communities across Canada, but primarily in the West and the Atlantic. An exception is Mountain Equipment Co-op with eleven outlets selling outdoor equipment in Canada's major urban centres. Mountain Equipment Co-op has risen rapidly and has more than 2.4 million members and sales of $227 million in 2006. (The members figure includes everyone who has ever purchased a membership share to shop at Mountain Equipment Co-operative; see the case study of Mountain Equipment Co-op at the end of chapter 7.)

While there are some countries in the world where co-operatives have had a greater presence in the consumer retail market (e.g., Denmark, Norway, Sweden, Hungary, Latvia, Singapore, and Kuwait), the pattern in Canada is not unique.

Financial Services

Financial services are provided through credit unions or caisses populaires, and as with user-based co-operatives in general, the members are the users of the service. Credit unions and caisses populaires across Canada operate within two systems, le Mouvement des caisses Desjardins (the Desjardins Group), primarily in Quebec but also in other parts of francophone Canada and branching into other regions as well, and credit unions affiliated with the Credit Union Central of Canada, predominantly in English Canada. The Desjardins Group had $144 billion in assets in 2007 and 5.8 million members in 549 caisses populaires (Desjardins, 2008). For 2006, the 485 credit unions affiliated with the Credit Union Central of Canada had 4.9 million members and assets of about $95 billion (Credit Union Central of Canada, 2007), although with the exception of Saskatchewan where credit unions have 35 per cent of the market, they lack the same penetration as in Quebec where Desjardins is the largest employer in the province.

A Closer Look: Desjardins

One of the best kept secrets in Canada is that Desjardins, the sixth-largest financial institution in this country, is at its core, a co-operative, and it bears the name of the founder of the country's first credit union or caisse populaire. Alphonse Desjardins, a journalist who was influenced by experiments in Germany, Italy, and France, with his wife Dorimène, co-founded Canada's first credit union (Caisse d'épargne Desjardins) in Lévis, near Quebec City (Desjardins, 2008; Kenyon, 1976). By 1909, there were over a hundred caisses populaires, most associated with Catholic parishes in rural Quebec.

At this point, Desjardins is much more than a credit union, and it is referred to as a financial conglomerate or 'Group' involving not only its network of caisses populaires and credit unions in Quebec, the Atlantic Provinces Acadian region, Ontario, and Manitoba but also a series of related services, mostly subsidiaries, for example: insurance (Desjardins Financial Security Life Assurance Company, Desjardins General Insurance, The Personal, Certas Direct Insurance Company, Fonds de sécurité Desjardins); asset management (Desjardins Asset Management; Desjardins Global Asset Management); brokerage and investment (Desjardins Securities); property Management (Desjardins Gestion immobilière); Venture Capital Management (Desjardins Venture Capital; Capital régional et coopératif Desjardins); Asset Custody (Desjardins Trust), Banking (Desjardins Bank in Florida).

In 2007, Desjardins had about 40,000 employees and served more than 5.8 million members. Unlike a bank, which pays its dividends to shareholders, Desjardins' dividends go to its members, $592 million in 2007, based on patronage or their use of services. Also, Desjardins' caisses populaires are governed by elected members, about 7,000, and this feature differentiates it from other large financial institutions and is why we refer to Desjardins as a social economy business.

Credit unions, like co-operatives in general, are formed around a common bond of association for their members. Many of the earlier financial co-operatives, particularly in Quebec and in the Atlantic Provinces, where the Antigonish movement led by Father Moses Coady took hold in the 1930s, drew their members from Catholic parishes. However, union locals, ethnic, professional and political associations also have had a history of organizing financial co-operatives. More recently, financial co-operatives have adopted a community bond of association, thereby making membership accessible to everyone desiring to participate. Vancity, the largest single credit union in Canada, started in Vancouver but since has branched out to the Fraser Valley and Victoria. The pattern among credit unions is one of consolidation and the use of a regional bond of association of increasing range. As this has occurred, the credit union difference has been called into question, as the impact of members in local communities is reduced. Interestingly, while credit unions had the qualities of a social movement in their formative period, where they made credit available to farmers and workers who could not access it through the banks, and still refer to themselves as a movement (note Desjardins' name, le Mouvement des caisses Desjardins), the most recent innovation in credit, micro-lending, grew out of a bank in Bangladesh, the Grameen Bank, and has evolved into a social movement that for the most part has bypassed credit unions (see chapter 8 for a discussion of micro-lending).

Insurance

Another financial service in which Canada's co-operatives have had success is insurance, but these organizations are subsidiaries of other co-operatives rather than being co-operatives with the policyholders as members. Co-operative-owned insurance companies are large and eight have over $19 billion in assets and provide service to 10 million policyholders (Co-operatives Secretariat, 2007a). The Co-operators, possibly the best known, was started in 1946 by the Saskatchewan Wheat Pool and currently is owned by The Co-operators Group, whose board consists primarily of major co-operatives across Canada (Co-operators, 2006). The Desjardins Group alone owns four insurance companies through the Desjardins General Insurance Group (Desjardins, 2008).

Ironically, the insurance organizations most akin to co-operatives, farm mutuals, operate apart from the co-operative sector, and are incorporated under a special section of the Insurance Act. Yet in a farm mutual, as in a user-based co-operative, the policyholder is a member with only one vote, regardless of the size and the number of policies held. (There are also life insurance companies that have a mutual structure; most of these converted to mutuals from joint stock companies to protect themselves from takeovers.) As early as the 1830s, farmers, as part of a rural tradition of mutual aid, began organizing mutual insurance to protect themselves against fires and accidents. The Canadian Association of Mutual Insurance Companies (CAMIC) represents ninety-eight property and casualty mutuals operating in rural areas across Canada; their members are 3.7 million policyholders, and the associated companies hold $4.4 billion in assets for their members (CAMIC, 2007).

Other Services

Co-operatives are best known for the aforementioned services, and organizations in those domains pack the most economic muscle and membership. However, the largest number of co-operatives in Canada is in a growing variety of services with a more recent history. One example is school supply co-operatives for materials like stationery and books, organizations found almost exclusively in Quebec, where eighty-seven such co-operatives operate. These co-operatives, branching out into services such as cafeterias and driver education, had over

508,000 member and revenues of $143 million in 2004 (Co-operatives Secretariat, 2007a).

There are 2,200 housing co-operatives, now the largest group in Canada, with about 114,000 members; 390 child care and nursery co-operatives with 34,000 members; and 98 health care co-operatives with 66,500 members. Some other service co-operatives are funeral services (56), primarily in Quebec but also in the Atlantic Provinces; water supply co-operatives (166), primarily in Alberta, Manitoba, and Quebec; natural gas and rural electrification co-operatives (124), almost exclusively in rural Alberta; recreational co-operatives (259), particularly in Saskatchewan, engaged in the management of community centres, skating and curling rinks, golf courses, campgrounds, and swimming pools; communication co-operatives in radio TV/cable and editing and publishing (103); community development co-operatives (300), predominantly in Saskatchewan, that foster local leadership skills and innovation and solving social and economic problems; and transportation co-operatives, primarily taxi, airport limousines, freight services, and a small number of car-sharing co-operatives in Toronto and Vancouver (62).

There are many services in which users are members of co-operatives. This model is relatively easy to organize because it requires minimal user commitment – a small membership share and the right to participate in the governance. However, most often members do not participate in the governance. Of the aforementioned services, housing, health care, and child care, will be discussed in greater detail in chapter 5 on public sector non-profits, as they also depend in part on government financing and policy direction.

Worker Co-operatives

In some ways, this is the most interesting of the co-operative models, but historically it has been the most difficult to organize and the least stable. In a worker co-operative the workers are the members, and the co-operative's purpose is to meet the needs of its workers, primarily for employment but in other ways. Worker co-operatives are an ideal expression of workplace democracy in that the workers are like citizens of a democracy, each with one vote in electing representatives from among their membership to the board of directors (Ellerman, 1990). This arrangement differs from either a user-based co-operative or a marketing co-operative, as in both of those cases the workers are employees of the co-operative and generally not part of the membership. (In a user-based co-operative, the employees could be members as service users, but not as workers.)

In Canada, worker co-operatives started forming in the nineteenth century, supported by the Knights of Labour, a very influential union group at that time, and the Iron Moulders International Union in Ontario (Kealey, 1980; Kealey and Palmer, 1987). Among the initiatives undertaken was the creation of the *Star*, the forerunner to Canada's largest daily newspaper, the *Toronto Star*. Other analysts were already drawing the conclusion that the worker co-operative could not succeed, a critique promoted by the Fabian theorists, Beatrice Potter (Webb) and her husband, Sidney (Potter, 1904; Webb and Webb, 1920, 1921). The critique was broad, but focused on inadequate finances that many agreed was a central concern. The Webbs' critique was very influential, and it turned the co-operative movement away from worker co-operatives to a consumer or user model.

Ironically, perhaps, the reason for the predominance of the user-based over the worker model may lie in its weakness as a co-operative: the minimal member commitment. The worker co-operative, by comparison, requires a large time commitment to decision-making and a substantial financial investment from members. For user-based co-operatives, relatively few members participate in the governance (board of directors, annual general meetings, and committees of the board), the membership fee is typically very small, and in addition users of the service can easily exit and take their business elsewhere, should they desire to do so. For members of a worker co-operative, their investment can make their exit problematic, and their investment is tied to their job, a form of double jeopardy that relatively few workers seem willing to accept.

In statistical terms, the worker co-operative is much less prominent than any of the other models, whether in business scale or membership. In 2004, there were 358 worker co-operatives with about 14,600 members and $474.4 million in revenues (Co-operatives Secretariat, 2007a). Most are in the province of Quebec, and 59 per cent of the revenues are from forestry co-operatives, largely in Quebec. Forty-one forestry co-operatives in Quebec are associated with their own federation, the Fédération Québecois des Coopératives Forestières, with 4,200 members and $310 million of revenues (Coopératives Forestières, 2007). The first forestry co-operative in Quebec started in 1938 and by 1970 there were 167, but under government pressure these were consolidated, as the co-operatives were required to enter into a management agreement with the government to have cutting rights to public lands.

Another cluster of worker co-operatives in Quebec are in the ambulance sector and organized through the Confédération des syndicats nationaux (CSN), one of the two major labour federations in Quebec. Outside of Montreal, these co-operatives, whose services are publicly funded, control close to 40 per cent of the market, and are dominant in such centres as Quebec City, Gatineau and Trois Rivières (Craddock and Vayid, 2004).

Most other worker co-operatives in Canada are micro businesses in such fields as fair trade and natural foods (see the case study of The Big Carrot at the end of chapter 1). Some are also branching into services through the Internet, for example, *Toronto the Better Directory* is an online branch of Libra Information Services, and includes listings of 'businesses dedicated to maintaining and building a progressive Toronto that is an inclusive, just and creative community' (Toronto the Better, 2008). The online business earns its revenues from the sale of shopping cards through which purchasers obtain discounts at the businesses listed in the directory.

The Canadian Worker Co-operative Federation, formed in 1990, serves as an umbrella organization, and co-operatives in Quebec belong to the Fédération québécoise des coopératives de travail. Quebec also has a worker-shareholder co-operative, a variation of the worker co-operative, which reduces some risk associated with the archetypical model. In this model, a group of employees purchase a block of the company's shares, thereby allowing them to have a voice at the board of directors. Some worker-shareholder co-operatives are established to prevent plant closings and others are undertaken as a means to encourage groups of workers to become investors in the business that employs them. Workers organized through a shareholder co-operative enter into an agreement with the other principals in the company. At of the end of 2005 there were a hundred such co-operatives operating in Quebec (LePage, 2006). This arrangement is similar to the popular employee stock ownership plans (ESOPs) in the United States; however, unlike most ESOPs, in a worker shareholder co-operative the workers have complete voting rights.

A second variation of the worker co-operative model in Quebec is the multi-stakeholder co-operative, also referred to as a *solidarity co-operative* in so far as it involves multiple stakeholders (workers, users, other community organizations) in the governance. Arguably, the multi-stakeholder co-operative is a distinct model, not a worker co-operative. The prototype occurred in the mid-1980s when The Co-operators Group, the holding company for Co-operators Insurance, initiated a restructuring at several subsidiaries including Co-operators Data (Jordan, 1989). These subsidiaries had three stakeholder groups – the employees, users of the service, and The Co-operators Group – each with defined rights. The Co-operators took this experiment further and proposed to the Ontario government in 1990 that it would create a non-profit auto insurer with three stakeholders: drivers, employees, and government representatives (Co-operators Group, 2007). The proposal was not accepted, and the experiment at The Co-operators other subsidiaries did not endure, but it sparked a lot of interest including at the International Co-operative Alliance, where the Chair of the Research Committee, Sven Ake Böök from Sweden, issued a challenge: 'Why not radically rethink the concept of ... membership? Why not try a more mixed membership ... so that it is possible to be a member ... as a user [of service], an owner, a financier, and as an employee' (1990: 41).

In Quebec, the challenge that Ake Böök issued was taken up, and in 2004 there were 121, multi-stakeholder co-operatives, most providing homecare to seniors and others in need (Co-operatives Secretariat, 2007a). Having a worker co-operative as part of a broader organization – as in a multi-stakeholder or a worker-shareholder co-operative – reduces the financial load for employees and the inordinate risk of a worker co-operative.

In spite of their limited impact in Canada, there are some strikingly successful examples of worker co-operatives internationally. The one most cited is the Mondragon Co-operative Corporation in the Basque region of Spain, an experiment in democratic worker ownership that has evolved from 1956 to become an international corporation with subsidiaries in eighteen countries including India and China. Sales in 2006 were 13.4 billion euros and there are 83,600 employees world-wide, 36 per cent of whom are members of the co-operative (Monasterio, Telleria, and Etxebarria, 2007; Mondragon Co-operative Corporation, 2007). Interestingly, Mondragon refers to itself as a 'neoco-operative' because many co-operatives have been consolidated into one group, thereby weakening the influence of individual members. Also, outside of the Basque region, the workers within the Mondragon system are in a conventional labour relationship, not members of the co-operative. Worker co-operatives have also evolved in industries in the Emilia Romagna region of Northern Italy (Earle, 1986). (For a more elaborate analysis of a worker co-operative, see the case study of The Big Carrot at the end of chapter 1.)

Second- and Third-Tier Models

The co-operative principles encourage co-operatives to work together, one method of doing so being tiering arrangements. In the typical co-operative (also, referred to as 'first tier'), members are individuals. In second-tier co-operatives, members are first-tier co-operatives, each with one vote. Examples of second-tier co-operatives referred to above are Federated Co-operatives and Co-op Atlantic, the wholesalers and co-ordinating organizations for regional systems of first-tier retailers. This same practice applies for credit unions, the first-tier organizations belonging to credit union centrals in their province, for example, the Credit Union Central of New Brunswick or the Desjardins Group in Quebec and other francophone communities in Canada. Umbrella organizations for first-tier co-operatives are common for each type of co-operative service. In addition, second-tier organizations can belong to a third-tier structure, as in the Credit Union Central of Canada, a confederation of provincial or second-tier credit unions. Some apex organization – the Canadian Co-operative Association and Conseil canadienne de la coopération – have members that are a mix of first- and second-tier co-operatives.

The tiering arrangement represents a type of functional integration in which co-operatives with common needs co-operate with each other through an apex organization that helps them with their service provision. Often apex organizations serve as the voice of the sector (its members) to government, seeking to represent their needs. Sometimes they provide practical services to member organizations such as assistance with loans, loan guarantees, and information. Interprovincial Co-operatives acts as brokers for national and international markets for regional second-tier food wholesalers that are its members. These second- and third-tier co-operatives serve similar functions as the business associations for private sector interests and also have parallels to the apex organizations for clusters of non-profits, for example, the Canadian Environmental Network and Canadian Ethnocultural Council (see chapter 6). Arctic Co-operatives Ltd., the case study at the end of this chapter, is an outstanding example of a second-tier co-operative, serving thirty-one member-co-operatives in Nunavut and the Northwest Territories.

Non-profits as Social Economy Businesses

As indicated in chapter 1, the Statistics Canada survey for the year 2003 estimated that 35 per cent of non-profit revenue was earned, 20 per cent from the sale of goods and services and 11 per cent from membership fees (Hall et al., 2005). This means that for 2003, more than $39 billion in non-profit revenues were earned, which is about 10 per cent more than that earned by co-operatives, but spread over many more organizations. In fact, if a small group of very large non-profits like universities and hospitals relying heavily on government funding are excluded, 43 per cent of non-profit revenues are earned. While small amounts might be spread across the 161,000 non-profits estimated by Statistics Canada, some non-profits operate either exclusively or primarily in the market.

This might seem odd, as the notion of *non-profit* appears inconsistent with the spirit of the market. The Canada Revenue Agency (2008) definition is: 'A non-profit organization (NPO) is a club, society, or association that's organized and operated solely for: social welfare, civic improvement, pleasure or recreation, any other purpose except profit.' The definition focuses on the functions of non-profits. The following is a definition that we propose, adapted from the Humboldt California Foundation (2007): *A non-profit is self-governing organization, including corporations without share capital, societies or trusts, but also unincorporated associations, formed not for private gain but for public or mutual benefit purposes.* This definition highlights the many forms that non-profits can take, including not being incorporated, and that public benefit and mutual benefit are not mutually exclusive; this definition could also be applied to co-operatives without share capital, but such organizations would also utilize the co-operative principles. Moreover, the definition highlights a key feature of non-profit corporations that differentiates them from other corporations in that they are without share capital. This feature is important because it means that all of the revenues go to costs associated with the service, and similarly, deficits, unless they are made up in the future or from reserves, involve service reductions. This dynamic is not a guarantee of virtue, as a non-profit could pay staff excessive amounts, but generally this is not the case, and more often the opposite is true, as non-profits lack sufficient resources.

According to Statistics Canada, 42 per cent of non-profits have revenues of $30,000 or less and another 3 per cent have absolutely no revenues. Organizations with small amounts of revenue are concentrated in sports, recreation, and religion, typically small congregations, and rely heavily on volunteers. In fact, 54 per cent of non-profits have no staff, and another 26 per cent have from one to four staff; in other words, only 20 per cent of non-profits have more than four staff. Two per cent of non-profits account for 71 per cent of the paid staff. Organizations with limited revenues and without paid staff rely on volunteers. In the section that follows, we discuss two groupings of market-based activities by non-profits: commercial non-profits and quasi-commercial non-profits. Unlike co-operatives, there is no detailed database of non-profits broken down by services, so this account is anecdotal.

Commercial Non-profits

Combining the words *commercial* and *non-profit* may be considered an oxymoron, because the public perception of a non-profit is the antithesis of commercial. Non-profits are associated with the provision of a service at cost; commercial, in contrast, is associated with pecuniary motives including profit that can lead to increased capital valuation and financial benefit to owners. Yet, for such reasons as tradition, the public perception of trust associated with non-profits, the income tax exemption for non-profits, and the liberty from shareholder pressure for management, there is a subclass of non-profits that earn their revenues in full from the market. Any surplus or net income is reinvested in the organization and also could allow for the expansion of the service.

One example of a commercial non-profit is the Canadian Automobile Association (CAA), a federation of nine affiliated clubs serving 4.9 million members across the country (CAA, 2007). The CAA was founded in 1913 and its services, which continue to expand, include roadside assistance (the primary reason for membership), travel planning and maps, and insurance. The organization also serves as an advocate to government on issues such as highway quality and is affiliated with the American Automobile Association (AAA) founded in 1902 by regional motor clubs. The CAA still promotes itself as a club and the users of the service as members, but membership rights, other than those associated with using the service, are not publicized, and member participation in the annual general meeting is unusual, a characteristic typical of commercial non-profits.

A second example is the Blue Cross (2007) organizations serving all parts of Canada and affiliated with the Canadian Association of Blue Cross Plans. These plans supplement Medicare and cover approximately seven million Canadians. Blue Cross plans in Canada represent 30 per cent of the supplementary health and dental market and generate in excess of $2 billion in annual revenue. The website for the apex group proudly declares that 'all Member Plans operate on a not-for-profit basis,' which for a health insurer is an image that builds trust and may help business. Blue Cross in Canada evolved out of a U.S. organization, currently the Blue Cross and Blue Shield Association, and, unlike Canada, includes some publicly traded affiliates.

Options for Homes (see the case study at the end of chapter 8) is another example of a non-profit business. By 2008, Options had developed eight communities of about 1,500 people in no-frills condominiums at the low end of the market. The approach, initiated by developer Mike Labbé in Toronto, is being replicated in other Canadian cities, including Vancouver, Montreal, Ottawa, and Waterloo.

These examples are but a subset of commercial non-profits that attempt to engage users, often defined as a membership, for such services as business travel, home repairs, home fuels, and education services including private schools. For organizations of this sort, there are advantages to the non-profit model that are beneficial to marketing their service.

Some such organizations provide much of their service by the Internet and might be classified as online social economy businesses. For example, Zerofootprint is a non-profit organization that attempts to determine the size of the environmental footprint and works with organizations to establish what carbon offsets are needed to nullify the environmental footprint (Dembo and Davidson, 2007; Zerofootprint, 2008).

Many such organizations offer web services, for example, Web Networks (2008) is a business that serves 'socially committed businesses' in such domains as health care, housing, and unions. Its services include website hosting, e-mail lists, action pages, secure forms, site searches for existing websites, and building a total Internet system. Web Networks operates from Toronto with about six full-time employees, but like Craigslist its interactions with clients are primarily through the Internet.

Some social economy businesses, for example Travel Cuts, have a hybrid arrangement combining a business within a non-profit organization that benefits from the business.

A Closer Look: Travel Cuts

Travel Cuts and Voyages Campus, a system of travel agencies across Canada, was founded in the mid-1960s by the Association of Ontario Student Councils, which subsequently merged into the Canadian Federation of Students. The intention behind Travel Cuts (2007) was to help students obtain discounts on airline and train tickets as well as the popular International Student Identity cards, but the orientation has broadened to the public at large. To that end, Travel Cuts is affiliated with a network of student travel agencies around the world.

Travel Cuts is a share capital company that is 76 per cent owned by the Canadian Federation of Students and 24 per cent by the Canadian Student Horizons Group, representatives of those organizations forming the board of directors in proportion to their shareholding. In addition to the direct benefits to students that Travel Cuts provides, the 'owners,' so to speak, receive 1 per cent of gross sales to students. Travel Cuts is but one of an array of programs offered by the Canadian Federation of Students, including discounts on cell phones through an arrangement with StudentPhones.com and the StudentSaver Card that can be used in seventy countries.

Another example of a hybrid arrangement is the University of Toronto Press (UTP), Canada's largest university press. UTP, as a not-for-profit corporation, operates a group of divisions as businesses: scholarly books, journals, reference books, the University of Toronto Bookstores, a campus printing operation, and a division that sells publishing distribution services to other publishers (Harnum, 2007). UTP owned a full-service printing business until January 2007, when it was sold. The Press undertakes one financial statement for all of its divisions, and through this process the other divisions subsidize scholarly book publishing, its primary mission and always a challenging market. As a not-for-profit, the UTP pays no business tax, and therefore is able to reinvest all of its net income in the organization. In this model, the businesses are not simply subsidizing the non-profit press, but form the sum total of its operations. Therefore, the University of Toronto Press and others like it (e.g., McGill-Queen's University Press) and elsewhere (University of Chicago Press, Yale University Press) might be viewed as commercial non-profits. They compete in the market through a group of business divisions contained within a non-profit, and like any other commercial enterprise – non-profit or business – the market becomes the measure of their viability.

Businesses owned by Aboriginal communities could be viewed as a hybrid arrangement. We discuss that model in chapter 4 as a form of community economic development because such businesses are set up for community benefit and often involve partnerships with government agencies, as is typical of community economic development.

Quasi Commercial Non-profits

Many non-profits fit this category, and some could be easily viewed as commercial non-profits, as the service users pay either the market rate or something akin to it. These organizations differ from commercial non-profits because some services are supplemented by volunteers, and they may combine their commercial services with charitable functions, a dual identity. The YMCA network is a classic example in that it is a recreational facility whose members pay to join, but it also has a charitable arm to subsidize low-income members. The Y also provides youth services to the homeless, child care, summer camps, employment training, settlement assistance to recent immigrants in need, and supports international development work. The Ys pay fees to the YMCA Canada (2007), the umbrella organization for sixty affiliates across the country, and these are part of an international network in 122 countries affiliated with the World Alliance of YMCAs. The Ys compete effectively in the commercial market – while private sector health clubs come and go, the Y is very stable. For its charitable services, the Ys across Canada mobilize contributions from their members, donations totalling $23 million and one million hours of volunteering. Through a funding arrangement with the Canadian International Development Agency (CIDA), YMCA Canada supports partnerships with Ys in other countries. The Y is a social economy business, but with a difference, and also a charitable organization; hence the label 'quasi commercial.'

The Y is but one of many non-profit programs oriented towards health and well-being and youth services. The roots for such non-profits are the 'worker improvement movement' in mid-nineteenth century England, and similar movements subsequently in the United States and Canada. As people shifted from the countryside to the city, there was concern about moral decay. With a view towards 'building character' in the younger generation, religious groups and do-gooders among the middle class started sponsoring organizations that, in the words of historian David Macleod (2007: 10), were 'intended to counter urban disorder and restore moral order in the community.'

Conclusion

In this chapter, we focused on social economy businesses – co-operatives and credit unions that sell their services to a membership, and commercial and quasi-commercial non-profits. The first part of the chapter attempted to differentiate between social economy businesses and businesses operating within the private sector that have strong social commitments (referred to as social businesses). That discussion indicated how increasingly businesses are attempting to acknowledge their social commitments and struggling with corporate social responsibility. That discussion also gives examples of some businesses that changed their fundamental characteristics to a point that approximated those of social economy businesses. Private sector businesses of this sort, albeit anomalous, straddle the line between the two types of organization. They are profit earning, but as in the case of Newman's Own redistribute their net income to charitable causes, or, as in the case of the John Lewis Partnership and Zeiss, have an ownership structure that approximates a non-profit because their shares are locked into a trust. Scott Bader, we argued, crossed the line, and embraced the co-operative form. The Grameen family of businesses serving the poor of Bangladesh also exemplifies how a private sector business can be guided by a social mission of alleviating poverty. These firms straddling the line between the private sector and the social economy describe the challenge in determining where the private sector ends and social economy businesses begin.

Given that some agricultural co-operatives, a form of social economy business, are able to demutualize and become private sector firms underlines this point. Nevertheless, we stick to our argument, presented in chapter 1, that organizations in the social economy share a set of common characteristics in varying degree, and that this pertains to social economy businesses, as these are organizations with social objectives that are owned by no one in the traditional sense; they depend to some extent on the volunteer services of members, minimally to serve on their board of directors and committees and in some cases in service provision; and they are centres of civic engagement through which members can share understandings with each other on issues of common concern and that they can elect a governance from among their membership. Arguably, social economy businesses set a higher standard for conventional businesses through democratic decision-making and commitment to a community. Arguably too, social economy businesses are influenced by conventional businesses in their practices and have moved away from their social ideals, and at the extreme, have incorporated as conventional businesses.

* * *

DISCUSSION QUESTIONS

1. Do you agree with our definition of social economy businesses as 'organizations that balance their economic and social mission and that earn either all or a sizable portion of their revenues from the marketplace'?
2. Should businesses such as Bullfrog Power, Ballard Power Systems, Newman's Own, and Craigslist be viewed as social economy businesses?
3. The International Co-operative Alliance definition of co-operative refers to them as a 'democratically-controlled enterprise.' Co-operatives that sell services to the community at large generally have low rates of member participation in decision-making, for example, participation in the annual general meeting. Is it still appropriate to view them as social economy businesses?
4. Worker co-operatives often have an active membership but they have had greater difficulty sustaining themselves than most forms of co-operatives have. Why do you think that this is so? Consider also worker co-operatives such as the Mondragon Co-operative Corporation that have been highly successful as businesses.
5. Is it appropriate to refer to a 'commercial non-profit,' as is done in this chapter?
6. Should non-profits that own businesses be viewed as non-profits? Is the non-profit simply a ruse to allow the business to avoid paying taxes?

* * *

Case for Analysis: Arctic Co-operatives Ltd.

Arctic Co-operatives Ltd. (ACL) is a service federation owned by thirty-one community-based co-operative businesses located in Nunavut and the Northwest Territories, a vast distance across Canada's north (ACL, 2007). The ACL system is the largest employer of Aboriginal peoples outside of government. ACL, as noted earlier in this chapter, is a second-tier co-operative, meaning that other co-operatives, rather than individuals, are members. ACL, with its home office in Winnipeg, combines the economic purchasing power of the thirty-one co-operative businesses and provides support to them in serving their members in an economically advantageous way. As noted in Exhibit 2.1, ACL has embraced eleven objectives that are economic, cultural, social, and environmental. Among its economic objectives are the sale of Aboriginal art for its member co-operatives at the best possible price, the purchase of goods and services that its member co-operatives need, and the provision of financing for its thirty-one member co-operatives through the Arctic Co-operative Development Fund, which it controls.

The thirty-one co-operatives are owned by the Inuit, Dene, and Métis peoples. A total of 21,000 people living in communities served by these co-operatives are members and owners, and, as in co-operatives in general, they hold one voting share that entitles them to participate in the governance, that is, 'one member/one vote.' In 2007, the co-operatives generated $146 million in revenues and employed 1,000 people in communities throughout the north.[2] The individuals who are member-owners of the thirty-one local co-ops receive patronage refunds based on use of the co-operatives' services. In 2007 local co-operative members received $5.8 million in patronage refunds.

In addition to the revenue reported by the thirty-one member co-operatives, ACL itself had revenues of $99 million in 2007, through its sales to its member co-operatives and to others in the marketing of members' art. In 2007, the thirty-one member co-operatives received patronage refunds of $2.6 million from ACL based on service use, and between 1986 and 2007 patronage refunds totalled $34.6 million.

---

2 Thanks to Andy Morrison, the CEO of ACL, for his feedback and assistance with the most current data on ACL. See also http://www.arcticco-op.com (accessed 3 July 2008).

The co-operative system in the Arctic has a financial arm, the Arctic Co-operative Development Fund, with the same board of directors, management, and staff as ACL. Its purpose is to provide financial services to the co-operatives so that they can be financially viable, follow good business practices, and grow. In 2007, the fund financed $20 million of the member co-ops' resupply purchases and provided a total of $27 million in financing. Since 1986, the Fund has advanced over $383 million to the thirty-one co-operatives. The Arctic Co-operative Development Fund earns interest from its loans to its member co-operatives, $2 million in 2007. However, since 1986, 64 per cent of all interest paid by member co-operatives to the Arctic Co-operative Development Fund has been returned as patronage refunds, $16.6 million in total and $1.2 million in 2007.

According to ACL's CEO, Andy Morrison, 'every year, [co-ops] across the Arctic are building infrastructure' (Obleman, 2008). In 2008, there were many infrastructure projects. They included the construction of a new co-op store in Hall Beach; renovations to hotels in Rankin Inlet, Pangnirtung, and Baker Lake; the construction of a new hotel in Pond Inlet as well as the building of a garage for fuel delivery vehicles in Gjoa Haven; and multi-unit housing in Repulse Bay. Most of the construction workers are local and they have four to six months of work. In addition, work has been completed on a warehouse in Cambridge Bay, and a four-plex and a Parks Canada building in Repulse Bay.

Backgound

The Inuit, Dene, and Métis were traditionally nomadic peoples; however, in the 1950s, they began to create and settle in communities to get education and health care. They formed businesses and structured them as community-owner co-operatives. They chose such a structure as it fit well with their own values and their 'sharing culture' (ACL, 2008; RDI, 2005). As well, the founding members did not want people from outside their culture to provide services. Rather, they wanted to do so themselves and wanted to use the profits to better the local communities by investing in more businesses and by creating employment.

The early co-operatives were based on traditional work such as fur harvesting, arts and crafts, and fishing. Now the co-operatives run retail outlets, hotels and inns, cable operations, construction and property rental businesses, airlines agencies, and freight hauling services. Among the most famous are Inns North, which is a chain of twenty-two hotels, and the West Baffin Eskimo Co-operative in Cape Dorset (2003), which has produced and sold prints and carvings since 1959.

As the activities of the co-operatives became more complex, the members saw a need for more service and technical support for their businesses. In response, they created a number of service co-operatives. 'These new [co-operative] federations enabled the small [co-operatives] to assist each other' (ACL, 2008). The first federation, created in the 1960s, was the Canadian Arctic Producers. In 1972, the Canadian Arctic Co-operative Federation was created, and in 1981, the two merged to become ACL. An important influence in creating these federations and Arctic Co-operatives Ltd. was Andrew Goussaert, a missionary who came to Canada in 1956 and worked with the Inuit in the Central Arctic. Andrew Goussaert was the first chief executive officer of ACL, and for his life's work he received the Canadian Co-operative Achievement Award in 2008.

Mission

ACL's mission is 'to be the vehicle for service to, and co-operation among the multi-purpose Co-operative businesses in Canada's north, by providing leadership and expertise to develop and safeguard the ownership participation of our Member Owners in the business and commerce of their country, to assure control over their destiny' (ACL, 2008).

The mission is supported by eleven equally important objectives. They cover economic, educational, human resource, and advocacy aspirations. They are presented in detail in Exhibit 2.1.

Structure

ACL is co-operatively owned and democratically controlled by the thirty-one autonomous co-operatives, which are grouped geographically into seven electoral districts. Each member co-operative is entitled to two voting delegates at ACL's annual general meeting. ACL's board of directors is elected by the delegates at the meeting; there are seven members, one from each of the seven electoral districts. ACL's CEO is appointed by the board (ACL, 2008).

* * *

DISCUSSION QUESTIONS

1. How does ACL's structure support the achievement of the organization's objectives, as outlined in Exhibit 2.1?
2. Could ACL have a different structure and still be effective? Why?

EXHIBIT 2.1 ACL'S 11 OBJECTIVES (ACL, 2008)

1. To improve the economic well-being of Co-op members by providing the highest long-term return for arts and crafts through the promotion and marketing of member produced products at the wholesale and retail levels.
2. To provide merchandise services in a most economical and efficient way, satisfying the consumer needs of the Co-operative membership and assisting the Co-operative retail stores to improve their market share by providing top quality products and services to their member/owners and their communities.
3. To improve the understanding and effectiveness of the Co-op Movement, by providing Co-operative training and education programs to inform Co-op members, their elected officials, and their employees of their roles and responsibilities.
4. To promote the orderly growth and financial success of the Co-operative Movement through the development and implementation of policies and practices that will generate adequate levels of earnings, members' equity, and other financial strengths to enable the Co-op Movement to improve the economic well-being of their member owners.
5. To provide an environment to promote the recruitment, development, and training of northern people in employment and management positions within the Co-operative Movement.
6. To provide leadership in the growth and development of the Co-operative Movement through evaluation and participation in appropriate business opportunities and joint ventures which offer benefits to our members.
7. To provide an environment for our human resources that will enable them to achieve their personal objectives while working to maximize their potential and meeting the economic and social objectives of the organization.
8. To provide management, operational, and technical support services to Co-operatives in the most economical and efficient way to

meet the needs of Member Co-operatives and to assist them in the management and operation of their business ventures.

9. To develop and maintain effective communications and member and public relations programs to increase awareness of the nature, aim, and role ACL and the Co-operative Movement play in our economy.

10. To represent the Co-operative Movement of Canada's north with government, Aboriginal organizations, and other agencies.

11. To conduct our affairs in an environmentally and socially responsible manner, ensuring compliance with the law and with due recognition given to the unique cultures and customs of Canada's north.

3 Community Economic Development

As noted previously, we have separated community economic development, or CED as it is commonly labelled, from social economy businesses, although as will be seen in the discussion that follows the line between these two areas of the social economy can blur. Nevertheless, we make this distinction on at least two grounds: first, community economic development is commonly associated with economic and social needs that are addressed only partially through the market. Many CED projects are in regions that have a below average standard of living or involve groups who experience extraordinary challenges. Therefore, special arrangements are created by government, foundations, or some other parenting organizations to support the initiative. We view social enterprises as a special case of community economic development, and therefore discuss this phenomenon separately in chapter 4.

Figure 3.1 situates CED in the overlap between the social economy, private sector, and public sector, a location indicating that CED initiatives embrace the distinctive characteristics of the social economy such as a strong social mission, but they also earn revenues from the market and require ongoing external supports, often from government.

A second feature of CED is its orientation towards a community, typically within a geographical locale. In stating this point, we recognize that community is in flux and increasingly refers to people who share a common interest, and increasingly through Internet interactions (Wellman and Gulia, 1999). However, the CED tradition maintains a geographical orientation, and even then it refers to communities of common interest.

For the Canadian Community Economic Development Network (CCEDNet, 2007), the apex organization for CED in Canada, 'CED can

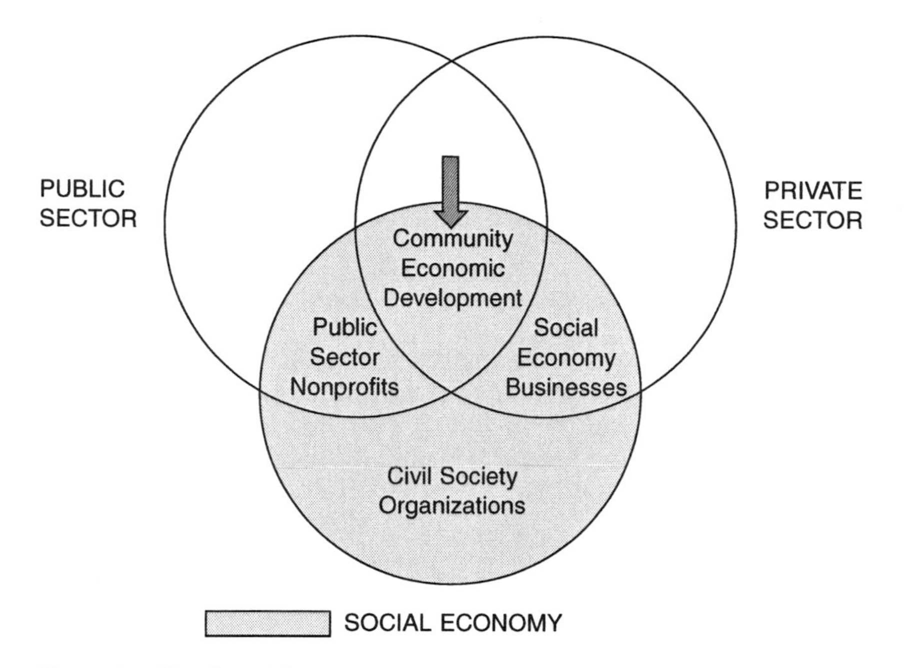

Figure 3.1 The Social Economy: An Interactive Approach

be defined as action by people locally to create economic opportunities and enhance social conditions in their communities on a sustainable and inclusive basis, particularly with those who are most disadvantaged.' The CCEDNet definition is activist in that it involves 'action by a people locally'; it focuses on the creation of 'economic opportunities,' as does the CED tradition in general; and it emphasizes 'those who are most disadvantaged,' often groups in need of affordable housing.

While there are similarities between CED and social economy businesses like co-operatives with share capital and commercial nonprofits (see chapter 2) in so far as both are engaged in the market in order to sell their services, social economy busineseses function without the ongoing external support required by CED initiatives, and they also may have greater mobility (less rootedness in one location) because of their need to be competitive within the market. Like commercial businesses in general, credit unions are merging into larger units, as are commercial non-profits. The market can influence whether a social economy business is maintained in its current form, modified, or closed completely. For CED initiatives, the workings of the market are a consideration, but the necessary supports are often linked to a particular place, and mobility for the participants beyond their local community could be problematic. The difference is one of degree, but it is nevertheless significant. In addition, CED organizations, although they may achieve independence from their parenting organization, continue to rely on ongoing supports, more so than social economy businesses do. In Canada, government agencies are an important support for many CED projects, and remain so, although if the project is relatively successful, government support usually decreases.

The root problem that spawns community economic development is social and economic inequality, a historic problem in capitalist economies and arguably a predominant characteristic of human societies in general. Canada has had an uneven mosaic of development with economic inequalities correlated with regions, race, ethnicity, and other factors. This dynamic is associated with the marketplace, which while stimulating productivity also leads to a highly unequal distribution of wealth and related benefits. Economic inequality in Canada appears to be worsening, even as overall wealth increases. According to one recent study that compared 1976–79 and 2001–04, the share of the national income earned by the top half of Canadian families increased from 73 to 79.5 per cent, with most of the increase going to the top 10 per cent; similarly, the share of the bottom half of families fell from 27 to 20.5 per cent, with most of the loss experienced by the bottom 20 per cent (Yalnizyan, 2007).

As in other countries, economic inequality in Canada is correlated with race and ethnicity, with the research indicating that relative to the norms, visible minorities earn much less money, experience greater levels of poverty, and experience less economic payoff for their education credentials (Galabuzi, 2001; Ornstein, 2000; Reitz, 2001). This point is underlined in related research (discussed below) for the Greater Toronto Area (GTA), whose population is nearly 50 per cent foreign born and increasingly made up of visible minorities.

Inequality is not something new, and for many generations it has been a topic of discussion in universities, governments, and community groups. John Porter's classic study, *The Vertical Mosaic: An Analysis of Social Class and Power in Canada* (1965), portrayed Canada as structured around a series of overlapping elites, heavily Anglo-Saxon and heavily concentrated in Toronto and Montreal. The issues that Porter raised were not simply Canadian but general characteristics in differing degree of capitalist economies – highly productive and highly inegalitarian, with wealth heavily concentrated in select commercial centres. A similar analysis on an international level is presented by Thurow (1996), illustrating how corporate elites are appropriating an excessive share of the new wealth that their firms are generating. A more recent study by the Canadian Centre of Policy Alternatives (CCPA) underlines this point, indicating that the salaries of Canada's hundred best-paid CEOs in 2007 averaged $10.4 million (ranging from $3 to $51.6 million) (Mackenzie, 2009). Put in perspective, this report indicates that these CEOs would require from 9:00 a.m. until 9:04 a.m. on 2 January 2009 to earn the same amount as the average Canadian in a total year (i.e., $40,237). The top eighty-nine CEOs earned the same amount as all of the city of Brandon, Manitoba's 41,511 residents combined. As illustrated in the financial collapse in the fall of 2008, exhorbitant CEO pay is not necessarily a reward for corporate performance. Without belabouring the point, even within a relatively wealthy country such as Canada, there are chronic and growing inequalities.

In response to market-based inequalities, governments, foundations, and community groups have attempted to reduce the associated hardships. In this undertaking, government social programs, United Way campaigns, and other forms of social giving might be viewed as a countervailing force attempting to smooth, in some small degree, the rough edge of a market economy. While this intervention takes many forms, in this chapter we look at some examples of community economic development initiatives involving government and other parenting organizations that attempt to support market-based initiatives by local community groups. Indeed, the field of community economic development is vast, and could in itself be the subject of a lengthy book. It is not our intention to capture all of community economic development in Canada. Our selection is illustrative, and inevitably important examples are missed. Other aspects of community economic development are discussed in chapter 4, on social enterprises, as well as in other parts of the book.

The remainder of the chapter is organized as follows: government-sponsored regionally based programs oriented to low-income communities including public sector non-profits that deliver these programs; community development corporations created by activists in communities in need; the performing arts as a form of CED; the underlying values of CED; and the conclusion.

Regional Programs for Low-Income Communities

Canada is made up of regions with varying degrees of prosperity, a pattern that has its roots in the birth of the country and has continued to the present, albeit with some shifts between the haves and have-nots. The mosaic of regional inequalities is well documented as is the history of government programs intended to address this problem (Baurnier, 1998; McGee, 1992; Phillips, 1982). Although some provinces have fared better historically than others, with Alberta, Ontario, and British Columbia having on average higher personal income and lower unemployment than Atlantic Canada, this type of description is misleading as within each province there is unevenness in the distribution of wealth, and the same can be said for urban centres as well. In Ontario, which has had a major share of Canada's manufacturing industries and which has been a favoured location of subsidiaries of multinationals, most headquartered in the United States, wealth is concentrated in the southwestern corridor (Toronto-Windsor) and the Ottawa region. With the decline of automobile manufacturing in Canada, Ontario's southwestern corridor is experiencing increased economic stress, and its privileged status within Canada may be changing. Other parts of the province – the resource-based north with many single-industry communities, and the east, relying on agriculture and light industry – have lacked the prosperity of the industrial belt and the capital region.

This pattern of regional inequalities exists throughout Canada. In Newfoundland and Labrador there is much greater prosperity in the Avalon Peninsula than in the rest of the province because St John's is the main commercial centre and the focus of government activity. In comparison with St John's, the Northern Peninsula, with its reliance on the depressed fishing industry, is impoverished, and even more so if the comparison is with the rest of Canada. In New Brunswick, there is much greater prosperity in Moncton, the primary commercial centre, than in the resource-based north. This same disparity exists between Cape Breton and Halifax in Nova Scotia, and West Prince County and Charlottetown in Prince Edward Island. Throughout Canada, there are similar poorer regions, for example, northern and northwestern Quebec, the Interlake region of Manitoba, parts of rural Saskatchewan, the interior of British Columbia, and vast parts of the North. In general, the most depressed areas are dependent on primary industries that are past their peak and related international price arrangements that are beyond their control. Yet some regions relying on primary industries do prosper when their resources are in demand, for example, oil in Alberta and Newfoundland and potash in Saskatchewan.

Charting the mosaic of economic inequality goes beyond a broad regional analysis because within relatively wealthy urban centres there are pockets of poverty, as has been carefully documented in a series of reports of the Greater Toronto Area by the United Way Toronto – *Decade of Decline* (2002); *Poverty by Postal Code* (2004); and *Strong Neighbourhoods: A Call to Action* (2005) – supplemented by the report, *Three Cities within Toronto* (Hulchanski, 2007), and the *TD Economics Special Report* (2007). The 2004 United Way report, in particular, highlights that the number of high-poverty neighbourhoods in the GTA has increased from 30 to 120 and are highly concentrated in the inner suburbs; these neighbourhoods have about 43 per cent of poor families; and that immigrant families (often visible minorities) account for two-thirds of the families living in higher poverty neighbourhoods. These reports agree that there is a growing gap between rich and poor and that poverty is becoming racialized (Galabuzi, 2001, 2006). Poverty in large cities can be more severe than in smaller communities with lower housing costs and informal support systems for services that require payments in urban centres. Similarly, within rural areas, there is unevenness in the standard of living, with the greatest poverty being found in Aboriginal reserves where unemployment can be the norm and where amenities taken for granted in other parts of the country may be absent.

This uneven mosaic is the context for government programs intended to reduce the impact of inequalities between communities, a portion of which bears on the social economy. The severe cutbacks in government social programs during the mid-1990s hampered CED efforts in Canada. It is ironic, perhaps, that Paul Martin as prime minister in 2004, announced a government program to assist the social economy, because as the minister of finance in 1995, he was the architect of huge reductions in social programs. In his 1995 budget speech, Martin boasted that 'relative to the size of our economy, program spending will be lower in 1996–97 than any time since 1951.' These sharp cuts in government programs were followed by a series of federal and provincial tax cuts of about $150 billion of revenue from 2002 to 2005, revenue that could have been allocated to social programs, including CED initiatives.

There still are differing government programs such as employment insurance (formerly unemployment insurance) and job training, which are of great importance for regions relying on seasonal industries, as well as equalization payments to the poorer provinces. Regional development programs that provide assistance to business in the poorer regions of the country are a critical support to community economic development. Although the primary orientation of regional development programs is private sector business, typically small business development, this funding can include CED initiatives in the social economy.

To make such funding available, the federal government has created a policy framework, funding allocations, and special agencies that evaluate proposals and work with organizations in their region. Historically, the federal government has experimented with various ways of delivering programs that promote community economic development in high unemployment areas. For example, in the late 1950s and through the 1960s, the federal government emphasized specific initiatives such as the Technical and Vocational Training Assistance Program, the Occupational Training Act, and the Agricultural Rehabilitation and Development Program (Beaumier, 1998).

By 1969 the regional development programs were consolidated within the federal Department of Regional Economic Expansion (DREE), with much of its effort focused on Eastern Canada, and particularly its urban centres. However, by the early 1970s, the federal government began questioning centralization, and from 1984 it signed Economic and Regional Development Agreements with the provinces, making regional development a shared responsibility. From 1987 there was a further restructuring of federal agencies into the Atlantic Canada Opportunities Agency (including sub-agencies such as Enterprise Cape Breton); Western Economic Diversification Canada serving the four Western provinces; FedNor for Northern Ontario; the Federal Office of Regional Development-Quebec; and later one agency specifically for Aboriginal businesses. In addition, the federal government established programs specifically for rural communities, the Canadian Rural Partnership, and another for Aboriginal communities through its department of Indian and Northern Affairs Canada – Community Economic Development Program and the Community Economic Opportunities Program – as well as the agency Aboriginal Businesses Canada (ABC). The provinces and territorial governments also have regional development programs: Regional Development Boards in

Newfoundland; the Community and Regional Development Act of Nova Scotia; the Saskatchewan program for Urban Community Development; and the Manitoba CED Framework.

These government supports are one context through which community economic development operates, although as mentioned, the primary orientation of these programs is support for conventional business development rather than the social economy, as the Atlantic Canada Opportunities Agency (2007) makes clear: 'This ACOA program is designed to help you set up, expand or modernize your business. Focusing on small- and medium-sized enterprises, the program offers access to capital in the form of interest-free, unsecured, repayable contributions. Non-profit organizations providing support to the business community may also qualify.' Government regional development programs in other parts of Canada are similar: the orientation is to the private sector, but the door is also open to non-profit organizations.

The primary mechanism through which government currently delivers its regional development programs is the Community Futures Development Corporations of which there are 268 spread across Canada: ninety in the four Western provinces; sixty-one in Northern and Eastern Ontario; sixty-seven in Quebec under the names of Société d'aide au développement des collectivités (SADC) or d'un Centre d'aide aux entreprises (CAE); forty-one in the four Atlantic Provinces; and the remainder in the Northwest Territories and Nunavut (Pan Canadian Community Futures Group, 2007). These are non-profit corporations with community boards that operate as agents of and within the broad policy guidelines of the federal government and its regional development agencies like the Atlantic Canada Opportunities Agency, Canada Economic Development for Quebec Regions, Fednor, Western Economic Diversification Canada, and within the funding allocations flowing from these agencies.

Referring back to Figure 3.1, these are public sector non-profits that operate in the overlap between the social economy and the public sector, and that function as intermediaries between the government and local communities that they serve, and in particular, small and medium businesses within the communities. With a board and employees from the local community, they are better positioned than government bureaucrats in Ottawa or even in regional development offices to deliver business development programs. These non-profits have an outreach within their jurisdiction that would be difficult to attain in a centralized system. For example, the East Algoma Community Futures Development Corporation covers a large region in northwestern Ontario. In addition to assisting businesses with their customer base and to expand, this organization lists a series of community development services to eighteen local communities. These services go beyond direct loans and include community Internet access, community promotion projects to enhance tourism, and downtown improvement projects. The Chinook Community Futures Development Corporation in southeastern Alberta emphasizes its training programs, resource library, and its camp for youth entrepreneurs. Throughout Canada, the programs are similar, with some regional variations.

In addition to the community development services through standard government programs and delivered by a Community Futures Development Corporation, non-profit corporations, referred to as community development corporations (CDCs), have also emerged to focus specifically on CED with a non-profit orientation. In contrast to the Community Futures Development Corporation, which is a non-profit created by government, the Community Development Corporation is created by community activists. Nevertheless, these corporations are predominantly in areas serviced by government regional development programs and have benefited from the funding associated with these programs, but they have a different focus than government centres and generally project a vision of a more democratic economy and egalitarian society.

Community Development Corporations

CDCs originated as part of the American civil rights movement of the late 1960s, and the desire to overcome the poverty experienced by Blacks and other impoverished groups living in ghettos of decaying cities. The idea was taken up in Canada and the CDC has become a vehicle through which community activists can channel their energies towards developing their communities (Perry, 1987). In Canada, the first CDCs were started by co-operative activists who wanted to assist local communities to overcome their economic and social problems. In contrast to most modern co-operatives, which focus on specific services for a defined group within a community – 'unifunctional' organizations in the words of Melnyk (1985) – the CDC takes a more holistic perspective and houses a broader array of services. This strategy involves support for businesses with a community orientation (see the discussion of social economy businesses in chapter 2), including non-profits of various sorts, co-operatives, and social enterprises, as discussed in chapter 4. One of the definitional challenges for this type of organization is that community per se no longer is clearly defined and, as noted, it tends to be based more on personal networks, often online, that span the globe. As such, the constituency base for a CDC can be much less clear than for co-operatives or other mutual associations. Often the membership is ad hoc and the governance may lack the representative structure of co-operatives. Although CDCs vary in their organization and programs, they have the common feature of a support system for related social enterprises and other non-profit organizations. In some cases, the CDC may plan local development itself and control the assets, either directly or through subsidiary corporations, as is illustrated by New Dawn Enterprises.

A Closer Look: New Dawn Enterprises

New Dawn Enterprises Ltd. of Sydney, Cape Breton, is probably the best known CDC in Canada and is a good example of such an arrangement. Formally incorporated in 1976 and believed to be the oldest CDC in Canada, New Dawn was rooted in the Atlantic co-operative movement, also referred to as the Antigonish movement (MacLeod, 1986), a populist social movement that responded to the ravages of the Great Depression by organizing credit unions and fishers' co-operatives, and that used an innovative adult education approach called 'kitchen-table meetings' to mobilize and educate community members (Welton, 2001). New Dawn's founder and early spiritual leader was Greg MacLeod, a coalminer's son who became a priest, university professor, and community activist.

New Dawn, a not-for-profit corporation which continues to grow and provide jobs in the Sydney/Glace Bay region, contains such services as: the Cape Breton Association for Housing Development and Pine Tree Park Estates Ltd. with 220 units of accommodation for low- and middle-income households; commercial real estate; Cape Care, a homecare and home nursing service employing more than 200 in 2005; New Dawn Guest Home, a thirty-bed residential facility; and Sydney Senior Care Home Living Ltd., a caregiving arrangement that permits people with disabilities to be housed in others' homes through an arrangement managed by New Dawn.

In addition, this CDC includes Highland Resources Ltd., a career college operated by New Dawn offering training and certification in such fields as welding, continuing care, and supervisory management; and the New Dawn Community Development Educational Foundation used to fundraise to support education; the Volunteer Resource Centre, an agency that organizes volunteers for Meals on Wheels programs and for other activities; and New Dawn Immigration Consultants, which works with immigrants to Cape Breton and organizes joint ventures with businesses in other countries (New Dawn, 2006).

To develop its program, New Dawn skilfully mobilizes local resources and government funding, tapping into programs that are available through the Atlantic Canada Opportunities Agency and other government agencies. It creates jobs in communities with very high rates of unemployment and develops services needed by local residents, thereby reducing the population outflow that plagues poorer regions.

New Dawn is the oldest CDC in Canada, but it is by no means one of a kind. Another innovative example is the Quint Development Corporation, which serves five core neighbourhoods of Saskatoon (hence its name, Quint). Quint's (2007a) mission is 'to strengthen the economic and social well-being of Saskatoon's five core neighbourhoods through a community based development approach.' Much more recent than New Dawn, Quint was formed in 1995 by community residents, but like New Dawn and other community development corporations in Canada, Quint is a hub for CED in the core areas of its community. Quint's basic initiatives focus on housing, as it is a fundamental need for persons with relatively low incomes. Its 2006 annual report (Quint Development Corporation, 2007a) indicates that in ten years since its inception, Quint has built housing co-operatives for ninety families (400 individuals); assisted thirty-seven families to own their own homes; renovated two apartment buildings with forty suites, and including a child care centre, family recreation room, and community garden; established a Male Youth Lodge for homeless and itinerant youth and provided employment training for the residents; and set up Pleasant Hill Place to house young, single mothers.

In addition, Quint has placed a heavy emphasis on jobs through its Core Neighbourhood at Work program that in 2006 assisted about a hundred residents to gain employment and over fifty residents to further their education. Quint views public education as an important part of its mandate, and distributes its newsletter, *QuintEssentials*, throughout the core area. Quint also has partnerships with other organizations with overlapping goals, for example, the Saskatoon Anti-Poverty Coalition, the Saskatoon Housing Initiative Partnership, the Rainbow Community Centre, the CED Network of Saskatchewan. It also has worked closely with the University of Saskatchewan to develop a module on CED practice and to create a model of community learning practice with health colleges. In other words, Quint has a comprehensive program and participates in many ways in Saskatoon's social economy.

In its 2006 annual report, Quint presented a plan to vastly expand its services within Saskatoon's core area – the Station 20 West Development Corporation (Quint, 2007b). This would be a 45,000 square feet Community Enterprise Centre that would combine retail and commercial office space. Occupants of this space will include the following: the Good Food Junction Co-operative Grocery Store and Café; CHEP (Child Hunger and Education Program) Good Foods Inc.; Heifer International; the University of Saskatchewan Outreach and Engagement Centre; the Saskatoon Community Clinic-Westside; the College of Dentistry, the College of Medicine, Saskatoon Health Region; and the Quint Development Corporation, as well as a commercial kitchen, a multi-purpose community room, drop-in child care space, and meeting rooms. The front of Station 20 is to be a town square where residents can gather, and the rear will contain a library branch and fifty-five units of affordable housing developed by the Saskatchewan Housing Corporation.

The provincial government did not uphold its $8 million financial commitment after the 2007 election led to the defeat of the NDP by the Saskatchewan Party. This is one of the unfortunate by-products of dependence on government financing that CED organizations experience. Quint, however, has persevered, and is implementing the plan in stages, with the development funding coming from concerned citizens, religious organizations, and a variety of other social economy organizations including Affinity Credit Union, the Canadian Union of

Public Employees, and the Saskatchewan Union of Nurses, in other words, other social economy organizations. One benefit from the province's withdrawal is that the resulting community mobilization has strengthened Quint and enhanced its visibility in Saskatoon.

New Dawn and Quint are just two examples of community development corporations found across Canada; among other such organizations are the following: Supporting Employment and Economic Development (SEED), Winnipeg; River Bank Development Corporation, Prince Albert; Community Action Co-operative, Regina; Community Ownership Solutions, Winnipeg; Corporation de développement communautaire Drummond, Quebec; Corporation de développement communautaire de Sherbrooke; CDC de la Pointe, and CDC Vallée de la Matapédia; and the New Westminster Community Development Society. Some are focused on the development of co-operatives specifically, such as the regional development co-operatives throughout Quebec (Coopérative de développement régional Saguenay-Lac-Saint-Jean/Nord-du-Québec), CDR-Acadie serving northern New Brunswick, or le Conseil de développement coopérative (Evangeline community of Prince Edward Island).

Quebec has an extensive network of community economic development corporations (Corporation de développement économique communautaire) in all major urban areas (e.g., Corporation de développement économique communautaire de la ville de Québec, Corporation de Développement Économique et Communautaire Montréal-Nord). These organizations, funded by the municipal, provincial, and federal governments, bring together many stakeholders who also take an active role in the corporation's development.

Many of the Quebec initiatives are affiliated with le Chantier de l'économie sociale, an umbrella association formed from the government of Quebec's Summit on the Economy and Employment in 1996. The Quebec government had a previous history of supporting local development initiatives through its network of regional development co-operatives (Coopératives de developpement régional) affiliated through la Fédération des coopératives de développement régional du Québec and le Conseil de la coopération du Québec (FCDRQ, 2007). The regional development co-operatives support worker co-operatives and co-operatives more generally. Le Chantier places greater emphasis on other forms of non-profit community economic development, and gradually has created a voice for such associations. Favreau argues that the organizations associated with the social economy in Quebec have gathered so much strength that they have created 'a new relationship between the economic and social sphere' (2006: 13), one example being the Fiducie du Chantier de l'économie sociale, or the Chantier Trust.

A Closer Look: Fiducie du Chantier de l'économie sociale, or the Chantier Trust

The $52.8 million trust fund administered by le Chantier makes 'patient capital' available to organizations in the social economy. Fiducie du Chantier de l'économie sociale, or the Chantier Trust, as it is known in English, received its initial impetus from the package of social economy funding announced by Liberal Prime Minister Paul Martin that led the federal department, Economic Development Canada, in 2005 to approve the initial capitalization of $22.8 million over five years (Mendell and Rouzier, 2006). This amount was supplemented by investments of $12 million and $8 million, respectively, from Quebec's two labour investment funds, Fonds de solidarité FTQ (Quebec Federation of Labour) and Fondaction (Confedération des syndicates nationaux). In addition, the Quebec government invested $10 million. The fact that union-controlled investment funds would collaborate with the federal and provincial governments on this initiative reflects the breadth of the coalition and the political strength of the social economy in Quebec. Nevertheless, government agencies remain the major players in this CED initiative in Quebec, as in other parts of the country.

A need faced by social enterprises that the Trust addresses is 'patient capital' – investments in an organization with 'a 15-year capital repayment moratorium' (Fiducie du Chantier, 2008). These investments do not involve ownership, as in privately owned businesses, and do not involve immediate repayment, as in loans from conventional sources. These investments take two forms: to finance costs related to the purchase and development of real estate needed by the organization; and operations capital needed to finance the cost of new products and equipment purchases.

None of the other provinces in Canada received funding under the federal government's social economy program before the opportunity was withdrawn by the incoming federal government under Steven Harper. However, le Chantier has given community economic development in Quebec a higher profile than elsewhere in Canada, and that might have been one reason that it succeeded in assembling its trust fund. Nevertheless, there are many impressive community economic development initiatives across Canada.

Some community development corporations go beyond projects with a business focus and include community safety, neighbourhood fix-up, and housing programs. In Winnipeg, the North End Community Renewal Corporation, a spin-off of SEED Winnipeg, addresses safety and neighbourhood improvement issues in Winnipeg's rundown north end; the West Broadway Community Development Corporation and Spence Neighbourhood Association focus on the rehabilitation of housing. Many of these CDCs operate within a provincial government program, for example, Neighbourhoods Alive!, which is oriented to specific neighbourhoods in crisis (Neighbourhoods Alive, 2007).

CED organizations also have taken on an important role in small towns, often primary-resource communities, which have lost key industries or experienced the effects of government restructuring and the related withdrawal. A major study of four such communities in Canada found that in response to the withdrawal of services, nonprofit organizations, relying heavily on volunteers, attempted to fill the void (Halseth and Ryser, 2006). That particular study involved Springhill, Nova Scotia; Tweed, Ontario; Wood River, Saskatchewan; and Mackenzie, British Columbia. These communities emphasized building partnerships between government agencies, universities, businesses, and non-profit organizations. However, non-profit organizations operating in rural towns tend to be small and rely heavily on volunteers, who can only be stretched so far.

These many examples illustrate the complex relationship of CED organizations in interacting with government. Whether CED initiatives are supported through government-sponsored Community Futures Development Corporations or whether they are creations of community activists such as the classic community development corporation, they rely to a substantial degree on government programs. Part of the mandate of the community development corporation is to assist the development of enterprises that earn a portion of their revenues from the market, yet they also have a transformative vision of the economy. Often this work involves supporting the development of social enterprises that serve groups on the margins of society. The developers for these types of organization go beyond community development corporations, but nevertheless, as discussed in chapter 4, they are an excellent example of the integrative function of CED activities in general.

Underlying Values

One of the debates within community economic development is whether this practice should be viewed as a mechanism for integrating communities and individuals on the margin into the mainstream or whether CED should be seen as the seeds of a new vision of society. Social enterprises in particular (see chapter 4) are often viewed as a type of community economic development activity to integrate persons on the margins within the economy. Bill Young, the CEO of Social Capital Partners, argues that mainstreaming should be a goal of community economic development. As part of his program at Social Capital Partners, he has worked out an arrangement with the Active Green + Ross chain for auto tires and automobile service and repair that has these stores hire people who have faced employment challenges for various reasons (Laidlaw, 2007).

This orientation is distinct from that of many activists who view community economic development as the seeds of a different economy. Le Chantier de l'économie sociale, for example, emphasizes the importance of democracy in the workplace and the community as a centrepiece of the social economy and community economic development. The Canadian Community Economic Development Network (CCEDNet, 2007), the umbrella organization for community economic development in Canada, also emphasizes these distinct values of CED: 'CED has emerged as an alternative to conventional approaches to economic development. It is founded on the belief that problems facing communities – unemployment, poverty, job loss, environmental degradation and loss of community control – need to be addressed in a holistic and participatory way.'

Another leader in this field, the Centre for Community Enterprise (2007) in Port Alberni (Vancouver Island), articulates similar ideals: 'To undertake and promote approaches to training, technical assistance, publishing, research, networking, investment, and public policy that foster creative, inclusive, and sustainable community economies, particularly among Canada's marginalized populations.'

These ideals, articulated by le Chantier, CCEDNet, and the Centre for Community Enterprise, are very much the norm in the CED community. The goal is not simply to create jobs and to build better housing for persons in need, but to create a more egalitarian and democratic society, and to create more sustainable communities. These goals are challenging when CED organizations rely so heavily on government for funding. The challenge is heightened also when these activities require collaboration with the private sector, as many CED activities do. Thriving communities require small business, but generally small business is the antithesis of a democratic workplace. These contradictions notwithstanding, there is a growing legacy of community economic development in Canada that illustrates its potential and even more so with greater investment. The examples discussed in this chapter are selective.

Although our classification of CED involves activities that engage with the market and earn a substantial portion of their revenues through the payment for services by the users or clientele, it is difficult, and indeed unusual, for these services to attain self-sufficiency. Where they do, it is often because they are heavily subsidized by sub-standard pay to the employees and heavy volunteer contributions. Governments, foundations, and other forms of financial donors typically participate in the start-up, and in varying degrees as the activity progresses. Volunteer contributions are standard, not only on the board but also in service provision.

In spite of its ideals, it is not evident that community economic development has much impact on the reduction of social inequalities. Viewed cynically, it could be argued that these activities smooth the rough edge of the capitalist economy, and in particular, the tendency of the market to create inequalities, and at a growing pace. The need is far greater than the services available through the social economy. Yet for the persons who are participants of CED initiatives, the benefits are tangible.

There is another benefit to these activities that bears mention. The projects that result from CED activities involve a relationship between a clientele and service providers ranging from granting agencies, paid staff in the development group, volunteers, and the community in which the project is embedded. The value added from these projects involves a large number of so-called intangibles, things that don't find their way into accounting statements because there is not a direct market exchange involved, but are of real benefit to the providers and the communities that house these projects. This issue will be explored in chapter 9, which addresses social accounting models. One of those models, the Expanded Value Added Statement (Mook, Quarter, and Richmond, 2007), indicates how intangibles, including volunteer contributions, can be presented within an accounting framework.

CED projects have benefits in addition to the service to the clientele. These initiatives engage people with each other in a constructive dynamic or form of civic engagement (see chapter 1). Putnam (2000) refers to this dynamic as social capital – social engagement, trust, and informal cooperation. Social capital is the stuff of strong communities, and like financial investments, it can create multipliers, as strong communities pull together and initiate new projects. Therefore, even though CED initiatives are not likely to remake a society and to negate the growing inequalities that are being created through the market and related government policies that have reduced the percentage of spending on social programs in relation to the size of the economy, they have an important role in reducing the hardships associated with social inequalities.

The Performing Arts

While it may seem unusual to characterize the performing arts as a form of CED, these activities are vital to communities. It is unimaginable to think of a community without theatre, music, and dance, even if it is amateur. Moreover, performing arts organizations fit the criteria of CED in that if they are formally incorporated, they are usually non-profits that earn a portion of their revenues from the market but also rely on external supports from government and foundations. Even small amateur performing arts organizations that are part of the informal economy purchase goods and services and may draw tourists to a community.

The performing arts represent a broad category that includes theatre, music organizations, dance associations, and opera companies, and are part of an even broader category labelled as culture that includes the visual arts, heritage institutions, book publishing, film and video distribution, television, radio, and movies. While the organizational arrangements for culture in general are varied, and involve a combination of private businesses, self-employment, Crown corporations, and non-profit organizations, the performing arts have a concentration of non-profit organizations supported by government, foundations, and private interests. Some performing arts groups such as small theatres in the informal economy are supported by donations from viewers and staffed by volunteers who engage in their practice for personal satisfaction. Nevertheless, as noted, such organizations bring tangible benefits to their communities.

The performing arts make significant economic contributions which are summarized regularly by Statistics Canada. The most recent figures show that performing arts had operating revenues in 2005 of $1.2 billion, of which slightly less than half were from non-profit companies. Among the non-profit organizations, theatre companies accounted for 48 per cent of revenues (Statistics Canada, 2007b). The data indicate that for 2005 theatre companies earned $282.5 million; musical theatre and arts companies, $69.4 million; dance companies, $80.2 million; musical groups and artists, $140.2 million; and other performing arts companies, $12 million.

Non-profit performing arts companies earned half of their revenues from the market, 42 per cent from ticket sales and 8 per cent from the sale of merchandise, but governments contributed 29 per cent and private sector businesses and individuals another 21 per cent (Statistics Canada, 2006c). Government support for the performing arts started declining in 1992–93, but earned revenues and donations from businesses and individuals increased (Statistics Canada, 2000). Recently, government contributions have picked up again and in 2004 increased by 7.2 per cent over the previous year (Statistics Canada, 2006d). Among governments, the provinces contribute the most, and Quebec invests more heavily than other provinces in the performing arts, accounting for 26 per cent of total operating revenue. This larger investment by Quebec probably reflects that province's desire to preserve its unique culture. Therefore, when the Harper government announced cuts to the performing arts in its 2008 election campaign, it provoked a sharp reaction in Quebec. For Canada as a whole, with the exception of opera, governments exceed corporations and individuals in their financial support of the performing arts (Statistics Canada, 2004a), although this estimate would not take into account the imputed value of volunteer contributions. Government support is typical of community economic development in general, not just the performing arts.

Given this government support, it is usual to view the performing arts as takers of community resources; however, there are a growing number of economic impact studies demonstrating the economic benefits of the performing arts (Kuly, Stewart, and Dudley, 2005; Trillium Foundation, 2003). For example, the 2008 Juno Awards were estimated to have brought $11.3 million of economic benefit to Calgary and the surrounding areas (Calgary Arts Development, 2008). The awards generated an estimated eighty-two full-time job equivalents and $1.7 million of tax revenue including all levels of government. Therefore, the arts and the support that they receive from government do have an economic benefit.

Government support for the performing arts is usually administered through arts councils, or public sector non-profits in our schema. The directory, *Associations Canada*, lists 150 arts councils, and many of these have affiliates (e.g., the P.E.I. Council of the Arts lists six affiliates), so the actual number of outlets is much larger. In addition, the Canada Council for the Arts (2007), a government agency discussed more in chapter 5, distributes grants in an annual competition, in 2004–05 distributing $132.3 million to the arts community.

At the federal level, the Canadian Conference of the Arts (2007), founded in 1945, speaks on behalf of the arts community and advocates for them to government. The members of the Canadian Conference of the Arts are a complex web of non-profit organizations from across Canada that acts as the voice of the arts sector. Many of these are professional associations and unions speaking on behalf of various forms of artists, for example, ACTRA, L'Union des écrivaines et des écrivains québécois, the Writers Union of Canada, and the Canadian Alliance for Dance Artists. In terms of our typology presented in Figure 3.1, these would be non-profit mutual associations of the type that proliferate in civil society (see chapter 6).

Non-profit performing arts companies spend 48 per cent of their revenues on personnel, primarily payments made to performing and creative artists. About 75 per cent of the workforce is on contract, and the paid workforce is declining whereas the volunteer workforce is on the increase (Statistics Canada, 2004a). The performing arts workforce, like that of non-profits in general, relies heavily on volunteers who represent about 41 per cent of the human resources (Statistics Canada, 2006c). Small theatre and small- and medium-sized music companies rely heavily on volunteers, and in those types of organization the number of volunteers has surpassed the number of paid persons (Statistics Canada, 2004a). These organizations engage volunteers out of necessity to sustain their viability and their ability to continue services to the community.

The non-profit performing arts companies have to watch their financial bottom line closely, as their potential to overcome any significant deficit is limited and constrains their future capacity. In 2004, non-profit performing arts companies as a group had a small operating deficit of 1.6 per cent, erasing a small surplus from the year before. In general, these companies operate on a very tight margin, and they are highly dependent on government and private donors to make ends meet. Their employees tend to be underpaid, and in effect subsidize their service, as do their volunteers who contribute without charge a major portion of their human resources.

Nevertheless, these organizations do a remarkable job of producing their events, and sustaining the communities that they serve. Statistics Canada (2006c) estimates that in 2004, 500 non-profit companies produced 43,730 performances at home and abroad, attracting an estimated 14.2 million spectators. This outreach into the community is all the more remarkable when considering that these figures do not include amateur and quasi-amateur groups that operate in the informal economy. Each of these non-profit companies is unique, and serves its particular community in its own way, but often the services go beyond simply performance and involve a broader array, as illustrated by the Saskatchewan Native Theatre Company.

A Closer Look: Saskatchewan Native Theatre Company

An innovative example of how a small theatre company survives on a combination of ticket sales and government grants is the Saskatchewan Native Theatre Company (2007). This organization, operating in Saskatoon since 1999, involves a professional theatre that derives revenue from ticket sales, and also has an arts education program that might be viewed as a form of arts therapy and training for Aboriginal youth. The arts therapy allows participants to 'discover themselves.' The Circle of Voices is a full-time accredited program that trains Aboriginal youth in theatre and helps them to gain cultural understanding. The Ensemble Theatre Arts Program (ETAP), another training program, lasts two years with an option for a third. The Saskatchewan Native Theatre Company also organizes a summer camp for youth 8 to 15 years of age, an after-school program, and artists' circles for aspiring artists. The company's outreach program brings theatre to remote communities, school gymnasiums, and other unlikely venues. The company hosts a venue at the Saskatoon International Fringe Festival. Like many theatre companies, it is unable to sustain itself from ticket sales and relies to an extent on government grants from Health Canada to support the youth training program.

The Saskatchewan Native Theatre Company is a great example of how performing arts groups serve their communities in many ways. Like CED organizations in general, they are sustained through revenues earned from ticket sales but also grants from government agencies, and donations from individuals and foundations, volunteer contributions and underpaid staff. While the performing arts have distinct features, they are also reflective of CED in general.

Conclusion

In this chapter, we have situated community economic development in the overlap between the social economy and the public and the private sectors (see Figure 3.1). For the most part, community economic development involves organizations such as non-profits and co-operatives that are within the social economy. These organizations earn a portion of their revenues from the market, sometimes in competition with other private sector firms, but they rely on support from government, and at times from corporations and individuals, both financial and volunteer labour. Community economic development serves a range of social functions. Although these functions differ, they have the common denominator of assisting those in need in a highly inegalitarian society. Some are regional development programs through which government partners with non-profit agencies to target poorer regions of the country. These programs focus on assisting small and medium businesses, but some make funds available to non-profits with a business idea. Community development corporations founded by community activists also target government programs to assist economically poorer areas in many ways including housing, employment, neighbourhood clean-up, and safety.

Another form of CED is social enterprises, to be discussed in chapter 4. There is much more that could be discussed such as local currencies, bartering arrangements, and practices that are associated with the informal economy. This is a rich and growing field that has emerged as a countervailing force to the inequalities generated through a market economy, and ironically has increasingly used the market in an attempt to reduce those inequalities.

* * *

DISCUSSION QUESTIONS

1. Is the definition of community economic development provided by CCEDNet adequate, in your view? If not, what changes would you suggest?

2. Is it appropriate to conceptualize CED as a hybrid arrangement bridging the private sector, government, and the social economy?
3. Discuss Canada's efforts at addressing regional inequalities using CED strategies?
4. Are community development corporations (CDCs) distinct from government-sponsored initiatives such as through Community Futures Development Corporations?
5. Is it appropriate to portray the performing arts as a form of CED? Why or why not?
6. Does CED represent the seeds of a new society or is it simply a form of mainstreaming?

* * *

Case for Analysis: Winnipeg Social Purchasing Portal

A social purchasing portal is a web-based business-to-business database (often called B2B) that links businesses and suppliers. A social purchasing portal adds to the B2B model by using suppliers that are local social enterprises that provide employment for those individuals who face some sort of employment barriers. It is founded on the premise of building relationships and partnerships by integrating a community economic development vision, business objectives, and government goals.

A social purchasing portal has three key attributes: (1) using existing purchasing of everyday business goods and services such as office supplies, catering, and couriers to create local economic and social value without added cost or loss of purchasing value; (2) enabling socially responsible purchasing to occur through blending business and social values; and (3) using a business model (not a charity model) to contribute to building a healthy community. A social purchasing portal 'facilitates the targeting of existing everyday business purchasing to suppliers of goods and services to blend business and social values' (Social Purchasing Portal [SPP], 2008).

The model is intended to be self-sustaining after the initial expenses are covered. In each community, a local organization acts as the lead agency. The website requires an initial investment of $10,000 to cover technology and content costs. Ongoing and operational costs include the salary for one person to maintain and to update the website and to support the community and business relationships. (LePage, 2004: 3).

Exhibit 3.1 illustrates the relationship between the purchaser, supplier, and employee participants of a social purchasing portal. A social purchasing portal is a win-win-win design as each participant wins – purchasers use their business expenditures to practice corporate social responsibility; suppliers have more access to markets; and employees who face employment barriers gain meaningful employment.

Canada's First Social Purchasing Portal

The first community in Canada to design and implement a social purchasing portal was Vancouver. It was launched in June 2003 and was supported in its start-up by the British Columbia Technology Social Venture Partners (2008), a network of senior technology leaders, whose mission is 'to catalyze significant, long-term positive social change by ... [encouraging] individuals to be well informed, effective and engaged philanthropists, and [by investing] time, expertise and money in innovative not-for-profit organizations while helping to strengthen them in the process.' In just over one year, the Vancouver social purchasing portal had a hundred purchasing businesses and almost fifty suppliers. As well, over fifty individuals have been hired. For example, Cook Studio Catering, a social enterprise, was able to hire five individuals to meet the growing demand for its services (SPP, 2008).

Winnipeg Social Purchasing Portal

The Winnipeg Social Purchasing Portal (WSPP) is one of eight social purchasing portals in Canada; the others are online in Toronto, Surrey, Fraser Valley, Calgary, Vancouver Island, Vancouver, and the Waterloo Region. Another ten communities are in the process of designing social purchasing portals.

The WSSP was created, in October 2004, from a partnership between two local organizations, that is, Supporting Employment and Economic Development (SEED)Winnipeg Inc. and the North End Community Renewal Corporation (NECRC). SEED's mission is 'to combat poverty and assist in the renewal of Winnipeg's inner city. [It does so] by helping individuals and groups start small businesses and save money for future goals. [It offers] business management training and individual consulting, access to micro-enterprise loans, [and] asset building programs' (SEED Winnipeg, 2008: 2). Similarly, 'NECRC [North End Community Renewal Corporation] is committed to the social, economic and cultural renewal of the North End of Winnipeg ... NECRC operates on principles of Community Economic Development using a development system approach to bring about renewal in the North End. [Its] four development themes ... community, business, employment, and housing combine to maximize the impact of our community initiatives' (NECRC, 2008).

The purpose of the WSSP is 'to enable business and non-profit organizations to work together to create meaningful employment opportunities while building stronger and healthier communities' (SPP, 2007a). WSSP has also created an employment exchange committee, which is a partnership among eighteen non-profit organizations that work with individuals who have faced multiple employment barriers. The exchange replies to job postings from supplier and purchaser partners to facilitate work opportunities for those individuals (SPP, 2007b: 2, 4).

WSSP's Supplier and Purchaser Partners

There are approximately thirty supplier organizations that participate in the WSSP. They offer a range of services such as chiropractic care, renovation and property management services, technology support, and catering. Their products include organic food, Aboriginal star blankets, natural clothing, and gourmet gift baskets. The organizations that purchase through the WSSP include universities, co-operatives, credit unions, consultants, accountants, and other private sector organizations.

In addition to creating the employment exchange committee, the WSSP has had a significant and positive impact on the economic well-being of Winnipeg. In three years, the WSSP has stimulated the following outcomes: (1) many of the supplier partners have had notable increases in the demand for their products and services; (2) forty-six new jobs have been created and 90 per cent of the newly employed are inner city residents, vulnerable youth, and others facing significant barriers to employment; and (3) many of the purchaser partners have increased their business transactions with the supplier partners and have indicated an interest in doing business with more social enterprises (SEED, 2008: 16).

Starting a Social Purchasing Portal

There are useful guidelines available in the public domain to create a social purchasing portal. Exhibit 3.2 presents a sample work plan that is the basis for the design and implementation of such portals across the country.

* * *

DISCUSSION QUESTIONS

1. Using the sample work plan in Exhibit 3.2, sketch out a plan for your community.
2. Why might social enterprises and businesses be reticent about participating in a social purchasing portal?

* * *

EXHIBIT 3.1 SOCIAL PURCHASING PORTAL DYNAMIC
(SPP, 2008)

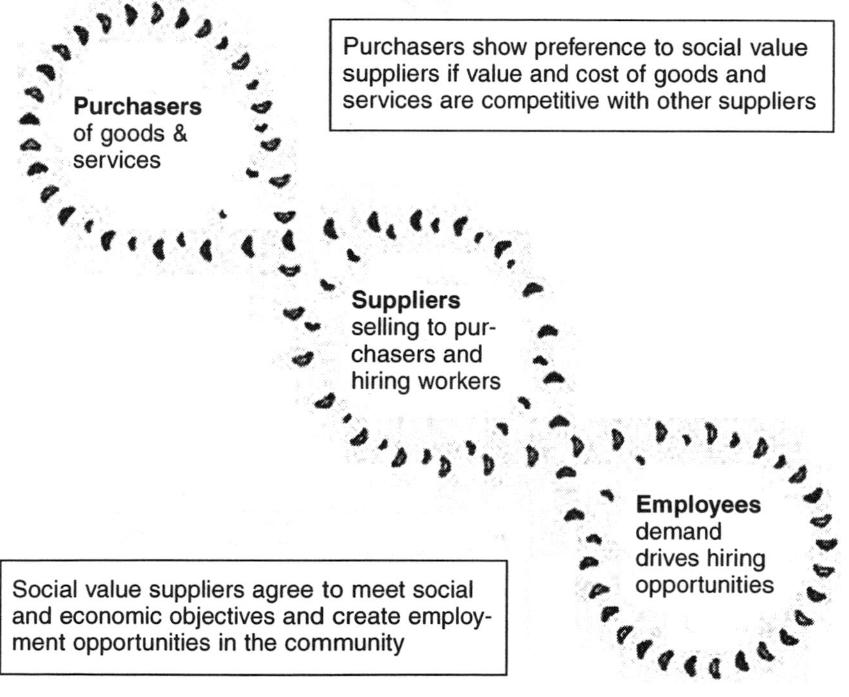

EXHIBIT 3.2 SAMPLE WORK PLAN/GOALS (LePage, 2005: 23)

(1) Purchasing Partner Agreements
- Arrange meetings and presentations with potential purchasing partners
- Engage initial purchasing partners, letters of commitment from six to twelve businesses
- Continual engagement

(2) Supplier Partner Agreements
- Arrange meetings and presentations with potential supplier partners
- Engage initial supplier partners, letters of commitment from six to twelve businesses.
- Continual engagement

(3) Employment Services Coordination
- Enter into local agreements to provide the employment coordinating role
- Employment opportunities posted and filled through participating businesses and community employment services

(4) Community Marketing
- Presentations and meetings with potential SPP partners and supporters: Chamber of Commerce, United Way, local business associations, etc.
- Monthly newsletter

(5) Site Technical Development
- Localize content – a content template will be provided as a basis
- Determine any local adjustments required for the database fields
- Coordinate with FTE and Communicopia.net on hosting arrangements, site development, and launch dates
- Ongoing maintenance and content updates

4 Social Enterprises

This chapter examines social enterprises, also known as a social business enterprise, social firm, non-profit enterprise, social purpose business, and social venture. A social enterprise is a form of community economic development in which an organization exchanges services and goods in the market as a means to realizing its social objectives or mission. In this sense it is similar to a conventional business, but it also requires external support in order to be sustainable and is established primarily to meet a social purpose. The chapter also looks at two other forms of enterprises: businesses owned by Aboriginal communities and online social enterprises. Related to social enterprise, the chapter also explores social entrepreneurship.

In our typology, we differentiate social enterprises from social economy businesses, as discussed in chapter 2. Social economy businesses earn their total revenues from the market much like a private sector business. By comparison, social enterprises generally earn a portion of their revenues from the market, and in contrast to social economy businesses, they usually require extraordinary assistance during the start-up phase and during subsequent operations, much like CED organizations in general. This support may be financial or involve the donation of goods and materials. As such, Figure 4.1 situates social enterprises as a form of community economic development. Some social enterprises may attain self-sufficiency without these extraordinary supports, but these are the exceptions. As they achieve self-sufficiency without extraordinary supports, they could also be classified as social economy businesses.

Social enterprises are often initiated by a parenting organization, most often a non-profit, and some (as discussed below) are simply a subsidiary of a non-profit that gives the main organization an income stream from the market to support its primary services. According to

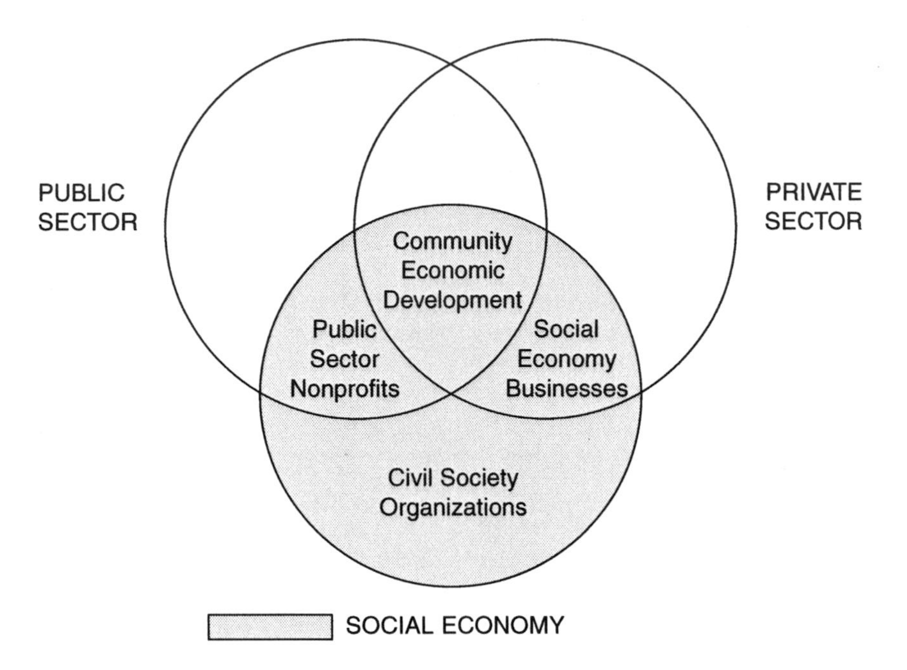

Figure 4.1 The Social Economy: An Interactive Approach

the *Canadian Social Enterprise Guide,* a social enterprise refers to 'business ventures operated by non-profits, whether they are societies, charities, or co-operatives' (Enterprising Non-Profits Program, 2005: 25). As the *Canadian Social Enterprise Guide* states, this is not a new idea – the Girl Guides baked and sold cookies in Regina in 1927. However, the idea of developing market-based solutions to social problems has attracted great interest since the 1990s. As governments seek to reduce their spending on social programs, the idea is appealing that these reductions can be compensated for, and perhaps even exceeded, through the market. Although advocates of social enterprises do not view themselves as being motivated by the neoliberal agenda of small government, the influence of these policies is a stimulus for the development of this form of organization.

Different Forms of Social Enterprise

In this chapter we discuss different forms of social enterprise including organizations oriented towards directly assisting persons with special challenges to become more self-sufficient. These may include persons with a psychiatric or intellectual disability, youth having difficulty in school, and groups that face discrimination both historically and currently, for example, Aboriginal peoples and recent immigrants, particularly members of visible minorities. These can be overlapping categories. The chapter is structured as follows: social enterprises set up primarily to train people with special challenges to enter the workforce; social enterprises creating employment, as distinct from simply training people; non-profits that house social enterprises usually to subsidize their services; non-profits that enter into arrangements with businesses to support the non-profit's services; businesses owned by Aboriginal communities; and online social enterprises. Social enterprises also collaborate with each other, for instance, through co-location, an issue that is discussed at the chapter's end.

Social Enterprises as Training Organizations

THE CONTEXT

Businesses created for persons marginalized from the mainstream labour force are a growing phenomenon. In the modern world, social changes have thrust the necessity for these organizations to the fore, one being the changing relationship between formal schooling and the economy. Over the years, there has been an extreme inflation of education credentials (Berg, 1970; Collins, 1979; Livingstone, 1999) so that extended schooling is a norm prior to entry into the workforce, even for relatively unskilled forms of employment. For youth who opt out of formal schooling before attaining sufficient credentials, the barriers to labour market entry can be formidable. Even with a family-supported stable living arrangement, they often are in need of assistance that will help them in the transition to employment and a career. These problems are compounded for persons from racial minorities and those with psychiatric, intellectual, and physical disabilities. Recent immigrants are increasingly persons of colour and persons whose first language is neither English nor French; large numbers come from Asia, the Caribbean, and South America rather than the British Isles and Western Europe. Some experience barriers in the recognition of their training and credentials, others arrive with skills that lead them into low-paying dead-end jobs. In addition to recent immigrants, Aboriginal peoples, particularly in Western Canada, are moving in greater numbers off First Nations communities into cities where they too experience discrimination in employment and housing.

Persons with psychiatric disabilities face a different type of challenge since the introduction of deinstitutionalization has created expectations that community-based forms of care in employment and housing will supplant the support provided through large-scale psychiatric facilities (Trainor, Pape, and Pomeroy, 1997). Expectations have been created for such persons to be integrated into the workforce, but in order for these expectations to be realized, special supports are needed. Some of these supports come from government agencies that address employment and housing needs, but more often than not government prefers to fund community partners to be service providers within the broad parameters of the program. Given this overall context, social enterprises have evolved in an effort to integrate these groups. Most social enterprises are non-profits, some are co-operatives, and others are registered as businesses, but almost all have a parenting organization – a non-profit organization or a government agency – that has taken the lead in setting them up. Social enterprises vary and include training organizations to help employees enter the workforce; these may be organizations to assist persons with a serious disability to find useful activities that also supplement their income, and organizations that can serve as a career and as a primary livelihood.

EXAMPLES OF SOCIAL ENTERPRISE TRAINING ORGANIZATIONS

The prototype of a social enterprise (although it predates the use of the label) is Goodwill Industries (2007), a non-profit founded in Boston in 1902 by a Methodist minister (Edgar Helms). It operates in twenty-four countries, and since 1935 in Canada (and as Renaissance in Quebec). Goodwill emphasizes employment training for persons on the margins of the workforce and derives its revenues primarily from retail outlets including the Internet (shopgoodwill.com) that sell donated clothes, shoes, and furnishings. In addition, community-based Goodwill organizations, each of which is autonomous, enter into contracts with government and businesses for janitorial and environmental services.

Goodwill is a source of transitional employment and training for persons who have difficulties entering the job market. Goodwill employs its clients at retail outlets, depots, and pick-up facilities, as well as additional contracts. The organization also has an assessment service and a search support for unemployed persons and creates opportunities for volunteers. The organization's philosophy is that 'when people start to work, people start to belong, to matter, and to connect. And as more people connect to their communities, communities get healthier and work better' (Goodwill, 2007).

Although Goodwill is relatively self-sufficient, it does (like social enterprises in general) depend on special supports, in this case large donations of goods from the community. Among the newer forms of social enterprises, the supports vary, but assistance from government programs, foundations, and parenting organizations is commonplace. Supportive federal government programs are under the Youth Employment Strategy involving thirteen different departments and addressing such issues as training, employment, housing, and health care. Many of the sub-programs are focused, for example, Targeted Wage Subsidies or the Skills Development program for persons eligible for employment insurance. The federal support programs are complemented by provincial programs, for example, the Government of Manitoba Community Economic Development Policy Framework. In response to community activists, the Manitoba government, starting in 1999, developed a policy framework and established a Cabinet Secretariat (the Community and Economic Development Committee of Cabinet) that coordinated cross-departmental collaboration in CED projects (Koystra, 2006).

Like Goodwill Industries, many social enterprises emphasize training. Part du Chef is a Montreal restaurant and catering business, with both sit-in and takeout services, that hires and trains persons with psychiatric disabilities. In addition to technical training needed for the profession, persons in the program are given training in job searching techniques, resume preparation, and high school classes so that they will have their diploma (Part du Chef, 2007). Part du Chef, located in a trendy office complex in the east end of Montreal that was formerly an industrial park, evolved over a period of twenty years from a meals delivery and janitorial service to the current more ambitious project.

Across Canada, Part du Chef is one of many social enterprises with a training emphasis, most often for youth but also for others facing special challenges. The Cook Studio Café (2007) in Vancouver's Downtown Eastside is a forty-five-seat café and has a takeout deli and bakeshop. In addition, this café is a training facility for youth at risk, preparing them to become cooks in their Youth Internship Program. Cook also puts on wellness, nutrition, and cooking workshops for local residents. Cook was initiated in 2002 by a local resource group, the NV Food and Service Resource Group, and funded by Human

Resource Development Canada through its Youth Employment Strategy program.

Kids in the Hall, a much celebrated Edmonton initiative visited by Queen Elizabeth in 2005 on her cross-Canada tour, is part of the same tradition as Part du Chef and Cook Studio Café. Kids in the Hall also works with youth at risk in the city's core, and the program includes six months of life-management skills training, job training, and paid employment. Life-management sessions involve topics such as budgeting, birth control, anger management, and communication skills. The employment portion of the program takes place in the full-service restaurant, Kids in the Hall Bistro. The program, originally a creation of the Edmonton City Centre Church Corporation, aims to help youth-at-risk develop skills that will enable them to get and keep a job (Miller, 2005).

The Potluck Café Society is of the same genre, a training program for at-risk residents of Vancouver's Downtown Eastside. The café has features of a business that provides meals to area residents, including discounts for low-income diners, and also discounted daily breakfast, lunch, and dinner. Potluck also does catering for a broader clientele. Potluck is but one of a group of social enterprises in Eastside Vancouver focusing on street youth and Aboriginal peoples. Among these organizations are the Portland Hotel Society, which works with people with substance abuse; the Call'n Post, which provides mailbox services, fax services, free Internet and e-mail, voice mail, desktop publishing, posters and business cards, photocopying, and other essential services for area residents; and the Picasso Café, which offers troubled youth training in the culinary arts (Social Enterprise Data Base, 2007).

In Saskatchewan, many of the youth training programs are set up as co-operatives, in line with that province's tradition. The Core Neighbourhood Youth Co-op (CNYC, 2007) is an umbrella association that operates sub-programs targeting youth in the core area of Saskatoon. One project, the Bicycle Co-op, involves a workshop through which participants fix their own bicycles and also learn to build bicycles using donated frames and parts. Built by the Power of Youth is a carpentry program that teaches a variety of carpentry skills and employs at-risk youth. Word on the Street is a highly innovative monthly journal, written entirely by at-risk youth and distributed to over ninety locations in Saskatoon.

In Metropolitan Toronto's highly cosmopolitan culture, the training programs have an ethnocultural emphasis, for example, Haween

(2007), a division of the Somali Women and Children's Support Network. Haween attempts to increase the employment opportunities of women refugees from war-torn Somalia through a number of programs such as English as a second language; business skills such as marketing, invoicing, and business administration; and practical skills such as sewing, pattern making, cutting, and designing; and through working in Haween Enterprises.

A major and long-time player in employment training in Toronto is the Learning Enrichment Foundation (LEF, 2008), which since 1978 has operated in one of the city's economically poorest areas that also attracts a disproportionate share of new immigrants. LEF has training programs for various forms of industry, construction, child care centres, cooking, and food services. LEF not only trains its clientele but also assists with employment through its networks and language training.

These examples are but a tiny sample of the array of programs available through social enterprises in Canada. It is estimated that there are more than 500 across Canada (Armstrong, 2007).

Social Enterprises Creating Employment

While many social enterprises are focused on training participants to enter the paid workforce, others represent relatively permanent employment for groups at risk. The jobs may be part-time, as is often the case with the cluster of organizations that employ people with psychiatric disabilities, for example, those associated with the Ontario Council of Alternative Businesses (Trainor and Tremblay, 1992). These include A-Way Express, a courier service that relies on public transportation; the Raging Spoon, a café and catering business; Abel Enterprises, which engages in woodworking and cabinet making; Crazy Cooks and Krackers Katering, both of which are catering businesses, and Fresh Start, which provides cleaning and maintenance work.

The participants in these organizations, many of whom subscribe to the label *consumer/survivors* (a commentary on having survived the treatments of the psychiatric system), may have limits on how much they can work, in part for health reasons as their conditions may be chronic, and in part for administrative reasons because with a chronic condition they would be on a pension that may be reduced in relation to their earnings. The pension also carries a pharmaceutical supplement for otherwise very expensive medications. Therefore, this type of social enterprise differs from those set up to train people in that their participants are more likely to be part-time.

Social enterprises are also created for other groups experiencing special challenges in the workforce, for example, persons with developmental disabilities such as Down's syndrome, some of whom may find work at Common Ground Co-operative, for example.

A Closer Look: Common Ground Co-operative

A variation of the social enterprises for persons with psychiatric disabilities is Common Ground Co-operative (2007), a Toronto-based organization that promotes the creation of 'self-employment initiatives for people with intellectual challenges.' Common Ground has over 100 members, many of whom volunteer for the board and its committees or on the business sites that are associated with it. Common Ground, since its inception in 2000, has established four enterprises: Lemon & Allspice Cookery and three Coffee Sheds. These enterprises are registered business partnerships owned and operated by the business partners (the people with intellectual disabilities), who are assisted by job coaches. Partners have regular meetings to make decisions about their work including how much to pay themselves. Common Ground, the umbrella organization for these businesses, is an incorporated co-operative without shares (also with a charitable registration to facilitate donations) that provides management services (administration, financial advice, education, and salaries for job coaches) to the four businesses through a services agreement with them. Through this support structure and the ongoing involvement of coaches, the partners in the businesses (people with intellectual disabilities) have been able to achieve a form of gainful employment.

An older version of this same model is Summer Street Industries in New Glasgow, Nova Scotia, operating since the mid-1970s. Its social enterprises for adults with an intellectual disability include a catering service and woodworking shop. The Summer Street enterprises and related programs serve as an outlet for 145 adults with intellectual disabilities (Enterprising Non-Profits Program [ENP], 2005). Other social enterprises of this genre are those owned by the Vocational and Rehabilitation Research Institute, Calgary. It owns and operates three social enterprises for persons with intellectual disabilities – a baggage cart retrieval service at Calgary International Airport, a bottle depot, and a public recreation facility designed for persons with disabilities (ENP, 2005). Among the many social enterprises across Canada, two in Winnipeg are exemplars in this field. Neechi Foods Co-operative, a small market operating in Winnipeg's north end since 1989, is an Aboriginal specialty store employing a group of local residents. Neechi has taken on a symbolic role for community economic development in Manitoba as its guiding principles with some minor adaptations have been embraced by other organizations as well as by the Manitoba government (Koystra, 2006). Inner City Renovation, featured at the beginning of chapter 1, is more recent than Neechi, but it too is based on a low-income workforce with a sizable number of Aboriginal people (Donkervoort, 2007a). Both of these are successful enterprises that have had an impact in Manitoba and other parts of Canada.

Other social enterprises follow in the same tradition of Inner City Renovation and Neechi in creating ongoing employment for persons on the margins of the workforce. United We Can Bottle Depot (2007) in Vancouver's Downtown Eastside was created by a non-profit, Save Our Living Environment (SOLE), committed to improving existing urban conditions by implementing sustainable practices. Through full refunds for bottles, the Depot supports many street people and 'binners.' Like many social enterprises, the Bottle Depot has struggled for financial self-sufficiency, but in 2007 it covered 65 per cent of its operating costs through handling fees paid by manufacturers. In addition to recycling containers, Save Our Living Environment has created the Crossroads and Lanes Neighbourhood Clean up Project, which removes litter and graffiti from the downtown core and also creates employment.

All of these organizations differ, but they share the goal of creating employment opportunities and training for persons on the margins. Essentially, social enterprises are integrating persons on the margins within the mainstream economy, although with their own unique touch. Unlike the organizations we have classified as social economy businesses in chapter 2, social enterprises rely on external supports, not only in their start-up, but also ongoing. Some attain a financial equilibrium that allows them to operate without external financial supports, but this equilibrium can involve relatively low salaries or ongoing part-time work.

Non-profits that House Social Enterprises

The examples to this point are of social enterprises that may be supported by other organizations to provide their services. This section addresses social enterprises that are embedded within non-profits to create an income stream that supplements the non-profit's services. The prototype is the Thrift stores set up by the Salvation Army to subsidize the cost of its many social services to the indigent within urban communities. Other non-profits, typically service organizations with a charitable status, have replicated this approach, in some cases simply copying the Salvation Army and in other cases reaching out to a different market – Goodwill Industries, St Vincent de Paul, Women in Need (the so-called W.I.N. stores), Beacon Community Services, Great Finds, Watoto (attempting to assist parentless children in Uganda), and the Habitat for Humanity ReStore. Many of these organizations originate in the United States and operate across Canada. Some share the same niche as the Salvation Army, others find a distinct market. The ReStore, which is associated with the entire Habitat for Humanity system, is like a miniature Home Depot, but with an emphasis on recycling and reuse, so that household building supplies and tools that are lying idle are resold, the revenues supporting Habitat's housing program. Some of the ReStore materials are donations from retailers such as Home Depot that discard end-of-line materials; others come from households clearing out unused items cluttering the cellar and attic.

It has become common practice for non-profits to house social enterprises to support their services. A distinctly Canadian example is SARCAN Recycling, set up by the Saskatchewan Association of Rehabilitation Centres, an association of seventy-three member agencies that serve people with developmental disabilities. In 1988, SARCAN was granted an exclusive contract to collect and recycle deposit beverage containers, a service that it provides through its member agencies and also through hiring their clients with disabilities. Through this service, SARCAN employs persons who would otherwise be on social assistance, and saves the province an estimated $2.5 million per year, and it generates revenues that it returns to the participating agencies and thereby supports its services (ENP, 2005).

Although the products may differ, the dynamic for all of these social enterprises is similar in that they subsidize part of the non-profit's services; the products that they sell are donated; the labour is predominantly from volunteers supplemented by paid management; and the purchasers combine their desire for modest prices with support for the agency from which they make the purchase. For these reasons, they differ from social economy businesses discussed in chapter 2.

This dynamic is also consistent with environmentalism in that a use is found for goods that previously might have become waste. For some such organizations, the revenue from the associated social enterprises forms a substantial portion of their overall budget. For example, the Victoria Hospice financial statement for 2005–06 indicates that 43 per cent of its total revenues are from 'donations, fundraising, and its thrift boutique.' Through calling the store a 'boutique,' the hospice has attempted to carve out a distinct market niche for its outlet. However, this should not create the impression that thrift stores are a pejorative; in fact, 'thrift' has created such a strong presence in the market that commercial retailers have attempted to co-opt the image.

Non-profits Entering into Partnership Arrangements with Businesses

Non-profits are utilizing these arrangements to generate revenue, but technically speaking it is not an example of a non-profit social enterprise but rather a non-profit entering into an agreement with private sector business that will generate income for the non-profit. Probably the largest of these arrangements is Savers, a U.S.-based multinational corporation that operates the Value Village chain in English-speaking Canada (Village des Valeurs in Quebec). Savers enters into an agreement with charitable organizations to pay them for boxes of used clothing that they deliver to Savers. This corporation works with more than a hundred charitable organizations in the United States, Canada, and Australia, and in total, it reimbursed them for more than $130 million in 2005 (Savers, 2007). In addition, it also sends to poorer countries used clothing that it feels is not suitable for its primary market. Savers was founded in 1954 by William Ellison, who had experience in the Salvation Army Thrift Shops, but unlike the Salvation Army, Savers is a profit-oriented business. A variation of this arrangement is the growing number of Aboriginal communities across Canada creating businesses that are owned by the band council or some related group.

Businesses Owned by Aboriginal Communities

This distinct group of businesses has arisen in large part because of land claim settlements in Aboriginal communities. As many land claim settlements still are in process, it is likely that this phenomenon will accelerate in the coming years. In brief, these are businesses owned by band councils, tribal councils, or land claim or development corporations (Anderson, 2002). They could be seen simply as a form of community economic development, but they also represent a form of entrepreneurship on the part of peoples attempting to overcome historic forms of oppression; hence, we consider them in this chapter on social enterprise. On the surface, they are similar to either social businesses or social economy businesses, as whether they are incorporated as businesses or as non-profit corporations they earn their revenues from the marketplace. However, these enterprises are not set up primarily to satisfy a set of shareholders; rather, their primary stakeholder is the Aboriginal community that established them, and supporting that community or band is central to their business plan.

A Closer Look: Makivik Corporation

Makivik Corporation (2008) is a non-profit organization created by the Inuit of Northern Quebec in 1978 to invest the $120 million received from the settlement. Makivik, governed by an executive committee and board of directors elected by the Inuit of Nunavik, is set up to further the development of the Nunavik region, and to that end it has a number of wholly owned for-profit subsidiaries: Air Inuit, a regional airline serving Nunavik; First Air, A Canadian domestic airline serving the Arctic; Nunavik Arctic Foods, a firm that harvests and markets caribou meat; Halutik enterprises, a fuel and heavy equipment firm operating out of Kuujjuaq; Nunavik Creations, a firm that creates clothing of contemporary and traditional styles; and Cruise North Expeditions, established for Arctic educational tours by international tourists.

Some of Makivik's ventures involve joint initiatives primarily with other Inuit development funds. For example, Pan Arctic Inuit Logistics, which operates and services military and air traffic radars in Arctic Canada, is owned by Mativik and six other Inuit development corporations in the four Inuit land claim settlement regions of Canada. Another joint venture is the Unaaq Fisheries, a shrimp-trawling firm, undertaken with the Qikiqtaaluk Corporation, another development corporation representing the Qikiqtaaluk region in the Nunavik settlement. Nunavut Eastern Arctic

Shipping, a sea shipping firm servicing Arctic communities with such necessities as fuel, is another of Makivik's joint ventures, as is Natsiq Investment Corporation, an investment fund to harvest seals and to develop international markets for seal products undertaken in conjunction with Makivik Corporation, Qikiqtaaluk Corporation, and Sakku Investments Corporation.

This brief discussion scratches but the surface of this intricate network of enterprises, but the bottom line is that they are not just businesses but guardians of a heritage and entrusted to earn revenues that will further the development of the communities that they represent by reinvesting in them. The reinvestment comes not only from the businesses that are set up through Makivik and the other similar development companies, but also through investing the land claims settlement money in domestic and international markets and using the proceeds to support Aboriginal communities. The reinvestment in cultural and recreational facilities in the communities is extensive.

This discussion has focused on the Inuit, but businesses owned either directly by Aboriginal communities or through development corporations that they create are a more general phenomenon across Canada that transcends the land claims settlements. Some of these businesses like casinos and tobacco retailing stir controversy, as there are social costs associated with the economic benefits. However, Aboriginal businesses are increasingly participating in the market economy both within their own communities and more generally. While much of this activity mirrors business enterprise in general, except that the owners are Aboriginal, some of it has a distinct character in that it is organized through a hybrid arrangement intended to promote the economic development of Aboriginal communities. The Cree Nation of Wemindji (at the tip of James Bay) owns the Tawich Development Corporation whose investments include transportation firms for the North and South; Air Wemindji, a bush-flight service for tourism, which outfits mining and exploration activities; Whapchiwem Helicopters; and a wholesale petroleum company which focuses on servicing the northern region (Wemindji, 2008).

The Osoyoos Indian Band Development Corporation in the Southern Okanagan region of British Columbia owns the NK'MIP Canyon Desert Golf Course, NK'MIP Construction Ltd., NK'MIP Vineyards,

NK'MIP Gas and Convenience Store, Nk'Mip RV Resort, the NK'MIP Cultural Centre, NK'MIP CELLARS (the first Aboriginal winery in Canada), NK'MIP Preschool and Daycare, Oliver Readi-Mix, Spirit Ridge Vineyard Resort and Spa, and the Mount Baldy Ski Corporation (Osoyoos Indian Band, 2008).

These examples are illustrative of a change that is occurring within Aboriginal communities and of a unique form of enterprise – businesses operating within the market, but also embedded within a community that they serve. The arrangement is a form of partnership and analogous to the relationship between a Crown corporation and the level of government that owns it.

Online Social Enterprises

The Internet is playing a greater role for social enterprises, and there are some that might be characterized as online social enterprises because the Internet is the primary vehicle for their commerce. This emerging form has many manifestations. The growing number of social purchasing organizations that arrange the sale of services from social enterprises to supportive organizations is one example (see the Winnipeg Social Purchasing Portal at the end of chapter 3). In Winnipeg, the Social Purchasing Portal, set up through SEED Winnipeg and the North End Community Renewal Corporation (NECRC), is a web-based system that allows Winnipeg corporations to purchase goods and services from inner-city and social enterprises that hire those who face barriers to employment (SEED Winnipeg, 2007).

While there is a long history of individuals applying social criteria to their purchases (the boycott of products from South Africa under Apartheid, the boycott of California table grapes in the late 1960s, or the selection of organic products), the Social Purchasing Portal is attempting to promote the same practice for businesses, and systematically, by using the Internet. This innovative approach allows purchasers to support service providers who share their values. A variation of this theme is Entrewomen.ca, an online source for women entrepreneurs through which they can make connections, acquire business information, and learn about opportunities. Entrewomen.ca is operated by the PARO Centre for Women's Enterprise (2008) in Thunder Bay.

Non-profit Internet providers are another example of online social enterprise. The Brant Free Net (2008) serves the Brantford, Ontario, region with a range of such services as Internet access, website design, website hosting, and web mail. This is but one of a group of free net services in Canada, including the following: the National Capital FreeNet, Victoria Free-Net, Web Community Resource Networks, Saskatchewan! Connected (serving Regina, Saskatoon, Moose Jaw, and Prince Albert). The latter operates as a public service organized by the government of Saskatchewan. Many of these services receive some government support as well as assistance from donors and volunteers, but membership fees and payment for service cover a portion of the costs. Some non-profits promote wireless systems, for example, Wireless Toronto and Wireless Nomad Co-operative have 'virtual tenancy' in the Toronto Business Development Centre, whose subscribers are also members of the co-operative.

Online systems have assisted Aboriginal communities in their community and economic development. An example is First Net, an online system established by the Mi'kmaq Nova Scotia First Net Committee representing the thirteen Mi'kmaq communities in Nova Scotia, including Cape Breton Island (Mi'kmaq First Net, 2008). First Net is a form of community informatics (Gurstein, 2000; Stoeker, 2005) as it links existing geographical communities and facilitates common projects one of which is a learning guide for public schools about Mi'kmaq culture. Another example is K-Net or Kuh-ke-nah Network.

A Closer Look: Kuh-ke-nah Network (K-Net)

Kuh-ke-nah Network (K-Net) is an Internet system involving sixty Aboriginal communities in Ontario, Quebec, and other parts of Canada (Fiser, Clement, and Walmark, 2006; K-Net, 2008). Most of the communities are very isolated and small and are in the Sioux Lookout district of northwestern Ontario, a vast sparsely populated area averaging only 0.5 people per square kilometre. Before the introduction of K-Net, most communities' external access consisted of one public pay phone. K-Net introduced broad band service that was superior to the norm in Canada's major cities.

This system had its inception in the mid-1990s, under the leadership of the Keewaytinook Okimakanak Tribal Council (the Northern Chiefs), who in partnership with federal government agencies, made available to participating communities a broad range of Internet services. These included telehealth applications for clinical consults, telepsychiatry, and various forms of diagnosis that otherwise would require air flights to distant centres. The nursing stations that handle routine medical examinations, homecare, and public health, and are funded by Health Canada, serve as a key K-Net link to health care specialists in distant centres. Through the use of such sophisticated equipment as an otoscope that reveals the ear drum and other cavities and the stethoscope that accesses heartbeat and breathing, physicians in distant centres provide clinical consults, telepsychiatry, and various forms of diagnosis.

Similarly, for education Kewaytinook Internet High School (KiHS), undertaken in partnership with Industry Canada, provides secondary school courses to grades nine and ten students through network access, thereby allowing them to remain in their home communities rather than go off to distant boarding schools.

K-Net has a decentralized structure that gives participating communities autonomy in adapting the system to their needs, a feature that is consistent with Aboriginal values and with the philosophy of community economic development.

K-Net and First Net are examples of community informatics in Aboriginal communities in Canada, but these innovative online systems are exceptional. The Aboriginal Canada Portal that tracks online connectivity for Aboriginal communities found that while 70 per cent had basic connectivity to the Internet, only 19 per cent had high speed services. Among remote communities north of 55 degrees latitude, 37 per cent have no connectivity and only 14 per cent have high speed access (Aboriginal Canada Portal, 2004).

Co-location and Social Enterprises

The concept of business hubs has a lengthy history, but this practice is more recent for social enterprises. Co-location offers opportunities for reducing rental costs and synergies due to services that are shared in common. There are some interesting models that have emerged, some including a mix of non-profit social enterprises and businesses with a social mission. In Toronto, the Centre of Social Innovation houses an impressive group of social enterprises and has related programs to assist their development. Some hubs focus primarily on the arts, for example, One West Hastings Media Arts Centre in Vancouver and Artscape and 401 Richmond in Toronto. Others are simply for non-profits providing various forms of service, for example, The Kahanoff Centre in Calgary, Windsor-Essex Nonprofit Support Network, Saskatoon Community Service Village, and the Queen St Commons in Chartottetown. Co-location offers opportunities for reducing rental costs and creating synergies for services and missions that are shared in common.

A variation of co-location undertaken by the Sage Centre (2008), with offices in Vancouver and Toronto, is an administrative home (as distinct from a physical space) for environmental and social justice projects that do not have non-profit incorporation and charitable status on their own. These projects become legally part of the Sage Centre and benefit from its administrative infrastructure including financial audits, reconciliation of banking statements, assistance with payables and receivables, and filing tax returns and charitable receipts for donations.

Social Entrepreneurship

Social entrepreneurship is a term often associated with social enterprise, although, as indicated in chapter 2, social entrepreneurship appears in differing contexts, not simply in relation to social enterprises (see also Clark and Ucak, 2006; Mair and Marti, 2006). Social entrepreneurship also is used in different ways: as a process or behaviour and in terms of outcomes (Mair and Marti, 2006).

As with many terms, there is no one definition of a *social entrepreneur*. Definitions range from 'merely the initiation and/or management of a social enterprise' to an individual or group who creates long-term, sustainable social change (Dees, 1998; Light 2006; Mair and Marti, 2006; Martin and Osberg, 2007; Peredo and McLean, 2006: 58).

The most widely cited contemporary example of a social entrepreneur is Muhammad Yunus, the founder and leader of the Grameen Bank, an organization that originated in Bangladesh and has since become the prototype of an international movement to make business credit accessible for people without economics means, predominantly women, who want to start or invest in their own business (Yunus,

1998). Yunus' remarkable achievements were referred to in chapter 2, and will be discussed further in chapter 8 under different forms of finance.

Dees (2001: 1), a pioneer in this field, defines the idealized social entrepreneur as one who makes fundamental changes in the social sector by:

- Adopting a mission to create and sustain social value (not just private value)
- Recognizing and relentlessly pursuing new opportunities to serve that mission
- Engaging in a process of continuous innovation, adaptation, and learning
- Acting boldly without being limited by resources currently in hand, and
- Exhibiting a heightened sense of accountability to the constituencies served and for the outcomes created.

The closer one gets to meeting all of these conditions, the closer one is to being a social entrepreneur.

Others provide similar criteria. Roger Martin, dean of the Rotman School of Management, University of Toronto, and Sally Osberg, president and CEO of the Skoll Foundation, promote the 'big bang' viewpoint of social entrepreneurship as 'forging a new, stable equilibrium that releases trapped potential or alleviates the suffering of the targeted group, and through imitation and the creation of a stable ecosystem around the new equilibrium ensuring a better future for the targeted group and even society at large' (Martin and Osberg, 2007: 5). From this perspective, social entrepreneurs are not simply leaders in an enterprise that combines both social and business goals, but are visionaries that articulate a model that moves the world. Other organizational leaders in this field have argued similarly. For example, the Schwab Foundation for Social Entrepreneurship refers to 'a pragmatic visionary who achieves large scale, systemic and sustainable social change through a new invention, a different approach, a more rigorous application of known technologies or strategies, or a combination of these' and states further that a social entrepreneur 'combines the characteristics represented by Richard Branson and Mother Teresa' (Schwab Foundation for Social Entrepreneurship, 2008). Using this standard, the list of successful social entrepreneurs is limited because the objective is not only to create a successful social enterprise but also for it to be an innovation that others replicate and that significantly changes the way the world operates.

Peredo and McLean (2006) present an alternative view of social entrepreneurship, which is more inclusive as it does not necessarily have to result in major social change. They argue that social entrepreneurship occurs: 'where some person or group: (1) aim(s) at creating social value, either exclusively or at least in some prominent way; (2) show(s) a capacity to recognize and take advantage of opportunities to create that value ('envision'); (3) employ(s) innovation, ranging from outright invention to adapting someone else's novelty, in creating and/or distributing social value; (4) is/are willing to accept an above-average degree of risk in creating and disseminating social value; and (5) is/are unusually resourceful in being relatively undaunted by scarce assets in pursuing their social venture' (2006: 64).

Using this definition, social entrepreneurs would include the late Paul Newman whose company, Newman's Own (discussed in chapter 2), donates all of its after-tax profits to educational and charitable organizations. Also included would be Eva Smith and Eva's, the social enterprise discussed at the end of this chapter that employs or trains youth.

Social entrepreneurship as an academic concept has been used to broaden understandings of how societies change and progress. Along these lines, Martin and Osberg (2007) argue that it is necessary to distinguish between different types of socially valuable activities such as providing social services, social activism, and social entrepreneurship. Social service provision is a small-scale activity that addresses an important issue, but does not result in a disruption of the status quo. Social activism is closer to social entrepreneurship: it results in a change in the way things are done, but does this indirectly by influencing others to take actions. Social entrepreneurship is direct action that creates a new and sustained equilibrium.

It is also important to analyse social entrepreneurship within the broader context in which it appears. Social entrepreneurs operate in wider institutional and political structures, and social entrepreneurship varies according to socioeconomic and cultural environments (Weerawardena and Mort, 2006). As Mair and Marti (2006: 40) state, the embeddedness of social entrepreneurship within a social structure 'implies that it is impossible to detach the agent (social entrepreneur) from the structure (community, society, etc.).'

Collective action and political engagement are important factors in the success or failure of social entrepreneurs (Parkinson and Howarth, 2008). Often, the concept of social entrepreneurship is seen to focus on individuals, and there is criticism of this point: 'Bias that comes from focusing on individuals is a tendency to ignore the role of organizations and the resources they provide for pattern-breaking change. Researchers have long known that successful ideas require a mix of talents rarely found in one person. Indeed, the most compelling research on business entrepreneurship suggests that successful change requires a stream of capabilities including leadership, management, marketing, organizational design, and finance' (Light, 2006: 4).

Interestingly, the review committee for the Nobel Peace Prize recognized this criticism by awarding the prize to both Yunus and the Grameen Bank. Yunus was the visionary who initiated the process; the idea could have not begun to achieve its current reach without the contributions of the many people who work through the Grameen structure.

An organizational perspective on social entrepreneurship arises from the research on community-based enterprise, which is defined 'as a community acting corporately as both entrepreneur and enterprise in pursuit of the common good' (Peredo and Chrisman, 2006: 2). Community-based entrepreneurship not only applies to market-based approaches, as do social enterprises in general, but also to community approaches that do not involve monetary exchange, as is not unusual in communities that are relatively impoverished. Innovation that is the centrepiece of social entrepreneurship need not involve the exchange of money. According to Anderson and Dees (2002: 192), 'Social entrepreneurship is about finding new and better ways to create and sustain social value,' not necessarily making money. This point is important because it bears on societies in which poverty is widespread, but innovative techniques help their members to survive, and it also bears on those in poverty in wealthier societies who may be limited in their ability to pay for services (Peredo and McLean, 2008). In these circumstances, innovation related to health, education, and shelter often does not involve monetary exchange.

Overall, the concept of social entrepreneurship and its varying manifestations motivates us to re-think and push our thinking about how to address social needs and effect social change. One challenge for practitioners and researchers in this area is assessing social performance and impact, an area we address in chapter 9.

Pulling It Together

Table 4.1 summarizes the differing expressions of social enterprise in relation to the target groups. The examples are selective, but nevertheless indicate the range of this growing phenomenon and its many target groups. Space does not permit the entire list. The left side of the table shows the differing expressions and contexts of social enterprises: training organizations, employment-creating organizations, subsidiaries of non-profits, businesses owned by Aboriginal communities, and online social enterprises. The top of the table shows the target groups: organizations that are oriented in general to people in need, and others that have a specific target such as persons with psychiatric disabilities, youth, Aboriginal peoples, recent immigrants, persons with intellectual disabilities, and women. Some organizations, of course, target more than one group. In addition to these target groups, some social enterprises focus on international development, for example, Watoto (attempting to assist parentless children in Uganda).

Conclusion

Within the framework of the social economy, social enterprises are viewed as a form of community economic development that relies in part on the market for revenues but also depends on government programs and support from foundations and individuals. The balance between market and other forms of support varies for different types of social enterprises, with some attaining near self-sufficiency and others relying heavily on ongoing supports.

This discussion of social enterprises focuses on organizations that address groups with extraordinary needs, as summarized in Table 4.1. Some of these organizations are for training purposes; others represent forms of employment. This chapter also discusses social enterprises set up to supplement the income of non-profit organizations so that they can maintain their other services; Aboriginal businesses owned by their community; and social enterprises that function primarily online. Some social enterprises band together through co-location to share resources that they may not have been able to access on their own.

The concept of social entrepreneurship was also introduced in this chapter.

Table 4.1 Different Forms of Social Enterprises by Target Groups

Different Forms of Social Enterprise	Target Groups						
	General	Psychiatric Disabilities	Youth	Aboriginal	Recent Immigrants	Intellectual Disabilities	Women
Training Organizations	Goodwill	Part du Chef	Cook Studio Café, Kids in the Hall, Core Neighbourhood Youth Co-op	Potluck Café Society	Haween, Learning Enrichment Foundation		PARO Centre for Women's Enterprise
Employment Creating	United We Can Bottle Depot	A-Way Express, Raging Spoon, Crazy Cooks, Krackers Katering		Neechi Foods Co-operative, Inner City Renovation		Lemon & Allspice, Coffee Shed, Summer St Industries, Vocational and Rehabilitation Research Institute	
Subsidiaries of Non-profits	Salvation Army Thrift Shops, Habitat Restore, St Vincent de Paul					SARCAN Recycling	Women in Need
Businesses Owned by Aboriginal Communities				Makivik, Air Inuit, Tawich Development, Osoyoos Indian Band Development			
Online Social Enterprise	Winnipeg Social Purchasing Portal and 7 others, shopgoodwill.com, Wireless Nomad Co-operative						Entrewomen.ca

* * *

DISCUSSION QUESTIONS

1. Do you agree with the definition of social enterprises in this chapter?
2. We argue that the individualistic concept of social entrepreneurship is inappropriate and it is important to look at the organizational and community contexts. Do you agree?
3. Are on-the-job training programs through social enterprises a realistic approach to reducing inequalities?
4. Are businesses for persons with serious disabilities an improvement over 'sheltered workshops'?
5. Is the distinction in this chapter between social enterprises and social economy businesses appropriate?
6. Is it appropriate to characterize businesses owned and operated through Aboriginal communities as a form of social enterprise?

Case for Analysis: The Print Shop at Eva's Phoenix

Introduction

The Print Shop is a social enterprise designed to train at-risk youth and to be a revenue-generating social service. It is both a training facility and a commercial print shop. It provides homeless and at-risk youth the opportunity to learn fundamental work and life skills. The Print Shop is located at Eva's Phoenix; see Exhibit 4.1 for a description of Eva Smith, her vision, and the structure of the organization.

Every quarter up to eight youth receive hands-on print training. While the youth are not paid, they receive such things as transit passes and honoraria for completed tasks and attendance. They are accountable for duties and responsibilities that mirror those of most printing operations. Even before the youth are hired, they job shadow to get an appreciation of working in the graphic communications industry.

The Print Shop is based on a blended-value proposition that entails social, economic, and environmental dimensions. It is dedicated to 'continuing asset building' so that the youth can become self-sufficient in the long term. Success is achieved if *both* the youth and the Print Shop develop self-sufficiency. In 2007–08, both the Print Shop and Andrew Macdonald were recognized by the Toronto Community Foundation's Vital Ideas and Vital People Awards.

Operations

The Print Shop specializes in 'trainee-friendly' print work, typically small-format printing jobs (11″ x 17″ and under) in one colour and two- to three-spot colour reproduction. It can work with most graphic design software programs. In-house graphic design work is also available. Commercial projects include business cards, letterhead, forms, and brochures. Finishing services include trimming, folding, scoring, perforating, and shrink-wrapping. The Print Shop occupies 800 square feet in Eva's Phoenix. It has four presses: an A.B. Dick 360, an A.B. Dick 9810, a Heidelberg QM-46, and a Multilith 1250, all with colour heads, and other donated equipment.

The Print Shop is supported by an advisory board that includes senior members of the graphic communications industry. The board provides advice on curriculum, employment opportunities, and technology. The Print Shop participates actively in the graphic communications industry; for example, it has had booths at trade shows.

Curriculum

The program lasts for twenty-three weeks and is offered in three stages: life skills training and counselling for three weeks; on-the-job print shop training for twenty weeks; and making job connections and developing careers in the last four weeks. Participants learn fundamental employability work habits (e.g., team work, attendance, punctuality, and safety) as well as a customer service orientation. Youth learn about the graphic communications industry and go on tours of organizations so that they can see where they might work after graduation. The Print Shop brings in peer mentors to assist both the trainees and the instructors with training and production. The peer mentors are themselves Print Shop graduates. Once the youth graduate, they stay connected to the Print Shop through a two-year follow-up program. They receive training in job planning and organization, prepress using various software programs on both PC and Macintosh platforms, small offset press operation, and binding and finishing.

Voices: Graduates

'My training at Phoenix Print Shop helped me get into higher education in visual communications. My Phoenix Print Shop Scholarship Award has helped me stay there.' – Rebecca

'I had serious problems with alcohol and was living on the streets. Two months after starting a substance abuse problem, I got a job at the Print Shop. I met great staff who listened to me and taught me the wonders of printing.' – David

'I was kicked out of my Dad's house at 19. I had nowhere to live. I now work as a junior pressman and live in a two-bedroom apartment and am a peer mentor at Eva's Phoenix.' – Reinieire

'At the Print Shop, you get respect and support and the teachers are really patient ... The staff advocates for me to employers – just because I'm deaf, it doesn't mean I'm dumb.' – Andrea

'It felt like there was family – it was mind-blowing.' – Noel

Voices : Advocates

'The real end product is the changed person – it's a very human enterprise. You can't do better than that!'
– Michael Rolph, former Business Manager, The Print Shop

'I believe that the social enterprise path ... has integrity as a "third way" of doing business and delivering social service.'
– Andrew Macdonald, Manager of Social Enterprise, Eva's Phoenix

'We have a great concern for the lack of entry level staff available to our industry. The Phoenix program is an excellent feeder system providing employers potential staff already knowledgeable in print processes.' – Brian O'Leary, Vice President, Kwik-Kopy

'There are few initiatives that encourage young people to consider printing as a career choice. Eva's Phoenix offers this advantage to the industry as well as providing guidance to homeless and at-risk youth by giving them structure, education, and a path to self-improvement.'
– Myrna Penny, Managing Director, PrintLink Canada

'This is a win-win partnership for Xerox and the Phoenix Print Shop. The graduate we hired has the right combination of a positive attitude and the critical skills and training necessary to enable him to "hit the ground running," and instantly contribute to our team.'
– Robert Wright, Manager of Customer Relations, Xerox

Financial and Human Resource Goals

Annual operating costs are approximately $180,000. The 2007 objective was to sell approximately $300,000 of print for a gross profit of $120,000 and a net loss of $55,000. The goal is to break even in fiscal 2009, with a stretch goal of 2008. Longer term (three to five years) the Print Shop wants the commercial department to generate a profit to help pay for a print training department. As the business grows the Print Shop also envisions hiring some graduates to join the team on a permanent basis.

Investors

Key investors include the Toronto Enterprise Fund of the United Way of Greater Toronto, Human Resources and Social Development Canada, Heidelberg Canada, St Stephen's Job Connect Program, the Scotia Capital Global Markets Group, and the Royal Bank of Canada Foundation. The Print Shop has been looking for other sources of funding and participated successfully at the first Canadian Social Investors Forum, held in April 2003. Ten community organizations participated and a hundred potential social investors attended. The ten organizations worked for three months with volunteer business coaches to develop their business plans.

* * *

DISCUSSION QUESTIONS

1. What is innovative in the design of the Print Shop?
2. How could the Print Shop achieve scale while being true to its social mission?

* * *

EXHIBIT 4.1 EVA SMITH'S LEGACY

Eva Smith (1923–1993) co-founded the North York Emergency Home for Youth, which was later renamed Eva's Place in her honour. Her passion was in helping people, especially urban youth, to use their skills to find solutions to their challenges. Now her passion lives through three shelters in Toronto, known jointly as Eva's Initiatives. Eva's Initiatives' mission is '[to] work collaboratively with homeless and at risk youth [aged 16 to 24] to actualize their potential to lead productive, self-sufficient and healthy lives by providing safe shelter and a range of services, [and to create] long term solutions for homeless youth by developing and implementing proactive and progressive services.'

In the Greater Toronto Area, there are ten thousand homeless and at-risk youth. Most are on the streets as they have suffered family breakdown and abuse. Many struggle with substance abuse problems and crime and prostitution are common. Eva's Place, Eva's Satellite, and Eva's Phoenix provide housing for at-risk youth. Eva's Phoenix is an innovative fifty-bed transitional housing and training facility in downtown Toronto. It was once a fire truck repair garage and has been redesigned as a set of ten townhouse units featuring private and communal living spaces. It has a main street that all the units overlook. Fifty youth apprenticed in the construction trades and helped to build the facility. Forty-one of the youth found work soon after completing the renovation. As one youth put it, 'I used to sleep under a bridge. Now I can build one.'

Eva's Phoenix has won many awards for its innovative design. As well, it has been recognized by the Toronto Board of Trade as an example of public-private partnerships. The approach to designing Eva's Phoenix is being developed for replication across Canada.

In addition to providing secure shelter for one year, Eva's Phoenix provides mentoring and training services. Youth are trained for employment in printing, culinary arts, network administration, or film production. *One Day, One Dollar* is a film about the realities of life for youth forced to live on the street because of the abuse they face in their homes.

5 Public Sector Non-Profits

Many non-profits, often with a charitable status, overlap with the public sector. Although they have a separate incorporation and their own board of directors, they rely on government agencies for a substantial portion of financing and are influenced in varying degree by government policies. Salamon (1987, 1995) labels this relationship with government as a partnership because non-profit organizations provide services to the public or specific parts of the public that are financed substantially by government and operate within a policy framework created by government. For government, it is advantageous to have non-profit agencies provide the services because they are located in the communities of the recipients, are more in touch with their needs, and therefore can deliver the services better than government administrators.

While the concept of a *partnership* that Salamon presents does capture the interdependence of government and public sector non-profits, partnerships can range from relative equality to gross imbalances of power with one dominant partner. Most often for public sector non-profits, government is the dominant partner, because, to borrow an oft-used idiom, 'He who pays the piper, calls the tune.' Put simply, without financial support, the delivery of these services is unlikely, and the agencies providing them would either fold or be fundamentally transformed. As will be illustrated, this relationship with government plays out in different ways; however, financial dependency and to some degree policy dependency are the norms.

Government does not formulate its policies in isolation but is influenced by community groups who deliver services in fields to which government contributes substantial funding. This influence might be viewed as a 'feedback loop,' with government agencies not obliged to

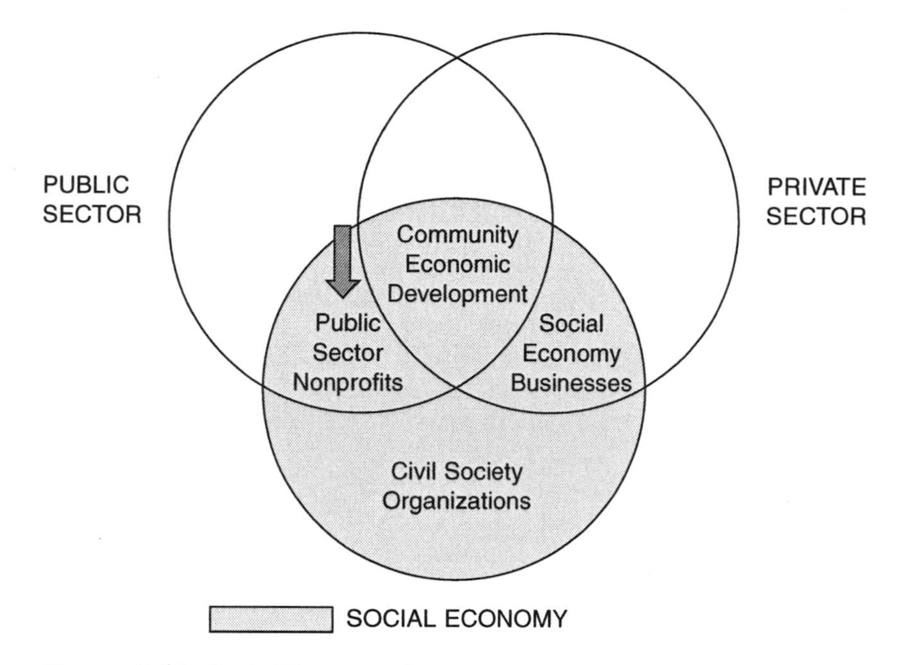

Figure 5.1 The Social Economy: An Interactive Approach

accept the feedback, but foolish if they ignore it completely. Arguably, the influence of community groups is less than ideal, but government's reliance on them to deliver services suggests that interdependence, not simply dependence, is the best descriptor of the relationship.

Some question whether public sector non-profits should be included within the social economy, because of their dependence on government. This viewpoint seems naive because in the modern world the public sector no longer is a distant monolith but a vast network of agencies with varying degrees of autonomy that participate within the communities in which they are situated. These agencies, operating within government policy frameworks and often with funding packages that they administer, work with public sector non-profits that provide related services and apply for ongoing financial support.

The term *quasi autonomous, non-government organizations* (QANGO) is often applied to public sector non-profits to underline their partnership or interdependency with government. Nevertheless, all have their own board of directors and therefore maintain an important degree of autonomy in how their services are delivered.

Public sector non-profits could be referred to as *intermediary organizations* in that they bridge a relationship between government and local communities in which service recipients are situated. We prefer intermediary organizations to a partnership because it characterizes the bridging role between government and local communities. Partnership, by comparison, focuses on the interaction between government and public sector non-profits only, and says less about the relationship to the communities that these organizations serve. Figure 5.1 situates public sector non-profits within the overall framework of the social economy, but as with other groupings in our typology, they are not homogeneous but could be sub-categorized as well.

Historical Context

Public sector non-profits are very much a product of the past sixty years or so and have evolved historically. An important historical account of this phenomenon can be found in the book, *An Essential Grace* (1985), by Samuel Martin of the University of Western Ontario, School of Business. Martin uses the label *humanistic services* and applies it to a broad array of work including health care, education, the arts, religion, and poverty relief. Martin argues that Canada has gone from a society in which non-profits providing humanistic services were financed largely by private charity to one in which government underwrites most of the costs.

Martin presents his analysis in four historical stages. Stage 1, found most often in rural communities, is characterized by personal and voluntary service between a benefactor and recipient, often involving people who know each other. Stage 2, characterizing the shift to a more urban environment, is still based on voluntary service, but unlike Stage 1 the services are institutionalized (e.g., hospitals, clinics, soup kitchens) and depend on the beneficence of groups bound by a common bond of association. Stage 3, reflecting the increased demand for services primarily in urban environments, recognized the limitations of ad hoc reliance on generous benefactors, and signalled the advent of organized federated fundraising campaigns (e.g., the United Way) and the need for government programs. Stage 4 involves the use of taxpayers and related social programs, including universal social programs such as health care and education, which become public rather than private goods. Social programs, managed by government in partnership with public sector non-profits, or intermediary agencies, are responsible for a growing range of services that Martin characterizes as 'humanistic.'

Government has created a broad array of universal programs in education, health, and welfare, financed through various forms of taxation. As taxes have increased, they have become the predominant form of payment for those services, dwarfing private contributions. Martin notes that in 1937, in the midst of the Great Depression that had already increased government involvement in the economy, the costs associated with public services were divided evenly between government and private donors. The ratio in favour of government has gradually increased so that by 1980 it was 4:1. In other words, about 80 per cent of the expenditure on public services is coming from governments through taxes. Martin shows that this pattern of increased payment through taxes pertains to every type of service. For such services as education and welfare, in which there is a lengthy tradition of government involvement, the ratio of government to private expenditure is 13:1. For health care, the ratio is 4:1, and for culture, defined broadly to include recreation and religion as well as the arts, government spent slightly more than private donors did.

In the period since Martin did his research, taxes remain the dominant form of payment for humanistic services, although the ratio for government-to-private expenditure has changed somewhat, for example, to about 3.5 to 1 for health care. Using the tax year 2003, businesses claimed just over $1 billion in charitable donations, about 15 per cent of the $6.5 billion claimed by individual taxpayers (Conn and Barr, 2005). While these are substantial sums of money and of great importance to beneficiaries, primarily larger non-profits, they are a small fraction of social program spending by government and of the gross domestic product (Conn and Barr, 2005; Easwaramoorthy et al., 2006). However, there has been some change in the role of government, and in particular since Paul Martin's watershed budget in 1995 that sharply reduced social program spending. These sharp cuts in government programs and subsequent tax cuts that reduced government revenues have proved challenging for public sector non-profits that are involved in humanitarian services. Nevertheless, the historical pattern that Samuel Martin discerned remains, with government as a major force in the financing and also in creating a broad policy framework for public sector non-profits. Put simply, government does not simply give funding but also creates some rules as to how it could be used.

During this neoliberal period, government has been more rigorous in enforcing the rules and it has shifted from grants for core funding to 'contracts' that require competitive review processes and evaluations when they are completed. Also, there has been some chipping away at universal programs and a push towards a model that relies more heavily on service users absorbing more of the costs. Similarly, greater pressure has been placed on non-profits to generate 'earned revenues' from the sale of services (see chapter 2 for social economy businesses and chapter 4 for social enterprises). Non-profits have also been pressured to tap a larger pool of donors of labour (volunteers) and finances. Nevertheless, government, at all levels, remains a major player in the provision of social services in Canada, and it does this with intermediary organizations that we label as public sector non-profits.

Sub-categories of Public Sector Non-profits

For simplicity, we use three sub-categories of public sector non-profits: (1) spin-offs from government that depend totally on a government program for their survival; (2) organizations created originally by government legislation, but that maintain relatively greater autonomy both in policy and finance than the spin-off organizations; and (3) organizations that were set up apart from government but because of the nature of their service, often to people with limited financial means, rely on government financing. It is the latter group that is the focus of this chapter, although we shall discuss these other categories briefly for illustrative purposes.

Spin-off Organizations

As government has moved away from direct service provision, it has spun off agencies that were previously part of the public service. The idea is to situate these agencies closer to the communities that they serve and to employ people who come from those communities, and in so doing strengthen the ties to local communities. In other words, even though the agency is operating within a government policy framework, often centrally created, the services are tailored to a degree to the needs of the local community. One example is the Community Futures Development Corporation, discussed in chapter 3, as an intermediary between the federal government and local communities.

These agencies have a funding allocation from the federal government and a relatively homogeneous set of services. There is a fine, perhaps indistinguishable, line between the Community Futures Development Corporation, which is a non-profit, and the Atlantic Canada Opportunities Agency, which is a federal government department, and Enterprise Cape Breton, a Crown corporation. All are in the same service and all are situated in regions that partake of the service, which increasingly is a pattern of government. All serve an intermediary role between government and local communities. However, the Community Futures Development Corporation is smaller and more integrated within local communities than the Atlantic Canada Opportunities Agency, serving the Atlantic region.

Another example of a spin-off agency is the Canadian Institute for Health Information (CIHI, 2008), a non-profit founded in 1994 with offices in Ottawa, Toronto, Montreal, Edmonton, and Victoria, that produces analyses of Canada's health services largely through bilateral agreements with federal and provincial government departments. This agency came about through an agreement between the federal government, provinces, and territories, and receives core funding for its services from these entities and their representatives (deputy ministers and directors of regional health authorities) who are on the board of directors. Analyses undertaken by the CIHI inform health policy as well as government spending on health care. Like other public sector non-profits, the CIHI is an intermediary to the public, including representative bodies such as the Canadian Medical Association. Although the CIHI, like the Community Futures Development Corporation, is a spin-off from government, it is much more independent in fashioning its analyses.

There is also variability in the degree of independence of government agencies, with those serving as intermediaries to the university and arts communities having a relatively high degree of autonomy. For example, the Social Sciences and Humanities Research Council of Canada (SSHRC) retains a surprising degree of autonomy in its services to the academic community. SSHRC was created in 1977 by an act of parliament to administer the allocation of funding for university research in the social sciences and humanities. The Canada Council for the Arts, a Crown corporation founded in 1957, has a similar role for the arts. From the way that these agencies function, one might expect that they would be non-profits, but in spite of their intermediary role, they are part of government and therefore not within the social economy, as we define it. However, their role bears mention because within the category public sector non-profits the line between the social economy and government can be difficult to discern. (Recall that in chapter 2, there was a similar discussion about the line between the social economy and the private sector.)

Organizations Created by Government Legislation but Have Shifted Away

Organizations legislated by government can change, and may not remain within the public sector. Some Crown corporations are privatized, for example, Air Canada, Petro Canada, the Potash Corporation of Saskatchewan, and as noted above, government agencies can be spun off. Many universities and health care settings such as hospitals and homes for the aged are legislated by government, but in spite of their dependence on government financing and the influence of some government policies, their relationship may change and they may shift away from the public sector. As noted, they are referred to as QANGO: quasi-autonomous, non-government organizations. In our analysis, we include them, but note that they are an intermediary or a bridge between the public sector and the social economy.

Universities are a prime example of non-profit organizations that have achieved greater autonomy from government both in their policies and financing in that they are earning a greater part of their revenues from other sources. Statistics Canada (2007a) data indicate that for Canada as a whole, transfers from government account for 54 per cent of university revenue, and for three provinces (Ontario, Nova Scotia, and New Brunswick) government transfers account for less than half of revenues. In addition, universities typically have a foundation with a charitable status to encourage contributions by donors for endowments of major capital expenditures, scholarships, and sponsored research chairs. Universities are largely self-governing institutions that have a high degree of employee participation in decision-making relative to workplace norms. It is common practice for university faculties to have governing councils and for university staff to have collective bargaining rights through union locals. Hiring committees generally involve representatives of faculty and other staff associations.

Nevertheless, universities do overlap in part with the public sector: government representatives often sit on the board of governors, government may regulate tuition fees, contribute a substantial portion of funding based on enrolment, and also support research. However, overlap with the public sector is not the same as being part of the public sector, like a government agency. Universities have one foot in the public sector, but another in the social economy, and hence the label public sector non-profit. Like other public sector non-profits, universities are an intermediary organization bridging the public sector with the social economy. Universities provide many forms of support that, if removed, would weaken the social economy greatly. Universities are of such importance to the social economy that they could be characterized as a hub.

Some forms of support are obvious: courses, degree programs, and certificates on non-profits, co-operatives, and the social economy. While these are far from the norm in the social sciences, they are nevertheless significant. Examples include the following: Dalhousie's Institute for Nonprofit Leadership; École des Hautes Études Commerciales (HEC), Université de Montréal; University of Cape Breton MBA in Community Economic Development; Institut de recherche et d'éducation pour les coopératives et les mutuelles de l'Université de Sherbrooke (IRECUS); Queen's University Public Policy and Third Sector Initiative; Schulich School of Business, York University, Nonprofit Management and Leadership Program; Saint Mary's University Master of Management in Co-operatives and Credit Unions.

In addition, there are many research centres in universities devoted to the study of the social economy and related organizations, some of which offer degrees as well. Some examples are: British Columbia Institute for Co-operative Studies, University of Victoria; Centre for the Study of Co-operatives, University of Saskatchewan; Mount Royal College, Institute for Nonprofit Studies; Ryerson University Centre for Voluntary Sector Studies; Carleton University and University of Ottawa Centre for Voluntary Sector Research and Development; and the Social Economy Centre of the University of Toronto.

Universities also house associations for students, faculty, and other employees that help sustain these groups, and for students in particular, these associations can be vital training for civil society. As an example, Student Affairs of the University of Toronto lists 1,178 organizations with official status. These associations bring together people with diverse bonds of association, for example, the Bulgarian Students' Association, Cancer Awareness Society, Coalition for Animal Rights and the Environment, Comic Book Club, and Cricket Club

(University of Toronto, 2008). These would only be a subset of organizations that students partake of. Increasingly, Internet groups are the way that students associate with each other, and also many associations do not bother obtaining official status.

Student associations serve as a training ground in civic engagement that carries over to society as a whole. Some student associations are simply extensions of larger associations, for example, the University of Toronto Campus Conservatives, the Green Party of Canada at the University of Toronto. There are also representative councils for various student bodies such as the Graduate Students' Union, Woodsworth College Students' Association, and Burwash Hall Residence Council. There are nineteen media organizations alone, including the *Varsity* newspaper (operating for 125 years), CIUT-FM 89.5 FM, and the University of Toronto Community Radio.

Universities not only serve as a vital training ground in civil society for students, but also for the staff who participate in governing councils for their faculty or department. Unions and other labour associations that collectively bargain the labour rights of staff groups are the norm. At the University of Toronto, there are twenty-one union locals representing staff interests, and in addition the University of Toronto Faculty Association bargains collectively for faculty and librarians. These unions are locals of larger labour organizations (e.g., the United Steelworkers, CUPE, and OPSEU), and the faculty association, along with representatives of other faculties across Canada, belongs to the Canadian Association of University Teachers, as well as the provincial affiliate, the Ontario Confederation of University Faculty Associations.

Not only is the university a hub for unions and labour associations, it affiliates with other organizations through such organizations as the following: the Association of Universities and Colleges of Canada representing ninety-two non-profit universities and colleges; the Council of Ontario Universities; the Association of American Universities; and the Toronto City Summit Alliance, the University of Toronto being one of the largest employers in the city. University staff and students are important contributors to the United Way campaigns and are an important source of volunteers for many social economy organizations. Volunteer groups, such as 'pro bono lawyers,' assist community groups that are unable to cover the market rate for legal fees.

Unravelling this web of associations that connect through the university would be a major undertaking, but the examples illustrate how the University of Toronto serves as an intermediary between the public sector and the social economy. The university serves as a hub for an array of civil society associations that are a training ground for students, a bridging mechanism for its staff, and a link to other universities, the municipality, and the surrounding region. The University of Toronto is not unusual in that regard, but reflects how universities across Canada are important participants in their communities.

Nor are universities sui generis among public sector non-profits. The same can be said of hospitals and other health care non-profits, libraries, museums, historical sites, and social planning councils. All serve as hubs for webs of associations and in so doing facilitate connections. Hospitals, for example, house associations for specific diseases that afflict their patients, as well as unions for their staff groups, and make organizational connections to other hospitals, related health care facilities, and the communities they serve. The players may differ from a university, but the pattern of serving as a hub for civil society associations is similar.

Therefore, universities and many other public sector non-profits, originally legislated by a branch of government, serve a critical role within the social economy. Some might argue that because they have one foot in the public sector, they should not be in the social economy. However, that same point could be made for social economy businesses that overlap with the private sector, for example, farm marketing and retail food co-operatives, credit unions, and commercial non-profits. If one views the social economy as a dynamic framework that interacts with the private and public sectors, this overlap is not problematic. However, if one views the social economy as a procrustean bed whose members must meet rigid criteria, then the overlap could be a problem. The view presented in this book is that the social economy is a dynamic framework, and understanding its interaction with the other sectors of the economy is essential to capturing its essence.

Organizations Set Up Apart from Government but with Ongoing Dependence

Society consists of many social service organizations for persons with limited finances and other extraordinary needs. Some are able to sustain their services through a combination of labour and financial donations, and therefore are considered in the next chapter on civil society. Others find a niche in the market to support a substantial part of their service, and therefore are social enterprises considered in chapter 3. The organizations to be considered in this section rely more heavily on government programs than social enterprises do. However, they still may earn part of their revenues from the users of the service. Knowing whether to classify them as public sector non-profits or as social enterprises is a judgment call, but in the examples that follow, it will be evident that they are highly embedded within a government program and, without government support, these services would likely end.

Three cases are considered within this context: non-market housing, health care, and child care. For each, the discussion analyses how community groups have organized public sector non-profits or intermediary organizations to lobby government to fund services for people in need. This dynamic is typical of public sector non-profits, even those set up apart from the public sector but relying heavily on its policies and funding.

Non-Market Housing

Housing is one of the most basic of human needs, and for individuals and families with low incomes affordable accommodation can be problematic. Traditionally, Canada has had a good standard of housing with a relatively high percentage of private ownership, good quality stock, and a relatively low rate of homelessness. However, two distinct factors – growing inequality of incomes and the escalating price of housing in urban areas such as Vancouver, Victoria, Calgary, Toronto, and Ottawa – have led to a lack of affordable housing for a growing number, and at the extreme a growing group of people at risk of homelessness, although other factors contribute to homelessness as well. The Canada Mortgage and Housing Corporation (CMHC, 2005a, b) defines 'core need' as circumstances in which housing costs exceed 30 per cent of a household's pre-tax income, and in addition if the housing size is inadequate and in disrepair. Using the 2001 census data, CMHC estimates that 26.3 per cent of housing did not meet at least one of these standards and another 3.8 per cent missed more than one of these standards.

Of the three criteria, affordability was the most widespread and affected 16.9 per cent of households, predominantly tenants in cities such as Toronto, Vancouver, and Calgary. Affordability needs were also over-represented among single-parent households. In a separate analysis, CMHC estimates that 5.3 per cent of households spent more than 50 per cent of their before-tax income on shelter (CMHC, 2005a, b). While a subset of those spending a large portion of their income on housing are making a life choice (e.g., to purchase an expensive home), about 12.3 per cent of households in Canada (nearly one in eight) have serious affordability problems (Luffman, 2006).

The pressure on housing prices in large urban centres has been accentuated by demographic changes such as reduced household size, more divorces, fewer and later marriages, more elderly people, fewer children, less doubling up, and earlier home leaving, factors that have led to smaller households (Statistics Canada, 2006b). In a long-standing process called 'gentrification,' higher income couples in urban areas renovate large, old houses, driving up the price and reducing the number of users because tenant space is removed (Fallis, 1990; Wyly and Hammel, 2001). This process not only escalates price increases, but it also squeezes the rental market, thereby increasing the amount that tenants have to pay.

The severity of affordability problems varies, the most serious being households with low incomes, and, at the extreme, people who are unable to afford a stable living arrangement, either hard-core homeless living on the streets and in shelters or persons a step above with 'no fixed address' relying on supportive friends and family. The number of persons relying on arrangements through the informal economy with family and friends should not be underestimated. A recent study in the United Kingdom estimates that 380,000 persons (the 'hidden homeless') rely on such arrangements as the couch and even the floor of family and friends (Robinson and Coward, 2003). There do not seem to be similar data for Canada, but it is widely recognized that couch hopping is manifest for persons on the margins, but with greater social supports than those who end up on the street. A much larger group than either the homeless or those with informal arrangements are tenants using a relatively large percentage of their income for rentals and therefore at risk of losing a stable housing arrangement.

Although there are differing analyses of what's to be done, there is broad agreement that government intervention is required to assist those with affordability problems. In many of Canada's largest cities, the so-called economic rent, or the price at which new accommodation can be rented or sold in order for developers to recover costs, exceeds the financial means of the average household. The private housing market functions well for luxury housing, for households with high incomes, or for people with substantial equity for such reasons as existing housing ownership, inheritance, or other forms of good fortune. Given these economic factors, developers are not meeting the need for a new stock of rental accommodation for households of modest means, and instead have diverted their resources to the condominium market and to high-end development.

Innovative market-based programs service some of the need. For example, the award-winning non-profit business, Options for Homes (see case study at the end of chapter 8), has created a highly innovative approach to building condominiums for persons whose income and savings are stretched by the private market. Another example is the award-winning program of the Labourers' International Union of North America, Local 1115, in Cape Breton that has seen the members build homes for each other that are financed through a fund based on a 25 cents per hour deduction from pay (Perry, 1994; Quarter, 1995). (The Cape Breton Labourers' Benevolent Fund is also discussed in greater detail in chapter 8 on innovative forms of finance.) Some people unable to buy into the private housing market might have the good fortune to be picked by charitable organizations like Habitat for Humanity, a program that amasses armies of volunteers to build homes for the working poor. However, there remains a large group in need that requires government intervention, particularly in expensive urban centres.

Government Involvement

The government presence in the Canadian housing market goes back until at least the Great Depression of the 1930s (Hulchanski, 2004; Rose, 1980). In 1938, the federal government passed the National Housing Act, and three years later it created a Crown corporation, Wartime Housing Limited, the forerunner to Canada Mortgage and Housing Corporation. From its inception, the primary thrust of government policy was support of the private building industry. Through the post–Second World War period until the mid-1960s, government policy had the goal of a home for every family (Rose, 1980). In support of the development industry, the federal government used the National Housing Act to lower interest rates, increase the amortization period, and reduce down-payment requirements, policies to encourage home ownership. Even after government modified its home ownership dream and included rental accommodation in the mix, its orientation was to support the private market through a variety of subsidies and tax expenditures to assist potential owners, subsidize renters, and create incentives for developers to supply the housing market (Hulchanski, 1990, 2001, 2002).

In spite of this partnership between government and the development industry, and its relative success in meeting the housing needs of Canadians, there were segments of the population that required a different approach, because the private market, even subsidized by government, was not satisfying their need for affordable housing. This gap in government policy gave rise to the social housing or non-market housing sector. Canada's social housing sector is one of the smallest among Western countries, but has grown largely because it develops affordable housing (Hulchanski, 1990, 2002, 2004).

Social Housing

Social housing, which is a catch-all for an array of housing arrangements, operates outside of the private market. It is labelled as 'non-market' meaning that unlike private market housing that is bought and sold according to market exchange, social housing is normally not exchanged, excepting in extreme circumstances in which the development no longer is feasible. The users or tenants of social housing generally are people of modest means who cannot afford housing in the private market.

The roots of the social sector are in housing directly owned by government and referred to as *public housing*. These projects, often of a large scale, were an attempt by government to meet the needs of the poor. The first major public housing project in Canada was Regent Park North in Toronto, built after municipal taxpayers endorsed a $6 million levy in 1947 (Rose, 1980). By the mid-1950s, public housing projects also had been built in St John's, Halifax, Hamilton, Windsor, and Vancouver. In spite of strong opposition at the municipal level to creating 'urban slums,' by the early 1970s over 200,000 units had been built (Hulchanski, 1990). Public housing is administered directly by a government agency, which serves as the landlord and oversees each development.

The problems associated with public housing led to a re-evaluation during the mid-1960s, and the idea evolved of smaller non-market communities that were more integrated into the surrounding neighbourhoods and were administered either by non-profit agencies or by the tenants themselves as a co-operative. Referred to as *social housing*, this model consisted of non-profit housing developed by agencies operating at arm's length from government, for example, municipal non-profit agencies, church, labour, native and co-operative groups (Banting, 1990; Sousa and Quarter, 2003). Essentially, a government department entered into a partnership with these non-profit organizations (e.g., the Co-operative Housing Federation of Toronto) in planning new developments. These organizations were an intermediary between the appropriate government agency and the tenants of the new development, and therefore were public sector non-profits in our classification schema, delivering a service within a government policy framework. Without the government program, their role dissolved. In expanding the existing non-market housing stock, social housing programs have supplanted public housing, adding about 250,000 units, but overall non-market housing remains a relatively small part of Canada's housing mosaic. Only 5 per cent of Canadian households live in non-market social housing, compared to an average of about 15 to 20 per cent in many Western European countries (Hulchanski, 2002, 2004, 2005, 2007).

Social housing is affordable to its users. If they lack the means to pay the housing charge without using more than 30 per cent of their income, normally they would receive a rent-geared-to-income subsidy. In addition, tenants have security of tenure, and when tenants move on, the units are transferred to others who qualify. A major advantage of social housing over private rentals is that the housing charge rises only to meet increased operating costs. With time, there is an increasing gap in the charge to tenants between social housing and private rentals in the same neighbourhood. Without rent controls and other forms of regulation of the private rental market, this gap would be even greater.

The Achilles Heel of social housing is that it requires a 'supply-side subsidy' so that the charge to tenants is affordable. Again, this is because in order for developers to recover the cost of building in some of Canada's large urban centres, the rent or housing charges would exceed the paying capacity of the average tenant. Over the years, these supply-side subsidies have varied in form, but in general the government has covered a portion of the building cost through mortgage subsidies or other similar arrangements, thereby making the units affordable to the tenants. This arrangement, which was enacted during the 1973–74 when the Liberal minority government depended on the NDP for support, continued until 1993 when the federal government opted out of social housing (except for a small program in Aboriginal housing) and downloaded the responsibility to the provinces (Prince, 1998; van Dyk, 1995). Some provinces have continued to assist the development of social housing, but the decision by the federal government to end its involvement greatly slowed the development process. In Ontario, where most social housing was being built, eight years of Conservative government, including the downloading of the program to municipalities who were ill prepared to administer it, ground new development to a near halt. Therefore, dependence on government finance, a salient feature of public sector non-profits, applies strongly to social housing.

Nevertheless, as long as income inequality and housing prices in urban centres continue to increase, social housing is an option that policy makers have to consider. Governments have struggled with the subsidies required by social housing through enacting administrative changes, a recent one being the convergence of the differing social housing models. For example, housing co-operatives, which traditionally decided on their new members, have been forced in some jurisdictions to utilize centralized lists for eligibility where tenants receive a rental subsidy, and non-profits and public housing have transferred greater control to tenants, including the right to have their representatives on the board of directors (Sousa and Quarter, 2003). One experiment that may lead to even greater convergence of these models was the conversion in 2003 of the Alexandra Park public housing project in downtown Toronto into a tenant-managed co-operative, Atkinson Housing Co-operative. Although Atkinson has many features of other housing co-operatives, it still operates within a public housing framework, and thereby could be labelled as a 'hybrid' arrangement (Sousa, 2006; Sousa and Quarter, 2005).

A Closer Look: Atkinson Housing Co-operative

The Atkinson experiment involves a community which is a veritable United Nations, but with the common denominator of low income. The conversion took ten years and was led at first by one of the tenants, Sonny Atkinson, who died before it was completed in 2003. The co-operative is named after him and represents a legacy of his commitment to seeing it through in spite of challenging negotiations with the provincial and then the municipal housing authority (after the province downloaded the responsibility of social housing onto municipalities in 2000). The conversion was supported through its ten-year process by the Co-operative Housing Federation of Toronto that assisted the tenants in understanding the concept of a housing co-operative and that trained the board members to assume responsibility for governing the development.

At the Atkinson Housing Co-operative, the tenants are selected from a centralized list maintained through the municipal housing authority. Once the tenants decide to move into the community they automatically become members of the co-operative, which differs from other housing co-operatives that are empowered to select their members according to their own criteria. As with other co-operatives the members elect their board of directors from among their group, a first for a public housing project in Canada. The co-operative has succeeded in negotiating greater security of tenure for the tenants so that if their income rises, they do not necessarily have to move out of the development, as is often the case in public housing. The board hires the co-operative's property manager or a property management company, which is accountable to it. Moreover, the co-operative makes decisions about most maintenance issues, wresting control from the municipal housing authority. However, the co-operative continues to rely on financing from the municipal housing authority for major repairs such as roof replacement and sidewalks.

The conversion of the Atkinson Housing Co-operative represents an opportunity for building a stronger community among disadvantaged and marginalized populations. In fact, this conversion appears to be an idea with legs, as the Manitoba Housing and Renewal Corporation is actively exploring the conversion into housing co-operatives of existing public housing properties in Winnipeg, and the idea is being considered in other cities as well.

As governments struggle with the housing challenges of those with low incomes, it is possible that the face of social housing will change further. However, as long as there is social need, it is unlikely that this form of housing will disappear. Even conservative politicians recognize that the market has its limitations when addressing the needs of persons with relatively low incomes.

Health Care

Unlike housing, which is a constant and essential need, health care, while it is also essential, tends to be an episodic need. Housing costs are constant whereas health care costs, excepting for seniors and others with chronic conditions, are more intermittent and less predictable, and in times of crisis outstrip the financial resources of all but the wealthy. Therefore, governments have had to intervene to insure the public against financial catastrophe in times of need.

In Canada, the first government plan related to health care became operational in 1947, after the Saskatchewan CCF (the forerunner to the NDP) passed the Hospitalization Act providing government insurance for hospital care (Taylor, 1978). By 1957 the federal government enacted its own plan and transferred funds to any province introducing comprehensive hospital insurance that was accessible to all residents and portable throughout the country.

Government health care insurance was expanded again in 1962 when Saskatchewan enacted the Medical Care Insurance Act (Medicare, as it became known), and four years later when the federal government legislated the National Medical Insurance Act. Since that time, there have been negotiations over the specifics of cost sharing between the federal government and provinces and other issues such as users' fees, but government finance has been the backbone of Canada's health care system, currently covering about 70 per cent of the total health care bill (CIHI, 2007).

Yet in spite of a strong government presence in finance, the delivery of health care remains largely private, under the control of physicians working on a fee-for-service basis, and with medications produced by the pharmaceutical industry. However, there are other important components of the health care system that are primarily in the social economy: non-profit hospitals, community health centres, addiction-treatment centres, and a network of other health care non-profits that raise funds and awareness about particular illnesses (e.g., the Canadian Breast Cancer Foundation). Therefore, like the Canadian economy as a whole, the health care system is a mixed model with crucial components of participation from government, the private sector, and the social economy.

Although some social economy organizations in the health care field function apart from government (e.g., associations for persons with particular illnesses and foundations that raise funds for various health care initiatives), government policy and finance are a major influence on health care organizations, many of which are public sector non-profits. Some, as discussed above, have their roots in the public sector, but others have evolved from the social economy, but because of the dominance of government finance and policy, have assumed intermediary roles between government agencies and the sectors of the public that they serve.

The mental health and addictions fields are ones in which community-based non-profits rely heavily on government finance and are influenced by government policy. With the deinstitutionalization of mental health, organizations were developed in the community to give voice to the concerns of users of the system, many of whom have low incomes and rely on disability pensions and other government-funded supports for housing and medication. For example, starting in 1991, the Ontario government funded the Consumer/Survivor Development Initiative (since renamed the Ontario Peer Development Initiative) with forty-two programs across the province. The Ontario Peer Development Initiative (OPDI, 2006) is a public sector non-profit that was spun off by the provincial government. By 2006, there were sixty consumer/survivor initiatives, all different, but all non-profit organizations relying on government funding to service their clientele. These are examples of public sector non-profits that are intermediaries between the provincial government and users of psychiatric services, that is, consumer-survivors. These initiatives are funded through Local Health Integration Networks throughout the province of Ontario and represent an impressive array of organizations, for example, consumer/survivor businesses (see chapter 3), drop-in centres, self-help groups, family networks, vocational training associations, advocacy organizations, and patient councils (OPDI, 2007).

Community Health Centres

Among the many debates in health care is whether efficiency would be increased through a delivery system of non-profit community health centres that place greater emphasis on health promotion and disease prevention and which encourage homecare as an alternative to hospitalization and nursing homes (Rachlis and Kushner, 1989). The community health centre has become a focal point for this alternative view of health care. The roots of the community health model can be traced to the Victorian Order of Nurses, started in 1897, when Lady Aberdeen (the wife of Canada's governor general of that time) was granted a charter by Queen Victoria to proceed with an organization of nurses. The Victorian Order of Nurses (VON, 2007) was inspired by the legendary Florence Nightingale, known as the 'lady with the lamp' during the Crimean War, and a leading advocate for improved public health in Victorian England. The Victorian Order of Nurses would treat those in need in their homes and in 'cottage hospitals.' The first of these, established in Regina in 1898, might be seen as the pioneer community health centre in Canada. By 1924, when the Victorian Order of Nurses turned its cottage hospitals over to local authorities, forty-three more had been established in communities and isolated areas across Canada.

The Victorian Order of Nurses was born because there was a lack of basic health services. The impetus for the more recent community health centre movement was also a lack of basic health services, but for different reasons. When Medicare was introduced in Saskatchewan in 1962, many doctors went on strike, forcing local communities to organize their own health care by forming Community Health Service Associations (Badgley and Wolfe, 1967). These associations, some of which are still operating, sprung from a grassroots movement based on an innovative form of mutual self-help. Writing just after the doctors' strike, Robin Badgley and Samuel Wolfe (1967: 102–4) described what appeared to be an incipient healthcare movement: 'The concept of consumer-sponsored group practice has captured the imagination of many of the general public and a sizeable number of doctors in recent decades. In Saskatchewan, this movement developed as a direct consequence of the doctors' strike.'

The Saskatchewan community health centres operate as consumer health co-operatives, with users being members with the right to vote at annual general meetings and with the right to influence the health policies of the clinic. Across Canada, there are fourteen health care centres organized as co-operatives (Craddock and Vayid, 2004), a subset of a broader grouping of non-profit community health centres. These organizations grant membership rights to users of the service that give them the opportunity to vote at general meetings and to elect directors from among their group.

The community health centre movement that evolved in Saskatchewan lacked the same fanfare as Medicare. The Saskatoon Agreement, which concluded the doctors' strike in 1962, spelled out the rights of the citizens of Saskatchewan to establish community health centres (Badgley and Wolfe, 1967). Like Medicare, though, their birth was painful and strongly opposed by the private-delivery system controlled by doctors. There was deep-seated animosity in the medical profession towards community health centres, for example, the denial of hospital privileges to doctors working in them. It was not until 1972 that these centres were funded directly for their services by the provincial Department of Health. Unlike Medicare, which doctors embraced when its financial benefits became clear, non-profit community health centres still are viewed with suspicion and as a threat to the autonomy of the medical profession. Community health centres are an excellent example of a public sector non-profit that serves as an intermediary between a government policy and financial framework and the public that they serve, but they are on the margins of the health care delivery system.

The community health movement was given a major boost when Quebec introduced in 1972 a publicly funded province-wide system of Local Community Service Centres (CLSCs) (Bozzoni, 1988; Désrosiers, 1978). The CLSCs combined primary health care and social services with a strong emphasis on homecare. The homecare programs emphasized prenatal and infant care, and many CLSC staff are nurses and social workers. The doctors at the CLSCs tend to be young general practitioners, disproportionately women, who are prepared to work on a salary and a thirty-five-hour week.

In contrast to most community health centres in Canada, which have evolved from the initiative of community activists but with the support of government programs, the CLSC system was a creation of the Quebec government and part of a plan to decentralize the coordination of health services. In that regard, it could be classified as a 'spin-off' from the public sector, much like Community Futures Development Corporation, discussed above.

Prior to its adoption by the government of Quebec, the CLSC model actually had the same community roots as other community health centres, as it was a creation of citizen movements working in the poor neighbourhoods of Montreal in the late 1960s. The forerunners to the CLSC were called *cliniques populaires* and were influenced by similar organizations in the United States that emphasized the promotion of health and the prevention of disease as well as basic health care. The first was at Pointe St Charles in 1968, with others to follow in St-Jacques, St-Henri, Centre-Ville, Hochelaga-Maisonneuve, and Centre-South (Pointe St-Charles, 2007). However, over the years, the cliniques populaires were integrated into the CLSC network established by the Quebec government. Each CLSC operated within provincial and regional policy frameworks, but had its own board, much like community health centres in general. Then in 2004, CLSCs were integrated with community hospitals and long-term care facilities to become sub-regional health and social service centres called CSSS. For CLSCs this change resulted in the loss of an autonomous board, a weakening of the local and community part of their programs, and a greater emphasis on standard forms of medical care (Kaufman, 2007).

The CLSC is an example of the vulnerability of public sector non-profits to changes in government policy initiatives. This relationship has been characterized as a partnership (Salamon, 1987, 1995), but as noted, government is the senior partner and in a position to change the program. While the CLSC was probably the most vulnerable of community health centres because it was created by the Quebec government, the pattern differs only in degree from community health centres in other parts of Canada. As in Quebec, the administration of health care has become regionalized, and community health centres have had to relate to regional health authorities, some losing much of their autonomy (Association of Ontario Health Centres, 2006). In Ontario, there are seventy-six community health centres, seventeen satellites, and ten Aboriginal health centres. However, of these centres, only twenty-five have independent community boards and the others are integrated within fourteen Local Health Integrated Networks across the province (Tetley, 2007). This same pattern can be found across Canada, although the labelling of the regional health authority differs.

Not only has there been an integration of community health centres within regional health systems, but there is also great variability in government support of local centres. In Ontario, there were no new centres through two consecutive terms of the Conservative government. However, with a more supportive provincial government and minister of health, the program has been renewed but without the community boards, the hallmark of this approach. Nevertheless, non-profit community health centres with a community board (including co-operatives) can be found across Canada. Their umbrella association is the Canadian Alliance for Community Health Centre Associations (CAMHC, 2006). These organizations largely supplement the predominant delivery of medical services, and therefore are tolerated. They play an important role, and also symbolize an alternative that could be activated, given appropriate circumstances.

Aboriginal Community Health Organizations

Aboriginal organizations have been adept at working with government programs to create public sector non-profits to service Aboriginal communities. Some, as noted above, are community health centres (referred to as Aboriginal Health Access Centres), and these have distinct features such as native healing and medicines (Association of Ontario Health Centres, 2006).

An innovative model is the National Aboriginal Health Organization (NAHO, 2008), founded in 2000 for 'influencing and advancing the health and well-being of Aboriginal Peoples by carrying out knowledge-based strategies.' NAHO has five member organizations: the Assembly of First Nations, the Congress of Aboriginal Peoples, Inuit Tapiriit Kanatami, the Métis National Council, and the Native Women's Association of Canada. NAHO receives its core funding from Health Canada, and utilizes this funding to provide information to Aboriginal communities across Canada on issues related to Aboriginal health and well-being. Among its publications is the *Journal of Aboriginal Health* for specialists in Inuit, Métis, and First Nations health, as well as traditional healers. In addition to its publications, NAHO operates a media centre that releases recent publications and reports for its constituencies. NAHO is among a group of Aboriginal organizations concerned about informing the Aboriginal peoples of Canada regarding their health options. In addition to working with Health Canada, NAHO is integrated within a web of health care networks, some Aboriginal. It works specifically with the First Nations Centre, the Ajunnginiq Centre, the Métis Centre, and the Canadian Health Network.

Like non-market housing, community health centres and related initiatives are vulnerable to government cutbacks and policy change. For example, the Canadian Health Network (2008), a project of the Canadian Public Health Association, another public sector non-profit, is designed to help Canadians obtain health information that they require through its website and related publications, or to quote its mission, 'to promote healthy choices' through access to more than '20,000' information sources. The government of Canada decided that this seemingly innovative project did not fit its priorities and cut the funding as of 2008.

Child Care

Child care is another area in which government policy and funding are important. Traditionally, child care in Canada has been a private concern of the family and for that reason Canadian governments have been reluctant to become heavily involved. However, as more women have become participants in the labour force, licensed child care centres have assumed a greater role. Much of this transformation has occurred since the late 1960s, but the tradition for child care centres outside of the home dates back to the nineteenth century when religious communities in Quebec established *salles d'asile* (Lalonde-Graton, 1986). These centres were financed primarily by Christian charity as a means of helping the poor. Child care centres were also stimulated by European education reformers and humanists, for example, Robert Owen, Johann Pestalozzi, and Wilhelm Froebel. These early reformers were not only interested in child care, as traditionally defined, but viewed the care of children as an educational process. Owen, in particular, was a strong proponent of early education, even from infancy, and in 1816 created the first known school for infants at New Lanark, Scotland, a model community that he established. In his 1813 book, *A New View for Society*, Owen, who considered education as a way of breaking down rigid class structures, emphasized the importance of infant education and also demanded universal public education, teacher training colleges, and adult education (Owen, 1969 [1813]).

The work of Owen, Froebel, and Pestalozzi could be viewed as the beginnings of early childhood education, as distinct from child care per se. Although we use the term *child care* in this book, a common labelling by people working in this field is early childhood education and care. One problem in utilizing 'early childhood education and care,' as the OECD (2004: 6) states in relation to Canada's system, is the following: 'The result is a patchwork of uneconomic fragmented services within which a small "child care" sector is seen as a labour market support, often without a focused child development and education role.' The OECD urges Canadian governments to make early childhood education a 'cornerstone of Canadian family and education policy.'

In Canada, the first early childhood schools appeared in the mid-nineteenth century, and they were oriented to children of the poor (Prochner, 2000). By the 1870s, private kindergartens, also associated with reformist movements, began to appear, at first for children from the middle and upper classes, but with the support of charitable organizations they became oriented to the children of recent immigrants. The first public kindergarten opened in 1883 in the Toronto Board of Education, and by 1900 there were kindergartens across the province for children from age three to five. By the 1920s, child care centres, sponsored primarily by charitable organizations, were set up for children, including infants, whose mother was employed (Friendly and Beach, 2005).[1] During the Second World War, when women entered the workforce in large numbers, the federal government initiated a cost-sharing agreement with the provinces (only Ontario and Quebec participated) and supported centres for children whose mothers were employed in essential war-related industries.

Drivers

There are at least two essential and interrelated drivers for the increased availability of licensed child care arrangements for children in Canada: greater participation of women in the paid workforce and government programs.

By 2004, women comprised 47 per cent of the paid workforce in Canada, a sharp increase from 37 per cent in 1976, and one of the highest participation rates in the world (Statistics Canada, 2006b). This dramatic increase applied even more so to women with small children, whose participation rates exceed the norm for women in general. In 2004, the paid workforce included 65 per cent of women with children under aged 3, 70 per cent of women with children aged 3 to 5 years, and 68 per cent of female lone-parent families. These statistics include women from age 15 and above; if only the prime work years, 25 to 54, are included, the participation rate for women in Canada was 81 per cent in 2005 (Statistics Canada, 2006b). In other words, the role change

1 This summary of the history of child care in Canada relies heavily on the account in Friendly and Beach (2005).

of women pertained most to those with small children, a marked difference from decades past.

Another Statistics Canada survey showed that 25 per cent of parents had child care arrangements from when their children were 6 months old, and that from ages 1 to 5 years about half of children were in such arrangements (the highest percentage at age 4) (Statistics Canada, 2006b) The data illustrate that the critical factor in whether children were in child care arrangements was if the parents were in the paid workforce or studying. Of single-parent families, 85 per cent of children were in a child care arrangement; for two-parent families, the comparable figure was 73 per cent. In both cases, there was a sizable increase from the previous survey, six years earlier.

This role change for women reflected the influence of the feminist movement and the changing conception of what it meant to be a woman. One manifestation of this cultural change is that the birth rate declined markedly, and in 2002 it was about one-third of what it was in 1959. The family has become smaller and thereby is losing internal child care supports from older children, particularly when the mother is working in the paid workforce. Similarly, the shift away from an extended family involving multiple generations in the same household has meant the loss of an unpaid source of child care. Today, the family unit is not only smaller but also much less permanent, more mobile, and in much greater need of external institutional assistance. The increased participation of women in the paid workforce created a need for child care arrangements in support of the parents.

The second driver – government financial and policy support – is equally important in stimulating the development of licensed child care arrangements. The government's role, as noted, goes back to the nineteenth century. In 1966, the federal government created the Canada Assistance Plan (CAP), another cost-sharing agreement with the provinces through which parents who met a needs' test would receive fees' subsidies for their children to be in public and non-profit centres. As provinces gradually bought into this arrangement, it stimulated the growth of child care centres. However, the primary orientation of the CAP equated government expenditures with welfare, much like social housing, and as distinct from universal programs such as Medicare or public education. The criticism of this orientation by government was presented in the 1986 *Report of the Task Force on Child Care*: 'The present state of childcare in Canada is on a par with the state of education in this country in the late 1800s and health care in the 1930s.

In a global perspective, Canada's child care and parental leave programs lag far behind systems operating in most western industrialized countries' (Status of Women, 1986: 3).

As mothers entered the paid workforce in increased numbers, middle-class parents who were ineligible for assistance under the CAP also required child care arrangements. To some extent, the government accommodated this need by making child care expenses deductible under the Income Tax Act and including maternity benefits for eligible new mothers within the Unemployment Insurance Act. Beginning with Quebec in 1979, the provinces began subsidizing the operating costs of child care centres in various ways. This increased funding was in response to pressure from community organizations specific to child care, for example, the Childcare Advocacy Association of Canada, supported by feminist groups such as the National Action Committee on the Status of Women, and others such as the Canadian Council on Social Development, the Canadian Labour Congress, and university-based programs such as the Childcare Resource and Research Unit of the University of Toronto. Put differently, one result of the first driver – the sharp increase in workforce participation rates of women – was the strengthening by women of child care advocacy groups (e.g., Association Québecoise des CPEs and the Ontario Coalition for Better Childcare) and feminist organizations, who worked hard to mobilize support. (The role of such non-profit mutual associations will be discussed in greater detail in chapter 6.)

These non-profit advocacy groups and governments across Canada have faced off for about the past forty years, with proponents arguing for a universal program for licensed child care, much akin to Medicare, and some governments being sympathetic but not following through. As early as 1970, the Royal Commission on the Status of Women called for a National Day-care Act (Friendly and Beach, 2005). At several points between 1984 and 1995, the federal government initiated efforts at reaching agreements with the provinces about a national child care program. However, this process was weakened by the tilt in power towards the provinces and the 1996 decision of the federal government to change its funding transfer arrangement from specific allocations under the Canada Assistance Plan to a block transfer for use at the province's discretion under the Canada Health and Social Transfer (Prince, 1998).

Finally, in 2004, the newly elected Liberal government made universal child care a priority in its throne speech and moved quickly to sign deals with each province. The plan was not only to greatly enhance the system of centres available to care for children but also to place a much greater emphasis on early learning, child development being one of the key principles on which the system would be built. The government committed $5 billion over five years for 250,000 new spaces in child care centres, but its stay in power was brief. The deal was quickly scuppered by the incoming Conservative government, and the funds were diverted to $100 per month payments to parents with children under 6 years of age to spend as they would like. The underlying philosophy, it seemed, was to encourage mothers to stay at home with their children.

The Results

As of 2007, Quebec is the only Canadian province with a relatively comprehensive child care program. In 2004, 43 per cent of the licensed child care spaces in Canada were in that province, and the government is working on a program of adding 20,000 additional spaces, thereby reducing waiting lists. Quebec's expenditure on licensed child care in 2004 represents 58 per cent of Canada's total and increased eleven-fold from 1991 (Friendly and Beach, 2005).

According to Statistics Canada (2005), of all children from 6 months to 5 years of age in a child care arrangement (i.e., other than from their parent or guardian), only 25 per cent were in a child care centre. The others were in such arrangements as care in someone else's home (a small portion of which would be licensed centres) or in the child's home by either a relative or non-relative. Most of these arrangements with family members or neighbours could be characterized as part of the informal economy. Only in Quebec, with the most developed government program, were child care centres predominant (41 per cent), and this includes child care for children in kindergarten. The other provinces ranged from 10 per cent in Saskatchewan to 28 per cent in Prince Edward Island.

Between 1971 and 2003, the number of licensed child care spaces in Canada increased by nearly forty-three—fold to more than 745,000, with community settings as distinct from licensed family arrangements comprising nearly 83 per cent of the total, or about five-sixths of the available spaces (Statistics Canada, 2006c). Of centre-based provision, 79 per cent are non-profit and the remainder, commercial. In fact, non-profit centres have represented 87 per cent of the growth in child care spaces since 1996, but since 2001 the largest share of the increase is in licensed family centres, largely in Quebec, and a departure from the pattern since 1971.

One reason for the increase in non-profit centres is that from 1997 Quebec mandated that its licensed child care centres (*centres de la petite enfance*, or CPEs) that supplemented the public education system be non-profit. The Quebec program, a combination of augmented public education supplemented by non-profit child care centres, involved the extension of kindergarten to a full day; half-day kindergarten for 4-year-olds supplemented by after-school child care programs; and eventually the availability from infancy of CPEs – the cost to parents normally being $7 per day, but with reductions for those with low incomes.

Within the child care advocacy movement, there is a debate as to whether this service would be better seen as an extension of public education or as distinct and carried on through non-profit child care centres. For example, in 1989 the Ontario Coalition for Better Childcare (1989: 5) criticized non-profit child care as an 'under-funded cottage industry' that relied too heavily on underpaid staff and the unpaid labour of overburdened parent volunteers. At that time, the Ontario Coalition of Better Childcare embraced the policy of a 'publicly operated universally accessible system for children 3.8 and over' (Ontario Coalition of Better Childcare, 1989: 9), but this issue remains controversial.

The participation of parents in supplementing the centre's services, while generally viewed as positive, is also controversial because it involves an additional task, often to mothers, who are already carrying a job in the paid workforce plus heavy responsibilities at home. Nevertheless, Quebec does mandate that at least two-thirds of non-profit centre boards consist of parent users. Parent boards of directors and volunteer participation are the norms for nursery school co-operatives as well as child care co-operatives for working parents, of which there are 386 in Canada (Co-operatives Secretariat, 2007a). These are often associated with a U.S. organization, Parent Cooperative Preschool International.

In summary, child care in Canada can be viewed as a hodge-podge, and excepting Quebec, reflects a lack of careful government policy. The arrangements that supplement the family are largely informal, and licensed centres are predominantly non-profits and municipal, but also include the private sector, which research suggests doesn't provide as high quality care (Cleveland and Krashinsky, 2004; Cleveland et al.,

2007). Government finance and policy are major drivers, as are the non-profit advocacy groups that lobby government to improve services. Today, licensed child care arrangements can be viewed as less of a welfare service than social housing but not as a universal program like Medicare or public education. The OECD (2004: 6) report on Canada states: 'National and provincial policy for early education and care for young children in Canada is still in its initial stages. Care and education are still treated separately and coverage is low compared to other OECD countries.' A follow-up study by the OECD (2006) ranked Canada last among fourteen countries in its expenditure on child care, at 0.2 per cent of GDP. Canada's child care expenditure was 10 per cent of Denmark's, the highest in the group, and about half of the OECD average. The OECD report urged Canada to bring its expenditures up to the average, as a means of improving the access to early childhood education.

Therefore, institutional child care in Canada is similar to social housing and health care in that for it to move forward, it requires an investment from government. Like social housing, governments, with the exception of Quebec, have not been forthcoming with the necessary investment. Child care centres rely on government investment to subsidize their building costs and to subsidize the user charges to parents with low to modest incomes. Like other public sector non-profits, they are heavily dependent on funding from government, both start-up and ongoing. The centres, once under way, have their own momentum, but their clientele require ongoing support.

Like social housing and health care, the child care networks have created intermediary organizations that lobby government on their behalf and also provide services to their members. An excellent example is the Child Care Advocacy Association of Canada.

A Closer Look: Child Care Advocacy Association of Canada

To realize the dream of universal early childhood education and child care, a large array of intermediary organizations work in this field, for example, the Canadian Child Care Federation and its provincial affiliates (e.g., Alberta Child Care Federation, Nova Scotia Child Care Federation), with the broad goal of achieving excellence in early learning and child care. Some organizations speak specifically on behalf of child care workers, for example, the

Child Care Human Resources Sector Council (CCHRSC). Child Care Advocacy Association of Canada and its affiliates promote 'a publicly funded, inclusive, quality, nonprofit child care system' (Childcare Advocacy of Canada, 2008). Started in 1982, this organization has affiliates across Canada that address similar issues at the provincial level, for example, the New Brunswick Child Care Coalition and the Alberta Child Care Network. Governments, including elected members of parliament and provincial legislatures, are the target of its initiatives. This has created sustainability challenges, as like many other intermediary organizations working in this field, Child Care Advocacy Association of Canada relies heavily on government contracts for its funding. Another sustainability issue for advocates is that just when a government-funded universal child care program was realized, the vicissitudes of politics led to its undoing. This is a challenge, however, for all public sector non-profit organizations, as government policy direction is subject to political change.

Conclusion

Public sector non-profits are an unusual grouping that some would view as being outside of the social economy. These organizations rely on government funding and are influenced by government policy. Some are spin-offs from governments that attempt to decentralize their services and locate their agencies more closely to communities that they serve. Others are creations of government that have achieved greater independence over the years, universities being a prime example. Most, however, are organizations operating within the community and are drawn into government's orbit because they serve clientele with low incomes who cannot sustain the cost of services (social housing and child care) or the costs can be extraordinary and beyond the means of all but the wealthy (health care). In response, these organizations attempt to generate larger government support either directly or through intermediary organizations. Public sector non-profits serve another function in that they can act as hubs for networks of non-profit mutual associations that we characterize as civil society organizations (see Figure 5.1). It is to that group that we turn next.

* * *

DISCUSSION QUESTIONS

1. Is it appropriate to view public sector non-profits, such as discussed in this chapter, as part of the social economy?
2. As Samuel Martin's historical account indicates, in the modern world, government financing has increased in importance for many types of services. What is your view of this trend? Can public sector non-profits function without this government support?
3. Social housing programs have attempted to operate apart from government, but they rely on government financing and are influenced by government policy. Is it appropriate to view such organizations as part of the social economy?
4. Community health centres also rely on government funding, as does health care in general. Should such organizations be viewed as agencies of government?
5. Early childhood education and care in Canada has been criticized by the OECD for insufficient government support relative to other Western countries. Would it not be better to view early childhood education and care as a form of public education, even from infancy?
6. Are there other services that should be included as public sector non-profits?

* * *

Case for Analysis:
Newfoundland and Labrador Arts Council[2]

Mission and Vision

The Newfoundland and Labrador Arts Council (NLAC) is a non-profit Crown agency created in 1980 by the Arts Council Act. NLAC's mission is to foster and to promote the creation and enjoyment of the arts for the benefit of the residents of Newfoundland and Labrador. It does so by operating financial assistance programs, providing various

---

2 We would like to thank Reg Winsor and Janet McDonald for their support and feedback.

services and resources, and partnering with both governments and communities to promote arts development.

According to G.M. Story, co-editor of the *Dictionary of Newfoundland English*, '[it] is our creative ability that ensures our survival as a recognizable people and culture, and enables us also to contribute to the enrichment of the nation of which we form a distinctive part' (NLAC, 2008a). NLAC was created to encourage artistic endeavours and to recognize and to stimulate Newfoundland and Labrador's rich and distinctive culture.

NLAC's vision states: 'Newfoundlanders and Labradorians are a creative, innovative and diverse people who participate fully in a healthy, vibrant arts and cultural community which is globally recognized for artistic excellence' (NLAC, 2008a). NLAC is governed by six core operating values: (1) it achieves its mission by working collaboratively; (2) it fosters universal access to the arts; (3) it supports artistic freedom of expression, diversity, and excellence; (4) it believes that art should be an economically viable activity; (5) it encourages dialogue with artists and other stakeholders; and (6) it follows principles of transparency and accountability in its reporting practices.

Legislative Framework

The Arts Council Act received assent on 28 May 1980. It defines the arts broadly to include theatre, dance, folk arts, literature, music, painting, sculpture, the graphic arts, crafts, and other similar and interpretive activities. The Arts Council Act created an Arts Fund that receives funding from the provincial treasury and an Investment Committee to manage the assets of NLAC. It created a volunteer council (board) of twelve members who are appointed by the provincial government through the lieutenant governor in council. Two members are representatives from the provincial Department of Tourism, Culture, and Recreation and the other ten are artists from a variety of arts and communities. The twelve members serve for three years and may seek reappointment for one more term. The chair of the council reports annually to the minister of tourism, culture, and recreation.

Programs

NLAC has several core programs. The Sustaining Program for Professional Arts Organizations program provides grants to support administration and project costs to professional arts organizations that further the arts in the province. In 2007, NLAC awarded $246,563 in total to twenty-one new artists and groups, forty-three established artists and groups, and seven non-profit arts organizations. The average grant was $2,118.

NLAC also provides Sustaining Grants with a guaranteed minimum of three years that are available to non-profit professional arts organizations for assistance towards administrative and production costs. NLAC also funds The Professional Festivals Program to support the operation of festivals or series that run during a concentrated period of time. Another of its core programs is the Cultural Assistance Plan for Emergencies that provides funding for artists who suffer severe illness, a debilitating accident, or other catastrophic event.

NLAC also hosts an annual gala to honour the recipients of its Arts Awards. The categories include the ArtsSmarts Arts in Education Award, Patron of the Arts Award, CBC Emerging Artist Award, Hall of Honour Award, Rogers Cable Arts Achievement Award, and Artist of the Year Award. Members of the arts community, arts organizations, and the public can submit nominations. In describing the recipients of the 2008 awards, Carmelita McGrath, Chair of NLAC, commented: 'This year's winners and all the finalists provide us with striking examples of the diversity and intensity of arts activity in our province. That's what these awards are all about – recognizing and valuing the creativity and commitment of artists whose work enriches our lives every day' (NLAC, 2007).

NLAC also supports three programs that have an educational mandate: ArtsSmarts, Visiting Artist Program, and the School Touring Program. In 1998, the J.W. McConnell Family launched ArtsSmart (2008), which is a national initiative to promote the active involvement of students in the arts through school-based projects. Its mission is to integrate art throughout school curricula, to stimulate children to do and to appreciate art. NLAC is the province's ArtsSmart partner, and between 1998 and 2007, it awarded $700,000 to schools throughout the province.

NLAC also provides funding for artists to visit schools. A teacher in any school in the provincial kindergarten to Grade 12 system can apply for a grant of $500 to cover artist fees, materials, and administration costs. As well, NLAC provides $60,000 annually for its School Touring Program, which gives financial assistance to professional artists and arts organizations for school touring productions that may encourage students' artistic interests.

Council Members

In November 2007, Carmelita McGrath was elected NLAC's chair. McGrath is an award-winning author and freelance writer and editor. She has also worked in research and education. According to McGrath, 'The arts in this province are an essential part of who we are and, increasingly, how we are seen by the rest of the world ... I believe that our biggest challenge now is to ensure that the arts and artists are recognized and adequately supported through the kind of focused investment we've identified in our Strategic Framework. We continue to work on program renewal and new initiatives with this goal in mind' (NLAC, 2008b).

The NLAC has two co-vice chairs, four other members from the arts community, as well as the deputy minister and the director of arts from the Department of Tourism, Culture, and Recreation. A staff of six people supports the council.

Strategy

As part of its twenty-fifth anniversary celebrations in 2005, NLAC undertook a major strategic review. The plan identified the issues, challenges, and opportunities for the arts in the province and identified four strategic goals supported by some strategic objectives. Its timeline included creating its first annual operational plan in 2006. Exhibit 5.1 presents the main elements of the plan.

* * *

DISCUSSION QUESTIONS

1. What are the advantages and disadvantages of NLAC's legislative framework?
2. What ideas do you have for implementing NLAC's strategy?

* * *

EXHIBIT 5.1 NLAC'S STRATEGY

The Arts in Newfoundland and Labrador: Issues, Challenges, and Opportunities

To ensure the strategic framework reflects the views and concerns of our stakeholders, Council conducted an extensive consultation with artists, representatives of artist organizations, community representatives and others. With the assistance of an external consultant, we analyzed 226 surveys, held community forums attended by 172 participants and carried out in-depth interviews with forty-three people. This consultation process provided a rich body of information and feedback for Council in the development of our strategic framework. The information forms a firm foundation for our activity plan under the Transparency and Accountability Act.

We also reviewed the status of the arts within a broader framework. Across Canada and around the world, artistic creation and enjoyment of the arts are recognized as key contributors to creative communities and healthy societies. Within our province, there is a growing recognition of the value of the arts. Parents are now demanding more artistic opportunities within schools for their children, recognizing that an understanding and appreciation of the arts spurs intellectual and creative development as well as greater respect for diversity and cultural identity. Community leaders recognize that participation in the arts within their own communities fosters community pride, identity, engagement and an enriched quality of life.

Despite these encouraging signs, artists continue to struggle, with the majority facing tremendous economic barriers. Within Canada, only 10 per cent of artists make a living exclusively from their art, a percentage that is also reflected in the province. Council funds about 70 per cent of all artists who apply to our granting programs but only to the level of about 30 per cent of the requested amounts. An average grant from Council is about $1,700.

This leaves artists in a particularly vulnerable position, especially given that the number of funding sources within the province is quite limited. In addition, the arts community, including arts organizations, competes with other sectors such as health and education for a limited public purse. Artists report a desperate need to generate greater economic viability for themselves through greater access to audiences within the province, throughout Canada and beyond. Artists also require a more responsive tax regime that provides incentives and/or deductions for export activity, materials, and other necessary tools to support artistic creation. Artists would also benefit from greater public awareness of the arts and increased access to their work province-wide within a culture that supports freedom of artist expression and diversity.

Artists and arts organizations expect Council to take a strong advocacy role by championing the arts and giving artists a strong, credible voice in public policy development. There is also a strong need for additional focus on professional development and mentoring, especially for emerging artists and those who live in rural areas. We also need to place more emphasis on engaging artists in supportive networks to enable access to information and resources and create a stronger sense of belonging to an arts community. Council has been weak in this area and requires additional communications staff and related resources to meet these important needs.

A critical strategic issue for Council is how best to direct limited grant funds. There is an acute awareness that existing funds are insufficient to meet basic requirements and that the number and scope of grant categories must be expanded. Grant programs must be supported by appropriate guidelines which respond to artists' needs as well as [to] the objectives of arts organizations. There is strong endorsement of Council's peer assessment process, though this too can be further strengthened to achieve higher levels of transparency and more effective feedback.

Throughout the process, we have identified opportunities to better focus and co-ordinate investments and programming through stronger collaborative partnerships with government, other arts organizations, communities, and other stakeholders. We firmly believe that these approaches will assist us all to build on each other's capabilities and energy for the benefit of all.

Finally, and perhaps most importantly, the Newfoundland and Labrador Arts Council enjoys the tremendous talent and energy of arts champions within government, other arts organizations and communities. The opportunity and challenge ahead is to build on this foundation to ensure that excellence in arts creation and public enjoyment of the arts become a shared vision for all of us in Newfoundland and Labrador.

STRATEGIC GOAL 1: Improve support for artistic excellence through focused investments

The primary function of the Newfoundland and Labrador Arts Council is to develop and administer granting programs for artists and arts organizations. Over the last 25 years, tremendous changes have occurred in the arts community with emerging art forms, technology and new media. Many artists are expressing interest in export opportunities. Emerging artists require mentorship and access to financial support. For artists and arts organizations alike, the needs are great, calling for increased funding and focused investments co-ordinated with a diverse partnership base.

Strategic Objectives

1. Intensify efforts to increase the Newfoundland and Labrador Arts Council's core funding to meet the needs of artists and arts organizations.
2. Work with other agencies to coordinate and maximize available resources.
3. Review and revise current funding programs to ensure a more comprehensive approach to meeting the needs of the arts community.
4. Place additional focus on professional development, both through collaboration with other organizations and through direct delivery.
5. Maintain the principle and strengthen the process of peer assessment.

STRATEGIC GOAL 2: Be an effective leader and advocate in fostering and promoting the arts in Newfoundland and Labrador

Currently within the province's arts community, insufficient research exists to monitor the growth and development of the arts. Inadequate resources for information and communications impact Council's ability to advocate effectively for increased arts investment and more responsive arts policy. Our stakeholders expect us to encourage collaboration among arts organizations, provide leadership on issues facing artists, and raise the visibility of the arts in public policy development.

Strategic Objectives

1. Through a Council Advocacy Committee, develop and implement a plan which raises awareness of the vital role of the arts in society and which strives to improve the status of artists.

2. Develop and implement a communications plan that promotes the role of the Newfoundland and Labrador Arts Council, and creates opportunities for artists to network.

3. Develop research capacity so that the Newfoundland and Labrador Arts Council is a credible and authoritative voice for public policy development.

STRATEGIC GOAL 3: Support public awareness and participation, community involvement, and education in the arts

Artists and other stakeholders believe that Council must play a stronger role in increasing public and community awareness of and participation in the arts. This reflects the important role the arts play in building vibrant communities and enhancing quality of life. The arts offer opportunities to deepen our appreciation of our diversity and heritages. Children and adults who are exposed to arts education broaden their understanding of the world and strengthen their capacity for creativity and innovation.

Strategic Objectives

1. Take a lead role in promoting the arts to build audiences and broad-based participation, and to reflect cultural and artistic diversity.

2. Create linkages among amateur artists and groups, community groups and professional artists to strengthen artistic practice and participation throughout the province.

3. Expand partnerships and diversify programs.

4. Strengthen and broaden the role of the professional artist in formal education and lifelong learning.

STRATEGIC GOAL 4: Ensure a high standard of stewardship, accountability and transparency in all Newfoundland and Labrador Arts Council operations

Public funds have been entrusted to the Newfoundland and Labrador Arts Council to support grant programs and operations. As steward for these funds, Council intends to strive for the highest standards of transparency and accountability. The intent of this strategic goal is to ensure that effective, efficient and responsive governance and operational processes are in place and are visible.

Strategic Objectives

1. Conduct an annual review and assessment of NLAC programs to ensure human and financial resources provide the greatest possible value and impact.
2. Ensure program information and processes are open, accessible and easily understood.
3. Consult with key stakeholders every three years as a basis for determining governance and operational strategy.
4. Ensure an effective and efficient governance model is in place to support program delivery.
5. Foster the development of an environment that supports Council and staff development and which is open and accessible to the arts community.

6 Civil Society Organizations

In chapter 1, we briefly discussed civil society organizations including some differing manifestations and some history. Civil society organizations are arguably the purest example of social economy organizations in that (unlike the previous four groupings in chapters 2 to 5) they neither overlap with the public sector nor with the market. In the latter part of the eighteenth century, scholars conceived of a social space distinct from the state that could serve as a means to counteract despotism (Keane, 1998). Among political theorists of the nineteenth century, Alexis de Tocqueville is most often associated with this viewpoint. In his travels to the United States, he was impressed with the voluntary associations and their role in sustaining political democracy (Tocqueville, 1969).

In chapter 2, we discussed social economy businesses that overlap with the private sector as they, like other businesses, compete in the market. In chapters 3 and 4 respectively, we discussed community economic development and social enterprises as initiatives that participate in the market, but also rely on support from government, not only when they are initiated but also on an ongoing basis. In chapter 5, we discussed differing manifestations of public sector non-profits: organizations that have one foot in the public sector and another in the social economy. These organizations serve the public, but they also rely heavily on government programs and funding.

By comparison and unlike the components of the social economy discussed in chapters 2 to 5, Figure 6.1 depicts civil society organizations as separate from either the public or private sectors. However, the separation in the figure could be misleading because as noted in chapter 1, civil society organizations relate to the public and private sectors in many ways. Chapters 1 to 5 refer in places to this integration, but this chapter shall develop this point further.

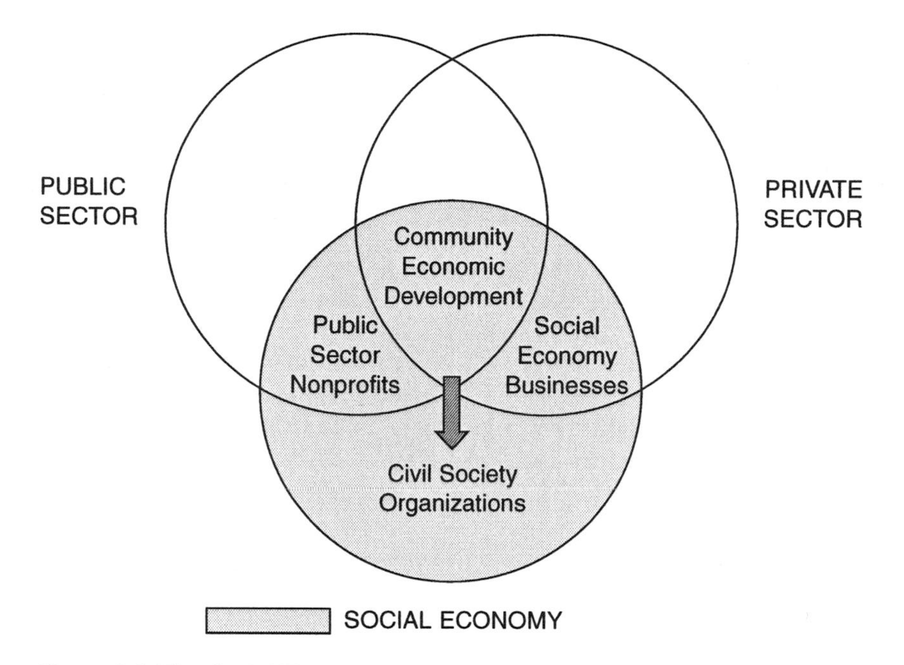

Figure 6.1 The Social Economy: An Interactive Approach

First, most civil society organizations are non-profit mutual associations whose members, employees, and volunteers (paid and unpaid human resources) work in either the private or public sector. Second, and related to the point above, the revenues for civil society organizations come from membership fees in mutual associations or from foundation grants and other forms of charitable donations to civil society organizations serving a public other than their membership. The members who pay the fees generally earn them in either the private or public sector and the contributions from foundations and other forms of donation are usually earned originally in those sectors of the economy as well. Also, foundations may invest a portion of their capital in the stock market. Third, civil society organizations provide services that contribute to a broad social infrastructure that supports society. As has often been said, the private sector is good at generating wealth, but much less successful at distributing it equitably. The resulting social problems are addressed in part by civil society organizations. Similarly, governments may attempt to represent the public will, but civil society organizations help to remind them what the public desires. Without belabouring the point, all parts of the social economy interact in a dynamic way with the private and public sectors, and with each other. Society can be carved up for social analysis, but the parts relate to each other. This may be self-evident, but nevertheless seems worth stating if only to prevent the naive view that the social economy exists in separation from the rest of society.

Civil Society Organizations: Differing Manifestations

In presenting the vast array of civil society organizations, we use two broad groupings: non-profit mutual associations that serve a membership and organizations that serve the public, either at large or specific publics of people in need. As will be seen, these categories, while useful for discussion purposes, are not entirely distinct. Non-profit mutual associations serve a membership, but the membership is a sub-group of the public, and in organizations with a broad membership (e.g., a political party) the distinction loses meaning. Moreover, some mutual associations are set up not only to serve the interests of their members but the public at large. Environmental groups are an example as are the large majority of other social movement organizations. Therefore, these organizations relate to more than one major stakeholder. Similarly, civil society organizations that serve the public, as distinct from their members, may not be relating to the public at large but rather to a specific public, for example, people with low incomes or persons with a particular disability. Within each of these groupings, there are many sub-groups that we discuss in greater detail below.

Non-profit Mutual Associations Serving Members' Needs

Mutual, meaning *shared in common*, is a form of association in which the members have common bonds, and they work together to achieve goals of mutual interest. Mutual associations embody the principle of self-help. For the founders, the organizing exercise can literally involve a self-help process. For those that follow, the self-help process that led to the organization's creation may not be as evident because the organization is already in place. They become beneficiaries of the organization and may be viewed as partaking of a social dividend resulting from the organization's creation. Nevertheless, mutual associations evolve from the contributions of second and subsequent generations. This is an oversimplification because organizations are not static but continue to develop and change over time.

Mutual associations are financed by fees or dues that members pay to cover the cost of the service, and they tend not to rely on government assistance. Some mutual associations are strictly voluntary and provide their services through the unpaid labour contributions of the participants, but for many the service costs are covered through a combination of fees that, if sufficient, may be used to hire employees and volunteer service (board of directors, if it is incorporated, and committees of the organization). Some characterize mutual associations as operating in the market, and this may be true of those in competitive market sectors. However, the mutual associations to be discussed in this chapter are not operating in competitive markets, as do social economy businesses (discussed in chapter 2), but are set up to meet the social needs of members within a non-profit value system. In effect, they provide a service that allows the members to connect with each other. Members, each with one vote, are responsible for the governance of the association, ensuring that its financial obligations are met, and ensuring that it is responsive to their mutual needs.

Mutual associations have a lengthy history extending to the early nineteenth century communal movements of Charles Fourier in France and Robert Owen in England, who envisaged a form of communal socialism. Mutuals also are rooted in anarchist philosophies (e.g., Peter Kropotkin's classic book, *Mutual Aid*). Co-operatives in general are founded on the principle of mutual aid (Craig, 1993; MacPherson, 1979) as are a myriad of non-profit associations whose members share a common bond. These include religious congregations, ethnocultural associations, unions, professional and managerial associations, social clubs, insurance and burial societies, and self-help groups; the list is lengthy and increasingly involves Internet associations. In Canada, there are well over 100,000 non-profit mutual associations and co-operatives (Hall et al., 2005).

Even though we use the term *mutual* in reference to associations that serve the needs of their members, as a rule such associations don't refer to themselves in this way. The exceptions are associations with services like burial and insurance. Many of these associations have their roots in the nineteenth and early twentieth centuries as newcomers to Canada organized services for each other. This was an era that predated government involvement in the provision of public services (see Samuel Martin's stage typology in chapter 5) and immigrant communities had to self-organize. While these organizations are not as prominent today, they still exist – for example, the All For One Mutual Benefit Society or Ivansker Mutual Benefit Society. Some are for people with a common origin in the 'old country,' such as the Sons of Scotland Benevolent Association or the Ukrainian Mutual Benefit Association of Saint Nicholas of Canada. Some use a variation of the name *mutual benefit*: for example, the Apter Friendly Society, Keltzer Sick Benefit Society, Zion Benevolent Society, and Benevolent Irish Society of Prince Edward Island.

In addition to these forms of associations, as mentioned in chapter 2, the Canadian Association of Mutual Insurance Companies represents ninety-eight property and casualty mutuals operating in rural areas across Canada. Many evolved from the self-organizing efforts in rural communities as farmers had to find ways to protect themselves against the vicissitudes of nature (CAMIC, 2007). We included that group of mutuals within chapter 2 because they are a form of business that serves a broad clientele as distinct from a defined membership with voting rights, as referred to in this chapter.

As mentioned, there are many different forms of non-profit mutual societies, each serving different member needs. In the following discussion, we subdivide mutual associations into two groups: those relating primarily to the economy and those that are primarily social.

Non-profit Mutual Associations Relating to the Economy

BUSINESS ASSOCIATIONS

There are thousands of associations formed by businesses with a mutual interest. These are non-profit member-based organizations financed through membership fees much like a union, professional association, or religious congregation, and their purpose is to promote the interests of the businesses that form them. Although business associations generally represent private sector interests, they do this through a structure that is common among non-profit mutual associations in that they are member financed and operate according to the principle of one member/one vote, with the member organizations electing representatives to the governance or board of directors from among their group. Business associations are often oriented to government; in effect, they make the case to government for the type of business they represent.

Not all business associations have only private sector members. Retail co-operatives, commercial non-profits, and government agencies can belong to business associations, and similarly retail co-operatives can form their own associations. These would not be referred to by the label *business association*, but rather as second- and third-tier co-operatives, as discussed in chapter 2 (e.g., the Credit Union Central of British Columbia, the umbrella organization for credit unions in that province).

Business associations can be general and involve all types of business within a particular community or region or specific and grouped according to a product or some other feature that businesses share in common. Among general associations, the chamber of commerce is the best known.

A Closer Look: Canadian Chamber of Commerce

The most basic business association in Canada is the Chamber of Commerce or board of trade, an association representing the interests of member businesses and found in every city and town throughout Canada, including sparsely populated areas (e.g., the Baffin Regional Chamber of Commerce). Local businesses join these organizations, which in turn communicate with members and advocate for them to the appropriate level of government and to international organizations, if appropriate. Associations Canada lists 983 chambers of commerce and boards of trade (Associations Canada, 2008). The website of the Canadian Chamber of Commerce (2008) describes its purpose as follows: 'Since 1925, the Canadian Chamber of Commerce has been the largest, most influential advocate for business in Canada. Founded with the aim of creating a strong, unified voice for Canadian business and a set of values from which policies encouraging prosperity would emerge, the Canadian Chamber of Commerce continues to be the only voluntary, nonpolitical association that has an organized grassroots affiliate *in every federal riding*' (emphasis ours).

Our emphasis on '*in every federal riding*' is deliberate as it makes clear the primary purpose of the chambers of commerce. There are provincial tiers (e.g., Nova Scotia Chambers of Commerce) representing businesses in their region, and the International Chamber of Commerce, which presents itself as 'the voice of world business championing the global economy' (International Chamber of Commerce, 2008).

The chambers of commerce are a broad and inclusive structure for businesses, whereas other business associations are more focused on particular types of enterprise, for example, the Canadian Federation of Independent Business (2007), which promotes itself as the voice of small firms in Canada, has more than 105,000 members, and lobbies all levels of government on their behalf. In contrast, the Canadian Council of Chief Executives presents itself as the voice of large corporations, its website boasting that its members 'collectively administer C$3.5 trillion in assets, have annual revenues in excess of C$800 billion, and are responsible for the vast majority of Canada's exports, investment, research and development, and training' (Canadian Council of Chief Executives, n.d.).

Other business associations specialize by market sector, for example, the Canadian Federation of Agriculture is the umbrella organization for agricultural producers. Founded in 1935, its members are provincial federations of agriculture (e.g., the Newfoundland and Labrador Federation of Agriculture) and major product-specific associations (e.g., the Dairy Farmers of Canada, Chicken Farmers of Canada, Canadian Sugar Beet Producers' Association), and it also includes the Coopérative Fédérée. Among business associations for agriculture, farm marketing co-operatives have a strong presence.

Many additional agricultural associations are more specialized, each seeking to represent its farmer members for such products as sugar beets, honey, roses, different breeds of livestock, and less common animals such as greyhounds, bison, and snails. Associations also exist for related products such as seeds, fertilizers, water wells, and for related services such as soil science, pest management, and plowing. The Canadian Organic Growers has affiliates across the country (e.g., Growers of Organic Food Yukon, and Canadian Organic Growers, on Vancouver Island), as does the Canadian Health Food Association with its network of retailers, wholesalers, distributors, and manufacturers.

The structure for agriculture is reproduced for every form of business, including the following: the Canadian Manufacturers and Exporters Association, the Tourism Industry Association of Canada, the Direct Sellers Association of Canada, the Canadian Film and Television Production Association, and the Association of Canadian Distillers. The complete list would fill many pages. However, the examples indicate how Canadian businesses have organized themselves through an intricate web of overlapping memberships, any one business belonging to many associations based on location, size, nature of product, and overseas markets. The tiers described above for the chambers of commerce and the Canadian Federation of Agriculture pertain to any major business associations. In addition, the web of business associations can interact with ethnocultural webs (e.g., the Belgian-Canadian Business Association, Canada-Singapore Business Association).

Business associations seek to assist their members through providing useful information to them and through representing their mutual interests to government, the public, and the media on such issues as taxation, environmental concerns, and other public policy issues. For example, in the midst of the public debate on the environment, the president and chief executive of the Canadian Council of Chief Executives, Thomas D'Aquino (2007), published an article in the *National Post* criticizing the Kyoto Accord. The Canadian Federation of Independent Business was created out of a tax revolt led by its founder, John Bulloch, and its website openly publicizes its benefits for small business: 'Persistent CFIB lobbying was instrumental in achieving the capital gains exemption, the small business reduced corporate tax rate, and beneficial changes to the Bankruptcy Act, the Small Business Loans Act and RRSP rules.' Many business associations advertise their role in lobbying for reduced taxation rates, reduced regulations, and other issues representing their members' financial interests.

In addition to business associations, other associations represent the interests of social economy and public sector organizations such as hospitals (e.g., Association des hôpitaux du Québec); libraries (e.g., Canadian Library Association); museums (e.g., Inuit Heritage Trust – Nunavut); school boards (e.g., Canadian School Boards Association, Newfoundland and Labrador School Board Associations, Quebec English School Boards Association); national parks (e.g., B.C. Recreation and Parks Association); science centres (e.g., Canadian Association of Science Centres); and zoos (e.g., Canadian Association of Zoos and Aquariums).

Umbrella associations representing member organizations are not limited to businesses but apply to every form of organization. In the modern world it is a normative practice. Organizations with a common bond utilize the space of civil society to join together with and to mobilize around their shared interest. The mobilization can take many forms, but most often it involves representing member interests to government and the public. Using civil society for this purpose not only pertains to associations of organizations but also of individuals – unions and other workplace groups such as management associations, as well as professional associations. We shall explore each of these arrangements in turn.

UNIONS

Unions and business associations can be at odds, but both are examples of civil society organizations based on the principle of mutual aid. In Canada, union locals generally do not incorporate, but they are formally structured workers' associations that operate as non-profits. They are set up to meet the needs of their members in contract negotiations with their employer (collective bargaining) on conditions of pay and work. They are a classic example of mutual aid in that members pay for the service through dues, usually deducted from their paycheques, and operate according to the democratic principle of one member/one vote in electing an executive to represent them. Like other civil society organizations, unions rely on unpaid labour contributions from members who assist the paid staff through participating in the executive, committees, and other activities.

According to Human Resources and Social Development Canada (2007), some 4.48 million Canadians belong to a union, and union membership represents 30.3 per cent of the non-agricultural paid workforce. These figures are for certified bargaining units only and do not include other forms of workplace associations that may bargain with employers, for example, the University of Toronto Faculty Association. In absolute numbers, 4.48 million represents a large growth of union membership from the late 1970s, but as a percentage of the workforce, union membership has declined, in particular in the private sector where the rate has fallen from 26 to 18 per cent in the past three decades (Statistics Canada, 2004b). Unionization in the public sector, by comparison, remains high and relatively constant at about 70 per cent.

There has been a marked change in gender composition of the unionized workforce in Canada with the rate among women tripling over three decades to about 30 per cent, about the same as men, who used to dominate the membership. This change is due in part to increased unionization among part-time and non-permanent workers and the expansion of unionization into the service sector, which is dominated by women. The other major change is that international unions have declined in influence from about two-thirds of unionized workers in 1962 to just over one-quarter. Unions headquartered in Canada now dominate in the Canadian labour movement.

In Canada in 2007, there were 14,742 union locals, the basic unit of a union. While some locals prefer to be independent (typically professional groups like university faculty), most affiliate with a central organization that assists with contract negotiations, research, and in strikes, should they occur. The nine largest unions, with which locals affiliate, represent more than half of unionized membership, and they are heavily concentrated in the public and service sectors of the economy. The Canadian Union of Public Employees (CUPE) with 548,880 members represents 12.2 per cent of Canada's unionized workforce, and together with the National Union of Public and General Employees (340,000 members), represent about 20 per cent of the unionized workforce in Canada. Other large public sector and social service unions are the Canadian Teachers' Federation (219,000 members), Public Service Alliance of Canada (166,960 members), Canadian Federation of Nurses (135,000), and Fédération de la santé et des services sociaux (117,130) (Human Resources and Social Development Canada, 2007). Given this pattern of public sector predominance, industrial unions are merging and some are organizing in the public sector and among public sector non-profits – the United Steel Workers of America is now the United Steel, Paper and Forestry, Rubber, Manufacturing, Energy, Allied Industrial and Service Workers International Union, AFL-CIO/CLC.

Like mutual associations in general, unions affiliate with each other in apex organizations, the Canadian Labour Congress (CLC) being the largest, with its member unions representing more than 70 per cent of Canada's union membership. The CLC speaks at the national level on policy issues such as taxation, pensions, and child care, and lobbies government on behalf of its member unions. The CLC has affiliates in each province (e.g., Manitoba Federation of Labour) and also connects with the labour movement internationally. In Quebec, the CLC affiliate, the Quebec Federation of Labour, competes with the Confédération des syndicats nationaux (CSN), which represents about 300,000 workers. In addition to the federal and provincial levels, unions across Canada associate with each other through municipal labour councils, whose objective, like provincial and federal apex organizations, is for members to aid each other around mutual concerns.

Unions in general have embraced what is referred to as 'business unionism' (a focus on pay, benefits, and conditions of work of their members). The apex organizations – national, provincial, and municipal – are the venue in which union leaders and delegates develop their position on issues. Mutual aid, labelled as *solidarity*, is a hallmark of unions in that their members are expected to help each other in their struggles with employers and governments. Unions and their apex organizations typically tackle a range of social issues such as universal child care, public pensions, and executive compensation. They support other organizations that tackle these issues most often through an arm's length relationship, but they may also be board members. For example, the Shareholder Association for Research and Education (SHARE), a Vancouver-based non-profit organization with a board of union members, presents resolutions at board meetings of corporations on concerns to the labour movement and also takes on a pension education function for the Canadian Labour Congress. Therefore, even though the focus among unions is the pay and working conditions of their members, they do address broader social issues and provide support for other related civil society organizations.

PROFESSIONAL ASSOCIATIONS

Unions bring together workers of either a particular workplace or of a group of workplaces (e.g., construction sites); professional associations by comparison bring together members from different workplaces who share either a common profession or a set of issues related to their profession (e.g., a learned society of scholars that organizes around a particular theme). Some associations are for well-known professions (e.g., the Canadian Medical Association, Canadian Bar Association, Canadian Association of University Teachers), but such forms of bonding extend to an amazing array of services (e.g., the Canadian Association of Professional Pet Dog Trainers; Cape Breton Professional Musicians Association; Canadian Society of Children's Authors, Illustrators and Performers; Canadian Cosmetics Careers Association Inc.).

Professional associations range in their degree of formality (some being incorporated with a professional staff and others being unincorporated and relying on volunteers to sustain the organization), but all embody the principle of mutual aid. Services of professional associations vary, but usually they include an annual conference and periodicals such as newsletters and journals. Increasingly, professional associations rely on the Internet to communicate through listservs, bulletin boards, blogs, and sophisticated websites that post information for members. Unlike conferences, which are episodic, the Internet facilitates ongoing communication.

Although professional associations differ from unions, some large professional associations negotiate fee schedules with government and thereby serve a quasi-labour function. This practice is followed by provincial medical associations (e.g., the Medical Society of Nova Scotia) that negotiate a fee schedule and track its enforcement on behalf of its members. It is a stretch to say that these associations are unions, but the fee schedule affects their income and arguably is analogous to a collective agreement between the Canadian Auto Workers and Air Canada. Larger professional associations may also certify their members, regulate their performance, and invoke sanctions when they are not meeting professional standards. The certification is needed to practise in the profession.

Larger professional associations typically have a national apex organization combined with provincial affiliates, and a maze of specialized associations. The Canadian Psychological Association lists thirty affiliates, some of which are large and have their own affiliates (e.g., Aboriginal Psychology, Adult Development and Aging, Brain and Behaviour, Clinical, Clinical Neuropsychology, Women and Psychology).

Associations for a profession can intersect with other bonds such as gender, race, and ethnicity that are common within civil society organizations (e.g., the Association québécoise des professeures et professeurs de français, Black Business and Professional Association, Association of Canadian Women Composers).

One form of professional association is for managers, for example, the Canadian Institute of Management which is 'dedicated to enhancing managerial skills and professional development' (Canadian Institute of Management, 2008). With seventeen branches across Canada, including small and isolated communities, the Canadian Institute of Management has an annual conference, professional training programs, and certification programs. Professional associations for managers usually are highly specialized (e.g., the Canadian Association of Chiefs of Police, Canadian Art Museum Directors' Organization, Canadian Golf Superintendents Association, Administrators of Large Urban Public Libraries, Union of British Columbia Indian Chiefs, Canadian Institute of Public Health Inspectors).

While it is unusual for people to belong to more than one workplace association, the average person may belong to several professional associations, reflecting not only his or her profession but also avocations. Given that professions have differing dimensions, an engineer might also be a manager, have an ethnocultural identification, and therefore belong to associations for each of these connections. Associations can also splinter by age (e.g., the Young Bangladeshi Canadian Professionals).

Professional associations mirror the modern world in that they represent a weakly linked mutual interest. Professional associations are a prime example of what Mark Granovetter (1973) referred to as the 'strength of weak ties' in that through enacting the principle of mutual aid, members can benefit from their common professional ties.

CONSUMER ASSOCIATIONS

Consumer protection in Canada comes from a combination of government agencies, industry self-regulation associations, and associations representing groups of consumers, some general and others product specific. Federal and provincial governments have consumer affairs units that attempt some oversight (e.g., the Office of Consumer Affairs in Industry Canada). One of its projects is the Canadian Consumer Information Gateway, a strategic partnership designed to create stronger consumer protections involving about 400 federal, provincial, and non-governmental agencies (Office of Consumer Affairs, 2008). There are similar agencies in Canada's provinces (e.g., British Columbia Business Practices and Consumer Protection Authority; Consumer and Commercial Affairs Branch, in Newfoundland and Labrador; and Office de la protection du consommateur, in Quebec).

In addition, the Crown corporation, the Standards Council of Canada, is a federal agency set up in 1970 responsible for establishing acceptable standards and for accrediting organizations that develop standards. The Standards Council of Canada participates in the International Organization for Standardization (ISO) and the International Electrotechnical Commission, which are leading international voluntary standardization bodies, as well as in regional standards organizations. It also encourages the adoption and application of international standards in Canada. The Standards Council of Canada represents this country on the ISO (2008), a non-profit network of the national standards institutes of 157 countries, with a central secretariat in Geneva, Switzerland, that coordinates the system. ISO certification indicates that a corporation has achieved particular standards, and therefore large corporations view it as assisting their credibility with consumers.

As noted, professional associations (particularly among elite professions) provide a degree of regulation, as do some business associations. Better Business Bureaus, non-profit organizations serving communities across Canada, are specifically set up to address consumer complaints about their member businesses, but compliance is largely voluntary. Better Business Bureaus certify businesses for membership, provide consumers with reports on their record, and attempt to resolve disputes between businesses who are members and consumers (Better Business Bureau, 2008). These non-profits are funded by their members who gain the benefit of being able to advertise that they have been certified by the Better Business Bureau.

In addition to government agencies, Crown corporations, international standards agencies, and business self-regulatory bodies, there are consumer-driven initiatives of various sorts, some general and others focused, but all intended to create greater consumer protections in the market. The Consumers' Association of Canada (2008), founded in 1947, and with provincial chapters, seeks to represent a wide variety of consumer concerns. The Consumers Council of Canada (2008) also strives to protect consumers, but structures itself as a partnership between consumers, business, and government. Many consumer protections associations are more focused on particular issues. Some examples include the following: the Automobile Protection Association, originally the publisher of the car buying guide, *Lemon-Aid* (now published directly by its author, Phil Edmonston); the Canada Safety Council, focusing on safety standards for driving, occupational health and safety, traffic safety, child safety, community safety, and home safety; the Canadian Council on Tobacco Control, formerly the Canadian Council on Smoking and Health, founded in 1974 by non-profit organizations such as the Canadian Cancer Society, the Heart and Stroke Foundation of Canada, and the Canadian Lung Association that were concerned about the adverse health effects of tobacco smoking; the Canadian Toy Testing Council, a non-profit operating since 1952, that tests toys and assesses their safety for use by children; the Media Awareness Network, a non-profit that creates media education resources related to a variety of media including the Internet so that children can 'safely and actively engage with media' (Media Awareness Network, 2008); and Safe Kids Canada, an organization working with about 1,800 community partners to promote safety and reduce injuries to children and youth.

In addition to these consumer protection organizations, consumers of particular products can protect themselves against excess charges through buying clubs, which are non-profit organizations that are similar to consumer co-operatives (discussed in chapter 2 under social economy businesses). Buying clubs are a self-organizing effort by groups of consumers to reduce prices by cutting out 'middle men' and profit. In Canada, some buying clubs are affiliated with the Ontario Natural Food Co-operative, a second-tier organization that serves consumer food co-operatives and buying clubs.

Associations for consumers have found it difficult to support their services through fees from individual consumers, and they have had to rely to some extent on support from government agencies and foundations. Nevertheless, these civil society organizations have an important role in informing consumers of their choices and creating greater public awareness, not simply for adults, but also for children and vulnerable groups who are at risk from particular products and services. Like business associations, unions, and professional associations, consumer associations relate to the economy. While business associations may be viewed primarily as providers of a voice for private sector firms, in contrast unions, professional associations, and consumer societies involve a countervailing force within civil society to corporate economic power and government agencies.

Associations of businesses, unionized workers, and consumers operate within civil society, but they represent their members primarily on economic issues and in relation to other sectors of the economy. The same is also true of some professional associations. By contrast, there are civil society associations for whom the member bond of association is undertaken to meet social needs with economics as a by-product. We now discuss some of the more prominent forms.

Non-profit Mutual Associations Focusing on Social Needs

RELIGIOUS CONGREGATIONS

The congregation or an association of people sharing a common faith is the basic unit of organized religion. According to the National Survey of Nonprofit and Voluntary Organizations conducted by Statistics Canada for the year 2003, there were 30,679 formally incorporated religious organizations (19% of all incorporated non-profits in Canada). Predominantly these were congregations but they also included various auxiliaries, for example, the Jesuits in English Canada, Sisters of Charity-Halifax, Missionaries of the Precious Blood (Hall et al., 2005). Ninety-four per cent of religious organizations have a charitable status, thereby allowing their members to gain a tax deduction for donations. Religious congregations have greater longevity than most forms of civil society organizations, more than half being in operation for forty or more years (Hall et al., 2005). They are found throughout Canada, with the lowest proportion in the territories and Quebec. The 2001 census indicates that 43.2 per cent of the population state that they are Roman Catholic, 29.2 per cent are Protestant, 1.6 per cent Christian Orthodox, and 2.6 per cent other forms of Christianity (Statistics Canada, 2001). There are 104 Christian denominations operating in Canada that service the religious needs of their members (National Council of Churches, 2005). In spite of the continued dominance of Christian religions in Canada, they are in decline as a percentage of the population. Other religions remain a relatively small part of the Canadian faith communities (Muslim, 2%; Judaism, 1.1%; Hindu, 1%; Sikh, 0.9%) but either are on the increase or relatively stable.

While identification with a religion remains predominant in Canada, and religious congregations are a major form of civil society organization, increasing numbers of Canadians disassociate themselves from religion. In the 2001 census, the next largest group after Christianity is those with 'no religion,' 16.2 per cent of the overall population, but 37 per cent of the people in the Yukon and 35 per cent in British Columbia. Those reporting no religion increased 31.7 per cent from 1991; prior to 1971, less than 1 per cent gave this response. Much like faith communities, people without religions can bond with each other in mutual associations (e.g., the Humanist Association of Canada with chapters across the country, Skeptics Canada, Freethought Association of Canada). Associations for atheists, agnostics, and others who disassociate themselves from faith communities are commonplace in universities (e.g., the University of Alberta Atheists and Agnostics, UBC Skeptics). Some religious congregations such as those associated with the Canadian Unitarian Council (2008), a spiritual community that has its roots in the Protestant religion and its reformist tradition and whose members embrace humanism in various forms, might be viewed as a bridge between faith communities and non-believers.

The rules governing religious associations vary, but generally they are similar to other mutual associations with a membership, each with one vote, that is responsible for the organization including its finances. Religions also involve the tiering arrangement common in mutual associations, with provincial, national, and international organizations. For example, the Canadian Unitarian Council is a member of the

International Council of Unitarians and Universalists. International affiliations are common also for non-believers (e.g., the Atheist Alliance International, International Humanist and Ethical Union).

Although the primary function of a religious congregation is to meet its members' needs around their shared faith, it can also serve other functions. In the National Survey of Nonprofit and Voluntary Organizations, 69 per cent of religious organizations stated that they serve not only their members but also the public (Hall et al., 2005). Many religious congregations get involved in community projects, but the exemplar is the Salvation Army (2008), operating in 400 communities across Canada and representing itself as the 'largest non-governmental direct provider of social services in Canada.' Its services include the following: disaster relief; clothing, food, accommodation, life skills training and counselling; camps for children; shelters and safe houses for the homeless; palliative care, corrections programs, child care and parenting programs for young parents; and its Thrift shops that generate revenues in support of its services. The Salvation Army might be viewed as a cross between a religious organization that serves its members and a social work agency that serves people in need.

On a smaller scale, other faith groups have attempted to become social service agencies to those on the margins of society. E4C (previously known as the Edmonton City Centre Church Corporation) is a registered non-profit charitable organization owned by a group of churches in the city and governed by an independent board of directors. E4C has established programs that focus on food security within Edmonton's public schools, special needs housing, and youth outreach. Employment training has become a key focus, which has resulted in the much celebrated social enterprise, Kids in the Hall (E4C, 2008).

Some religious organizations participate in broader coalitions set up to address social issues. The Vancouver Food Providers' Coalition (2008) focuses on issues related to the 'provision of emergency food and other services to people in need in Downtown Vancouver.' The coalition includes government and social service agencies and representatives of religious organizations.

Kairos Canada (Canadian Ecumenical Justice Initiatives), a coalition of churches created in 2001, works with partners in Africa, Asia-Pacific, Latin America, and the Middle East to 'address global, national and local peace and justice issues' (2008). Its agenda is more political than the other examples referred to and focuses on social justice issues in Canada and internationally, for example, ecological justice, corporate accountability, international human and Indigenous rights, poverty in Canada, refugees and migration, and trade, debt, and international finace. Kairos was created out of the merger of ten former church-related coalitions including the Interchurch Coalition for Human Rights in Latin America, the Task Force on the Churches and Corporate Responsibility, and the Aboriginal Rights Coalition. Its members include representatives of the major Christian churches in Canada (e.g., the Anglican Church of Canada, United Church of Canada, Canadian Catholic Organization for Development and Peace) as well as some smaller church groups (e.g., the Mennonite Central Committee Canada, Religious Society of Friends [Quakers]).

ETHNOCULTURAL ASSOCIATIONS

As is often stated, Canada is a nation of immigrants who have settled in waves since the sixteenth century alongside communities of Aboriginal peoples scattered throughout a vast land. In the 2001 census, nearly eighteen million Canadians (about 61% of the population) identified at least one specific ethnic origin. About 11.3 million people (38%) gave more than one response (Statistics Canada, 2005). Recent immigrants are heavily concentrated in cosmopolitan cities like Toronto and Vancouver, where people from more than a 100 different countries of origin can live and work adjoining each other. In Toronto, for example, 81.5 per cent of the population identified with an ethnic group in the 2001 census. For Vancouver it was 80.8 per cent; Winnipeg, 77.8 per cent; and Edmonton, 74.3 per cent. These urban centres are attractive to newcomers because they are more likely to be with family members and others from the same country of origin who share their mother tongue and customs. After the first generation, newcomers to Canada tend to move outside of their ethnic enclaves, but many still maintain ties with their culture of origin and turn to mutual associations that help their members relate to each other and provide services that they require. Some organizations are clubs for persons whose roots are elsewhere (e.g., the Portuguese Club of London, Red Deer Danish Canadian Club, Swiss Club Saskatoon, Vatnabyggd Icelandic Club of Saskatchewan). The list could be lengthy.

The social infrastructure created by ethnocultural groups can involve an elaborate network of services, and among the larger immigrant groups there can be hundreds of mutual associations for these services. Let's take the Italian community as an example. In the 2001 census, 1.27 million Canadians stated that they are of Italian origin, and they were heavily concentrated in Toronto (429,380) and Montreal (224,460), but with substantial numbers in Ontario's other urban centres and also in Vancouver. Like other immigrant groups, people of Italian origin came in waves, largely in search of economic opportunity. The first known Italian to visit Canada was Giovanni Caboto (also known as John Cabot), who it is believed landed near Bonavista, Newfoundland, in 1497. Italians came to Canada at various points from the seventeenth century onward, but the largest immigration occurred following the Second World War through to the mid-1960s, when opportunities in the construction trades proved attractive (National Congress of Italian Canadians, 2008).

Italian Canadians, like other ethnocultural groups, are bound by an intricate web of mutual associations, some of which include the following: social clubs (e.g., Ottawa St Anthony's Italia Soccer Club, Lega Di Bowling Di Castropignano); business associations (e.g., Canadian Italian Business and Professional Association, Italian Chamber of Commerce in Canada); professional associations (e.g., Association of Italian-Canadian Writers, Canadian Society for Italian Studies); cultural promotion organizations (e.g., Istituto Italiano di Cultura, Italian Canadian Cultural Association); historical societies (e.g., Monte Cassino Society, Anglo-Italian Family History Society); communication and media organizations (e.g., *Corriere Italiano, Il Cittadino Canadese*); schools (e.g., Dante Alighieri Italian School, Italian School of Calgary); seniors associations and centres (e.g., Villa Colombo); religious organizations (e.g., Italian Church of the Redeemer); social service organizations (e.g., Order of Sons of Italy in Canada, Istituto Nazionale di Assistenza Sociale); and sociopolitical groups (e.g., National Congress of Italian Canadians, Italian Canadian Women's Alliance). Many of these organizations have affiliates and subgroups, for example, the Canadian Italian Business and Professional Association has chapters wherever there is a significant Italian Canadian populace.

Moreover, this web of mutual associations is not particular to Italian Canadians but can be found in every ethnocultural group in varying degrees, depending on their numbers, wealth, and degree of integration. The Chinese Canadian National Council (CCNC), formed in 1979 as a response to a program on CTV that portrayed Chinese Canadians unfavourably, has chapters in each province (e.g., the Chinese Association of Newfoundland and Labrador) as well as in cities with large Chinese immigrant communities (CCNC, 2008). The CCNC Toronto

Chapter has links to a network of social service agencies for members of its community, for example, the Chinese Interagency Network of Greater Toronto, which is an umbrella organization of thirty-three social and health service agencies, as well as the Alternative Social Planning Group, which is a coalition of organizations promoting equity issues. Some of the CCNC's undertakings are political campaigns that bridge mutual associations from many ethnocultural communities, for example, the Colour of Poverty campaign focuses on the preponderance of visible minorities below the low-income cutoff (CCNC Toronto Chapter, 2008).

Similar networks of mutual associations are found for almost every ethnocultural group, the norm being an apex organization, provincial, regional, and municipal chapters, and an array of service associations interconnected to this quasi-political structure. The Assembly of First Nations has twenty-four regional affiliates (e.g., Council of Yukon First Nations, Union of New Brunswick Indians), each with its own interconnecting groups. Some apex organizations speak for relatively large and established ethnocultural groups (e.g., the Canadian Polish Congress, Portuguese Canadian National Congress, Ukrainian Canadian Congress). Others are relatively new and small (e.g., the National Council of Barbadian Associations in Canada, United Macedonians Organization of Canada).

Thirty-two apex organizations for ethnocultural groups are members of the Canadian Ethnocultural Council (CEC, 2008), a non-profit mutual association formed in 1980 that endeavours to 'ensure the preservation, enhancement and sharing of the cultural heritage of Canadians, the removal of barriers that prevent some Canadians from participating fully and equally in society, the elimination of racism and the preservation of a united Canada.' The CEC lobbies the federal government on multiculturalism and equity and sponsors forums, for example, 'Trafficking in Persons.' The CEC represents a positive commentary on the Canadian experience in multiculturalism in that organizations representing groups with a history of violent and seemingly intractable conflict elsewhere (e.g., the Canadian Jewish Congress, Canadian Arab Federation, Council of the Muslim Community of Canada) are able to work together in solving problems of mutual concern.

SOCIAL CLUBS

Social clubs are formed around differing bonds of association, sometimes more than one, that their members share in common. The human imagination is the only limitation on the range of social clubs – they number in the thousands and the variation is incredible. Some social clubs are based on bonds of associations such as ethnicity and religion and have been referred to previously; others such as service clubs and some fraternal orders serve a dual function of meeting their members' needs and public service and are discussed later in this chapter. In this section we focus on social clubs that serve their members' mutual needs and are not referred to elsewhere in this book. Many social clubs are incorporated and may include a charitable status as well, but others are not and range from those that are duly constituted (with by-laws and an executive elected by the membership) to those that are less formal but that nevertheless have an ongoing presence that transcends individuals coming and going.

Sampling the vast array of social clubs in Canada would be overwhelming and our discussion just sketches the landscape. For example, sixty competitive sports federations are affiliated with Sport Canada, a government agency. Each federation has an elaborate network of clubs through which people participate, some of which are elite, but most of which could be characterized as recreation or perhaps recreation with a competitive bent. These federations are not only for the well-known sports such as hockey, baseball, and basketball, but also for activities that capture less attention such as boccia, broomball, ringette, and taekwando. The clubs for these sports are non-profit mutual associations supported through fees paid by the participants and their parents and heavily assisted by volunteer contributions from team coaches; in fact, the Statistics Canada survey of non-profits estimates that 23 per cent of the volunteer hours (460 million hours) contributed in 2003 were for sports and recreation activities (Hall et al., 2005).

An Ipsos-Reid Survey done in 2003 indicates that 69 per cent of Canadians between the ages of 12 and 21 participate in organized sports, and that 38 per cent participate at least once a week (Sport Canada, 2008). Each sport affiliated with Sport Canada has its own organizational structure, often one that is quite elaborate. For example, Hockey Canada, the apex organization, with affiliates in each province, estimates that 4.5 million Canadians participate in organized hockey as players, coaches, officials, and administrators (Hockey Canada, 2007).

In addition to federations affiliated with Sport Canada, many others attract large numbers of participants. There are about 335 bridge clubs in Canada affiliated with the American Contract Bridge League (ACBL, 2008) through which players, some very regular, earn points. Other clubs, less competitive, are not sanctioned by the ACBL, but nonetheless draw large numbers of participants.

Similarly, there are about 140 chess clubs affiliated with the Chess Federation of Canada (2008). The Canadian Correspondence Chess Association is the official body for persons wanting to participate in chess by post, e-mail, or web-server. Increasingly, chess is being played in clubs that function on the Internet, and for those who prefer playing chess alone, that too is available.

In addition to clubs for competitive activities, others are just recreational. The following are some examples of such clubs and their activities or focus: automobile clubs (e.g., the Alberta Pioneer Auto Club, Dodge Brothers Club Inc.); birding clubs (e.g., Feather Fanciers Club, Manitoba Canary and Finch Club); stamp/coin clubs (e.g., Moncton Coin Club, Prince Edward Island Numismatic Association); dog (kennel) clubs (e.g., Fundy Trail Beagle Club, Moncton Retriever Club); clubs focusing on other animals (e.g., Nova Scotia Hereford Club, Edmonton Trout Club); dance clubs (e.g., Calgary Folk Club, Federation of Newfoundland and Labrador Square Dance); naturalist clubs (e.g., North Okanagan Naturalists Club, Chilliwack Hiking Club); clubs for people with disabilities (e.g., Hebrew Club for the Blind, Disabled Skiers Association of B.C.); genealogy/history clubs (e.g., Société d'histoire de Lachine, New Brunswick Genealogical Society); esoteric clubs (e.g., Canadian Tire Coupon Collectors Club, Montreal Science Fiction and Fantasy Association); gardening clubs (e.g., Alpine Garden Club of BC, Japanese Gardeners Association Bonsai Club); book clubs (e.g., Esquimalt High Brow Society, Calgary Readers); and other kinds of clubs (e.g., Air Sailing Club, in Guelph; Nova Scotia Horseshoe Players).

The examples scratch but the surface of a network that sustains Canadians from coast to coast. The examples do not include large groupings such as fraternities and sororities that are commonplace in universities or the network of 1,600 Royal Canadian Legion clubs for 400,000 members who share the bond of being veterans of war. While the Royal Canadian Legion is probably the largest network of social clubs in Canada, it is by no means one of a kind. The Canadian Kennel Club (2008), an organization that registers pure bred dogs, organizes shows, and serves an educational function, has 25,000 individual members and over 700 clubs across Canada.

Social clubs, like other forms of mutual associations, often are organized into provincial, national, and international tiers. The Royal Canadian Legion (2008) organizational structure takes on the character of a military operation with the dominion command, provincial commands, district commanders, zone commanders, and the local branch. While other clubs bypass the military labelling, the organizational arrangement is similar. The Canadian Railroad Historical Association (2008), a mutual association operating since 1932 that is dedicated to 'the preservation and dissemination of information concerning railway heritage in Canada,' has thirteen divisions. The Federation of B.C. Naturalists boasts forty-five clubs as members and thirteen others that are affiliated. In other words, just as the clubs referred to above bring individuals together, the clubs themselves belong to networks that bring like-minded organizations together. Both the clubs for individuals and the related networks with which they affiliate are reflective of mutual aid: individuals and clubs coming together to meet shared needs.

SELF-HELP GROUPS

All non-profit mutual associations are based on mutual aid, or groups of people with a shared need coming together to help each other, but some organizations are referred to as 'self-help' groups. The 'self-help' tradition involves people suffering from an addiction, health, or social challenge coming together to share their common concerns and to support each other in seeking improvement in their lives. In a self-help group, the members identify with and find common cause with peers who are living with similar challenges (Borkman, 1999). Trust is a central mechanism in the success of self-help groups in that the members not only identify with each other but also feel comfortable discussing concerns that can be quite personal (Ryan, 2007). Many self-help groups (commonly referred to as support groups) are a supplement to services provided by professionals, for example, women with breast cancer are encouraged to join a support group with others suffering from a similar plight so that they can share their experiences and learn from each other.

Among the best known of self-help groups is Alcoholics Anonymous, an international organization that has spawned other organizations using a similar approach.

A Closer Look: Alcoholics Anonymous

Alcoholics Anonymous (AA, 2008) was started in 1935 by a New York businessman and an Ohio surgeon who were alcoholics. It operates in 180 countries and estimates its membership at over two million, even though it does not keep formal membership lists. AA groups are primarily self-organizing, but they operate within a supportive organizational arrangement whereby groups in the same area set up an 'intergroup' office that assists new groups, and they also choose delegates to an annual General Service Conference. In Canada, AA intergroup offices are throughout the country and are organized by large areas. For example, British Columbia and the Yukon make up Area 79, which includes 700 AA groups in forty-six districts as well as an Area Committee with representatives from each of the districts and members of the General Service Committee (AA B.C./Yukon, 2008). Within Canada, there are 5,277 AA groups estimated to have more than 102,000 members (AA Information, 2008).

AA groups are organized around a twelve-step process that utilizes a combination of self-confession, group support, and religion (though AA disavows the latter). A key feature of the process is participants acknowledging in front of their group that they are alcoholics and also accepting that even if they are able to overcome their problem they remain vulnerable to reverting to alcoholism, hence, the label 'recovered alcoholics' is suggested for those who have their drinking under control. Participation in AA is limited to alcoholics, but two spin-off self-help groups are Al-Anon for the families of alcoholics, and Alateen, for teenagers who have alcoholic parents. In Al-Anon, relatives and friends of alcoholics 'share their experience, strength, and hope in order to solve their common problems' (Al-Anon/Alteen, 2008). Alateen applies this same process to teenaged family members of alcoholics.

The twelve-step approach also has been applied to other addictions (e.g., Gamblers Anonymous, Overeaters Anonymous, Narcotics Anonymous, Cocaine Anonymous, Marijuana Anonymous, Neurotics Anonymous, Emotional Health Anonymous, Sexaholics Anonymous, Sexual Compulsives Anonymous, Clutterers Anonymous, Smokers

Anonymous, Nicotine Anonymous). The imagination is the only limitation.

While the twelve-step approach has had a major influence on self-help groups for addictions, other approaches are used too, not only for addictions but for other challenges as well. The Seventh Step Society of Canada, modelled after a program started in Kansas and operating in Canada since 1973, uses a self-help approach to prevent recidivism among ex-convicts. Interestingly, the seventh step is a commitment to the self-help movement: 'We pledge ourselves to help others as we have been helped' (Seventh Step, 2008). Many other self-help groups are for people struggling with different health concerns (e.g., the Arthritis Self-Help Group, Inc., Barrie Post Polio Association, Irritable Bowel Syndrome Self Help and Support Group). There is a national infrastructure of organizations affiliated with the Canadian Network of Self-Help Centres to help people find a self-help group for their needs (e.g., the Self-Help Resource Centre of Greater Toronto, Self-Help Resource Association of British Columbia). The Self-Help Connection Clearinghouse Association of Dartmouth helps people in Nova Scotia find common cause through more than 500 groups for 'abuse, anxiety, stress, depression, manic depression, addictions, bereavement, eating disorders, parenting, caregiving, heart and stroke, cancer and divorce' (Self-help Connection Clearinghouse Association, 2008). The Calgary Association of Self Help (2008) focuses on mental health issues, and one of its objectives is 'peer support and mutual aid.' Similarly, a central tenet of the Ontario Peer Development Initiative (OPDI, 2007) for persons with mental health disabilities is self-help and peer support, as reflected in the programs of affiliated organizations such as the Mood Disorders Association of Ontario, Waterloo Region Self-Help, Cambridge Active Self-Help.

Many self-help initiatives are related to social challenges rather than addictions and health concerns. Parents without Partners is an international non-profit network, originating in New York in 1957, that brings together through chapters single parents with children, support groups being one of its services. Parents, Families and Friends of Lesbians and Gays PFLAG (Canada), which has branches in sixty communities across Canada, offers social support for persons with questions about gender issues. The Association of Parent Support Groups of Ontario has support groups for parents with disruptive children. The average person faces many challenges in a lifetime, and self-help groups allow people with a shared concern to learn from each other and gain support through the process.

Increasingly, people are turning to the Internet for self-help groups, not only for addictions such as those addressed through the twelve-step approach but for other health problems and social concerns as well. These online groups allow for greater anonymity than the typical face-to-face group, and therefore might be a better way for some people to begin to get help. In addition, they are more practical for people in isolated locations and for people who have other commitments that may not allow them to meet face-to-face regularly (Cooper, 2004).

The Online Intergroup of Alcoholics Anonymous is the support structure 'to serve all online AA Groups in the rapidly growing online Fellowship' (AA, Online Intergroup, 2008). Some online AA groups advertise themselves for gays, lesbians, or loners. There are also online support groups for alcoholics such as the Alcohol Help Centre that vary from the AA approach. Self-help groups for various forms of cancer are available through the Internet, for example, Breast Cancer Nova Scotia has an internationally recognized online support group (Breast Cancer Action Nova Scotia, 2008). The Alzheimer Society of Canada offers an online forum for persons with the disease and care-givers (see http://www.alzheimer.ca/forum). The organization Little People utilizes the popular social networking site, Facebook (see http://www.facebook.com/), and has a second online group, Parents of Little People 2 (at http://groups.yahoo.com/group/parentsoflittlepeople2/).

There are websites devoted to helping people with health challenges to find compatible support groups (see http://www.patientslikeme.com). The large Internet organizations such as Google, Yahoo!, and MSN assist with the technical creation of online self-help groups (see http://groups.google.com/). People who are interested in facilitating online self-help groups can go to the Internet (see http://www.mentalhelp.net/selfhelp/selfhelp.php?id=863) and get tips for running online support groups.

Even though online self-help and support groups are a relatively recent phenomenon, they have become a powerful social force that cannot be dismissed as a passing trend. An Ipsos Reid national survey conducted on 4 October 2007 indicates that 37 per cent of Canadians have visited online social networking sites and online social communities and 29 per cent have a personal profile on at least one site (Ipsos News Centre, 2007a). Moreover, the time investment in these sites averages 5.4 hours per week, not an insignificant amount. Similarly, the Pew Internet and American Life Project reports that 80 per cent of

American Internet users have searched for health information online and that some also participate in online communities (Boase et al., 2006). Yahoo! alone listed 154,176 groups in its health and wellness section on 15 March 2008, though it is not clear that all of these are bona fide self-help groups (Yahoo!, 2008). While some are sceptical about the value of online self-help groups, there is every reason to believe that they will continue to develop and find more applications.

Civil Society Organizations that Serve the Public

In the introduction to this chapter, we indicated that our discussion of civil society organizations would proceed within two broad groupings: non-profit mutual associations serving members' needs and civil society organizations that serve the public. Most of the chapter has been devoted to the first group, but in this second section we turn to civil society organizations serving the public. As noted, the line between these two groups is not always clear; for example, religious congregations, whose primary function is to serve their members' spiritual needs, also engage in public service. Similarly, the Canadian Labour Congress whose primary function is to represent affiliated unionized workers and their interests also speaks on behalf of working people more generally. Therefore, mutual interest associations whose primary function is to serve their members' needs may also attempt to speak on behalf of a broader public, as do civil society organizations whose primary function is to serve the public. Even for this latter group that we now turn to, their members may derive some personal benefit from their service, or what Andreoni (1990) has called the 'warm-glow giving.' That said, our focus is on a group's primary intent, taken at face value. We subdivide the category civil society organizations that serve the public into two: sociopolitical organizations that address issues of public concern and public service organizations that mobilize their membership to create public goods, usually for persons with major social needs.

Sociopolitical Organizations

By sociopolitical organizations we mean associations that advocate for a particular issue or set of concerns of public interest and that mobilize a membership around the advocacy strategy. Many such groups have a limited agenda and focus on issues that are of immediate and direct concern to themselves and a specific public. Ratepayer associations are a widespread example, often addressing municipal issues of direct concern to their neighbourhood, although they may affiliate with a broader federation such as the Confederation of Resident and Ratepayer Associations in Toronto. Other groups focus on a limited set of issues that affect them directly (e.g., business improvement area associations, tenants associations, parent-teacher associations, or Home and School associations). Occasionally, issues addressed by organizations of this sort attract broad public interest even though the issue is specific to a locale. For example, the decision by the Vancouver Island Health Authority to close a needle exchange in Victoria has been a source of ongoing controversy among community groups and was front-page news in the *Times Colonist* newspaper that serves the city (Lavoie, 2008). The Needle Exchange, operated by AIDS Vancouver Island, was evicted from its current site because of neighbourhood complaints. While the value of the exchange in preventing the spread of HIV is not in dispute, residents prefer that it be situated elsewhere, or at least 'not in my backyard.' This is an example of a resident concern attracting broad public interest; the issue is local, although the phenomenon is commonplace.

Unlike neighbourhood, tenants, and parents associations, most other sociopolitical associations prefer to speak for a broader public that they purport to represent. Even though associations may have a defined membership, sociopolitical organizations tend to view the membership as a subset of a broader group for whom the membership either speaks or to whom it attempts to relate. Political parties are an example, perhaps the most formal, in that they have members who pay a fee and within that broader group a cadre of activists who serve as executive members of riding associations and as volunteers during election campaigns, but their primary purpose is to mobilize public support during elections. In order to become the government or even to have representation, the support from voters must exceed the number of members. For example, the Liberal Party of Canada received 4,479,415 votes in the 2006 federal election, but its party membership ranges from about 100,000 to 250,000 depending on whether there is an election or a leadership campaign.

This same principle applies among sociopolitical organizations attempting to shift social norms on issues such as the environment, the role of women in society, gay and lesbian rights, disability issues, smoking, other human rights issues, or Canada's military mission in

Afghanistan. Civil society is the space for associations not necessarily in agreement with each other that mobilize around these issues.

Although all of these social issues are important, and there are many others that could have been mentioned, the environment is the issue du jour in Canada and internationally. An Ipsos Reid poll in 2007 found that 85 per cent of Canadians expressed concern about climate change (Ipsos News Centre, 2007b). In other words, environmental organizations are working in fertile ground, reflecting in part their educational activities and activism. In Canada, environmental organizations are affiliated with the Canadian Environmental Network, embracing about 700 organizations ranging from major groups with millions of members (e.g., Greenpeace, Friends of the Earth, the Sierra Club, World Wildlife Federation) to highly specific issue groups (e.g., Edmonton Trolley Coalition, Nova Forest Alliance, Safe Water Group of Prince Edward County, North Saskatchewan Watershed Alliance). A detailed case study of the Canadian Environmental Network is presented at the end of this chapter.

An example of an environmental organization operating within the Canadian Environmental Network is Evergreen, the subject of a detailed case study at the end of chapter 9. Evergreen, started in 1991, is a 'national non-profit environmental organization with a mandate to bring nature to our cities through naturalization projects' (Evergreen, 2007), and it has become a major environmental force in a short time.

Most other movements have a similar arrangement to the environmental movement and also have an apex organization with a web of interlinked organizations focused on specific tasks. For the feminist movement, the apex organization is the National Action Committee on the Status of Women (NACSW, 2008), which has 700 affiliated groups. Civil society also has contrary associations such as Real Women of Canada (2008), promoting itself as 'Canada's alternative Women's Movement' and emphasizing a conservative agenda of family values, marriage, and opposition to abortion. This type of difference, at times bitter, is typical of civil society, in that it is a forum for dialogue, debate, and division. Even within organizations with a relatively common cause, differences of opinion are the norm. Some coalitions are organized by province (e.g., the Coalition for Lesbian and Gay Rights in Ontario; British Columbia Coalition of People with Disabilities). Others rely to a degree on a civil society organization with a broader mandate (e.g., the B.C. Human Rights Coalition).

Canadians also participate in international human rights organizations, either through the head office or through a Canadian affiliate. Amnesty International, with about 2.2 million members in 150 countries, engages Canadians in its human rights campaigns, including the 67,000 who belong to Amnesty International Canada (Amnesty International Canada, 2008).

One method of mobilization used by Amnesty and by sociopolitical organizations more generally is the Internet. An early expression of an online sociopolitical organization was the Free Burma Coalition, organized originally by a graduate student at the University of Wisconsin (Zarni, 2000). Such mobilizations are now commonplace with organizations such as aavaz.org regularly circulating petitions on issues (e.g., a call to the Chinese government for restraint in response to protests in Tibet; a call for an immediate ceasefire in the conflict in Gaza between Israel and Hamas) (Avaaz.org, 2008). The Make Poverty History (2008) coalition utilized the Internet to put pressure on the government of Canada to allocate its budget surplus for social programs that would reduce inequalities. TakingITGlobal (2008) is a social networking site with about 200,000 members that engages young people around the world in self-education and in campaigns on such issues as HIV/AIDS and climate change.

Public Service Organizations

There are many different types of public service organizations funded by donors – individuals including their members, corporations, and foundations – whose primary function is to serve a segment of the public in great need. One the oldest form of public service organization is the fraternal and service club whose members engage in community service. The participants may gain ego awards and possibly career credits, but the organization's manifest purpose is community service. Most fraternal organizations are international with Canadian chapters or clubs, although some are specifically Canadian, for example, Kin Canada (formerly the Kinsmen and Kinette Clubs of Canada).

Among the larger international clubs through which Canadian chapters have been organized are the following: Lions Clubs, with 44,500 clubs and more than 1.3 million members in 202 countries, with a focus on programs for preventable blindness including Lions Eye Bank of Alberta (Lions Club Canada, 2008); Kiwanis (2008) , with 8,000 clubs in ninety-six countries and about 260,000 adult members (the first Canadian club was formed in 1916 in Hamilton), emphasizing service to children and youth through special programs like the Kiwanis Music Festival and through its Service Leadership Programs and youth clubs; the Rotary Club (2008), started in 1905 and in Winnipeg in 1910, now with 32,000 clubs in more than 200 countries and over 1.2 million members world-wide, with an emphasis on attempting to eradicate polio worldwide; Shriners (2008), a fraternal group associated with Freemasonry, has 375,000 members in 191 chapters in the United States, Canada, Mexico, and Panama, and known for its twenty-two children's hospitals (including one in Montreal) serving more than 865,000 children; the Knights of Columbus (2008), an organization formed in 1881, and in 1897 in Canada, with 1.7 million members who are Catholic men engaged in community service in 13,000 councils.

Most fraternal orders are rooted in Christianity, even if they have become secular, but some such as B'nai B'rith are Jewish. Others formed in the United States, with chapters in Canada, relate to their members' country of origin (e.g., the Sons of Scotland, Sons of Norway).

Among the more recently formed public service organizations is Habitat for Humanity (2008), renowned for its work in building housing for the working poor. Since its founding in 1976 by a devout Christian family, Linda and Millard Fuller, Habitat has built more than 200,000 houses, sheltering more than one million people in about 3,000 communities worldwide, including parts of Canada. Habitat has a remarkable legacy of mobilizing volunteers and donors to build its dwellings for families with low incomes.

Many civil society organizations in public service focus on very specific health problems. The large organizations are household names such as: the Canadian Cancer Society, the Heart and Stroke Foundation of Canada, and the Alzheimer's Association of Canada. In addition, there are other organizations for afflictions that are less well known, for example, the Canadian Association of Pompe, Canadian Lyme Disease Foundation, Canadian Association for Tay-Sachs and Allied Diseases, ALS Society of Canada, Turner Syndrome Society.

Cancer, which includes many diseases, has associations for each disease, and multiple associations for pervasive forms affecting the breast and prostate. Although disease associations differ, the common denominator is that they are civil society organizations serving the public, an important group being those who have the affliction, and they are supported primarily by donations from individuals, foundations, and corporations, and heavily supported by volunteers who are an important part of their human resources. Some have research and public education functions, particularly the better endowed.

Civil society organizations serve the public in other ways as well. People suffering from food insecurity – families on social assistance, pensions, and the working poor (about 40% being children) – have access to a network of about 650 food banks in Canada that are supported by a combination of corporate food donations, financial donations from corporations and individuals, and generous labour contributions from volunteers. The Canadian Association of Food Banks (2008) estimates that more than 750,000 people partake monthly of food bank services across Canada. For the Greater Toronto Area alone, the Daily Bread Food Bank (2007), the umbrella organization, estimates more than 900,000 users for 2006–07.

Other social services relying on some combination of government funding, donations, and volunteers might be viewed as straddling the line between civil society organizations and public sector non-profits. The extensive network of rape crisis centres and transition houses across Canada falls into this category (see the Canadian Association of Sexual Assault Centres, 2008), as does the network of women's centres for other services (e.g., Lesbian Mothers Support Society, Downtown Eastside Women's Centre in Vancouver serving as a drop-in). Indeed, many community centres across Canada are of this nature (e.g., GLBTTQ Community Centre of Ottawa, and the Jane/Finch Community and Family Centre in an economically poor area of Toronto).

A fascinating relatively recent example of a non-profit public service organization that operates online is Wikipedia, the international encyclopedia. It is owned by a foundation, Wikimedia, founded in St Petersburg, Florida in 2003 and currently in San Francisco, which receives its funding from donors (Wikipedia, 2008). Wikipedia functions with a small cadre of employees, and is produced largely by volunteers, 75,000 active contributors, who have produced about nine million articles in 250 languages. Early in 2008, about 2.3 million articles were in English. The website is accessed by people around the world and is good example of grassroots mobilization through a civil society organization serving the public, in this case a very broad, international public.

Conclusion

Civil society organizations, as we have characterized them in this chapter, are a broad phenomenon covering many different types. We have used two general categories – non-profit mutual associations serving members' needs and civil society organizations that serve the public. We have also subdivided these groupings: for mutual associations we used two broad categories of economic and social; for civil society organizations serving the public, we subdivided them between sociopolitical organizations and public service groups. As noted, this classification system is not air-tight; some mutual groups such as religious congregations engage in public service, and some such as unions can also take on sociopolitical functions. Similarly, members of civil society organizations serving the public may gain some direct benefit because altruism can be imperfect (Andreoni, 1990). Moreover, as discussed above, civil society organizations are not an end unto themselves but relate to other parts of society. Some, such as business associations, could be viewed as fronts for private sector firms.

Sociopolitical associations attempt to mobilize public opinion, not simply within civil society, but also in an effort to change social policies and to shift social norms. Many of the associations to which we have referred have been quite successful in this endeavour.

* * *

DISCUSSION QUESTIONS

1. Is it appropriate to think of a social space such as civil society that is distinct from the other parts of the social economy?
2. This chapter covers a broad range of organizations. Is it appropriate to consider all of them as part of civil society?
3. Are business associations simply extensions of private sector firms? Is it appropriate to consider them part of civil society?
4. What about associations whose sole interest is to preserve social norms rather than to challenge them? Should they be considered part of civil society?
5. Some would say that civil society organizations lack a sufficient economic function to be considered part of the social economy. Do you agree?

6. Is the distinction between organizations that serve their members and those that serve the public appropriate? Is there a better way of classifying these groups?

* * *

Case for Analysis: Canadian Environmental Network

Nothing we could write would begin to capture the extensive array of environmental organizations in Canada. However, a snapshot could be obtained through the approximately 700 member organizations of the Canadian Environmental Network (CEN) and its regional networks in each of Canada's provinces and the Yukon. The CEN is a public sector non-profit, funded by the federal agency Environment Canada as well as by some contracts with other government agencies (CEN, 2008). The CEN has operated since 1977 as a bridge between governments, federal and provincial, and environmental organizations who mobilize members around particular issues. The CEN came about because the many environmental organizations across Canada wanted a mechanism to improve their communication with government. Therefore, the CEN could be viewed as a mechanism through which civil society organizations fighting ecological issues could have an impact on government policies. Although Environment Canada is the primary agency with which the Canadian Environmental Network works, it also undertakes contracts and consultations with other federal agencies because the environment is such a pervasive concern. Its provincial networks serve a similar function for provincial governments. The CEN also facilitates communication between member groups through an electronic weekly newsletter, annual conference, annual general meeting, and a database that it produces. Much of the CEN's activities are organized through caucuses on such issues as atmosphere and energy, biological diversity, biotechnology, environmental planning and assessment, environmental economics, environmental education, agriculture, forests, health, mining, toxics, and water. While CEN members engage in a collaborative approach through activities associated with the network, they are also independent and can choose to engage in confrontation in order to highlight issues that are of concern to them. For example, Friends of the Earth International (2008) in conjunction with Sierra Legal filed a lawsuit on 28 May 2007 that would require the government of Canada to respect its commitments under the Kyoto Accord.

Among the 700 organizations that are members of the Canadian Environmental Network, some are large and well known and others slug it out in the trenches on highly specific issues. The larger organizations participate internationally, as environmental concerns are worldwide. Greenpeace (2008), for example, has 2.8 million members in forty countries, a far cry from its beginning in 1971, when a small group set sail from Vancouver in a fishing boat to embarrass the United States over nuclear tests in Amchitka, Alaska. Friends of the Earth International (2008) operates in seventy countries and with more than two million members; founded in 1978, it addresses such issues as climate change, universal water security, and energy conservation. The Sierra Club (2008), another leader in the environmental field, differs from the norm; rather than being founded in the 1960s and 1970s, when concern for the environment was starting and growing, this U.S. organization dates to 1892. It boasts 1.3 million members, and chapters throughout Canada are affiliated with the Sierra Club Canada. The World Wildlife Federation (2008), devoted to the protection of nature since its inception in 1962, operates in 100 countries and has nearly five million members, including the Canadian Wildlife Federation. Nature Canada (2008), or the Canadian Nature Network, is an umbrella organization for a network of provincial affiliates (e.g., the Federation of B.C. Naturalists), each of whom has associated nature clubs. The network has about 100,000 members devoted to the preservation of natural life.

While the large federations gain much of the publicity on environmental issues, there are many small organizations, run largely by volunteers, which attempt to raise public awareness through tackling specific causes in their region and which challenge government policies. It is impossible to do justice to this network, but some very select examples, such as the following, give an idea of the breadth of issues that they support: rivers (e.g., Rivers Without Borders); professional support (e.g., the Canadian Environmental Law Association); education (e.g., the Saskatchewan Boreal Forest Learning Centre); youth (e.g., the Arctic Youth Network); transportation (e.g., the Edmonton Trolley Coalition); health issues (e.g., the Environmental Health Association of Nova Scotia); trees (e.g., the Carmanah Forestry Society); water (e.g., the Safe Drinking Water Foundation); watersheds (e.g., the Red River Watershed Alliance); clean air (e.g., Pollution Probe); site preservation (e.g., the Friends of Clayoquot Sound); food (e.g., the Winnipeg Community Gardening Network); trails (e.g., the Halifax North West Trails Association); renewable energy (e.g., Citizens For Renewable Energy); animal preservation (e.g., the Cariboo Chilcotin Conservation Society); waste reduction (e.g., the Ontario Toxic Waste Research Coalition); mining (e.g., Bedford Mining Alert); recycling (e.g., the Computer Recycling Society of Canada); international concerns (e.g., the Antarctic and Southern Ocean Coalition); support groups (e.g., Physicians for Global Survival); and miscellaneous (e.g., Citizens Against Burning of Tires).

While the organizations participating in the Canadian Environmental Network and its provincial affiliates are largely self-governing, and they challenge, at times militantly, government and corporate policies that are inconsistent with their environmental values, their apex organization is funded by government and seeks to work with government as a means to influence its policies. Some might argue that these roles are inconsistent.

* * *

DISCUSSION QUESTIONS

1. Is it appropriate for a sociopolitical group like the Canadian Environmental Network to be funded by government? Does this weaken its potential to pursue its own goals?
2. Given the experience of the National Action Committee on the Status of Women, which had much of its funding pulled by government, does the arrangement entered into by the Canadian Environmental Network leave it vulnerable?

PART 3

Critical Issues

7 Organizational Design and Governance Strategies

The chapter has two main objectives: (1) to highlight the range of organizational strategies and design choices in the social economy, and (2) to present the current thinking and practice of governance in the social economy. As governance crises shook the for-profit sector, there was an associated concern about the governance practices of the social economy, in particular, the effectiveness of non-profit boards. Concern about the well-publicized fundraising practices of Mothers Against Drunk Driving Canada, the misrepresentation as a national organization of the Montreal Society for the Prevention of Cruelty to Animals (Montreal SPCA), and negative publicity about the administrative costs of some other charities has focused more attention on the governance practices of the sector.

A Closer Look:
Montreal Society for the Prevention of Cruelty to Animals

The Montreal Society for the Prevention of Cruelty to Animals (Montreal SPCA), legally known as the Canadian SPCA, has a mission to protect animals against negligence, abuse, and exploitation, to represent their interests and ensure their well-being, and to raise public awareness and help develop compassion for all living creatures. It fulfils its mission by dealing with 25,000 animals a year, advocating for animal sterilization, ensuring good animal adoptions, and prosecuting cases of cruelty to animals. The Montreal SPCA's board has eight to twelve members whose function is 'to plan and direct policy, make decisions and be responsible to the organization and community it serves, so that the stated purposes, goals and objectives of the organization can be attained' (SPCA Montréal, 2008).

In 2007, the organization faced a barrage of criticism after it solicited funds under its legal name, as many donors thought they were giving to a national organization, not a local one. The Canadian SPCA raised about $1.6 million from donors outside Quebec. The then executive director, Pierre Barnoti, defended the use of the charity's legal name for its fundraising drive. Barnoti had also registered the name SPCA International for donations that would go to the Montreal SPCA. The organization, however, does not use its legal name when fundraising in Quebec. Barnoti's salary, reputed to be $120,000, was also a source of concern. In March 2008, after thirteen years as the head of the Montreal SPCA, Barnoti went on sick leave, and he was fired on 23 July that year. According to current board member, Raymonde Plasse, the firing of Barnoti and the election of a new board are creating a new culture in the Montreal SPCA, which should help to restore confidence in the organization (Parent, 2008).

However, Canada has not had the governance scandals that have hurt the U.S. non-profit sector: 'The Canadian system seems to work. While Canadian charities spend only a small fraction of what their U.S. counterparts do on compliance, polls show that citizen confidence in Canadian charities remains high' (Rosen, 2002).

The 2006 survey of 3,864 Canadians by the Muttart Foundation and Ipsos Reid supports the view that we still have confidence in our charities – 79 per cent of the respondents said that they had trust in charities, and 27 per cent indicated that they had a high degree of trust. Virtually all Canadians (93%) agreed that charities are important, with half (51%) strongly agreeing. Even so, 62 per cent object to charities hiring commission-based fundraisers, and 87 per cent believed that more attention should be given to how charities spend their money. Hospitals were the most trusted type of social economy organization (Muttart Foundation, 2006).

Types of Organizational Design

The chapter rests on a contingency view of organization design, which in short asserts that form follows function. In other words, there is no one best way to design an organization. 'Contingency means that one thing depends on other things, and for organizations to be effective, there must be a goodness of fit between their structure and the conditions in their external environment [and other factors such as strategy and age]' (Daft, 2007: 27). Many social economy organizations operate in institutional environments that are dynamic, if not turbulent. They are often profoundly dependent on government funding, which can and does change as governments change. In Canada, there have been significant reductions in governments' funding of the social sector over the past twenty years (Elson, 2008). As well, the environment is characterized by the presence of multiple stakeholders, multiple goals and metrics, and increased competition for limited sources of funds. As a result, strategic choices may change over time and organizations will have to change their designs to fit their evolving strategies.

Strategic Choices

While there are various typologies of strategic choices, the one developed by Miles and Snow (1978, 1984) seems to have the most explanatory value for the social economy. They argue that there are the following four strategic types: (1) prospector, an innovating risk-taking strategy; (2) defender, a stability-seeking strategy; (3) analyser, one that combines the prospector and defender strategies by trying to maintain a stable focus while innovating at the edges; and (4) reactor, a reactive response to the exigencies of the environment.

Social economy organizations have been found to change their strategies depending on the demands of their environments. Of the four strategic choice types, Akingbola (2006) found that the analyser and the prospector strategies were most often used in the seventy-nine social economy organizations he studied. He notes that organizations were not just reacting to changes in government funding but were managing their strategic choices purposefully. He notes further that '[more] than ever, nonprofit organizations are adept at being strategic and at aligning their strategies with changes in [their environmental domain]' (2006: 265).

The different strategic choices require different design choices, if the strategies are to be successfully implemented. The prospector type requires a flexible structure with strong research capacities; the defender type requires a bureaucratic design with an efficiency orientation and with close employee supervision; the analyser type requires a design that has both flexibility and tight control – a loose-tight design (Daft, 2007). However, the appropriate design choice, that is, the one that fits, does not guarantee that the organization will be successful. Appropriate organizational design choices are therefore necessary but not sufficient for successful strategy implementation. While structure needs to follow strategy, it is important to note that existing structures can constrain an organization's ability to see strategic choices, and therefore can limit strategizing.

What are the options in selecting an organizational design? While the human imagination is the only limitation, Mintzberg (1981) has developed a typology comprising the following five fundamental organizational designs.

Organizational Design Choices

Organization theorists have long recognized the importance and impact of organization design. Proper design choices can provide organizations with strategic advantages in executing their mission. Organizations can and do suffer if their design does not support the achievement of the mission.

Mintzberg (1981) has identified some key organizational configurations or types of organizations, each of which forms a gestalt that needs to be internally consistent. He first identified five configurations: simple structure, machine bureaucracy, professional bureaucracy, adhocracy, and divisionalized form. Each is described briefly here and illustrated with organizations from the social economy.

As the name suggests, the *simple structure* is simple with one large unit and one or two managers. Little is formalized and there is little or no planning. Most organizations start as simple structures and those that operate in simple, dynamic environments retain their simple structure. Small community-based organizations such as children's sports leagues are often simple structures. The *machine bureaucracy,* however, has an elaborate administration with many rules and standard operating procedures. Machine bureaucracy is a rigid structure that fits best with mass production activities. Some would argue that organizations like the United Nations fit many of the characteristics of the machine bureaucracy. A *professional bureaucracy* uses the standardization of skills rather than the standardization of work processes or outputs for its coordination. That is the fundamental difference between the professional and machine bureaucracy configurations. As well, power accrues to the professionals whose expertise is used to accomplish the work of the organization. The world-renowned Hospital for Sick Children in Toronto is a typical professional bureaucracy. Interestingly, its emergency department was redesigned and now resembles an adhocracy.

An *adhocracy* is essentially a project-focused organization of teams of multi-disciplinary experts. Adhocracies are designed to foster innovation in complex ways: 'It is a tremendously fluid structure, in which power is shifting and coordination and control are by mutual adjustment' (Mintzberg, 1981: 10). Lastly, the *divisionalized form* is not a 'complete form, but a partial structure, superimposed on others' (ibid.: 9). For example, the University Health Network in Toronto, consisting of three local hospitals, each a professional bureaucracy, appears to be a divisionalized form.

As well, Hegelsen (1995), based on her work at the *Village Voice* newspaper in New York City, identified another organizational type that she calls the *web of inclusion*. It is more circular than hierarchical, and builds from the centre out, spinning new threads of connection and reinforcing existing strands. Any weakness at the centre or the periphery hurts the web. Wei-Skillern and Marciano (2008) have researched networked non-profits such as Habitat for Humanity Egypt and Guide Dogs for the Blind Association in the United Kingdom. They conclude that 'non-profits that pursue their missions through networks of long-term, trust-based partnerships consistently achieve more sustainable mission impact with fewer resources than do monolithic organizations that try to do everything by themselves' (2008: 43).

While Hegelsen's work is based on a bricks-and-mortar organization, it seems to fit virtual organizations as well. Social economy organizations are becoming more virtual, creating content-rich websites to support their work. TakingITGlobal, for example, is using a social networking approach to engage students and teachers in Canada and the world to effect social change (Trevison, 2008). Some social economy organizations are only virtual (Ryan, 2005); Kiva.org, for example, is perhaps the best known.

A Closer Look: Kiva

Kiva's mission is 'to connect people through lending for the sake of alleviating poverty' (2008). Kiva is a person-to-person micro-lending website that works through a four-stage process (2008):

1 Lenders browse profiles of entrepreneurs in need, and choose someone to lend to. When they lend, using PayPal or their credit cards, Kiva collects the funds and then passes them along to one of its microfinance partners worldwide.
2 Kiva's microfinance partners distribute the loan funds to the selected entrepreneur. Often, its partners also provide training and other assistance to maximize the entrepreneur's chances of success.
3 Over time, the entrepreneurs repay their loans. Repayment and other updates are posted on Kiva's website and e-mailed to lenders who wish to receive them.
4 When lenders get their money back, they can re-lend to someone else in need, donate their funds to Kiva (to cover operational expenses), or withdraw their funds.

Global Agents for Change, a youth-managed micro-credit fund in Vancouver, is administered through Kiva. 'By the end of its [Vancouver to Tijuana fundraising] bike ride, [it] expects to have approximately $100,000 under management by the youth of [Global Agents for Change], lent and re-lent though Kiva' (Avery, 2008: ID12).

It is important to reinforce the point that design choices matter and that an organization's design choice that is out of sync with its environment, its mission, and its strategy will make it difficult to be effective. As well, it is important to distinguish between *effectiveness* and *efficiency*. The two terms are often used interchangeably and their meanings are obscured. Effectiveness means 'doing the right thing,' while efficiency means 'doing things right.' As a result, it is possible for an organization to be effective and not survive just as it is possible for an organization to be efficient but not have its desired impact.

Frumkin and André-Clark (2000) alert us to the perils of the efficiency trap whereby an organization works to become efficient but does so at the cost of its mission. They argue that non-profit organizations therefore need 'strategy grounded in values' (2000: 157). Non-profit organizations are prone to mission creep when they face demands from their funders for greater accountability and other external pressures and must fight that tendency (Alexander, 2000).

The Salvation Army is recognized for being both effective and efficient. According to Peter Drucker, a legendary thinker in the fields of non-profit *and* for-profit management, the Salvation Army is 'by far the most effective organization in the U.S. No one even comes close to it in respect to clarity of mission, ability to innovate, measurable results, dedication and putting money to maximum use. Those are his principal criteria: clarity of mission, innovative ability, clear definition of results and willingness to measure performance ... And when it comes to measuring results, it has one of the highest performance rates at the lowest cost' (cited by Lenzner and Ebeling, 1997).

Board Design and Governance

The chapter now looks at issues of board design and governance, first for non-profit organizations and then for member-focused organizations such as co-operatives and non-profit mutual associations. The board of directors is the official governance of social economy organizations, and it can play a central role in their mandate to ensure that they achieve their missions. Understanding and then applying typologies, such as those developed by Miles and Snow (1978) and by Mintzberg (1981), enable organizational actors to make informed strategic and design choices. The typologies also provide some guidance in what might be the expected outcomes of their choices.

NON-PROFIT BOARDS

Brown and Iverson (2004) found that non-profit organizations which followed a prospector strategy (innovating and risk-taking) sought to have boards that were expansive, inclusive, and involved non-board members in committees. In other words, such organizations tried to make their board structures flexible so that they could carry out their mission. Their research demonstrated that 'strategically different non-profit organizations (prospectors and defenders) exhibited predictable structural patterns' (2004: 394–5). It is important to remember that the patterns are predictable.

One of the fundamental requirements of a registered charity in Canada is an independent board, comprised of volunteers. Gill (2005) has identified nine main types of non-profit board designs:

(1) Operational, the board both governs and manages the organization
(2) Collective, the board and staff, together, make decisions about the organization
(3) Management, the board manages the operations with the help of staff
(4) Constituent representational, board members represent their constituencies
(5) Traditional, the board governs and oversees operations through committees, and management is delegated to staff through the executive director
(6) Results-based, the board sets a direction and is focused on achieving performance targets
(7) Policy governance, the board governs through policies designed to achieve the organization's mission
(8) Fundraising, the board – essentially a foundation – serves at an arm's length from the non-profit organization
(9) Advisory, the board, often selected and dominated by the executive director, governs nominally.

Three board types – traditional, policy governance, and results-based – will be described in more detail here as they are common in practice and in aspiration. In a traditional type, the board oversees operations but delegates management activities to the executive director (ED). The ED does much of the organizational planning and then the board vets and approves the plans. The board committees are functionally designed to mirror the key management functions. Policy governance boards, by comparison, govern through organizational goals (or ends), and the ED has the power to determine the means that are to be used for achieving the ends. Task forces are established to support the board's work. The board's principal role is to monitor policy compliance. (Later in the chapter, the Carver model of Policy Governance®, which has had considerable impact in the field of organizational governance, is described.) A results-based board is focused

Table 7.1 Key Attributes of Three Types of Boards

	Traditional	Policy Governance	Results-Based
Focus	Operations	Ends and Governance	Vision and Results
Leadership	Executive Director (ED) dominant	Board deals with ends (purpose) and ED means (implementation)	ED and board partnership
Planning	ED leads; committees vet; board reviews and approves	Board deals with ends (purpose) and ED means (implementation)	ED leads; board engages and links organization to community
Committees	Parallel management functions	Task forces	Board dominant; sets direction; monitors and reports on results
Accountability	ED reports to stake-holders	Board monitors policy compliance	Executive commit-tee members are core advisers

Source: Adapted with permission of the author, M. Gill *Governing for Results: A Director's Guide to Good Governance* (Victoria: Trafford Publishing, 2005), 41.

on setting a clear direction for the organization and for ensuring that the organization gets a good 'return' on its investment. The board and the ED work in partnership while taking on different aspects of the organizational planning process. In a results-based board, the board is dominant: it sets direction and assesses the extent to which the organization has achieved its results. Table 7.1 highlights the key attributes of the three board types.

There seems to be a relationship between organizational size and board type (Gill, 2005). Simple structures are likely to have operational, collective, or management board types, while machine and professional bureaucracies are likely to have traditional, constituent representational or governance board types. In designing a suitable board, there are three key questions that need to be answered: (1) Which decisions does the board want to make and which does it want to delegate? (2) How much involvement does the board want to have in the operations of the organization? (3) How will the reporting relationship between the board and the staff be defined? (United Way of Canada, 2008).

It is worth noting that '[no] single approach to governance has proven suitable for every organization' (Gill, 2005: 42). Girls Incorporated of York Region is an organization whose board is actively engaged in organizational design and the development of board governance.

A Closer Look: Girls Incorporated of York Region®

The programs of Girls Incorporated of York Region® (GIYR) focus on leadership experiences, athletic skills, economic literacy, self-reliance and life skills, and science, math, and technology. GIYR's mission is '[empowering] girls to realize their full potential through gender specific programming that inspires all girls to be strong, smart, and bold.' GIYR achieves its mission by running gender-specific programs for girls, ages 4 to 18 years, that promote awareness and self-discovery in such critical areas as self-esteem development, sexuality, career choices, peer pressure, and body image (Girls Incorporated of York Region, 2008). GIYR has been very effective in its programming; for example, between 2007 and 2008 it served more girls than the other Canadian Girls Inc. affiliates.

GIYR was founded as the Big Sisters of York in 1979 but elected not to join in the 2001 merger between Big Brothers and Big Sisters. Instead, the agency, recognizing the unique needs of girls, looked at opportunities to work with other organizations that had girl-focused programming. In 2002, the agency began the process of becoming an affiliate of Girls Incorporated®, a multinational organization with over 140 years of experience and, soon after, GIYR received full affiliate status.

In the past two years, the board of GIYR has been challenged and guided by its chair to engage in reflection and action to improve board processes (Singh, 2008). GIYR's executive director has also worked to support the board development process. Board education has become a priority. One key outcome of the process has been setting up small committees that have a specific functional focus, such as fund development. As well, the board is using various outreach approaches to increase the pool of potential volunteers for the board and its committees. The GIYR board is transitioning from a traditional board design to one of policy governance. As board development has become a central strategic focus of the GIYR board, it expects that its design will change over time.

Non-profit Governance

There is a burgeoning literature about good governance in the social economy. This chapter will highlight only the most current thinking. A recent far-ranging Canadian study (Bugg and Dalhoff, 2006) provides some useful insight about current trends in board governance. The study identifies eight key trends: (1) increased focus on governance; (2) increased demand for, but reduced supply of, qualified directors; (3) rising expectations and requirements for non-profit directors; (4) increased demand for efficiency and effectiveness; (5) more emphasis on process and organizational culture; (6) increased demand for accountability and transparency; (7) increased emphasis on performance measurement; and (8) increased attention to risk management.

These trends will have an impact on the organizational design of boards and the development of good governance practices. For example, Bugg and Dalhoff (2006) note that changing demographics require boards to become more diverse to represent better their stakeholders and the community at large. This is particularly important for boards that are not elected by a broad membership. For boards of this sort, often public sector non-profits such as hospitals and universities, it is important for the members to make an effort to reflect the diversity of the surrounding community and the primary stakeholders for their organization. They also note that a change in the funding environment, such as greater demands for accountability and transparency from donors, will require boards to engage in governance practices with high degrees of transparency and accountability.

In addition, there are specialized organizations designed to educate both the for-profit and non-profit sectors, and they are also increasingly important in helping board members to design effective strategies to respond to the trends. Education is essential for boards to be effective because in the social economy board members are volunteers who require training for their role. For some types of service, this training and ongoing support comes from umbrella organizations to which other organizations providing service belong (see the discussion in the earlier chapters on second- and third-tier organizations). Member education is one of the co-operative principles, and generally this is applied through apex organizations (e.g., the Co-operative Housing Federation of Toronto) making available training for board members. The United Way organizations across Canada also carry out this function to a degree through specialized workshops that they offer.

Altruvest Charitable Services (Altruvest) and Institute of Corporate Directors are two organizations that are working to increase board effectiveness through education and knowledge creation. The two organizations serve a valuable purpose as they provide the capacity to counter Drucker's provocative observation that '[all] nonprofit boards have one thing in common. They do not work' (Drucker cited in Laughlin and Andringa, 2007: 1).

A Closer Look: Altruvest Charitable Services and the Institute of Corporate Directors

Rob Follows founded Altruvest in 1994. As part of his fundraising work for Altruvest, Follows and his life partner have climbed to the summit of Mount Everest! Altruvest is a registered charity whose 'mission is to expand the talent pool, and enhance the governance skills of charitable sector boards and senior leaders, fostering more effective charities and stronger Canadian communities by building capacity in the sector by introducing new volunteers to board service, training charity senior leaders on board governance and leadership and by being a public advocate and thought leader for good governance' (Altruvest Charitable Services, 2008). Altruvest runs three programs: BoardMatch Fundamentals, BoardMatch Leaders, and its new program called BoardWorx Executive Director, which focuses on enhancing the skill sets of senior staff in the charitable sector.

The Institute of Corporate Directors (ICD) is a member-based organization that provides education about good governance in both the for-profit and the social sectors. Its mission is 'to represent the interests of directors – to foster excellence in directors to strengthen the governance and performance of Canadian corporations. [It] will achieve this mission through education, certification and advocacy of best practices in governance' (Institute of Corporate Directors, 2008). Among the ICD's core programs is one that addresses good governance practice in the non-profit sector.

Non-profit Governance Models

In this section, two current non-profit governance models are discussed: Carver's Policy Governance® Model, and the Leadership as Governance Model.

Carver's Policy Governance® Model (Carver Model)

The Carver Model, developed in 1990, has received much support and, more recently, some criticism. While its initial focus was on the for-profit sector, it has been refined for non-profit organizations. It is described, perhaps immodestly, on the Policy Governance Model website as 'the world's most complete theoretical foundation for the board's governance role in business, nonprofit (NGO), and government organizations' (Carver and Carver, 2008). The Carver Model is a universal set of prescriptions of good governance. The model begins with the view that ultimate organizational authority rests with the board, which is to ensure that the organization accomplishes its mission. In other words, 'the organization ... accomplishes the intended results for the intended people at the intended cost or priority' (Carver and Carver, 2001).

According to the model, '[policy governance] demands that the board's primary relationship be outside the organization – that is, with owners' (Carver and Carver, 2001). In the case of non-profit organizations, the owners are seen as the community, although ownership in this case would be more of a metaphor than a proprietary right. The board, therefore, is to serve as both the servant of the community and as the leader of the non-profit organization. Carver also suggests that the board should act as a surrogate for external market forces by setting the organization's mission and services (Brown and Iverson, 2004).

The Carver Model recommends that a position be created to which the board can delegate the management of the organization. The model's preferred term for the single point of delegation is the CEO but it is, more typically among non-profit organizations, the executive director. In this model, '[the] board creates the CEO; the CEO does not create the Board' (Carver and Carver, 2001). However, the board also delegates to the organization's leader the responsibility to manage and to execute board policy.

At the core of the Carver Model is the ends/means distinction. It defines purpose narrowly: the board defines which social needs are to be met, for whom, and at what cost. Or, as Carver puts it, (1) what results for which (2) recipient at what (3) worth. These three types of decisions are called ends. The ends are essentially the mission and vision of the organization. All other decisions are called means. Therefore, '[policy governance] boards develop policies that describe their values about ends, executive limitations, governance policies, and board-staff linkage. Each policy type is developed from the broadest, most inclusive level to more defined levels' (Carver and Carver, 2001). Carver's ends-means distinction is designed to enable boards to have the necessary oversight for good governance while allowing the organization to execute its mission flexibly. The Carver Model also puts significant emphasis on the importance of board self-evaluation and recommends a self-audit activity at every board meeting.

The Carver Model has been challenged for its rigidity and its 'one size fits all' universalist approach that does not account for the contingencies of organizational age and size (Armstrong, 1998). Armstrong also criticizes the model for ignoring human nature. Another critique of the Carver Model (Institute on Governance, 2008) argues that 'Carver makes high demands of the people in the system. Critics have pointed out that the model needs ideal board members to function, ones that truly know the organization and possess exceptional understanding of the organization's strengths and weaknesses. Board members of this calibre might be difficult to find.'

As well, the empirical evidence does not indicate that the Carver Model is any more effective than other models of governance (Brudney and Murray, 1997). While there is still further need to assess empirically the value of the Carver Model, non-profit organizations as different as Niagara College, Scouts Canada, and the Ontario Literacy Coalition have adopted it.

A Closer Look: Ontario Literacy Coalition

The Ontario Literacy Coalition (OLC), founded in 1988, is a member-based charitable organization that promotes and supports literacy and works with literacy organizations, learners, and others committed to literacy. Its mission 'is to find effective and respectful ways to help people in Ontario who have literacy challenges,' and its vision is 'a future ... of Ontario where people with literacy challenges have access to high quality supports and opportunities, and can find the information they need' (Ontario Literacy Coalition, 2008). In 2008, the OLC had 320 members, both individuals and organizations. The work of the OLC focuses on general adult literacy, labour market literacy, family literacy, English as an additional language, and professional development. Its primary activities are raising awareness, developing research and resources, and communication and coordination.

When the OLC started, it had a ten-person board elected by a majority of those in attendance at the inaugural annual general meeting. The staff was structured as a collective so that all reported directly to the board. As the OLC grew, it moved away from its collective organization design to one that was managed by an executive director (ED). Various advisory and working groups were created as well. In 2001, the members voted to further refine the OLC's organization design and also adopted the Carver Model for the board. According to the former chair of the OLC board (Kaattari, 2008):

> Moving to the Carver model is an important shift from the way that many Boards have historically worked. It can involve a fair amount of work to make the transition. But the rewards are well worth it. You can be clear about what skills you need at the Board table and recruit for them. As a Board, you will give very clear directions to your ED and very clear performance indicators. You have also given your ED the trust and flexibility to do what he or she has been hired to do.
>
> The Board decides what the organization should achieve and the ED decides how to get the work done. The Board then monitors to make sure that the ED does, in fact, get the work done.

Leadership as Governance Model

The Leadership as Governance Model argues that there are three types of governance: fiduciary, strategic, and generative (Chait, Ryan, and Taylor, 2005). Each type is necessary but alone is not sufficient for good governance.

Fiduciary Type

Fiduciary governance requires the board to behave with due diligence and to serve as the sentinel of an organization. It is designed to prevent the misuse of resources, ensure that the resources are used appropriately, keep the organization on mission, and ensure that the members of the board act in the interests of the organization. Acts of fiduciary governance include budgeting, auditing, investment, and program review. Its work is operational and uses financial and other metrics to address and/or prevent problems. Many pension funds and endowments, for example, are governed by fiduciaries. In short, fiduciary governance asks, 'What's wrong?'

Strategic Type

Strategic governance goes beyond the compliance requirements of the fiduciary type. It involves discovering and setting strategic direction. '[The] board's attention shifts from conformance to performance, and the [board members'] perspective changes from "inside out" to "outside in"' (Chait, Ryan, and Taylor, 2005: 51). The board and the ED work in partnership to shape strategy and to review its implementation and its results. It uses strategic indicators and competitive analysis as its metrics. In short, strategic governance asks, 'What's the plan?'

Generative Type

Generative governance, the most complex of the three types, is a process of reflective leadership practice. It is particularly important in complex, risky, and ambiguous situations where there is the potential for significant conflict, but where the desire for consensus is high and the board is making a decision that is not readily reversed. Its work is to discover issues and to make sense of them for the organization. It

Table 7.2 Some Key Differences between Fiduciary, Strategic, and Generative Types of Governance

	Fiduciary	Strategic	Generative
Purpose/ Activity	Stewardship of tangible assets	Strategic partnership between board and Executive Director	Source of leadership
Work	Oversees operations	Shape strategy and review performance	Recognize problems
Principal Role	Sentinel	Strategist	Sense-maker
Key Question	What's wrong?	What's the plan?	What's the question?
Metrics	Facts, figures, financial reports	Strategic indicators and competitive analysis	Learning

Source: Based on R.P. Chait, W.P. Ryan, and J. Taylor, *Governance as Leadership: Reframing the Work of NonProfit Boards* (Hoboken, NJ: Wiley, 2005), 132.

uses organizational learning as its success indicator. In short, generative governance asks, 'What's the question?'

To conclude, fiduciary governance spots problems, strategic governance solves problems, and generative governance frames problems (Ashraf, 2008). Table 7.2 highlights some of the key differences between the three types of governance.

The Leadership as Governance Model is trying to use a 'triple-helix' approach to governance. Chait, Ryan, and Taylor (2005) present a helpful example that highlights the use of the three types of governance in practice. What follows is an abbreviated version of their example.

Imagine you are on the board of an arts museum and have decided to lend a significant number of your organization's Impressionist paintings collection to another museum. In your sentinel (or fiduciary) role, you need to address such questions as the travel-worthiness of the art, the security arrangements for the art, and the costs and benefits of the plan to your organization. In your strategist (strategic) role, you need to address such questions as how the absence of your paintings will affect your visitor rate, how your museum's reputation will be affected, and what partnerships your museum might consider. In your sense-maker (generative) role, you need to address such questions as what you will do if the financial arrangements are not acceptable, if you will lend art to the highest bidder, and what sort of museum (traditional or avant garde) you want to be.

The Leadership as Governance Model, by focusing on the importance of the generative type of governance, adds a significant emphasis on a board's role to learn and to develop further the organization's mission. The generative role requires a different mindset, in short. Chait, Ryan, and Taylor (2005: 123, 131) urge board members to pose 'catalytic questions' such as: (1) Have we clarified (or muddled) organizational values and beliefs? (2) Have we clarified (or muddled) the organization's vision? (3) Have we discovered new ends as we have modified the means? (4) Have we reframed important problems? (5) What do we know now about governing that we did not know before? (6) What did we once know about the organization that is no longer true? (7) What did we once know not to be true about the organization that is now true?

The Leadership as Governance Model sets the bar high, and a question often asked is if the generative element of the model is both too demanding and impractical to achieve. The evolving governance of The Big Carrot (discussed in the Case for Analysis at the end of chapter 1) is a useful illustration of generative governance. Over twenty-five years, the members have experimented with and learned from different decision-making approaches.

While the Leadership as Governance and Carver Models seem complex, and perhaps even daunting, it is important to remember that good governance is achievable. According to Murray (2008), non-profit boards that have a practical – rather than an ideological – function tend to operate more effectively. This view implies that non-profit boards will have to strive to find a balance between passion for the mission, which can become ideological, and the achievement of the mission, which requires a focus on dispassionate execution. Such a balance can be tricky to achieve.

According to Plumtree and Laskin (2003), moving to a formal approach to governance is facilitated by several key success factors including the following: the recognition that there will be growing pains and that the process takes time; a clear understanding of the board's rights and responsibilities and those of the executive director; and ongoing communication between the board chair and the executive director. They go on to note that 'most organizations find that a collaborative board-staff relationship yields positive results. But occasional difficulties should be expected and should be managed constructively by both board and staff' (2003: 6).

Board Design and Governance for Member-Focused Associations

Many organizations in the social economy are set up to serve a membership and therefore embody the principle of mutual aid (Kropotkin, 1989; MacPherson, 1979). These include co-operatives, credit unions, and the many forms of non-profit mutual associations, for example, social clubs, religious congregations, ethnocultural associations, professional, labour, management, and consumer groups. The list is extensive, and these organizations are discussed in chapters 1 to 5, with chapter 5 in particular focusing on civil society organizations (see Figure 5.1). Most organizations of this sort derive their revenues from membership fees, but some such as co-operatives and credit unions sell their services in the market and are therefore classified as social economy businesses.

The board design of member-focused associations can be classified using the Gill (2005) typology described earlier in the chapter. Smaller organizations will tend to use a collective board design in which the board and staff, together, make decisions about the organization. They may also use a management board design in which the board manages the operations with the help of staff. Larger organizations will tend to use more elaborate designs such as a constituent representational design through which board members represent their constituencies. They may use a traditional design in which the board governs and oversees operations through committees, and management is delegated to staff through the executive director. Larger organizations may also use a results-based design in which the board sets a direction and is focused on achieving performance targets. It is important to note that the board design choices are a function of two related organizational contingencies: size and age. Chaves and Sajardo-Moreno (2004), further, note that as organizations in the social economy grow in size and complexity, the managers of the organizations play an increasingly prominent role in their governance.

In addition, when designing the right kind of board, member-focused associations need 'to face the challenge of the integration of values with value, and vice versa' (Malo and Vézina, 2004: 132). Many of the organizations described in chapters 1 to 5 seek an appropriate balance of their democratic values with the economic value that they are trying to achieve for their members. For example, feminist organizations have historically attempted to use a collective board (Rothschild-Whitt, 1982).

Governance for Member-Focused Associations

All organizations face a particular governance challenge in that they must attempt to meet the needs of their members, who much like the citizens in a democratic society are entitled to one vote at the annual general meetings and in committees. Co-operatives, as noted in chapter 2, embrace seven principles, and a key one is democratic member control.

While members may choose not to participate in the governance, they are entitled to, and often they exercise this entitlement when they are displeased with decisions undertaken by the organization. People who belong to a union or other form of labour association have likely experienced that the typical meeting is poorly attended, but when there are contract negotiations and the contract is less than expected, members will participate and with much energy. While there is no rule of thumb for member participation, a key consideration is the importance of the issue to the members.

Associations that address issues related to work, housing, and child care will often have an active membership, as do second-tier organizations in which the members are other organizations (e.g., a credit union central). For associations through which consumers purchase products like banking services and food, most members are inactive, save an activist group that acts as a proxy for the larger group's interests. If this proxy breaks down, the less active group may vote with their feet to take their purchases elsewhere, that is, exit the organization. Therefore, governance in member-focused associations is very challenging in that the board and management must be in tune with members' aspirations, even the aspirations of those members who limit their participation to using the services. Spear (2004) argues that members do not exert much influence over the boards of member-focused associations. In his view, 'the low level of membership activity in consumer/user co-operatives and mutuals raises questions about the extent to which board members may be considered representative, and the extent to which the democratic process gives a mandate to the elected board' (2004: 55).

Member-focused associations differ from conventional businesses in four important ways:

(1) As noted, the primary purpose of member-focused associations is to meet the common needs of their members, whereas the

primary purpose of most investor-owned businesses is to maximize profit for shareholders. Arguably, in order to meet shareholder needs, they must also satisfy consumers, but shareholder interest is salient. In effect, a conventional business is a piece of property owned by private interests often in the form of shareholders. A member-focused association may own property but it is in the service of its mission of member service.

(2) Member-focused associations use the one-member/one-vote system, not the one-vote-per-share system used by most businesses. This difference is fundamental and underlines the point that democratic governance is the lynchpin of a member-focused association.

(3) Member-focused associations may share surplus earnings among their members on the basis of how much they use the services (i.e., patronage). In a conventional business, surplus earnings are referred to as profits, and they belong to the owners, often based on the number of shares they hold.

(4) Member-focused associations are embedded within a community, and their membership is a proxy of that community. As noted in chapter 2, another of the principles embraced by co-operatives is 'concern for community.' This principle can be extended to all member-focused associations. By comparison, except for small businesses, conventional businesses have weak links to communities and increasingly so as commerce becomes less place based and relies on international markets. Large corporations such as banks attempt to disassociate themselves completely from a place by substituting acronyms for the place in their name (e.g., Bank of Montreal/BMO). Credit unions, by comparison, proudly associate themselves with a place, for example, Vancity, Coast Capital, Evangeline.

Issues of governance in member-focused associations are highlighted in several of the Cases for Analysis including Mountain Equipment Co-operative at the end of this chapter, The Big Carrot (chapter 1), and Arctic Co-operatives Ltd. (chapter 2). While the issues vary by organization, the common denominator is that the members, each bearing one vote like the citizens of a democracy, elect the board, or official governance, from among their group. This right is fundamental to a member-focused association, and underlines its difference from a conventional business. The Guelph Campus Co-operative is an illustration of governance in member-focused associations.

A Closer Look: Guelph Campus Co-op

Founded in 1913 by seven students and known as the Ontario Agricultural College Co-op, '[its] main purpose was to provide a cost-effective and structured business on-campus that would sell students their textbooks and supplies. As the only other bookstore was downtown, the Guelph Campus Co-op (GCC) provided a valuable service' (GCC, 2008a). The board of directors was elected from the student community and Co-op alumni. Its current mission (GCC, 2008b) states:

> We are a student owned and controlled co-operative, committed to upholding and promoting the seven principles of co-operation in all that we do.
>
> - To serve the best interests of the membership by operating effectively in areas significant to student life.
> - To acknowledge and support the active contributions students have made, and will continue to make, within our community.
> - To cultivate student leadership, participation, empowerment, self-sufficiency, and responsibility.

The GCC runs two businesses: a bookstore and affordable accommodation for students in houses and apartments near the University of Guelph campus. In 2007, the GCC redesigned one its buildings to be fully accessible for students with disabilities. It includes such features as an elevator and barrier-free appliances and bathrooms. GCC is also committed to green building and is redesigning its buildings to be environmentally friendly.

The GCC's annual general meeting is held in September and twelve members are elected to its board of directors. Any member of the GCC is entitled to run for the board. The terms are two years, and after finishing a term, any member is eligible for re-election. The board elects a president, treasurer, and secretary. The executive committee consists of the president, treasurer, secretary, and the past president. Both the board and the executive committee meet monthly.

To participate meaningfully, members need to become knowledgeable about their association so that they can contribute ideas and make informed decisions. According to the Ontario Worker Co-operative Federation (2008), 'good collective decisions require well-researched information and good communication between the board of directors, [management] and membership.' There has been increasing attention to how better engage association members in exercising their rights as well as their responsibilities.

Fairbairn (2004), whose research focuses on co-operatives, identifies different forms of participation, for example, attending and voting at meetings, participating in education and training, investing and patronage, and interacting with staff and fellow members. He goes on to suggest that 'relying on elections is too easy: people are not excited by formal democratic processes ... the onus is on the co-operative to show it understand its members' (2004: 31). Côté and Fairbairn (n.d.) have developed a useful tool to assess and to improve democratic functioning in co-operatives. They have developed measures to audit what they call co-operative cohesion, associative practices, and the type of environment in which a co-operative competes. To assess co-operative cohesion, the audit looks at the degree to which members share values, the degree to which members understand the business, and the extent to which the organization's strategies are effective. To assess associative practices, the audit looks at the extent of member education, the degree of communication with and information for members, the degree of member consultation, and the type of decision-making processes. To understand a co-operative's competitive environment, the audit requires a SWOT analysis. (A SWOT analysis is a tool to help organizations diagnose their current situation by identifying their Strengths, their Weaknesses, the Opportunities they have and the Threats they need to understand. The results of the analysis are used inform their strategic choices.) Once the audit is completed, a co-operative is able to determine its degree of democratic functioning and then use the findings to improve its democratic decision-making. This audit can be extended to member-focused associations more generally, as they embody the same structure as a co-operative.

Employee Participation in Governance

Social economy organizations, like conventional businesses and government agencies, have employees who generally operate outside of the governance body. Increasingly, organizations are striving for 'flatter structures' that give greater decision-making latitude to employees (Bernstein, 1982; Benet, 2006). For organizations with unions or other forms of workplace association, employee rights are negotiated by the bargaining unit with management. There is a surprisingly high rate of unionization in the social economy; Akingbola (2005) estimates the rate to be 40 per cent of the workforce. The unionized workforce is most prominent among the large public sector non-profits such as hospitals and universities, but it is strong among social service agencies in general.

In addition, there are some interesting examples of democratic governance in the social economy that include employees, not simply in the various forms of workplace participation that are becoming more commonplace in conventional businesses, but also in the formal governance, the board of directors.

The two forms that bear special mention are the worker co-operative (see chapter 2) in which the members are the employees, not the users of the service, as in most co-operatives, and the collective, as found in some non-profits, for example, feminist collectives.

As noted in chapter 2, worker co-operatives are an anomaly among co-operatives in that the members are employees, not consumers or users of the service. Excepting the worker co-operative, employees in a co-operative have a conventional relationship to management, as is found in businesses in general. Some may participate in the governance as consumers of the service, but they have no special rights as employees other than those that may be negotiated through a collective agreement by a union or another workplace association that represents them. In a worker co-operative, employees do have membership rights, a primary one being one vote each to participate in the governance and to elect a board of directors that will represent them (Ellerman, 1990). The Big Carrot case is an example of how a worker co-operative functions.

This form of governance also raises issues about participation by employees who are not on the board. As the case of The Big Carrot indicates, this can be challenging because when employees are also owners in common, there is an expectation that their views are taken seriously. As a result, organizations of this sort often experiment with structures, because striking a balance between employee participation and management's ability to function is important. The Big Carrot, for example, started as a collective in which every decision involved all of the members, but this soon became impractical as the business expanded and professional management was required. The organization has tried various structures including whether the office manager should be a member or external to the organization, whether the manager should be on the board, varying forms of decentralization, etc. Heather Barclay, the current president and office manager of The Big Carrot, highlights the challenge: 'There always seems to be a constant "pull" between the necessity for a hierarchical system to run the business and the need for the "equality" of the membership. In members meetings, we are all equal but as soon as we go downstairs our roles shift. This can and often has led to some conflict, especially for those members that do not hold managerial positions.'

Barclay presents the fundamental governance dilemma for worker co-operatives and other democratic workplaces: an appropriate balance between sufficient hierarchy that allows management to make business decisions and opportunities for employees to participate to a degree that management is representing their aspirations. There does not appear to be an ideal solution to this dilemma, but the fact that such organizations can compete effectively in the market is noteworthy.

The collective, as found among feminist non-profits, is a variation of a worker co-operative, the difference being that such organizations are small by intent and unlike a business like The Big Carrot, generally do not aspire to expand (Rothschild-Whitt, 1982). Feminist collectives tend to be small service organizations (e.g., rape crisis centres) and attempt to engage all members in decision-making. Management, under such circumstances, is challenging and conflict can be commonplace (Mansbridge, 1982). Arguably, conflict may be viewed as a by-product of democracy, but organizations functioning in the market have to make timely decisions. Nevertheless, through employee participation, workplace collectives attempt to obtain a buy-in so that when a decision is made there will be greater commitment among the employees.

Examples of employee participation in the governance of an organization are by no means mainstream, either in the social economy or in the private sector and government. However, they are leading edge and therefore deserve discussion. These examples are not limited to the social economy, as isolated cases can be found in the private sector as well (see chapter 2), for example, a small number of democratic employee stock ownership plans in the United States (Quarter, 1995). However, worker co-operatives and feminist collectives are outstanding examples of this model. In this regard, organizations in the social economy can also be viewed as a laboratory for innovation and experimentation.

Other Issues in Governance

There are many other issues related to governance that could be discussed, but we would be remiss to omit two in particular: board succession and selection of the executive director.

Non-profit boards may experience significant turnover as the members are volunteers, who may experience burnout or who may simply decide that after one term they want to move on to other activities. In addition, the organization's stakeholders (or their relative power) may change, and this could affect how board members perceive their involvement. Due to a stakeholder change, the organization can change its emphasis, and this could affect whether some board members want to continue. Board members of social economy organizations are expected to put in much time and insight into their roles. They have significant responsibilities: as directors, they are responsible for the good governance of the organizations, and they can be liable for any significant organization problems. Increasingly, boards in the social economy are developing formal nominating committees to plan for board succession. As well, they work with organizations like Altruvest, described above, to recruit and to attract potential board members. Also, a common practice of boards of social economy organizations is to stagger the term so that only part of the board's membership changes over at the annual meeting. Otherwise, continuity between policies could be adversely affected.

As the board is responsible for hiring the ED, it needs to develop a succession plan to ensure that the organization has a smooth transition when its ED leaves. Boards often avoid succession planning as they do not want to offend the ED, and the ED avoids raising the issue lest the board becomes concerned that the ED is about to leave (Gottlieb, 2006).

The challenge of ED succession may be even greater than that of board succession. Many EDs are expected to retire soon and there are not enough generation X-ers to replace them (Hall, 2006). Furthermore, it is well recognized that being an ED is a tough job that may not appeal to many. 'The growing complexity of managing ... and the long hours that many, if not most, executives are required to put in turn off many staffers who otherwise might be recruited to the position' (Hall, 2006: 2). A recent study of thirty-two leaders of Canada's charities and non-profit organizations, undertaken by Zarinpoush and Hall (2007), identified finding skilled managers and leaders as their greatest challenge. Gay Lea Foods Co-operative is one organization that has implemented a thoughtful and thorough approach to finding a new CEO.

A Closer Look: Gay Lea Foods Co-operative Ltd.

Gay Lea Foods, founded in 1958, is a co-operative owned by over 1,200 farmers, approximately one-quarter of Ontario's dairy farmers. Gay Lea Foods has five production facilities in Toronto, Mississauga, Guelph, and Teeswater producing milk, dips, cream, butter, sour cream, whipped cream, cottage cheese, and skim milk powder. In 2008, it was recognized as one of the Greater Toronto Area's Top 50 Employers (Gay Lea, 2008).

In 1972, Gay Lea Foods created a system of membership representation that consisted of two zones with thirty delegates per zone. The delegates' responsibilities are to attend quarterly meetings, recommend policy changes to the board, and assist in the development of the membership (Guy and Pletsch, 2003). Gay Lea Foods is governed by a nine-person board, which is supported by several committees, including an audit committee. It is managed by a team of the CEO and four vice-presidents.

The selection process of the CEO involved various levels and individuals, both at Gay Lea Foods and external organizations. The process has been characterized as intense and necessitating much soul searching (Guy and Pletsch, 2003: 5). The process had five phases: (1) learning from the 1995 CEO search, (2) an assessment of Gay Lea Foods' strategic strengths and weaknesses, (3) selection of a recruitment firm and of an internal facilitator and specification of the attributes for the ideal candidate, (4) interviews with six external and two internal candidates, and (5) multiple rounds of voting. According to a member of the audit committee, '[the] final selection discussion was very exhausting, and next time we should have more time between interviews' (Guy and Pletsch, 2003: 10). Gay Lea Foods hired Andrew MacGillivray, one of the six external candidates, in 2003, to be president and CEO, and he continues in those roles in 2008 (Gay Lea, 2008).

Conclusion

This chapter has described a range of organizational designs in the social economy. It has emphasized the importance of organizations having the right design to fit the demands of their environment and mission. The chapter then delved into the designs of non-profit boards to highlight their critical role in social economy organizations. Again, there is a range of designs and there is no one best way to design.

The chapter then presented two current models for board governance – the Carver Model and Leadership as Governance Model – both of which require more empirical examination. It then discussed the requirement for and the actual use of democratic decision-making processes in member-focused associations, including co-operatives, and employee participation in the governance. The chapter concludes with a discussion of two key governance issues in the social economy: board and ED succession.

* * *

DISCUSSION QUESTIONS

1. In your view, is one board type more effective than another? Why?
2. What are the strengths and weaknesses of the Carver Model?
3. What are the strengths and weaknesses of the Leadership as Governance Model?
4. How are member-focused associations different from other organizational types?
5. What can member-focused associations do to enhance membership participation in the democratic decision-making processes?
6. Is democratic governance practical in a modern economy?

LEARN MORE

If you want to learn more, visit these websites:

- www.altruvest.org
- www.blumbergs.ca
- www.boardsource.org
- www.charityvillage.com/cv/research/index.asp
- www.coopscanada.coop.

* * *

Case for Analysis: Mountain Equipment Co-op[1]

On 11 February 2008, Mountain Equipment Co-op (MEC) received two governance awards: it was the overall winner of the Conference Board of Canada/Spencer Stuart National Awards in Governance for its implementation of a sustainability strategy. MEC also received the top honour in the non-profit category (Awards, Conference Board of Canada, 2008a). The other contenders in the non-profit category were Bloorview Kids Rehab, Heart and Stroke Foundation of Canada, and the Saskatchewan Indian Gaming Authority.

There are six criteria, or principles of good governance, that the Awards in Governance Advisory Board (Conference Board of Canada, 2008b) uses to assess organizational innovations in governance:

1) Leadership and stewardship: ensuring strategic direction and planning, planning for succession and renewal, overseeing risk management and implementing internal control
2) Empowerment and accountability: delegating authority, allocating responsibilities, and establishing effective accountability
3) Communication and transparency: determining information flows, and communicating with and reporting to shareholders and stakeholders
4) Service and fairness: setting an example in corporate social responsibility, providing ethical leadership, and promoting environmental sustainability

1 We would like to thank Ben Hudson of MEC for his prompt assistance in providing information about the Annual General Meeting.

5) Accomplishment and measurement: monitoring and overseeing management, selecting organizational performance measures, evaluating the board, CEO, and individual directors
6) Continuous learning and growth: promoting a culture of innovation and developing and training directors, executives, and employees.

MEC's board was praised for its proactive leadership approach to sustainability. It was recognized for developing 'a focus on a key dimension that will contribute to the organization's success and [providing] leadership ... by establishing policies, committing to a solid long-term vision ... and then working with management to achieve success' (Conference Board of Canada, 2008c: 18–19).

Background

A group of students at the University of British Columbia founded Mountain Equipment Co-op in 1971 and sold sporting equipment that was not readily available such as avalanche beacons, ice crampons, and climbing rope. The students charged a one-time lifetime membership fee of five dollars. MEC, structured as a retail co-operative, has become Canada's largest supplier of outdoor equipment. It has more than 2.8 million members in 192 countries, eleven outlets in Canada's major urban centres, and its 2007 sales were about $240 million.

Values

MEC has articulated nine values to guide its actions. They are quality, integrity, co-operation, creativity, leadership, sustainability, stewardship, humanity, and adventure. MEC's Charter (2008a), which was developed as part of its Futures Project, outlines its vision as follows:

> We aspire to be the most viable, vibrant outdoor retail business in Canada. We want to bring about a future where Canadians of all ages, and especially our youth, play outdoors in self-propelled ways more often and in ever-increasing numbers; have access to a comprehensive, carefully nurtured network of parks, wilderness, and outdoor recreation areas; and have a connection to nature that is stronger than ever. We want MEC and our members to set examples that inspire other organizations

> and individuals towards environmental, social, and economic sustainability. In short, we want to leave the world better than we found it.

MEC's roots are symbolized in its logo, two mountain peaks. In 2007, MEC joined 1% for the Planet, an alliance of 500 organizations in twenty countries that pledges 1 per cent of its annual gross sales to environmental causes. MEC will donate an estimated $2.25 million to environmental causes in 2007 (Canadian Co-operatives Association, 2007). In 2006, MEC published its first annual accountability report and was the only Canadian retailer to receive the Award for Best First-Time Report from the Association of Certified Chartered Accountants and was ranked first by Jantzi for sustainability in the retail sector (Parshad, 2007).

In late 2007, MEC received kudos when it became the *first* major Canadian retailer to stop selling products that contain Bisphenol A. Patagonia was the only other major North American retailer to stop selling such products. Bisphenol A is used in clear hard plastic reusable bottles, and has been found to affect brain development (Science Daily, 2005).

MEC takes a green building approach when it builds or renovates its retail outlets. Its buildings are on the leading edge of green building design and technology in North American retail organizations. Its Toronto store, for example, has many green features such as reused structural timber from demolished buildings, natural lighting through high efficiency double-glazed windows, reduced energy use in the heating and cooling systems, and a rooftop garden. The building is 35 per cent more energy efficient than a comparable conventionally designed retail building (Five Winds International, 2003).

Governance

MEC's website is not just a virtual retail arm. It is both an advocacy and governance site. It provides detailed information about its governance model at the web page Home/About MEC/Directors, Election and AGM. Anyone over 16 who has been a member of MEC for at least six weeks is entitled to vote. Approximately 100 people attend the AGM (annual general meeting) in Vancouver. MEC, as a co-operative, is obligated to inform its membership of its board election. MEC communicates through e-mail, classified advertisements, and an election booklet. It sends out its booklet to approximately 200,000 members who are selected on criteria such as members who have voted before, purchased merchandise recently, and other member engagement activities. The elections are open for six weeks. The website also provides a candidate comparison tool.

In 2008, of a total of 34,308 votes, 31,812 were cast electronically, 2,411 were cast over the telephone, and 55 were cast through the mail. The vote is tallied and audited by Price Waterhouse Coopers. Telus provides the electronic voting site: each member is given a random personal identification number so that she or he is only able to vote once.

The board consists of nine members who serve staggered three-year terms. Three directors from across Canada are elected to represent members-at-large, that is, directors who do not represent just their regions. Directors each serve for a term of three years, and they may stand for re-election for a second term with a maximum term limit of seven consecutive years. After a break of at least forty-eight weeks, a director may again stand for election.

According to outgoing board chair, Linda Bartlett, the board has the following three principal responsibilities (MEC, 2008b):

> First, to ensure the organization is well managed and operates to meet the hopes, dreams, and aspirations of the owners – you and the other members who shop there. Second, to exercise control over MEC's assets and ensure they are used effectively. The third: to look at the long-term view and try to make sure MEC remains relevant ten and twenty years from now.

A Board member has the following obligations.

> The Directors have been elected by the members of MEC to represent their interests. While B.C. laws and MEC bylaws and rules define the manner in which MEC will conduct its affairs, the role of the Board of Directors is to provide leadership and to speak for the members in governing the direction that MEC pursues as an outdoor retailer ...
>
> [Directors are] responsible for (1) always acting in a manner which they believe is in the best interest of MEC as a whole; contributing to discussions as part of decision-making and respecting Board decisions on all issues; (2) maintaining relationships with staff so as to develop trust and respect, but avoiding personal relationships that may affect objectivity in making decisions affecting MEC; (3) respecting the confidentiality of in-

camera Board discussions and privileged information; (4) providing leadership to ensure that employees are viewed as an integral part of MEC, and are treated fairly and equitably; and (5) making certain MEC has clear long, medium and short-term plans that can be developed and measured realistically.

The website also provides information to help its members submit special resolutions for consideration at MEC's annual general meeting. To pass, a special resolution requires 75 per cent majority of the votes, cast by paper, online, and interactive voice technology. All members have the right to propose a special resolution. The member must get the support of five other members to have the resolution considered at the AGM. At the 2008 AGM, the board tabled one special resolution to make clearer the duration of a director's term. To pass, an ordinary resolution requires a simple majority of the votes cast at the annual general meeting.

The MEC board has developed practices and processes designed to foster governance excellence. They include the following (MEC, 2008b): (1) providing information to members as to what skills the board is looking for, so members can make thoughtful decisions when voting for new directors; (2) assessing at the beginning of each board year the skills that directors bring to the board across a broad range of board competencies and addressing any gaps; (3) conducting an annual review of how the board, as a whole, is functioning; (4) conducting anonymous, confidential peer evaluations to provide feedback to each director on his or her performance; and (5) building leadership capacity through a board leadership development program.

* * *

DISCUSSION QUESTIONS

1. Do you think that the criteria that the Awards in Governance Advisory Board uses to assess organizational innovations in governance are appropriate?
2. If you were a member of MEC's board, what do you think would be your most important duties? Why?

* * *

8 Financing

This chapter explores issues around financing in the social economy. The unique characteristics of social economy organizations in relation to this issue are discussed, as well as the challenges that arise as a result. The chapter also outlines some of the innovative funding mechanisms that have arisen in the past two decades to overcome these challenges and move forward financing programs for social economy organizations.

Social economy organizations have less access to financing than for-profit organizations, which can borrow funds through various forms of debt financing such as mortgages and debentures by putting up their assets for collateral. For-profits can also raise funds by issuing shares. Shareholders are effectively owners of the corporation and benefit through the appreciation of the corporation's market value and through any dividends the corporation pays from its profits. For short-term financing, also known as working capital, banks provide loans and revolving credit.

Co-operatives incorporated with share capital can issue a public offering statement to raise money through the sale of shares. In Ontario, for instance, a registered co-operative can issue membership shares, and class A (supporters) and class B (members) preference shares (New Economy Development Group [NEDG], 2006a).

Other social economy organizations, particularly non-profit corporations, non-profit co-operatives, and social enterprises, are more limited in their financing options as they typically do not have collateral, a challenge also faced by small and medium-sized enterprises in the business sector. A defining characteristic of a non-profit corporation is that they are an organization without share capital. This means that they do not have owners in the usual sense and that they cannot raise share capital as in a for-profit business. This constraint creates difficult challenges for organizations in their start-up phase and for those that lack a track record (Social Investment Organization [SIO] and Riverdale Community Development Corp. [RCDC], 2003).

Mendell, Lévesque, and Rouzier (2001) outline several additional difficulties faced by social economy organizations in financing their activities:

1) As the primary objective of social economy organizations is not financial, in general they do not generate a competitive rate of return on investment. This reduces the number of institutional and individual investors they can access, who are looking for a high rate of return.
2) Banks consider most social economy organizations as too small or too risky to justify setting up a small loans program for them.
3) Many individuals running social economy organizations have little experience dealing with the market economy.

Indeed, financing is one of the biggest concerns facing social economy organizations (Barr et al., 2006; Mendell et al., 2001). In a 2003 survey of formally incorporated non-profits, 48 per cent of responding organizations reported they had difficulty obtaining funding from government and individuals; 42 per cent said they had difficulty earning revenue in the market (Imagine Canada, 2006a).

Sources of Revenue for Social Economy Organizations

According to the National Survey of Nonprofit and Voluntary Organizations (NSNVO), non-profit organizations reported annual revenues of $112 billion in 2003 (Imagine Canada, 2006b). Excluding hospitals and universities, the main source of these revenues came from earned income (43%), followed by government (36%), gifts and donations (17%), and other sources (4%) (Hall et al., 2004). When hospitals and universities are included, the mix changes to the following: government (49%), earned income (35%), gifts and donations (13%), and other income (3%).

In addition to government funding, earned income, and gifts and donations, social economy organizations can access financial resources from community-based investment vehicles, credit unions, and social venture capital funds. Other more limited sources include banks, socially responsible investment funds, labour sponsored investment funds, and institutional investors such as pension funds (Hebb et al., 2006).

Financing is provided by all sectors: public, social economy and private, as well as from pooled sources. Pooling resources generally involves more than one sector coming together to provide opportunities and share risk.

One unique type of finance which plays a key role in financing the social economy is called social finance. Social finance is distinct from other forms of financing in that its intention is to support organizations in developing a social impact, and it seeks and prioritizes social and environmental goals as well as financial ones (Draimin and Jackson, 2007; TSA Consultancy, 2003). For example, Vancity offers a shared growth term deposit and a shared world term deposit to investor-savers who want to earn a competitive rate of return from a fund that finances community development projects in British Columbia and internationally. Some distinct features of social finance are the following (TSA Consultancy, 2003: 5–6):

- The mission of social finance is to use financial tools to achieve sustainable and equitable development.
- Its long-term vision is to increase social capital.
- It has numerous channels of delivery, each of them with different methods and forms of behaviour, acting in different ways, but together they give rise to an identity that is specific to social finance.
- The profession of social financier consists of funding activities and people that benefit their communities and societies.
- Social finance providers prioritize those organizations or individuals which are most excluded from mainstream services, and these are the target groups of the services provided.

Sources of Financing through the Public Sector

Government Funding

Governments are important sources of financing for social economy organizations (Hebb et al., 2006). Provincial governments provide the most financing to the social economy, through grants, loans, loan guarantees, and special tax treatment (ibid.). The Quebec government is a leader in this area, with its targeted programs for social economy organizations, for example, the Réseau d'investissement social du Québec (RISQ), created in 1997 by le Chantier de l'économie sociale. More recently, as noted in chapter 3, the Quebec government has invested $10 million in the Fiducie du Chantier de l'économie sociale, or the Chantier Trust, a pool of more than $53 million to support investment in social enterprises. The Quebec Network of Community Credit also receives support from the Government of Quebec, as do Local Development Centres (LDCs). Most provincial governments provide financing for local development funds as well as technical investment tax credits.

A Closer Look:
Réseau d'investissement social du Québec

The Réseau d'investissement social du Québec (RISQ) is a non-profit capital venture fund that offers loans and loan guarantees of up to $50,000 exclusively to social economy organizations. It also offers technical assistance in the form of funding up to $5,000 for pre-start-up support such as developing a business plan or undertaking a market and feasibility study. Technical assistance funding is only repayable if the project is successful.

The fund's principal investors include the Royal Bank of Canada, the Confédération des caisses populaires et d'économie Desjardins du Québec, la Banque Nationale du Canada, Bank of Montreal, Alcan Aluminum Ltd., le Groupe Jean Coutu (PJC) Inc., la Fondation Marcelle et Jean Coutu, le Cirque du soleil, and the Quebec government.

Since its inception in 1997 to 30 June 2005, RISQ provided $7.4 million for 180 capitalization projects, and just over $930,000 for 188 technical assistance projects. As a result, over 4,400 full-time and part-time jobs were created.

The federal government of Canada makes financing available through regional and Aboriginal development agencies such as the Community Futures Development Corporation, already discussed in chapter 3. It also set up the Business Development Bank of Canada (BDC), established over sixty years ago to offer consulting services, financing, and venture capital to small businesses. At the community level, the BDC provides financing for Aboriginal entrepreneurs through its Aboriginal Business Development Funds. The loan amounts vary from $5,000 to $20,000 with repayment terms of two to three years depending on cash-flow expectations. In total, $1 million will be allocated to four funds. Three funds have already been established in the following locations: in Port Alberni in partnership with the Nuu-chah-nulth Economic Development Corporation; in Fort McMurray in partnership with Keyano College; and in Edmonton with the Apeetogosan (Métis) Development Inc. (BDC, 2002, 2006, 2008).

The federal government is also a funding partner of the Native Venture Capital Limited Partnership of Quebec (Socit de Capital de risque autochtone du Québec), the first venture capital corporation in Canada dedicated to First Nations entrepreneurs. Other partners include Fonds de solidarité de la Fédération des travailleurs du Québec, the Mouvement Desjardins, the Native Benefits Plan, the Aboriginal Capital Corporations, Société de crédit commercial autochtone (SOCCA), the Corporation de développement économique montagnaise (CDEM), and the government of Quebec. In total, the fund consists of $6 million in investment capital that is used to fund First Nations businesses and communities (Indian and Northern Affairs Canada, 2002).

For co-operatives, the federal government provides funding through its Co-operative Development Initiative (CDI), a joint program between the co-operative sector and the federal government Co-operatives Secretariat. It provides funding for advisory services, and for innovation and research projects for co-operatives in Canada. Its primary administration is regional, but 6 per cent of its budget is dedicated for worker co-operatives and is administered nationally by the Canadian Worker Co-operative Federation. From 2003 to 2008, CDI distributed $15 million helping to create 135 new co-operatives and assisting 1,000 more (CCA, 2008). Projects received funds of between $5,000 and $75,000 per year. (Information on the program is made available on the Co-operatives Secretariat Website at http://coop.gc.ca/.)

The Co-operative Development Initiative national advisory service arm is called CoopZone and is located in Calgary. It is managed jointly by the Canadian Co-operative Association and the Conseil Canadien de la Coopération, and their website at www.coopzone.coop is their primary information source. Here you can find information about starting and improving a co-operative, as well as educational training materials and notices of related workshops and seminars. The Coop-Zone also has a database of developers in all regions of Canada who are available to help co-operatives with any of their development needs.

The Co-operative Development Initiative is managed by the Co-operatives Secretariat. The six priority areas for funding are: (1) adding value to agriculture; (2) improving access to health care and home care; (3) fostering economic development in rural, remote, or Northern communities; (4) promoting the development of Aboriginal communities; (5) supporting the integration of immigrants into Canadian communities; and (6) supporting community solutions to environmental challenges.

A Closer Look: Co-operative Development Initiative

Some examples of co-operatives that have benefited from Co-operative Development Initiative (CDI) funding include the following (CCA, 2007c; Co-operatives Secretariat, 2008):

Western Log Sort and Salvage Co-op. Every year, thousands of cubic metres of logs are left adrift on the Fraser River in British Columbia. This usable wood is going to waste since salvagers, also known as beachcombers, are paid very little for logs they pick up. CDI funding was used to develop and launch a receiving station for salvaged logs, as part of a venture of the Western Log Sort and Salvage Co-op called Wood Not Waste. The Wood Not Waste program is adding value to salvaged wood and ensuring that these logs are put back in the marketplace rather than going to waste. In addition to the ongoing employment opportunities for salvagers, this project has an enormous environmental impact as the Fraser River is a critical habitat for millions of waterfowl and shorebirds and is the largest salmon-producing river in the world.

Taxi Co-op. Taxi Co-op was started to purchase an existing taxi business on the outskirts of Calgary as well as to develop a new business within the city of Calgary. It has approximately twenty-two drivers and five owner/employers. CDI assisted with the start-up of the co-op, which involved incorporating, developing a business plan, and looking at several options for purchasing existing businesses.

Planet Bean. Planet Bean retails and wholesales gourmet fair trade organic coffee and other fair trade products in the Ontario market. Through CDI funding, Planet Bean examined various expansion strategies, developed a longer-term business plan, and articulated a plan for future expansion. A feasibility study for an additional coffee bar in Guelph was also part of this plan, as was the development of additional roasting capacity to increase sales in both the wholesale and retail aspects of its operations.

Healthy Minds Co-operative (N.S.). Incorporated with the help of CDI, Healthy Minds Co-op is an innovative health care service in Halifax working to meet the needs of people afflicted with mental illness and brain disorders. Healthy Minds unifies mental health consumers and advocates for improved service, while educating the public about mental illness and brain disorders.

Sources of Financing through the Social Economy

Philanthropy through Community Foundations

Community foundations are locally run public foundations that administer endowments to support charitable activities in their area. Canada's first community foundation, the Winnipeg Foundation, was founded in 1921. There are now over 160 community foundations in Canada, and in 2007 they held assets of almost $3 billion and made contributions to charities in the amount of $176 million (Community Foundations of Canada, 2008).

The Vancouver Foundation is the largest community foundation in Canada and one of the largest in North America. The Vancouver Foundation is a registered charity and as such is exempt from income taxes. The income from its funds is used for charitable purposes in British Columbia. In 2007, the Vancouver Foundation had assets of $785 million, administered endowment funds for over 400 non-profit agencies, and distributed $60 million to registered charitable organizations (Vancouver Foundation, n.d.).

The Vancouver Foundation supports a neighbourhood small grants program, which in turn supports resident-led grassroots activities that enhance their local neighbourhood; a youth homelessness initiative in Vancouver; the Giving in Action Society that provides grants to help families who have children or adults with developmental disabilities at home; and the MEDICI program that helps arts and cultural organizations improve their capacity and long-term financial stability.

Donors who wish to set up their own endowment fund within the Vancouver Foundation choose the type of fund they would like to establish: a donor-advised fund where they select charities or projects themselves; a field-of-interest fund where funds are dedicated to a general area, like arts and culture or animal welfare; or a community-impact fund, where money is pooled with others to address emerging community needs. Corporations can also outsource all or part of their charitable giving program. For example, Mountain Equipment Co-op's endowment fund for the environment is administered by the Vancouver Foundation (n.d.).

Venture Philanthropy

Venture philanthropy is a method of funding non-profit organizations viewed with both an investment and a philanthropic lens. In addition to requiring certain returns or results, venture philanthropists also give strategic and operational support.

Social Capital Partners (n.d.), founded in 2001, is based on this concept. Social Capital Partners was looking for new ways to apply venture philanthropy in the Canadian context. They started by consultating leaders in the non-profit sector and found that traditional funding mechanisms were counter-productive to sustaining long-term change that would help people develop paths towards self-sufficiency. Non-profit organizations that were dependent on government and foundation funding were restricted in terms of meeting their missions. They also found that alot of time and energy was devoted to fundraising, and little funding was available for organizational capacity building or for measuring long-term outcomes. Overall, as Social Capital Partners puts it: 'Frankly many charitable organizations have become better at meeting donors' needs than the needs of the populations they are trying to serve.'

As a result of these consultations, Social Capital Partners set up their investment approach based on the social enterprise model, with a focus on investing in enterprises that hire disadvantaged groups while providing relevant social support services. As they explain on their website: 'Our hypothesis is that if you can create viable businesses that balance a financial bottom line while providing support services and employment opportunities for a marginalized or at-risk population, the opportunity would exist for social organizations to maintain more control over their destiny while continuing to achieve their social goals.'

In order to select its first project, Social Capital Partners held a business plan competition with a $15,000 prize and a chance of up to $1 million of funding. From over 100 entries, Inner city Renovation Inc., a professional renovations company based in Winnipeg, was selected as the winner (for A Closer Look, see chapter 1 of this book). Key to the operation of Inner City Renovation (ICR, 2007) is the support provided for its workers, for example, trades training that allows the workers to rebuild their lives in a sustainable way as well as the use of role models. Social Capital Partners no longer has an active investment in Inner City Renovation, but continues to support it through its board. Inner City Renovation is now intending to become a worker-owned company.

Social Capital Partners' latest projects are investments in franchises to reduce some of the risk associated with starting a new business. It will make available up to $300,000 per franchise in financing with the stipulation that at least 50 per cent of the employees are hired through community programs that serve people facing employment barriers. Bill Young, the president of Social Capital Partners, refers to this process as 'mainstreaming.' To date, Social Capital Partners has worked with two franchise systems: Active Green + Ross (six franchisees) and Two Men and a Truck (one franchisee).

Micro-finance

Micro-finance and community loan funds are two examples of social finance (TSA Consultancy, 2003). Micro-finance aims to provide small loans, also called micro-loans or micro-credit, to poor and low-income people to start income-generating projects and small businesses. The best-known microfinance institution is the Grameen Bank in Bangladesh, which won the 2006 Nobel Peace Prize along with its founder, Muhammad Yunus, an economist who serves as the bank's managing director.

The Grameen Bank has a structure similar to a credit union in that it is owned by its members, predominately women. The first loan was made by Yunus from his own pocket in 1976: $27 to a group of women to purchase raw materials for their trade and thereby eliminate the need for intermediaries who were exploiting and impoverishing them by raking off their profits. Since then, Grameen has provided loans of over U.S. $5.2 billion to more that 7.2 million borrowers, 97 per cent of whom are women, in more than 82,000 villages in rural Bangladesh. Repayment rates are near 100 per cent (Yunus, 2003). Another distinct feature of the Grameen Bank is that it has invested in a network of services for the villages and regions in which their members live. There are twenty-five such organizations, some examples being: Grameen Krishi, which provides training and investment in improving agricultural practices; Grameen Shakti, which provides energy services with an emphasis on solar; and Grameen Phone, a provider of cell phone services (Yunus, 2007).

The investment in these twenty-five organizations is a classic example of a financial institution using its surplus earnings to engage in community reinvestment or community economic development. Not only has the Grameen Bank done this within Bangladesh, but it has also been a leader in spawning an international movement, not simply through leading by example but by also investing in Grameen Trust, which engages in training, technical assistance, and financial support for microfinance around the world. Today, micro-credit programs are offered in over 100 countries, including Canada, and Muhammad Yunus and Grameen Bank are very much their inspiration.

Micro-credit in Canada differs to a degree from the Grameen example and probably is more akin to first-entry loans for self-employed people with a business idea. Success with the first loan can lead to larger loans. However, the micro-program serves as a first step – a bridge to more conventional loans for the self-employed and small business people.

In Canada, several credit unions have started micro-credit programs. Alterna Savings, based in Ontario, offers the Community Micro Loan Program and the Immigrant Employment Loan Program. The Community Micro Loan Program provides loans of between $1,000 and $15,000 to low-income, self-employed individuals, who would not otherwise have access to credit from a financial institution. Successful applicants are also expected to take a business training program. The loan interest rate is set at variable prime plus 6 per cent, and there is also a 6 per cent administration fee. The Immigrant Employment Loan Program is operated in partnership with the Maytree Foundation and offers immigrants and refugees loans for training or upgrading their skills to increase the likelihood that they can find employment in Canada in their field of expertise (Alterna, n.d.).

Vancity Credit Union offers micro-loans of $5,000 and up that have helped more than 800 British Columbia entrepreneurs with over $13 million in assistance (Vancity, 2008a). These loans are based primarily on a business owner's character and viability of the business, as opposed to the availability of collateral to secure the loan.

Also in British Columbia, Coast Capital Savings offers micro-loans of up to $35,000 through a program it operates in partnership with Western Economic Diversification Canada. According to its annual report, Coast Capital provided twenty-three micro-loans totalling over $410,000 in 2007, one example being the social enterprise, Concrete Works (Coast Capital, 2007). Its innovative idea was to dramatically polish new or existing concrete in order to increase its light refraction, or amount of shine. By doing this, the environment is brightened by 20 to 30 per cent, saving on the amount of lighting fixtures needed. This process also increases the wear resistance of the surface, leading to more years of useful life of the flooring (Concrete Works, n.d.).

In Quebec, Desjardins offers what it calls solidarity products to both individuals and to businesses. In partnership with budget consulting organizations, it administers a Mutual Aid Fund of small loans, often around $500, to individuals with a repayment period of up to twenty-four months. For businesses, it has a micro-loan program for individuals or groups who cannot access traditional credit networks. These loans are also accompanied by close guidance to help recipients carry out their business project (Desjardins, n.d.).

While most micro-lending in Canada is oriented towards local communities, one organization, Kiva, uses the Internet to encourage micro-loans to people in poorer countries. This innovative idea (discussed in chapter 7) involves the transfer of funds from richer to poorer countries online to bridge distances (Kiva, 2007).

Micro-finance is generally thought of as having a major influence on poverty reduction strategies, primarily in developing economies but also in wealthier countries. Its appeal appears to be the emphasis on the market – poverty can be reduced through creating a new class of entrepreneurs, it is believed – a strategy that fits well with the neoliberal focus on reducing the role of government. More recently, a critique has emerged from researchers and practitioners engaged in international development work that questions the effectiveness of micro-finance. The critique raises some fundamental concerns, for instance, as discussed in the collection, *What's Wrong with Microfinance?* (Dichter and Harper, 2008). The critique's primary thrust is that micro-finance, while providing some short-term income, is not an effective poverty-reduction strategy. Micro-loans, while classified by their proponents as business credit, are argued to be analogous to consumer loans in that all they lead to in the short term is a small increase in purchasing power by the recipients. Critics argue that the success stories that have emerged may have done so anyway through other available lending sources, if micro-credit programs were unavailable. Group-based micro-finance, which transfers collection tasks from the micro-finance institution to the borrowers, is criticized as being less empowering than lending on an individual basis (Harper, 2008). Interest rates vary, but are generally high and, in some cases, usurious (Epstein and Smith, 2007; Rao, 2008; Shakya and Rankin, 2008). Even so, repayment rates in micro-credit programs are very impressive (about 95%) even with high interest charges, an indication that the borrowers must benefit to some degree (Emran, Morshed, and Stiglitz, 2006).

Nevertheless, micro-credit has become an international movement. In the modern world, typically ideas move from the wealthier to poorer nations, and not always for the better; but in the case of Grameen banking, the opposite has been the case. Grameen has spawned similar programs, not only in poor countries where the basic model has been applied, but also in wealthier countries such as Canada where the Grameen philosophy has been adapted and applied by lending institutions operating under the philosophy of community financing.

Financing for Home Ownership

Although there are a number of organizations providing funding assistance for low-income people to start their own businesses, or receive training so they can gain meaningful employment, there are few that offer financing to support home ownership. Options for Homes, a non-profit organization, is the exception. Options for Homes helps medium- to low-income people develop no-frills condominiums through a housing co-operative model that converts to a regular condominium association upon completion of the project. The key to its success is an innovative financing mechanism that functions as a second mortgage, which purchasers do not have to pay back until they sell or rent their units. This lowers the carrying costs of ownership, and brings home ownership within the means of people with much lower incomes. More details on the Options for

Homes financing model is found in the Case for Analysis at the end of this chapter.

Most examples of financing for home ownership and other forms of tenancy (see chapter 4) involve external organizations. However, an innovative, albeit small-scale example originates in Cape Breton and involves a form of mutual self-help by the members of a union local involved in the construction business, as detailed below.

A Closer Look:
The Cape Breton Labourers' Benevolent Fund[1]

The Labourers' International Union of North America, Local 1115, in Cape Breton, Nova Scotia, has developed a highly innovative model of mutual aid. Union members have deductions of 25 cents per hour from their paycheque (currently negotiating an increase to 50 cents per hour), which flows into the Cape Breton Labourers' Benevolent Fund and is used to build houses for the members. By 2008, the fund had financed new homes – three-bedroom bungalows – for twenty-four members of the union. When a house is built, the members of the union contribute and are paid for much of the labour. To date, an estimated 13,420 days of work have been created both in construction and administration. The Cape Breton Labourers' Benevolent Fund and the associated Cape Breton Labourers' Development Company have won three awards for their work. In 1991 they were the first initiative from outside the United States to be recognized for outstanding achievement by the National Congress for Community Economic Development. A year earlier, they were honoured by Canada Mortgage and Housing Corporation as the best financing and tenure program in Canada. They were also recognized for their achievements by the Nova Scotia Department of Housing and Consumer Affairs.

1 The information on the Cape Breton Labourers' Benevolent Fund was taken from the book, *Crossing the Line* (1995), by Jack Quarter, and through an interview with Jolene MacNeil, the fund's administrator.

Capitalization through Public Offering

Co-operatives incorporated with share capital have the ability to raise money through a public offering of shares. This is the route that La Siembra and Just Us worker co-operatives have taken in order to grow their businesses.

La Siembra Co-operative Inc. was founded in August 1999 in Ottawa as a worker co-operative with share capital. It sells organic fair-trade hot chocolate, chocolate, and sugar products under the Cocoa Camino brand. It is a highly successful and award-winning organization, with yearly revenues that grew from almost $87,000 in 2001 to nearly $2.2 million in 2005, with an increase in share capital from $15,000 to $627,000 in the same period (NEDG, 2006a). Revenues are continuing to rise; in 2006 they were almost $4 million (La Siembra, n.d.).

In order to raise this capital, La Siembra had to amend its articles of incorporation (that limited them to 25 shareholders previously) and prepare an offering statement to sell class A preferred shares, which it did in three provinces: Ontario, British Columbia, and Quebec. Through these offerings, it was able to raise approximately $500,000 in a three-year period (2002–05). Although the logistics of meeting different filing and reporting requirements in three provinces were challenging, there are few alternatives for organizations such as La Siembra to raise capital. It is at the point now where it needs to access even larger pools of capital, but feels it has few options to be able to do so if it remains as a worker co-operative (NEDG, 2006a).

Just Us! Coffee Roasters, a worker co-operative in Nova Scotia, is undergoing a similar process. It is seeking to raise $300,000 by selling $1,000 common membership shares for a related co-operative called Just Us! Fair Trade Investment Co-operative Limited. Just Us! (2008) continues to grow, with sales increasing from almost $1 million in 2000 to over $5.5 million in 2007. To grow even further, the co-operative is considering expanding its chocolate factory, developing an organic dairy, and improving its information technology.

Credit Unions and Caisses Populaires

As you learned in chapter 2, credit unions (caisse populaires in Quebec) are financial co-operatives set up to meet the financial needs of their members. Credit unions and caisse populaires offer many of the same products and services as do for-profit financial institutions, however, with some major differences – they are owned by their members and work for the economic and social betterment of their members and the economic development of the community. Each member has one vote, and is entitled to participate in the annual general meeting and run for elected officer positions. A portion of the surplus that is earned goes back to the community and to their members through patronage shares, which are proportional to the volume of business undertaken with the credit union or caisse populaire that year (see www.desjardins.com). Patronage dividends are an important difference from banks, whose dividends are based on the shares held by investors not use of the service by consumers.

The very first caisse populaire in Canada was set up in Lévis, Quebec, by Alphonse and Dorimne Desjardins in 1900 (Desjardins, 2008). The Desjardins Group today is the sixth largest financial institution in Canada, with 5.8 million members and assets of $144 billion in 2007. In the same year, it returned more than 60 per cent of its surplus to the community including patronage dividends to its individual members of $592 million and donations to the community of $72 million (Desjardins, 2008). It is also heavily involved in international development and micro-finance, supporting over 2.5 million people in over fifty countries throughout the world (Desjardins, 2006; Desjardins Développement International, 2007).

Financial co-operatives focus on loans to members, but they also can provide services targeted to social economy organizations. The Evangeline Credit Union (2008) in Wellington, Prince Edward Island, is well known for its reinvestment in various forms of community enterprises (Wilkinson and Quarter, 1996). This credit union, formed in 1970 through a merger of two smaller credit unions, is the lynchpin for a co-operative infrastructure that serves the tiny Acadian villages of Wellington, Mont Carmel, and Abram's Village, among others. Often referred to as the 'co-operative capital,' these tiny villages have fourteen co-operatives, offering services from the cradle to the grave, with 7,435 members and 233 employees, and assets worth $66 million (Conseil de développement cooperative, 2008).

This same form of reinvestment in local communities is found in other Acadian communities throughout Atlantic Canada. The Fédération des caisses populaires acadiennes, centred in Caraquet in north-eastern New Brunswick, has set up a venture capital fund that supports local development including social economy organizations. Examples of this link between credit unions and social economy development can be found in other parts of Canada as well. Fairbairn, Ketilson, and Krebs (1997) detail this link in Saskatchewan, where credit unions have the strongest presence outside of Quebec.

Among credit unions in the west, Vancity serves many social economy organizations through community business banking (see A Closer Look: The Co-operative Auto Network), grants, and partnerships. For example, it partners with B.C. Technology Social Ventures Partners and the Vancouver Foundation in the B.C. Social Enterprise Fund, which provides grants to B.C.-based non-profits that are generating earned income in supporting social and environmental change.

A Closer Look: The Co-operative Auto Network

From one Pontiac Firefly to a fleet of 227 including the latest in hybrids, the Co-operative Auto Network has grown substantially since it was incorporated in 1996. A non-profit co-operative owned by its members, the Network operates in British Columbia in the Lower Mainland and on Vancouver Island. Its start-up financing came from Vancity Credit Union and the Co-operators, and it also received a marketing grant from Environment Canada (Dauncey, 2004). The Network has been debt-free for several years and is now self-sufficient, with members' user fees covering 100 per cent of its operating costs. Any surplus at the end of the year goes to purchasing new vehicles, outreach, or updating office supplies (Jensen, 2001).

By 2004, total revenues for the Co-operative Auto Network exceeded $1 million. Its financial stability allows the organization to grow and innovate. It obtains new vehicles through leasing and buying, with about 20 per cent of the cars now owned by the Network. It averages one car for every twenty members, and gets about fifty new members every month. The Network also has secured from Vancity a $500,000 revolving line of credit with a favourable interest rate (NEDG, 2006b).

To join the Co-operative Auto Network, members pay a $20 registration fee and $500 for a refundable share. As the Network is a non-profit, neither dividends are issued nor is interest accrued on the shares. If a member leaves the co-operative, 100 per cent of the share value is refunded, less any outstanding charges. Members also pay a low monthly administration fee as well as an hourly and per kilometre usage fee. This covers vehicle maintenance, gas, insurance, cleaning, BCAA membership, and parking. Cars can be booked by the hour or for longer periods.

Charity Banks

In some countries, there are banks operated as non-profits, known as charity banks. For instance, in the UK there is The Charity Bank, in Ireland, Troidos, and in Italy, Banca Etica. Here in Canada, there is one under development, called Vartana. Vartana seeks to be a bank 'of, by and for the voluntary sector' (Vartana, n.d.). The bank already has many prominent backers, and has an agreement with the Vancity subsidiary, Citizens Bank of Canada, with a separate Board of Directors.

Vartana was originally proposed by a 23-year-old, Queen's University student, Aaron Pereira, as a federally regulated banking institution for charities and non-profit organizations (Waldie, 2004). The idea came to Pereira a few years earlier, when he ran into difficulty arranging short-term credit for a charity called CanadaHelps (2008). that he and two friends were starting. Mainstream banks were leery of lending to non-profit groups as they were perceived to be high risk and did not have a consistent cash flow.

Vartana is a Sanskrit word meaning the intersection of community and commerce. It is a registered charity, and all surplus earnings will be reinvested into non-profit organizations. Its mandate is to provide products, services, and advice grounded in an understanding of the voluntary sector and its needs, and it is geared towards small- to medium-sized charities and other non-profit organizations. Its financial products will include deposit products (operating and savings accounts, guaranteed income certificates), credit products (lines of credit, demand and term loans, mortgages, credit cards), and financial advisory services. Initially the services will be available online and through telephone banking, with plans to expand and accept deposits from the general public.

Sources of Financing through the Private Sector

Labour-Sponsored Investment Funds

Labour-sponsored investment funds have been controversial from a business viewpoint and also because many have been taken over by management interests to take advantage of associated tax credits (Hebb and Mackenzie, 2001). Nevertheless, among those that are functioning as were intended, there is evidence of support for organizations in the social economy.

The intended mission of a labour fund is to create and maintain jobs, while realizing a return for investors. In Quebec in the early 1980s, a deep recession resulted in a high unemployment rate, and the closing of many small- and medium-sized businesses. It was at that time that an investment fund controlled by the Quebec Federation of Labour (Fonds de solidarité FTQ or the Solidarity Fund, as it is widely called) was created, which would invest venture capital into small- and medium-sized enterprises in Quebec. Its objectives are the following:

- To invest in Quebec businesses and provide them with services to further their development and to help create, maintain, and protect jobs in Quebec
- To promote the economic training of workers in order to enhance their contribution to Quebec's economic development
- To stimulate the Quebec economy by making strategic investments that will benefit both workers and businesses
- To foster awareness and encourage workers to save for their retirement and help grow the economy by purchasing fund shares.

Since it was launched, the fund has helped create or maintain more than 125,000 jobs and nearly 1,900 companies in all sectors of the economy (QFL, 2007a). As at 31 May 2008, its assets totalled $7.3 billion (QFL, 2008), and in 2007, it invested over $665 million in more than 140 companies (QFL, 2007b).

Another labour-sponsored fund based in Quebec is Fondaction, sponsored by the other major labour federation in Quebec, Confédération des syndicats nationaux (CSN). Fondaction invests in companies that are committed to participatory management, operate in the social economy, practise environmental stewardship, and are concerned with more sustainable development. Fondaction supports nearly 100 companies with investments generally between $2 million and $5 million, and thus creates or maintains thousands of direct and indirect jobs (Canada Business, 2007).

For companies that need smaller investments, the Fondaction has created two partner funds (Canada Business, 2007):

- The Fonds de financement coopératif, which invests between $100,000 and $250,000 in co-operatives and other companies in the social economy
- Filaction, the Fonds pour l'investissement local et l'approvisionnement des fonds communautaires, which finances projects ranging from $50,000 to $150,000.

The Working Opportunity Fund in British Columbia is owned by seven trade unions representing 460,000 employees in British Columbia. It has been operating since 1992, and in 2007 had 50,000 members and assets of $400 million. Half of its assets are invested in small- and medium-sized B.C. businesses (GrowthWorks, 2007) The fund also helped to created the Shareholder Association for Research and Education (SHARE), an organization that operates in partnership with the Canadian Labour Congress, and engages in shareholder action strategies such as child labour campaigns (Quarter, Carmichael, and Ryan, 2008). The Working Opportunity Fund (2007) also has a charitable donation program, which is funded by 0.5 per cent of the securities of the fund. The aim of the program is to support charities in the areas of science, technology, and innovation.

Responsible Investment

Assets invested according to socially responsible guidelines have increased substantially in Canada as more pension funds, mostly in the public sector, adopt socially responsible investment practices, or SRI, as they are called. From 2004 to 2006, SRI assets in Canada increased from $65 billion to $504 billion (Social Investment Organization, 2007).

In addition to this general trend, social economy organizations in particular, are expressing greater concern for the responsible investment of their surpluses, reserve funds, and endowments. In the United Kingdom, a survey of large charities found that 55 per cent had a formal policy on responsible investing, with the most common form (51%) being negative screening (i.e., sanctions such as withdrawal or investment boycotts of companies who invest in particular industries such as tobacco and military production), followed by indirect engagement with companies through fund managers (28%). The most important reason these charities gave for developing an ethical policy was to avoid investments that conflicted with their aims (Kreander, Beattie, and McPhail, 2006).

Indeed, more and more social economy organization are engaging in an investment approach for their surpluses, reserve funds, and endowments known as 'mission-based investing.' Mission-based investments are not a distinct range of products or a market segment, but rather an approach that 'targets a market rate of return and also helps a foundation to achieve its mission' (New Economics Foundation, 2008: 9). This positive screening approach looks at whether or not an investment contributes to the organization achieving its mission and is closely related to another approach known as 'program-related investments.' However, the key difference is that program-related investments are part of an organization's programming strategy, thus a lower rate of return is acceptable.

The United Church of Canada invests its pensions and foundation funds in a balanced fund made up of companies with 'best of sector' track records in environmental stewardship, occupational health and safety, community consultation, employee relations, product safety, and ethical business practices. The investment policy, developed by the United Church of Canada Foundation (2001: 1) and Michael Jantzi Research Associates, specifies positive and negative screening criteria: 'The criteria are intended to honour the Church's desire to invest its funds in a manner consistent with both its values and mission, and the fiduciary responsibilities of the trustees of the funds.'

At the end of 2007, the foundation had investments from fifty-eight United Church organizations valued at $15.45 million. Its average return over the past five years was 10.46 per cent (United Church of Canada Foundation, 2008).

Tides Canada (2006) invests all of its financial assets using socially responsible investment principles. In 2006, these assets amounted to $15.3 million. Its investment managers are instructed by Tides to invest in organizations 'whose policies and practices are consistent with our mission to build a more just and sustainable world ... [and] to ensure that our investments do not contravene the work of our grant recipients, charity and non-profit partners, and donors' (Tides Canada, n.d.: 1). In order to do this, both goals and screens are used. Tides' goals are to invest in organizations that demonstrate that (ibid.):

- Their products and services contribute to basic human needs, including consumer health and safety.
- They exhibit superior performance in the protection of basic human rights, and the hiring, training, and promotion of minorities and women.
- They exhibit innovation with respect to products, which protect or enhance the environment, and/or which evidence superior performance relative to waste utilization and pollution control.
- When operating internationally, they meet the local standards of host countries for all of the above social and environmental dimensions.

Tides uses screens to avoid investing in organizations with the following characteristics (Tides Canada, n.d.: 1):

- Their products and services are unsafe in normal use (such as tobacco and gambling).
- They are weapons systems contractors or derive more than 10 per cent of their gross revenues from defence contracting or sub-contracting.
- They do not practise responsible corporate governance.
- They broadly violate fair labour practices.
- They have a record of failure to abide by federal, provincial, and local environmental regulation and/or are participating in nuclear power plant technology. (This screen could be re-evaluated if nuclear technology evolves.)
- They are responsible for systematic human rights violations or contribute to repressive governmental practices. These screens will also be applied to government debt where appropriate.

The Atkinson Charitable Foundation (n.d.), was founded in 1942 by Joseph Atkinson, the former publisher of the *Toronto Star*, Canada's largest newspaper. With $60 million in assets in 2007, it pursues its mission not only through its programs, but also through its mission-based investment policy including proxy voting and shareholder engagement. For Atkinson, this means engaging with companies who appear to rely on contingent work or precarious employment. For example, 'retailers, hotels and other employers increasing their use of temporary or part-time workers not covered by benefits or statutory entitlements; property management, construction, and other companies contracting through intermediaries such as temp agencies and independent subcontractors, often blurring the legal relationships and responsibilities of the employer; and consumer retail supply chains that exploit agricultural, transportation and forestry workers.'

Institutional investors such as pension funds play an important role in responsible investment and in supporting the social economy. In Canada, one example of this is the regional and social targeting by the Caisse de dépôt et placement du Québec, the organization that manages Quebec's public pension plans (Quarter, Carmichael and Ryan, 2008). In 2005, Quebec's government approved an act with respect to the Caisse that specifically states that part of the Caisse's objectives is 'contributing to Québec's economic development.' The Caisse de dépôt et placement du Québec (2007) has pursued this commitment through Quebec investments including private equity, equity markets, fixed income and currencies, and real estate. In 2007, this amounted to about 17 per cent of its total investments at fair value.[2]

Another example is the role of unionized labour pension funds in supporting economically targeted investments, or ETIs. *Economically targeted investment* is defined as 'investment designed to produce a competitive rate of return commensurate with risk as well as create collateral economic benefits for a targeted geographic area, group of people, or sector of the economy' (Bruyn, 1987: 6). In Canada, the real estate development company, Concert Properties (2007), is an example of an economically targeted investment. Concert was established in 1989 and is owned by twenty-six union and management pension funds. Its original mandate was to provide economically priced rental housing in British Columbia, but it has since expanded its real estate activities to include condominiums and commercial properties in three provinces: British Columbia, Alberta and Ontario. Since 1989, it has

2 As at 31 December 2007, the Caisse had total investment assets of $222.8 billion, including total assets in Quebec of $37.8 billion. This was made up of private equity ($6.0 billion), equity markets ($2.4 billion), fixed income and currencies ($22.4 billion), and real estate ($6.9 billion). Assets are classified as a Quebec investment if the head office of the company is located in Quebec, or in the case of real estate investments, the property is located in Quebec.

constructed over 8,000 rental and condominium homes, and in doing so created more than 15.2 million person-hours of on-site employment.

The use of pension funds for economically targeted investment is more fully developed in the United States, in particular in real estate where, like Concert Properties in Canada, pension funds have pooled their investments, for example, the AFL-CIO Housing Investment Trust, which has created 'over 80,000 units of housing, approximately half of which are affordable to low- or moderate-income households' (AFL-CIO Housing Investment Trust, 2007). The trust invests in mortgage securities that finance housing development, but adds the condition that the developer must employ union labour – an important collateral benefit for the sponsors. In addition to real estate development, economically targeted investments by pension funds also involve regional and social targeting. CalPERS (California Public Employees' Retirement System) targets a portion of its investments for California (11% by 2004), and in 2002 CalPERS began to target underserved areas of the state (Manley, Hebb, and Jackson, 2008).

Pooled Sources of Financing

Community Investment Funds

Community investment funds are defined as: 'a pool of capital that is used to make loans and/or loan guarantees and/or equity capital, in conjunction with technical assistance, to low income individuals, micro enterprises, affordable housing project, non profits, environmental projects and community asset development initiatives ... Those who invest in community investment funds want their money to create local jobs, enterprises, affordable housing, essential community services, and provide financial services to low-income individuals' (SIO and RCDC, 2003: 3).

Community investment funds have arisen because of the difficulties that social economy organizations face in accessing funding, especially in the start-up of new organizations. Often these funds pool resources from community groups, co-operatives, non-profits, financial institutions, government, and private individuals. In 2006, there were fifty-seven community investment funds in Canada, with assets totalling $809 million (SIO, 2007).

Many of these funds are part of a network called the Canadian Community Investment Network Co-operative (CCINC), started in 2004 as a means of collaboration among Canadian community financing organizations. Formally incorporated as a co-operative, CCINC now has twenty-five organizations as members and allies. Members include community loan funds, micro-loan funds, peer loan funds, social investors, co-op funds, financial institutions with community investment programs, and community futures development corporations. As a member, each organization is entitled to full participation at democratically run membership meetings and can run for election to the board of directors. The network itself has the following five goals: (1) to promote the alternative community investment sector; (2) to support the sustainability and growth of member organizations and the sector; (3) to work to increase the amount of accessible and affordable capital for use by member organizations; (4) to improve the capacity of practitioners through improved practice and information sharing; and (5) to work with all levels of government to improve the regulatory environment for community investment in Canada.

One of the members of CCINC is the Canadian Alternative Investment Co-operative (CAIC), started in the 1980s by a number of religious communities that wanted to pool their funds and make investments that support positive social change and promote alternative economic structures. In 2008, CAIC had forty-eight organizations as members and a lending pool of approximately $7 million. It provides mortgages of up to 75 per cent of the appraised value of property to charitable organizations, loans for social and affordable housing initiatives, and social enterprise financing in the form of loans and equity investments (CAIC, n.d.; CCINC, n.d.).

Yellowknife Glass Recyclers, a worker co-op, is an example of an organization that benefited from CAIC funding. It received a loan from CAIC to help develop marketing materials, expand its website, and grow its operations. The Bread of Life Centre in Port Alberni, British Columbia, received a first mortgage from CAIC that allowed it to purchase a building for its Soup Kitchen and Thrift store. The Christie Ossington Neighbourhood Centre in Toronto also received mortgage funding from CAIC so it could buy the building it was renting at the time.

Social Enterprise Funds

Social enterprise funds help individuals put together a business plan to start a social enterprise and offer capital funding when the enterprise is ready to scale up. Social enterprises have both financial and social goals. An important component is also educational, and mentors help with business expertise as well as educational seminars.

One example is the Social Enterprise Fund (SEF, n.d.), a joint initiative of the Edmonton Community Foundation, the City of Edmonton, and the United Way of Alberta. It was started in February 2008, but took eight years to get off the ground. It aims to become an $11 million fund, with $21 million in loans in its first five years.

The Social Enterprise Fund offers non-profits and social enterprises flexible term loans along with business expertise and educational seminars. The SEF has several financial packages with flexible terms, near prime, for example, the following:

- Housing or mission related: up to $500,000, 1-year term
- Building purchases: up to $250,000, 10-year term
- Existing social enterprises: up to $150,000, 5-year term
- New social enterprises: up to $50,000, 8-year term

The Social Enterprise Fund also offers Path to Loan grants of up to $10,000 to help with project planning, consultation, feasibility analysis, and business planning, and these can cover up to 50 per cent of total costs. Some of the Edmonton organizations that have benefited from the Social Enterprise Fund are Women Building Futures, Kids in the Hall Bistro, Habitat for Humanity Restores, and Earth Water.

Community-Based Financial Institutions

The Fiducie du Chantier de l'économie sociale (2007), or Chantier Trust, makes loans to social economy organizations with a fifteen-year capital repayment holiday. This is also known as 'patient capital.' The Trust acts as an intermediary between the financial market and social economy enterprises, and by socializing risk and offering a diversified portfolio, it is able to lower financing costs.

As noted in chapter 3, the fund's primary contributors are the following: the federal government department, Canada Economic Development, which provided a non-recoverable contribution of $22.8 million; the Fonds de solidarité FTQ; the government of Quebec; and Fondaction, the Fonds de développement de la CSN pour la coopération et l'emploi, which respectively contributed $12 million, $10 million, and $8 million in the form of debentures.

The Trust offers loans of between $50,000 and $1.5 million through two investment forms:

- Operations Patient Capital: to finance costs related to the working capital fund, market launching of new products, and the acquisition of office and computer equipment, automotive equipment, machinery, and tools. Operations patient capital is unsecured.
- Real Estate Patient Capital: to finance costs directly related to the acquisition, construction, or renovation of real estate assets such as land, building, and warehouses. Real estate patient capital is secured by a real estate mortgage subordinate to real estate mortgages that may be held with other lenders.

Loans can represent no more that 35 per cent of project-related costs. The first round of funding totalled $4.7 million and was divided among fourteen social economy businesses in Quebec (Fiducie du Chantier, 2008). Among the organizations funded in the first round were Le Recycle-Centre, which received $350,000 of their total project cost of $1.9 million to expand and renovate their premises; Coopérative de l'Université de Sherbrooke, which received $250,000 out of a total project cost of $1.45 million to make leasehold improvements and purchase equipment for its co-operative bookstore and computer services; and Les Serres coopératives de Guyenne, a greenhouse and tomato production facility, which received $250,000 out of a total project cost of $1.68 million to purchase equipment.

Conclusion

This chapter discussed the many manifestations of financing for social economy organizations, with a focus on the growing and impressive array of mechanisms within and related to the social economy. However, it is noteworthy that much of the funding for social economy organizations comes from either government or from conventional sources in the private sector like banks. Recall that in Figure 1.1, where we presented the social economy using a Venn diagram, we argued that this is appropriate because it emphasizes the interaction between the social economy and the private and public sectors. Nowhere is this truer than in finance. In chapter 3, we described the important role of regional development agencies, financed by government, in community economic development. Organizations such as the Atlantic Canada Opportunities Agency (discussed in chapter 3), while set up primarily to finance conventional businesses, play a critical role in funding community economic development within the social economy. Similarly, as discussed in the Case for Analysis at the end of chapter 1, the Federal Business and Development Bank played a critical role in the expansion of The Big Carrot. Nevertheless, within the social economy, a growing and diverse array of financial institutions are making available micro-credit and other forms of development funds, and also setting an example in how responsible investment can be undertaken. In this regard, organizations within the social economy may be viewed as a model that could influence the practices of other sectors of the economy.

This point then underlines a fundamental feature of the social economy: it is different in key respects but it is part of a broader economy and a broader society. It is dependent on the private and public sectors, but it interacts and influences those other sectors in important ways, not only in providing a social infrastructure but also in modelling approaches that some would argue are worth emulating.

* * *

DISCUSSION QUESTIONS

1. In your view, are special funding programs needed for social economy organizations in general? If not, are they needed for specific forms of organizations?
2. Is it logical to refer to a form of financing that is social, in other words, social finance?
3. Is the Cape Breton Labourers' Benevolent Fund a generalizable approach or one that is specific to a particular culture?
4. Should social economy organizations be less dependent on government funding?
5. Is venture philanthropy an oxymoron?
6. Can credit unions/caisses populaires and conventional financial institutions assume a more important role in financing social enterprises?

* * *

Case for Analysis: Options for Homes

Financing is a major challenge in developing housing for persons with moderate and low incomes, particularly in large cities. One response to this problem is non-market or social rental housing. However, these programs are dependent on government subsidies, and therefore are very vulnerable to the whims of government policy change. In 1993, when the federal government decided to disengage from social housing and download the responsibility to the provinces, many development groups that had been providing social housing folded.

Michel Labbé worked for fifteen years for one of these development groups, Lantana Non-profit Housing Corporation. Lantana had partnered with Canada Mortgage and Housing Corporation and other government agencies to develop non-profit and co-operative housing targeted primarily at persons with below average incomes. When the federal government stopped funding these projects, Labbé was determined to find another solution that did not rely on government funding. Based on some work he had done in Johannesburg, South Africa, he felt that it was more cost effective to focus on affordable ownership than affordable rental accommodation.

In comparison to renting, homeownership also brings many personal and societal benefits. Some of these include the following (MacNeil, 2004):

- Positive impacts in personal well-being, fulfilment, self-esteem, sense of control and stability
- A more vested interest in the community where homeowners live and more concern for what goes on around them
- Higher participation levels in community life and local activities leading to an improvement in neighbourhood and community quality of life
- A greater likelihood of voting in elections than renters
- When low-income renters become homeowners, there is a shift in thought processes, attitudes, and level of responsibility. People shift from being clients of social services to being partners in their communities.

Thus was the beginning of Options for Homes, an innovative, award-winning social enterprise incorporated in 1992 as a non-profit organization under the Corporations Act of Ontario. Its purpose is 'to disseminate information and to provide advice and to assist in the development of residential non-profit concerns and undertakings that will produce housing at cost' (Evenson and Millar, 2005: 33).

Options for Homes acts as a contracted development consultant to help moderate to low-income homebuyers organize as a building co-operative that will develop and purchase condominiums. Essentially, the building co-operative is transitional and dissolves once its obligations to the condominium are completed. The model's uniqueness stems from a financing technique explained further on in the case involving a second mortgage arrangement with an arms-length non-profit organization called Home Ownership Alternatives.

Fifteen years after its beginnings, Options for Homes has been the driving force in helping over 1,500 people and families in eight developments in the Greater Toronto Area own their own homes. Developments following the Options model have also been completed in other areas such as Montreal and Waterloo.

Governance

Options for Homes is designed as a workers' collective that selects its Board of Directors from among its employees. To be considered for membership on the Board, an employee has to work for the organization for five years. As of 2003, Options for Homes had a Board consisting of three persons.

Although situated in the same building, Home Ownership Alternatives, the financing arm for the Options, has a separate board of fifteen directors: seven members appointed from the community sector; four from among the building co-operatives and condominium projects financed by Home Ownership Alternatives; and four members from the co-operative sector.

The Options for Homes Model

The Options model can be broken down into three main areas: (1) Development and construction; (2) Organization; and (3) Financing. While each component, on its own, is not unique, the way they are combined is distinctive in the Canadian housing market.

DEVELOPMENT AND CONSTRUCTION

The key to a successful Options project, and also its greatest challenge, is finding affordable land. Options seeks out possible locations in up-

and-coming neighbourhoods. Some sites found in the past were owned by the federal government agency, Canada Lands (e.g., a development south of the former Downsview airport in Toronto) and were essentially dormant. Given the nature of Options' business focus, Canada Lands has been willing to delay the payment for the property until condominiums are completed, thereby reducing the development costs.

For the construction process, Options has developed a long-term business relationship with Deltera Ltd. and its sub-contractors. Deltera is the same company that builds for Tridel, an award-winning developer based in Toronto. As a result, Options has been able to build units with high quality work and design, on time and within budget. In addition, because of Deltera's track record and reputation, bonding securities are not required, which provides significant savings for the owners.

ORGANIZATION

Once a potential site has been found, Options for Homes undertakes a marketing campaign to bring together potential buyers. Flyers are distributed in the neighbouring communities inviting people to attend a sales presentation close to the construction site. At the presentation, non-commissioned sales agents, many of them owners in other Options developments, answer questions. Potential buyers are invited to purchase an information package for $100 that goes into more detail and provides all the necessary legal information and forms to start the purchase process. It also provides them with a personal appointment with a sales agent to answer any further questions. Once the forms are signed, buyers have a 10-day cooling-off period if they wish to reconsider their decision. If they go ahead with the purchase, they then automatically become a member of the building co-operative development corporation that will develop the project.

For a fee of 2 per cent of the overall capital cost of the development, Options for Homes acts as a consultant to the building co-operative. It finds contractors, architects and lawyers, arranges financing, and provides marketing for the project. A review of its operating results in 2005 found that Options operates frugally, with modest costs, compensation arrangements and lower fees than would be found in for-profit development companies (Evenson and Millar, 2005).

Together, members of the co-operative and Options staff finalize the new development. More importantly, at monthly meetings the incoming owners have input into the design and décor of their condominium and the building itself. The building co-operative is in place until the development is completed and all of the contractual obligations have been met, at which point it dissolves. When the building is completed, it is registered as a condominium and each co-op member becomes an owner of a condominium suite. Final closing consists of the discharge of the construction loan, mortgage registration by the individual purchasers, and registration and assignment of the second mortgage to Home Ownership Alternatives. Essentially, the development becomes the owners' responsibility at that point: the members of the condominium elect a board of directors that assumes legal responsibility, and Options staff moves onto its next development, though it remains available for advice to the condominium. The condominium is then no different legally than any other condominium development, though its history as a building co-operative differs from the typical condominium.

The dissolution of the building co-operative typically takes three years. After all the contractual obligations are met, any remaining assets are distributed back to the members of the co-operative or are used to further the development of other co-operatives. In previous projects, members have used these funds to finance building improvements, issue individual rebates, and provide a fund to help low-income people buy homes (Gibney, 2003). Recently, the funds have also been used to provide solar heating and car sharing for the developments as well as to expand the model internationally.

FINANCING

Options' third function is to facilitate an innovative financing mechanism through Home Ownership Alternatives for initial purchasers, similar to a second mortgage. The amount of this alternative second mortgage is determined by taking the difference between the basic purchase price of a unit, less its basic cost. Typically, this amounts to about 15 per cent above the basic cost.

The basic purchase price is determined by an independent appraisal of the unit's expected market value, and is based on market prices and comparables. The purchaser is not able to negotiate the unit's basic purchase price. The basic cost of a unit is the estimated cost of construction pro-rated to each unit, and exclusive of any upgrades. The total purchase price then amounts to the basic cost plus the amount of the second mortgage and any extras (Evenson and Millar, 2005). However, the purchaser is not required to make any payments on the alternative second mortgage unless the unit is sold or rented. This also prevents the unit from being 'flipped' by speculators (Guthrie, 2006).

This alternative second mortgage essentially represents part of the profit a private condominium developer would receive on the sale of units (Evenson and Millar, 2005). Upon resale, these deferred profits plus a proportion of any appreciation in the unit are paid to Home Ownership Alternatives. Any proceeds to Home Ownership Alternatives must be used to develop subsequent affordable housing projects. In 2008, Home Ownership Alternatives held assets of $38 million plus access to additional cash of $12 million.

Affordability of Housing

Purchasers of Options' homes have annual incomes as low as $20,000, with some as high as $100,000 and must make a minimum five percent down-payment. Options estimates that the total savings per unit in the Greater Toronto Area averages about $40,000. The affordability of these condominiums for moderate- to low-income purchasers is accomplished in three ways (Evenson and Millar, 2005):

1. Condominiums are produced at a lower cost (about 15% lower) than private, for-profit developments through significantly lower marketing and administration costs, more modest suite finishes, and few common amenities. Deferred fees and land costs also contribute to lower development costs.
2. An alternative second mortgage is offered that requires no payments until the unit is resold, thus reducing monthly carrying costs.
3. As there are fewer amenities and common areas, monthly condominium fees are also lower (about 10–20% lower than other modest similar units).

Current projects are also taking advantage of Canada-Ontario Affordable Housing Program – Homeownership Component funding, and seeking municipal concessions on land and fees. Options is also pursuing external financial contributions from corporations, banks, and pension funds with the intent of creating a pool of funds that could be used to further reduce the amount of downpayment required by a low-income purchaser (Evenson and Millar, 2005).

Key Success Factors

Michel Labbé, the visionary behind Options, attributes two main factors to a successful Options project: (1) land and (2) a motivated individual to lead the process. 'The biggest challenge is finding patient landowners,' he says. 'We could be doing twice as many buildings if we could get more land. Because we're non-profit we don't have large amounts of money. So we buy residual land' (Greer, 2005: N11). Finding a highly motivated person to lead the development project is also key. In both Waterloo and Montreal, projects have been successful expressively because of this.

What's Next

Labbé views Options as not simply a model for Canada but also one that is global in its reach. In this regard, he is working with groups in Jamaica, Uganda, and Romania to implement their own version of Options. His vision also does not stop at home ownership. He sees the Options model as applicable to other areas such as financing green energy and alleviating poverty.

* * *

DISCUSSION QUESTIONS

1. Draw up a plan to replicate the Options model in your neighbourhood.
2. What other uses do you see this model of financing applicable to?

LEARN MORE

If you want to learn more, visit these websites and sources:

- City of Toronto. (2007). Affordable Housing Committee Agenda. 13 Nov. Retrieved Aug. 25, 2008 from http://www.toronto.ca/legdocs/mmis/2007/ah/agendas/2007-11-13-ah05-ar.pdf.
- CMHC-SCHL. (2002). A Housing Legacy in the Making. Retrieved Aug. 25, 2008 from http://www.canequity.com/mortgage-news/archive/2002/pdf/housing_legacy_in_the_making.pdf.
- Evenson, J., and Millar, D. (2005). *Assessment of Options for Homes*

and the 'Options' Model for the Production of Low-Moderate Income Ownership Housing. Toronto: Canadian Urban Institute. Retrieved Aug. 25, 2008 from http://www.canurb.com/media/pdf/Options_Study2005.pdf.
- Gibney, D. (2003). Santa comes to Shermount – Santa's sack full of cash. *Toronto Star,* 20 Dec., N15.
- Greer, S.S. (2005). No-frills housing choices. Affordability, close-knit communities draw residents back to the basics. *Toronto Star,* 31 Dec., N11.
- Guthrie, S. (2006). Affordable and Accessible Housing in the Upper Fraser Valley: Issues and Opportunities. Retrieved Aug. 25, 2008 from http://www.uwfv.bc.ca/FVHRP%20Final%20Report%2026Feb06.pdf.
- MacNeil, M. (2004). Affordable Homeownership Study Prepared for the City of Calgary. Retrieved Aug. 25, 2008 from http://www.calgary.ca/docgallery/bu/cns/homelessness/ah_homeownership_study_short-04.pdf.

Additional Websites

- Deltera Website. http://www.deltera.com/case_studies/case_study_03/
- Home Ownership Alternatives Website. http://www.hoacorp.ca/
- Options for Homes Website. http://www.optionsforhomes.ca/
- Peter F. Drucker Award Website. http://www.innovation-award.ca/story7845.html?Page=story.htmlandIdeabookID=901
- University of Water Faculty of Environmental Studies Cool Job of the Month. http://www.fes.uwaterloo.ca/cooljobs/labbe07.html

Video

- *Michel Labbé, Social Entrepreneur of the Year Finalist.* (2007). Available online at http://www.youtube.com/watch?v=xs09or0C-gw

* * *

9 Social Accounting and Accountability

> Social accounting is what you get when the restrictions on conventional accounting are removed. It is thus a universe of all possible (organizational or entity) accountings which is only limited by our imaginations.
>
> – Gray (2000)

> Accountability is about holding people to account for their impacts on the lives of people and the planet.
>
> – AccountAbility (2005)

When social economy organizations prepare conventional accounting statements, they use formats developed for profit-oriented businesses. Yet, as we know, the primary mission of social economy organizations is social, and as such their accounting statements miss a critical feature – that their social impact is a vital part of their performance story. In addition, social economy organizations rely in varying degrees on volunteers and members, yet the value of this unpaid service is normally excluded from accounting statements.

Indeed, conventional accounting reflects primarily the needs of owners and managers of profit-oriented businesses (Hines, 1988; Morgan, 1988; Tinker, 1985). However, there is nothing inherent in accounting that limits it to this set of interests. Social accounting has attempted to reorient accounting to a broader set of social variables and social interests.

Experimentation with different social accounting statements emerged in the 1970s as public demand for information related to the social impacts of expenditures grew (Dilley and Weygandt, 1973). At that time, predictions were made that social audits would be required for businesses within the next ten years (Linowes, 1972). These were pioneering attempts, but all focused on the business sector (see Abt and Associates, 1974; Belkaoui, 1984; Estes, 1976; Flamholtz, 1985; Linowes, 1972; Seidler, 1973). Although these attempts did not take hold in the accounting world, they have inspired the re-emergence of social accounting in the twenty-first century, including models that apply to social economy organizations (Mook, Quarter, and Richmond, 2007; Quarter, Mook, and Richmond, 2003).

There are varying definitions of social accounting. All share the common features of expanding the range of criteria that are taken into consideration when measuring performance and looking at the organization in relation to its surrounding environment, both social and natural. Additionally, they stress that the audience for social accounting is broader and may differ from that for other forms of accounting. We define *social accounting* as 'a systematic analysis of the effects of an organization on its communities of interest or stakeholders, with stakeholder input as part of the data that are analyzed for the accounting statement' (Mook et al., 2007: 2). Mook et al. also argue that accounting is a driver of behaviour, and that social accounting can be used as a driver of social change.

Inherent in the social accounting approach is a stakeholder perspective in both looking at how stakeholders contribute to the organization and how they are impacted by it. Freeman (1984: 46) presents the most widely used definition of a stakeholder: 'any group or individual who can affect or is affected by the achievement of the organization's objectives.' This definition casts a wide net and is refined by Clarkson (1995), who subdivides stakeholders into primary and secondary. In his words, 'A primary stakeholder group is one without whose continuing participation the corporation cannot survive as a going concern' (1995: 106). He identifies primary stakeholders as: employees, customers, suppliers, investors, and governments and communities that supply laws, regulations, infrastructure, and markets.

Clarkson's list is directed to profit-oriented businesses, but it can be adapted for social economy organizations. For example, volunteers and members play a more important role. We also include the community and the natural environment to signify their importance both to the organization and to a social accounting framework. That said, accounting, and particularly social accounting, also has an obligation to go beyond mirroring the power dynamics of an organization, internally and externally. The accounting analysis should present the organization within its broadest context and should examine its impact on a variety of stakeholders, including those with the least power.

In this chapter, we will look at how social accounting can be used to better tell the performance story of social economy organizations. We will consider the role of accounting in accountability and control and also in driving behaviours that move us towards the economic, social, and environmental sustainability of the organization and of society. The challenges and opportunities of this type of accounting are also discussed.

From Conventional Accounting to Social Accounting

The prevailing definitions of conventional accounting present it as identifying, gathering, measuring, summarizing, and analysing financial data in order to support economic decision-making (American Accounting Association, 1990, 1992). Overall, accounting education treats the discipline as a neutral, technical, and value-free activity, and presents accounting decisions in businesses as being made to achieve the goal of maximizing shareholder wealth (Ferguson et al., 2005, 2006; Hopwood, 1990; Lewis, Humphrey, and Owen, 1992). This traditional approach to accounting is reflected in teaching and professional development, which tends to focus on technique acquisition (Gray, Bebbington, and McPhail, 1994; Roslender and Dillard, 2003).

Sustained criticisms to conventional accounting emerged in the 1960s and 1970s and gave birth to a second approach known as *critical accounting*. Scholars of critical accounting began to systematically question the assumptions underlying conventional accounting, arguing that accounting practices are neither objective, neutral, nor value-free, and that they create, sustain, and change social reality (Cooper and Neu, 1997; Craig and Amernic, 2004; Gray, 2002; Hines, 1988; Hopper, Storey, and Willmott, 1987; Llewellyn, 1994; Lodh and Gaffikin, 1997; Mathews, 1997; Morgan, 1988; Tinker, 1985). For instance, critical accountants argue that, by the very act of counting certain things and excluding others, accounting shapes a particular interpretation of social reality. This interpretation, which corresponds to particular assumptions about how society functions and should function, has in turn implications for decision-making and policy (Hines, 1988; Tinker, Merino, and Neimark, 1982).

Critical accounting also urges us to reflect on the conditions and consequences of accounting, and to consider accounting within a broad, societal context (Lodh and Gaffikin, 1997; Roslender and Dillard, 2003). Critical accounting asserts that organizations have an impact on a wide group of stakeholders and that accountability to these groups is a desirable democratic mechanism (Gray et al., 1997).

Critical accounting seeks not only to understand the world but also to change it, a fundamental difference from traditional accounting. In theory, critical accounting aims to 'engender progressive change within the conceptual, institutional, practical, and political territories of accounting' through all evaluative forms of social praxis (Tinker, 2005: 100). Yet, this goal is hypothetical more than real, as most often, critical accounting theorists develop critiques without suggesting alternative models to address issues of economic, social, and ecological justice in everyday life (Cooper, 2000; Cooper and Hopper, 2006; Dey, 2000, 2002; Gray, 1998). This emphasis on theoretical critique does not detract from the merits of critical accounting. In fact, its contributions have raised important insights to understanding accounting frameworks and practices from a critical perspective. However, for the most part, this approach does not provide accountants with working strategies and tools that challenge traditional accounting practices. This is precisely the intent of social accounting.

Social accounting shares most of the critiques raised by critical accounting, but at the same time provides a working framework that considers a broader range of factors and actors in the accounting process. This broadening is of particular importance to social economy organizations because the statements used in traditional accounting were developed for profit-oriented businesses and then applied to other organizations. Therefore, by creating alternative accounting frameworks, social accounting addresses an important need. It is a broad term that includes a variety of alternative accounting models, including expanded value added accounting, environmental accounting, and sustainability accounting.

Social accounting has been criticized in both traditional accounting and in critical accounting literatures. The traditional response relates to Friedman's (1970: 32) often quoted statement on corporate orientation: 'There is one and only one social responsibility of business – to use its resources and engage in activities designed to increase its profits so long as it stays within the rules of the game, which is to say, engages in open and free competition without deception or fraud.'

From this perspective, social responsibility is narrowly constructed to mean the maximization of profits, and thus any focus outside of this is not in the best interest of the firm.

From a critical accounting standpoint, social accounting is sometimes seen as a discourse that legitimizes the status quo, does not question the role that capitalism plays in perpetuating unequal and exploitive social relations, and provides an illusion that progress can be made by corporations (Everett and Neu, 2000). Lehman (1999: 220) goes even further and states: 'The procedural and instrumental tendencies within reform accounting models can stall the construction of more critical and interpretive models.' Indeed, it is becoming more apparent that the current form of capitalism, 'based on private property rights, growth and expansion, competition, maximizing consumption of non-essentials, maximizing returns to shareholders and directors and so on,' is not sustainable (Gore, 2006; Gray, 2005; Gray and Milne, 2004: 73; Robèrt, 2000).

This critical accounting perspective lends itself to a form of nihilism because it does not give accountants any agency to contribute to social change through innovating accounting frameworks and practices. We argue instead that accountants have the option of continuing with the current accounting systems that sustain the status quo or creating more democratic, transparent, and participatory accounting practices in the context of a broader strategy for social change. The assumption underlying the approach presented in this chapter is that accounting can be an agent of social change, and, moreover, this point is of particular importance to accounting practices for social economy organizations, which as noted, are set up for different purposes than profit-oriented businesses.

Before we look at some of the innovations in social accounting, we return to the concept of accountability and discuss how it applies to social economy organizations.

Social Economy Organizations and Accountability

It is important to note that accountability in social economy organizations differs from that in the private and public sectors. In the for-profit sector, organizations are ultimately accountable to one stakeholder, the shareholder or owner, whose primary concern is return on investment, and the competitive marketplace provides a mechanism for accountability (Herzlinger, 1996), In the public sector, governments are held to account to voters by mechanisms such as political constituencies, public mandates, oversight agencies, media scrutiny, and checks and balances (Kearns, 1994).

For social economy organizations, there are multiple accountabilities involving numerous actors, mechanisms, and standards of performance (Ebrahim, 2003a). To add to the complexity, there are member organizations, service organizations, and network organizations with differences in mission, philosophy, structure, and standard operating procedures (Ebrahim, 2003b). As you know from the earlier chapters, organizational form also varies and includes various types of non-profits, co-operatives, credit unions, and organizations formed as for-profits, but with a social mission. Generally, for social economy organizations, there are four important issues to address in terms of accountability: effectiveness (achieving mission), efficiency (getting the most out of resources), risk (minimizing), and corruption (guarding against individuals benefiting excessively) (Herzlinger, 1996).

Approaches to accountability can be either reactive or proactive. Reactive responses often occur as a result of internal crises, damage control, shifting societal values and expectations, or obligations such as with grants and contracts. These obligations are typical for public sector non-profit organizations, community economic development organizations, and others relying on external funds (Abraham, 2006). For example, outside stakeholders such as funders establish rules to monitor organizations and ensure they are in compliance with those rules (Ebrahim, 2003a). Each funder may have its own rules and reporting requirements. Accounting is thus used as a way of tracking and monitoring how the organization spends the funds that have been entrusted to it. Proactive accountability is driven by the desire to influence and shape the environment in which the organization operates. In some cases, it is done to define and shape standards that eventually may become mandated.

Accountability mechanisms can be functional or strategic. Most common accountability mechanisms are functional, such as accounting for fund expenditures or to seek out cost efficiencies. Most often, these mechanisms are designed to support and facilitate organizational objectives, and take a short-term perspective on impacts. Strategic mechanisms, by comparison, are more visionary and require a broader approach. This may involve umbrella organizations in national-level policy debates to support or facilitate the pursuit of sector objectives or the development of long-term approaches to sustainability (Ebrahim, 2003a; Gray, 2000; Mook and Sumner, 2010).

Social accounting can be connected to both accountability and control. Social accounting designed to support and facilitate organizational objectives includes: assessing risk, managing stakeholders, image management, public relations, seeking out efficiencies, and maintaining legitimacy. Social accounting designed to support and facilitate the pursuit of societal objectives would include stakeholder rights to information, transparency, openness, and describing the social and environmental costs of economic success (Gray, 2000). Sustainability is an example of a societal objective, indeed a highly important social objective, and social accounting for sustainability is discussed next.

Social Accounting for Sustainability

Sustainability is a relatively new term in the English language, first used in 1970s. During this decade, a number of events paved the way for its acceptance. In 1972, the United Nations Conference on the Human Environment launched the word. In addition, the OPEC oil crisis, beginning in 1973, stimulated a debate about the future of natural resources. At the same time, the Club of Rome, an informal international organization made up of scientists, educators, economists, humanists, industrialists, and national and international civil servants, published *The Limits to Growth* (Meadows et al., 1972) that highlighted the dangers of exponential growth in a resource-limited world. These crises demanded a concept that could highlight the need for a systematic response – the concept of sustainability (Sumner, 2005). This debate is crucial to the social economy as its ultimate aim is a more sustainable society, one that is socially responsible, economically fair, and environmentally viable.

The defining moment in the sustainability debates was undoubtedly the *Report of the World Commission on Environment and Development* (WCED) in 1987, commonly known as the Brundtland Report. The report defined *sustainable development* as 'development which implies meeting the needs of the present without compromising the ability of future generations to meet their own needs' (WCED, 1987: 1). Far from advocating any limits to growth, the report called for a new era of growth, a position that accounted for its overwhelming popularity among politicians, economists, and business elites. Although the report brought sustainability to international attention and made it a household word, its definition was still vague.

Sustainability is widely applauded, but it is also a source of confusion because most cannot explain its meaning (Sumner, 2005). Indeed, achieving sustainability in its biological sense is impossible and unrealistic as almost any action will deplete the biosphere to some degree (Gray, 1992).

One way of understanding sustainability is through the idea of the civil commons, defined as 'any co-operative human construct that protects and/or enables the universal access to life goods' (McMurtry, 1999: 1). Many social economy organizations are part of the civil commons. In other words, the civil commons is what people ensure together to protect and further life, as distinct from money aggregates (McMurtry, 1998). From this understanding, we can define *sustainability* as a set of structures and processes that build and protect the civil commons (Sumner, 2005). The structures can be either formal or informal, as long as they build the civil commons. Formal structures include governments, as well as many social economy organizations. Informal structures centre on traditions and customs such as mutual aid and neighbourliness. The processes involve forms of ongoing development such as teaching, learning, researching, writing, collaborating, and decision-making, as long as they build the civil commons. These structures and processes work together dynamically to build the co-operative human constructs that protect and enable universal access to life goods – the essence of sustainability.

If sustainability involves a set of structures and processes that build the civil commons, and social accounting influences and analyses, through stakeholder engagement, the resulting effects of an organization on its communities of interest or stakeholders, then social accounting for sustainability is a process that influences and analyses, through stakeholder engagement, whether or not an organization contributes to building the civil commons, and the resulting effects on its communities of interest or stakeholders (Mook and Sumner, 2010). Thus, if we understand sustainability as oriented towards life values, instead of monetary values, we can take actions that aspire towards sustainability, promoting individual, community, and environmental well-being. Social accounting provides a tool and process that allows us to examine how organizations build, protect, and enable structures that drive behaviour towards or away from sustainability (Mook and Sumner, 2010). For example, social accounting could include analysing and reporting fair wage and benefit packages for paid employees, skills development programs for volunteers, ethical purchasing policies, and the responsible use of non-renewable energy.

Another framework that provides a clearer concept of sustainability is the one developed by the Natural Step, and which is described in more detail later in this chapter. Briefly, the Natural Step framework is based on the natural laws of science and outlines the system conditions for sustainability to occur (Robèrt, 2000: 245):

> In order for a society to be sustainable, nature's functions and diversity are not systematically subject to:
>
> I. increasing concentrations of substances extracted from the Earth's crust;
> II. increasing concentrations of substances produced by society;
> III. physical impoverishment by over-harvesting or other forms of ecosystem manipulation; and that
> IV. resources are used fairly and efficiently in order to meet basic human needs worldwide.

Social accounting would then report on how an organization's activities contribute to unsustainability, with the intention of driving behaviours that would then minimize these impacts (Chester and Woofter, 2005; see also A Closer Look: Connecting the GRI to the Natural Step Framework below).

Overall, social accounting for sustainability can be seen both as a process and as a tool for connecting the social economy and sustainability, and for contributing to increased human and environmental well-being. It can model sustainable behaviour, reward movement towards sustainability, and discourage movement towards unsustainability. It serves to move organizations away from the approach of making the wrong things 'less bad' (eco-efficiency) to doing the right thing in the first place (eco-justice) (McDonough and Braungart, 2002: 76). In this way, social accounting for sustainability can ultimately be understood as accounting as if sustainability mattered – as if economic, social, and environmental sustainability were the reasons for, not the casualties of, doing business (Mook and Sumner, 2010).

Voluntary Accountability Standards

As concerns grew in the mid-1990s over the quality of various approaches emerging for social and ethical accounting, auditing and reporting, several non-profit organizations began to work on establishing voluntary accountability standards that could be applied internationally. Three of the most common accountability frameworks for sustainable development are AccountAbility 1000 (AA1000), Social Accountability 8000 (SA8000), and ISO 14001. These are discussed next.

AccountAbility 1000

The non-profit organization, AccountAbility, was founded in 1996 as the Institute for Social and Ethical AccountAbility to promote accountability for sustainable development. Some of its founding members were The Body Shop, the European Institute for Business Ethics, the accounting firm KPMG, Oxfam, and Shell. Over the next few years it brought together business, academics, and practitioners to work collaboratively to create a standard to 'support organisational learning, performance and progress towards sustainable development by improving the quality of social and ethical accounting, auditing and reporting' (AccountAbility, 2007). The result was the AA1000 Framework that was launched in 1999. Subsequently, AccountAbility has also launched the AccountAbility Rating that provides a public rating of the world's fifty largest companies, using as a basis the AA1000 standard, the AA1000 Standard for Stakeholder Engagement (2005), and a Certified Sustainabilty Assurance Practitioners Program (2005).

AccountAbility defines accountability as having the following three components:

- *Transparency:* accounting to stakeholders
- *Responsiveness:* responding to stakeholder concerns
- *Compliance:* complying with legal requirements, standards, codes, principles, policies, and other voluntarily commitments.

The principle of inclusivity is integral to all components of the AA1000 Framework. Inclusivity refers to the reflection of the needs and aspirations of all stakeholder groups at all stages. The Framework is divided into three broad categories:

- Scope and nature of process: completeness, materiality, regularity, and timeliness
- Meaningfulness of information: quality assurance, accessibility, and information quality

- Management of process: embeddedness and continuous improvement.

Using these principles, AccountAbility outlines five key stages an organization should go through to create a quality social accounting process: planning, accounting, collecting information, auditing and reporting, and embedding. In all stages, stakeholder engagement is a crucial component. Under planning, the organization is expected to establish commitment and governance procedures, identify stakeholders, and define and review values. In the next stage, accounting, issues are identified, the scope of the process is determined, indicators identified, information collected and analysed, and targets and an improvement plan are developed. From there the organization moves into the auditing and reporting stage. A report is prepared and audited, communicated to the stakeholders, and feedback is actively sought. Systems are also developed to embed the process into the organization's culture (AccountAbility, 1999).

The AA1000 Framework also covers both internal and external audits as a key component to an organization discharging its accountability. Although the Framework does not aim to provide a definitive guide to the format or content of a social report, or to assess performance, it does help to create a framework against which performance can be positioned and against which accountability can be understood.

Two important contributions of the AA1000 process are stakeholder engagement and assurance. In 2005 AccountAbility issued AA1000SES, its Stakeholder Engagement Standard, to help organizations systematically identify and map its stakeholders. In order to do this, six criteria are considered: responsibility, influence, proximity, dependency, representation, and policy and strategic intent (AccountAbility, 2005).

The AA1000AS is AccountAbility's Assurance Standards document. The AA1000AS is the only international standard specifically focused on sustainable development. The purpose of conducting an assurance review is to gauge the accuracy and completeness of the information presented. Assurance can be conducted internally or externally by an independent body. An assurance report provides an opinion on the completeness and reliability of a social accounting report, and is audited to give it credibility. It also provides valuable insights on management systems, data collection, and related processes (Scott and McGhee, 2008).

The AA1000AS presents guidelines for external assurance providers. In order to comply with AA1000AS, an assurance statement must include the following (Scott and McGhee, 2008: 20):

- A statement on use of the AA1000 Assurance Standard, including how the assurance provider applied the AA1000 principles of materiality, completeness, and responsiveness
- A description of work undertaken and a description of level of assurance pursued
- Conclusions as to the quality of the report and underlying organizational processes, systems, and competencies
- Additional commentary, including suggestions for improvements in the organization's corporate social responsibility (CSR) reporting.

SA8000 Standard

Another voluntary auditable certification standard commonly used for the ethical sourcing of products and goods and workplace conditions is Social Accountability 8000, or SA8000. It was created by the non-profit Social Accountability International (formerly the Council on Economic Priorities Accreditation Agency), an organization that is advised by members from business and the social economy, including Amnesty International, Maquila Solidarity Network (Canada), Legacoop (Italy), and Toys 'R' Us (United States).

SA8000 is based on the conventions of the International Labour Organisation (ILO), the Universal Declaration of Human Rights, and the U.N. Convention on the Rights of the Child. It covers the following elements (SAI, n.d.):

- *Child labour:* No workers under the age of 15 years; minimum lowered to 14 for countries operating under the ILO Convention 138 developing-country exception; remediation of any child found to be working
- *Forced labour:* No forced labour, including prison or debt bondage labour; no lodging of deposits or identity papers by employers or outside recruiters
- *Health and safety:* Provide a safe and healthy work environment; take steps to prevent injuries; regular health and safety worker

training; system to detect threats to health and safety; access to bathrooms and potable water
- *Freedom of association and right to collective bargaining:* Respect the right to form and join trade unions and bargain collectively; where law prohibits these freedoms, facilitate parallel means of association and bargaining
- *Discrimination:* No discrimination based on race, caste, origin, religion, disability, gender, sexual orientation, union or political affiliation, or age; no sexual harassment
- *Discipline:* No corporal punishment, mental or physical coercion, or verbal abuse
- *Working hours:* Comply with the applicable law but, in any event, no more than 48 hours per week with at least one day off for every seven-day period; voluntary overtime paid at a premium rate and not to exceed 12 hours per week on a regular basis; overtime may be mandatory if part of a collective bargaining agreement
- *Compensation:* Wages paid for a standard work week must meet the legal and industry standards and be sufficient to meet the basic need of workers and their families; no disciplinary deductions
- *Management systems:* Facilities seeking to gain and maintain certification must go beyond simple compliance to integrate the standard into their management systems and practices.

As of 31 March 2008, 1,693 organizations in sixty-four countries and sixty-one industries, employing 872,052 people, had been certified to SA8000 standards (SAAS, 2008, http://www.saasaccreditation.org/certfacilitieslist.htm). The largest number of accredited facilities was in Italy, India, China, and Brazil.

Firms such as Coop Italia, which are SA8000 certified, have obtained considerable improvements in working conditions. Coop Italia is the largest Italian retail chain, has over 6.5 million members, and employs over 54,000 people. Under their private Coop label they distribute fair trade products, organic foods, eco-labelled products, Forest Stewardship Council (FSC) labelled goods, and Dolphin Safe/Friend of the Sea. Additionally, Coop Italia products are free of genetically modified organisms (GMOs), and cosmetic products are certified as 'not tested on animals' (Tencati and Zsolnai, 2009). Since becoming the first European company to be certified in 1998, Coop Italia has inspired many other Italian companies to do the same. Today in Italy, over 800 companies are SA8000 certified.

ISO 14000 Standards

The International Organization for Standardization (ISO) is a non-profit network of the national standards institutes of 157 countries, one member per country. Its central secretariat is located in Geneva, Switzerland. ISO is the world's largest developer and publisher of international standards for many areas, including food technology, environmental protection, oil and gas, shipbuilding, and building construction.

The series of standards relating to environmental management is ISO 14000, which covers environmental management systems, environmental auditing, eco-labelling, life cycle assessment, environmental aspects in product standards, and environmental performance in evaluation. ISO 14000 standards can be applied to large businesses, small and medium enterprises, social economy organizations, communities, and the public sector (Baxter, 2004). The standards are based on a national consensus derived from stakeholder consultations.

ISO 14001, the international specification for an environmental management system (EMS), was first launched in 1996. It sets out guidelines to help organizations take a systematic approach to identifying the environmental impact of their activities, set environmental objectives and targets, and demonstrate their progress towards these targets to stakeholders. It does not, however, specify how the organization should go about meeting those requirements. New ISO 14000 standards (14064 and 14065) provide tools for greenhouse gas accounting, verification, and emissions trading.

In the year 2006, almost 130,000 ISO 14001 certificates were issued in 140 countries (ACNeilson, 2007). Although the standards are voluntary, in order to be accredited as ISO 14001 compliant, an organization must be audited by a certified ISO 14001 auditor. This same practice is applied for accreditation under AA1000 and SA8000.

Accountability standards offer guidelines to help organizations develop their approach to social accounting and to standardize approaches across organizations, but they do not specify formats. Social accounting, which we turn to next, does present models.

Social Accounting in Practice: Three Approaches

In different parts of the world, organizations are incorporating social accounting in their daily practices. Among social economy organizations, three approaches are beginning to be implemented: (1) the Global Reporting Initiative (GRI); (2) The Natural Step (TNS); and (3) the expanded value added statement (EVAS).

The first two approaches are generally found in what we call 'supplemental social accounting' reports, which separate financial and sustainability reporting (GRI, 2000, 2005; New Economics Foundation, 1998; Sillanpää, 1998; Zadek, 1998).

The last approach, the EVAS, integrates social, environmental, and economic data. In other words, the economic, social, and environmental dimensions are not supplemental to the financial accounts; rather, together they are integral. We use the term *integrated social accounting* to refer to this approach.

Global Reporting Initiative

The first social accounting approach, the Global Reporting Initiative, or GRI, is used by organizations in the for-profit, public, and social economy sectors. The GRI does not challenge conventional accounting formats, but provides a framework to communicate economic, social, and environmental performance in order to measure, disclose, and discharge accountability (GRI, 2006: 40): 'Sustainability reporting is the practice of measuring, disclosing, and being accountable for organizational performance while working towards the goal of sustainable development. A sustainability report provides a balanced and reasonable representation of the sustainability performance of the reporting organization, including both positive and negative contributions.'

Stichting Global Reporting Initiative[1] is the non-profit organization that coordinates the networks that come together to develop the Global Reporting Initiative framework. It is headquartered in the Netherlands, and its mission is 'to create conditions for the transparent and reliable exchange of sustainability information through the development and continuous improvement of its Sustainability Reporting Framework' (SGRI, 2007). The organization was started in 1997 as a partnership between the Coalition for Environmentally Responsible Economies (CERES) in Boston and the United Nations Environment Program (UNEP). It published its first guidelines in 2000. Today, using a global, multi-stakeholder consensus-seeking approach,

1 Stichting is the Dutch word for 'foundation.'

the guidelines are now in their third version (G3), and numerous sector supplements have been developed to provide specialized guidance. One sector supplement under development is for non-profit organizations. More than 1,000 organizations (private, public, and social economy) have self-declared their use of the GRI guidelines in their sustainability reports. Many others use the guidelines on a more informal basis.

The GRI framework also provides important guidance on the materiality aspect of social and environmental reporting, as discussed below. Its ultimate goal is to develop globally accepted sustainability reporting principles (GRI, 2002).

MATERIALITY

Accounting bodies have issued statements on materiality as they relate to the financial accounts. The Canadian Institute of Chartered Accountants refers to materiality in section 1000.17 of its Handbook (CICA, 2003): accountants are to use professional judgment in deciding if an item of information or its aggregate that is omitted or misstated would influence or change a decision.

The International Accounting Standards Board (IASB, 2006: 15–16) also defines materiality: 'Omissions or misstatements of items are material if they could, individually or collectively, influence the economic decisions of users taken on the basis of the financial statements. Materiality depends on the size and nature of the omission or misstatement judged in the surrounding circumstances. The size or nature of the item, or a combination of both, could be the determining factor.'

Materiality is also an important concept in sustainability reporting, but it is concerned with a wider range of impacts and stakeholders. When determining materiality for a sustainability report, both external and internal factors are taken into account (GRI, 2006: 9):

External Factors

- Main sustainability interests/topics and indicators raised by stakeholders
- Main topics and future challenges for the sector reported by peers and competitors
- Relevant laws, regulations, international agreements, or voluntary agreements with strategic significance to the organization and its stakeholders
- Reasonably estimable sustainability impacts, risks, or opportunities

(e.g., global warming, HIV-AIDS, poverty) identified through sound investigation by people with recognized expertise, or by expert bodies with recognized credentials in the field.

Internal Factors
In defining material topics, internal factors taken into account include:
- Key organizational values, policies, strategies, operational management systems, goals, and targets
- The interests/expectations of stakeholders specifically invested in the success of the organization (e.g., employees, shareholders, and suppliers)
- Significant risks to the organization
- Critical factors for enabling organizational success
- The core competencies of the organization and the manner in which they can or could contribute to sustainable development.

These are important guidelines that, if followed, help organizations avoid producing reports that are just simply public relations exercises, or 'greenwashing.'

INDICATOR PROTOCOLS
The Global Reporting Initiative provides protocols for indicators in six dimensions: economic, environment, human rights, labour, product responsibility, and society. Each dimension is then divided into aspects, and each of the aspects is further divided into core and additional indicators. The indicators were determined by a network of thousands of individuals from sixty countries through a consensus-seeking process. Core indicators are those that have been identified as being of interest to most stakeholders and assumed to be material unless deemed otherwise. Additional indicators are those that may be material so some organizations, but generally not to the majority. In total, seventy-nine indicators have been developed, forty-nine core and thirty additional.

A Closer Look: Stichting Global Reporting Initiative

Stichting Global Reporting Initiative, a non-profit organization and part of the social economy, issued its first Sustainability Report in 2007, covering the years 2004 to 2007 (SGRI, 2007). The report provides a good example of the steps taken and information provided by a social economy organization in engaging stakeholders and determining what economic, social, and environmental aspects of the organization were material enough to include in a sustainability report.

As an organization, as of 30 June 2007, Stichting Global Reporting Initiative had a board of directors of thirteen members, a stakeholder council consisting of forty-six members, a technical advisory committee of ten international experts, over four hundred organizational stakeholders, and a staff of twenty-six full-time and six part-time. Of the staff, seven are permanent and the remainder are on contract or volunteer. Revenues for 2006–07 amounted to $4.1 million, while operating costs were $2.4 million and employee wages and benefits, $1.6 million.

One of the important characteristics of social accounting is the engagement of stakeholders in the entire process. Using the criteria of 'influenced by or influences' performance and goals, Stichting Global Reporting Initiative identified five internal stakeholders and seventeen external ones.

Six hundred and sixty-seven individuals in the five internal stakeholders groups were asked by questionnaire to identify from a list, the ten most important and material economic, environmental, and social performance aspects of Stichting Global Reporting Initiative as an organization. The list of potential items of material importance was composed of all the categories, or aspects as they are called in the GRI. Those aspects that received at least 20 per cent of the total number of possible votes were included in Stichting Global Reporting Initiative's reporting. In total, twenty-one aspects were selected from the sixty-seven responses to the questionnaire (a 10 per cent response rate). The Stichting Global Reporting Initiative's Sustainability Reporting team also evaluated each selected aspect for materiality, as described previously, and as a result two more aspects were added.

The next step was to consider all the core indicators associated with the twenty-three aspects selected by the stakeholders. The applicable indicators were also subjected to the materiality test, with the result that twenty-nine indicators were deemed material. You can access the report online for actual results, but some examples of the indicators are the following:

- Economic performance (EC1): Direct economic value generated and distributed, including revenues, operating costs, employee compensation, donations and other community investments, retained earnings, and payments to capital providers and governments
- Emissions, effluents, and waste (EN16): Total direct and indirect greenhouse gas emissions by weight
- Transport (EN29): Significant environmental impacts of transporting products and other goods and materials used for the organization's operations, and transporting members of the workforce
- Employment (LA2): Total number and rate of employee turnover by age group, gender, and region
- Occupational health and safety (LA7): Rates of injury, occupational diseases, lost days, and absenteeism, and total number of work-related fatalities by region
- Diversity and Equal Opportunity (LA14):Ratio of basic salary of men to women by employee category
- Community (SO1): Nature, scope, and effectiveness of any programs and practices that assess and manage the impacts of operations on communities, including entering, operating, and exiting.

The strength of the GRI framework is its focus on stakeholder engagement and on materiality. Although there are many indicators, the framework in which they are set helps to make their complexity manageable and easy to understand across organizations. One limitation is that it is unclear how each indicator actually contributes to achieving sustainability, and although the GRI alludes to placing an organization's performance in context with larger societal issues, contextual indicators are not included in the indicator protocols.

The Natural Step Framework

Another approach to social accounting is the Natural Step Framework, developed in Sweden in 1989 by Dr Karl-Henrik Robèrt, a medical doctor and cancer scientist. He worked with over fifty Swedish scientists to develop a consensus document that described how the biosphere functions, how society influences and is a part of natural systems, how societies are threatening these systems, and what opportunities exist to reverse unsustainable behaviours.

The Natural Step framework uses the idea of the funnel as a metaphor. As it stands now, we are steadily accumulating waste while at the same time resources are diminishing and the Earth's population is rapidly increasing. In the funnel, the space becomes narrower and narrower. The idea is to move towards opening up the funnel again through altering our current emphasis on economic growth and meeting the system conditions described below (Broman, Holmberg, and Robèrt, 2000).

The framework itself consists of three components (Robèrt, 2000). The first is to understand the state of our ecosphere[2] today in light of the decline of its capacity to support our economies as they operate, and ultimately life itself. The over-harvesting of forests, croplands, and fisheries means that ecosystems require more and more resource throughputs such as fertilizers and pesticides in order to produce similar levels. This also means, however, that ecosystems are being subjected to increasing concentrations of polluting substances linked to climate change.

The second component is the idea of 'four system conditions' for sustainability. Based on the natural laws of science, Robèrt outlines the system conditions for sustainability to occur (Broman et al., 2000; Robèrt, 2000: 245):

> For a society to be sustainable, nature's functions and diversity must not systematically be subjected to:
>
> 1. Increasing concentrations of substances extracted from the Earth's crust
> 2. Increasing concentrations of substances produced by society
> 3. Physical impoverishment by over-harvesting or other forms of ecosystem manipulation
> 4. The unfair and inefficient use of resources in order to meet basic human needs worldwide.

---

2 The ecosphere is the space above the earth's crust (lithosphere) until the outer limits of the atmosphere.

The third component suggests strategies to move forward. This involves questioning activities in terms of the second component above, for example, are we systematically decreasing our demand for fossil fuels and unnatural compounds? Are we taking advantage of the low-hanging fruit, for example, by becoming more efficient in the use of resources?

This framework then serves as a tool or compass for organizations to set their strategic direction. Once organizations understand the framework and their role in it, they undertake a baseline assessment, noting where they are contravening the principles of sustainability. From there, they envision a future where the organization is complying with system conditions, and design a program for change that will take them from where they are today to their future vision (Broman et al., 2000).

This is the process followed by the Co-operators and hundreds of other organizations and municipalities including IKEA, the town of Canmore, Alberta, the Atlantic Canada Sustainability Initiative, the resort municipality of Whistler in British Columbia, Santropol Roulant in Montreal, the village of Teslin in the Yukon, the Co-operative Housing Federation of Canada, and the government of Canada.

A Closer Look: Natural Step Canada

Natural Step Canada is a national non-profit organization founded and incorporated in 1996. It provides sustainability training for businesses and community groups, as well as community-wide and regional capacity building and engagement programs. It is one of eleven international offices of The Natural Step founded by Karl-Henrik Robèrt. In 2006, it had a staff of six, and financial expenditures of $564,250. In addition, it received in-kind donations of furniture, equipment, venues and hosts for meetings and workshops, advice, and volunteer time (Natural Step Canada, 2006).[3]

Following the framework that The Natural Step uses to train others organizations, Natural Step Canada started by looking at the gap between its vision of a successful, sustainable non-profit,

3 The value of these was not included in their report.

and where they currently were. The key areas addressed were: use of energy and resources, waste produced, and the ways that they affected others' abilities to meet their fundamental needs (TNS, 2006). As a result, Natural Step Canada decided to take action in the following areas:

- Choosing a central office location so that employees can bike or walk to work
- Using public transportation as much as possible when biking or walking aren't possible
- Using teleconferencing instead of travelling to meetings whenever possible
- Offsetting work-related travel and events with the aim of being carbon-neutral in 2007
- Minimizing paper use by electronic newsletter and document distribution
- Using washable plates, cutlery, and glassware for all board and staff meetings and trainings
- Banking with a co-operative financial institution that is highly committed to social and environmental responsibility
- Screening investments for environmental and social factors
- Purchasing environmentally friendly office and cleaning supplies
- Serving local, organic food for Ottawa events and board meetings
- Purchasing fair-trade coffee and teas for staff and office guests
- Providing free or cost-reduced presentations and workshops to groups interested in sustainability

Taking It Further:
Connecting the GRI to the Natural Step Framework

One of the main criticisms of sustainability reports is they have nothing to do with sustainability (Gray, 2000). As part of their Master's program in Strategic Leadership towards Sustainability at the Blekinge Institute of Technology in Karlskrona, Sweden, Ronan Chester and Jennifer Woofter (2005) took up this challenge and evaluated the 2002 *Global Reporting Initiative Sustainability Reporting Guidelines* against the

Natural Step principles of sustainability. By doing this, they created indicators based on science that would report the organization's contribution to unsustainability. Examples of these indicators, which they call GRI+, included the following principles (Chester and Woofter, 2005: 27–8):

PRINCIPLE ONE

Report on how your organization contributes to systematically increasing concentrations of substances extracted from the lithosphere: (1) mining of metals or minerals; (2) extraction of petroleum-based materials; (3) reliance on metals, minerals, or petroleum-based materials in manufacturing, logistics, etc.; and (4) life cycle analysis of relevant metal/mineral/petroleum products.

PRINCIPLE TWO

Report on how your organization contributes to systematically increasing concentrations of substances produced by society: (1) carbon dioxide, (2) nitrous oxides, (3) chlorofluourocarbons (CFCs), and (4) any other persistent unnatural compounds.

PRINCIPLE THREE

Report on how your organization contributes to systematically increasing degradation by physical means: (1) strip mining; (2) timber harvesting; (3) land use changes; and (4) biodiversity.

PRINCIPLE FOUR

Report on how your organization contributes to conditions which systematically undermine people's capacity to meet their needs: (1) child labour; (2) women's rights; (3) human rights, and (4) fair wage.

Expanded Value Added Statement Accounting for Social Value Added

The expanded value added statement (EVAS) is an integrated approach to social accounting, and focuses on economic, social, and environmental impacts, instead of just the 'bottom line' of financial surpluses or deficits (Mook, 2007). For instance, an EVAS analysis of a housing co-operative was able to identify key aspects of the organization's functioning that were not apparent from traditional financial statements alone (Richmond and Mook, 2001). These key aspects included the impact of unpaid labour (i.e., volunteers), the role of the organization in providing employment, skills development, personal growth for its members, and the contribution of the organization to society through service provision and tax payment.

The expanded value added statement puts together information from audited financial statements along with monetized social and environmental data. Value added is a measure of wealth that an organization creates by adding value to raw materials, products, and services through the use of labour and capital. In contrast to profit, which is the wealth created for only one group – owners or shareholders – value added represents the wealth created for a larger group of stakeholders including employees, society, government, and the organization itself. Indeed, traditional accounting for socially minded organizations falls short in two important areas. First, traditional accounting is incomplete as it ignores a significant source of inputs, in particular, volunteer labour. Second, it is incomplete as it ignores a significant part of its outputs, particularly social and environmental outputs. Because of these two features, traditional accounting leaves much to be desired in helping socially minded organizations measure their performance according to their combined social and economic objectives.

The EVAS also emphasizes the collective effort needed for an organization to achieve its goals, viewing each primary stakeholder as important to its viability as a socially and economically responsible organization. For example, including volunteers and society as stakeholders presents an alternative perspective of an organization than focusing solely on its ability to spend its financial resources. By combining financial and social value added, the EVAS also emphasizes the interconnectedness and interdependence of the economy, community, and environment (Mook, Quarter, and Richmond, 2007).

DETERMINING A MARKET VALUE FOR OUTPUTS

Determining the market value for the outputs of a for-profit firm is relatively straightforward – it is simply the amount of revenues received through sales, or in other words, the amount people have paid for those goods or services in the market. However, for some social economy organizations revenues are seen as inputs[4] and the term *outputs* is generally used to mean the direct products of its activities,

4 The characterization of revenues as inputs might not apply to all non-profits, e.g., those that earn their revenues from market transactions.

for example, such services as mentorship and counselling for clients or running a soup kitchen.

Determining the market value for the outputs of a social economy organization presents special challenges because some of its goods and services may not involve market transactions, and non-financial items such as contributions of volunteer labour are generally ignored. In order to assign a comparative market value (a reasonable rate if it were exchanged in the market) to the outputs of non-profit organizations, the following procedure can be used (Richmond, 1999):

- Look to the market to find a comparative market value for similar goods/services produced in the private sector (e.g., for a non-profit organization delivering employment training services, the cost of similar private sector training could be used).
- If there are no equivalents in the private sector, compare with public sector goods (in the case of employment training, the cost of federal employment training programs could be used).
- If that value is not available, compare with other non-profit sector goods/services, using fees that they receive from government for providing the services. For example, a comparison could be made with fees paid by a government department to an employment-training agency to provide specialized training. In this case, the fees actually do go through the market. However, it has been argued that because the service is delivered by a non-profit organization, which is subsidized by government and uses volunteers, the fees for the service are not an accurate reflection of their real cost in the market.

Another method is to assign the value according to the cost of the resources going into creating the goods and services plus the value of in-kind and volunteer contributions. This can also be thought of as the revenues that might be received in the market, less the allocation for profit.

Estes (1976) also proposed a number of techniques to assign a monetary value to outputs. His examples are largely in relation to profit-oriented businesses, but they are also relevant to social economy organizations.

Surrogate Valuation. 'When a desired value cannot be directly determined, we may estimate instead the value of a surrogate – some item or phenomenon that is logically expected to involve approximately the same utility or sacrifice as the item in which we are interested' (Estes, 1976: 110). He gives the example of estimating the value of building facilities loaned to civic groups and suggests as a surrogate the rent that would be paid for commercial facilities of a similar quality. Another example is establishing a surrogate value for the personal growth and development of volunteers from participating in a non-profit organization. As a surrogate, we use the cost of a community college course in personal development.

Survey Techniques. This procedure involves asking participants what a service is worth to them. To assist in establishing an accurate estimate, Estes (1976) suggests using, as a prompt, a list of either prices or consumer items and asking the respondents to situate the service in relation to others on the list.

Restoration or Avoidance Cost. 'Certain social costs may be valued by estimating the monetary outlay necessary to undo or prevent the damage' (Estes, 1976: 115). Road salt corrodes automobiles, but frequent washings can prevent the damage, something that can be easily priced. Similarly, it is possible to estimate the cost of restoring environmentally damaged land to either industrial or residential use. In the event of a plant closure, many governments require a cleanup of the work site to residential standards, a liability that can be determined.

A Closer Look: Community Village

Community Village, part of a master-planned community, is a composite of four interrelated organizations: an economically targeted investment, a non-profit community police centre, a non-profit neighbourhood house, and the municipal government. This case study of Community Village is in part based on a real community located in Vancouver (Mook, 2007).

The social accounting statement developed for Community Village included several social and environmental aspects: the impact of transit-oriented development; opportunities for an active lifestyle; crime prevention measures; and the impact of making environmentally conscience decisions in purchasing energy-using devices. In order to place a value on these impacts so they could be included in the social accounting statement, the researcher looked to a variety of sources (Mook, 2007).

Valuing Impact of Transit-Oriented Development. The data used to estimate values for the impact of transit-oriented development were taken from two sources: Statistics Canada census data from 2001 for an area adjacent to rapid transit was used to determine the percentage of residents who used public transit to commute to work; and an extensive study of individual and societal transportation cost factors was used to estimate a value for this benefit (Litman, 2005).

Valuing an Active Lifestyle. To estimate the value of an active lifestyle, census data and two academic studies were used. One study looked at effects of physical inactivity on coronary artery disease, stroke, colon cancer, breast cancer, type 2 diabetes or mellitus, and osteoporosis, and estimated the cost of physical inactivity to the Canadian health care system (Katzmarzyk, Gledhill, and Shephard, 2000). The same study found that reducing physical inactivity by 10 per cent has the potential to reduce these expenditures by 7 per cent.

Valuing Cost of Crime. Using data from Statistics Canada, the average direct cost of property crimes in Canada and the associated cost of pain and suffering were determined (Brantingham and Easton, 1998; Leung, 2004). Crime rate data were obtained from the Vancouver Police Department Planning and Research Section (City of Vancouver, 2003).

Valuing CO_2 Emissions and Electricity Costs. To place a value on reducing CO_2 emissions, eleven alternatives were considered, which provided rates ranging from U.S. $11 a tonne to U.S. $835 a tonne. The rate used in this study was an average of these rates, Can $45.79 a tonne (Wigle, 2001). A CO_2 equivalent emissions factor for electricity was obtained from Natural Resources Canada, as was the national average cost of electricity (Natural Resources Canada, 2006).

ESTABLISHING A MARKET VALUE FOR VOLUNTEER AND MEMBER CONTRIBUTIONS

In order to place a value on volunteer labour and member contributions, there are two general schools of thought. The first is based on what economists refer to as 'opportunity costs' and the second is 'replacement costs.'

The opportunity costs approach assumes that 'the cost of volunteering is time that could have been spent in other ways, including earning money that could, after taxes, be spent on desired goods and services' (Brown, 1999: 10). Because time might have been spent generating income, the opportunity cost is tied to the hourly compensation that volunteers normally receive from paid jobs that they hold. However, this procedure could be problematic from an organization perspective because the skills associated with a volunteer service may differ substantially from those for which a salary is being received (Brown, 1999). The hourly rate that Bill Gates received from Microsoft for his services would not be an appropriate standard if he were to spend a day volunteering at a local food bank. An opposite problem might arise if the food bank volunteer were unemployed and, therefore without an hourly wage. It would be incorrect to suggest that the service is worth nothing. After considering the complexities of estimating opportunity costs, including the portion of a paid worker's hourly wage that goes to taxes, and after adjusting for any fringe benefits, Brown (1999: 11) suggests that volunteer time 'be valued at roughly one half to six sevenths of the average hourly wage.' In her view, higher values should be applied when volunteers have increased responsibilities relative to their paid work and lower values should be applied in the opposite circumstance.

Variations of Brown's (1999) procedure to estimate opportunity costs of volunteers were undertaken by Wolfe, Weisbrod, and Bird (1993) and Handy and Srinivasan (2004). Wolfe et al. estimated the marginal opportunity costs by asking volunteers what they would have received if they had worked additional hours for pay. Volunteers not in the labour market (retired, students, unemployed) 'were asked what they believed they could earn if they decided to seek paid employment' (1993: 31). Handy and Srinivasan (2004) also asked volunteers to estimate how much their tasks were worth, thereby arriving at a lower figure than the marginal opportunity cost. These procedures vary, but they share the common feature of looking at the value of volunteering from the perspective of the volunteer and what an hour is worth to that person.

The second approach is called the replacement cost method. This method looks at volunteer value from the perspective of the organization. This procedure, which is favoured by the accounting profession in cases where estimation for volunteer value is permitted, assumes that volunteers could be replaced by wage earners as substitutes in terms of skills and productivity.

There are three approaches to estimating replacement costs: the generalist approach; the specialist approach; and the modified specialist approach (Mook and Quarter, 2004). The *generalist approach* makes the assumption that all volunteer tasks should be treated equally, and is the simplest of the three methods to apply. For example, the Independent Sector, an advocacy organization for non-profits in the United States – utilizes the average hourly wage for non-agricultural workers published in the *Economic Report of the President*, plus 12 per cent for fringe benefits (Independent Sector, 2008). For Canada, Ross (1994) suggested a weighted average of hourly and salaried wages based on Statistics Canada data for employment earnings. He calculated both national and provincial averages.

The *specialist approach*, by comparison, targets the value of a volunteer's role to the market value of the exact task (Brudney, 1990; Community Literacy of Ontario, 1998; Gaskin, 1999; Gaskin and Dobson, 1997; Karn, 1983). For example, Community Literacy of Ontario uses an hourly rate for volunteer literacy workers based on a survey of the average annual salary of full-time support staff of ninety-four community organizations that supply training. Its strength is its precision – comparisons are made for each volunteer task and the market rate for paid work in that category is used. These rates can be found in labour market data generated by government agencies. The limitations are that organizations may not have access to the information needed to make such comparisons and may lack the personnel do the analysis.

The *modified specialist approach* targets the rate for a volunteer task to an organization as well as to the general skill level of the volunteer task. This approach is simpler than the specialist approach and, arguably, more practical. One method is to use the Statistics Canada wage rates based on the North American Industry Classification System (NAICS). This classification system (jointly developed by the statistics agencies of Canada, the United States, and Mexico) classifies organizations (such as businesses, government institutions, unions, and charitable and non-profit organizations) according to economic activity.

The NAICS classification combines all levels of tasks for a class such as sub-sector 624, social assistance. This sub-sector includes organizations engaged in a variety of services such as food and housing within the community and emergency and other forms of relief both to the individual and family. The NAICS classification combines all the tasks for a sub-sector and puts forward an average wage rate for all levels of occupation in that category, making its subsequent use straightforward. For volunteer activities requiring a high level of professional skills, the rate for salaried employees can be used. For those activities requiring basic skills, the rate for hourly employees can be used. For those activities using a mixture of skills, the two rates can be averaged.

A Closer Look: Canadian Crossroads International

Canadian Crossroads International (CCI) is an international non-profit that recruits, trains, and places volunteers from Canada and twelve partner countries in international development projects and internships in those countries, as well as in community development projects within Canada. Its mission is 'to create a more equitable and sustainable world by engaging and strengthening individuals, organizations and communities through mutual learning, solidarity and collective action' (CCI, 2007). CCI is funded primarily through the Canadian International Development Agency (CIDA) and through fundraising.

Each year, CCI recruits, trains, and sends over three hundred volunteers on international development projects and internships in partner countries and Canada. Participants are matched to a variety of community-based activities run by local non-governmental organizations working to address community needs in the areas of health (HIV/AIDS), basic education, sustainable resource management, youth/children, and capacity building of local organizations. Pre-departure orientation, post-placement debriefing and re-entry training, fund-raising, civic engagement, and education on development issues are all integral components of a CCI placement or internship. Travel, accommodation, and related costs are paid by CCI. Volunteers also serve as trainers, on the board of directors, and on eighty different national, regional, local, and country committees governing the various programs.

Statistics Canada wage rates based on the North American Industry Classification System (NAICS) were used to place a value on volunteer contributions of hours for their accounting statement. The activities of the majority of the volunteers of CCI were classified under NAICS sub-sector 54, 'professional, scientific and technical services.' This category includes organizations engaged in activities in which knowledge and skills are the major input and in which much of the expertise requires a university or college education. For the twelve months ending 31 March 2007, the wage rate for hourly paid employees in this category for Canada was $18.54. For salaried employees in this job category, the hourly equivalent was $31.56. For volunteer activities requiring a high level of professional skills, the rate for salaried employees was used. For those activities requiring basic skills, the rate for hourly employees was used. Using these rates, the total value of volunteer contributions was calculated to be $2,402,299. Financial revenues for the same period were $4,967,474. Together, these amounted to $7,369,773, with volunteer contributions comprising almost one-third of the total resources.

PUTTING TOGETHER AN EVAS: PARO CENTRE FOR WOMEN'S ENTERPRISE

In 2007, Carleton University researchers applied the expanded value added method to The PARO Centre for Women's Enterprise, a non-profit organization located in Thunder Bay, Ontario (Babcock, 2007). PARO was started in 1995 to serve communities across the northern Ontario region in order to 'empower women within their communities, strengthen small business and promote community economic development (CED) through integrated and women-centred program delivery' (PARO, 2008). It provides training and business coaching, organizes networking events and peer lending circles, and operates a retail store with the goal of increasing the self-sufficiency and success of women, families, and communities in the North.

For the fiscal year analysed,[5] PARO received $440,019 in revenue, of which $439,493 was spent on programming and administration, and the remainder transferred to its surplus account for the following year. Of those expenses, $254,364 went to employee wages and benefits for 10.5 full-time equivalent paid employee positions. The remainder, $185,129, was spent on purchasing external goods and services.

Six social value added factors were quantified for PARO (for detailed calculations, see Babcock, 2007).

5 Due to a change in fiscal year end, the period covered by this analysis is 11 months rather than the typical 12 months.

1) The skills development of the eighteen volunteers, both board members and non-board members, was measured, and a cost of one course at the local community college ($275) was used as a proxy value. The total of this was calculated to be $4,950.
2) Artisan volunteers who sold their products at the PARO retail store did so at a lower commission rate, and the value of this was estimated to be $1,100.
3) Volunteer hours were determined for board members, non-board members, and artisans. The nine-member board contributed 678 hours in the fiscal period analysed, while non-board members contributed an additional 661 hours. These hours were calculated to have a replacement value of $12,120 and $10,905 respectively. Artisans working in the PARO retail outlet volunteered 1,386 hours, which was valued at $13,860. The total value of volunteer hours thus was $36,885.
4) A value was also placed on the mentorship that the 150 loan circle members received, considered equivalent to a membership at the local Chamber of Commerce ($230). This amounted to $34,500.
5) In additions, speakers at PARO conferences frequently waived their speaking fees, which would have been $20,000.
6) The executive director of PARO frequently provided unpaid consultations and support to other organizations in the CED sector, to the amount of $35,200 for the fiscal period, based on a total of 880 hours multiplied by $40 per hour.

In total, the social factors that were quantified amounted to $132,635. This is the amount that will be shown in the 'Social' column in the EVAS presented here in Table 9.1.

The expanded value added statement consists of two sections: value added created and value added distributed. The first section estimates the value added created by the organization and the second shows the distribution of the value added to the key stakeholders associated with the organization. For the analysis of the value added that is created by the organization, the table is divided into three columns: (1) financial, using information from audited financial statements; (2) social and environmental contributions for which a market-comparison monetary value is estimated; and (3) combined (the addition of the first two columns).

The second part of the statement shows how the value added that was created is distributed to different stakeholders. For instance,

Table 9.1 Expanded Value Added Statement (Partial) for PARO for the Period Ended 31 March 2006[a]

		Financial	Social	Combined
Outputs		$447,019	$132,635	$579,654
Purchases of external goods and services		$192,655		$192,655
Value Added Created		$254,364	$132,635	$386,999
Stakeholders				
Employees	Wages and benefits	$254,364		$254,364
Volunteers	Skills development (1)		$4,950	$4,950
Artisan member volunteers	Lower commissions (2)		$1,100	$1,100
Program participants	Volunteer contributions (3)		$36,885	$36,885
	Mentorship (4)		$34,500	$34,500
	Donated speaker time (5)		$20,000	$20,000
CED sector	Consultations (6)		$35,200	$35,200
Value Added Distributed		$254,364	$132,635	$386,999

[a] As PARO was in the process of changing its year-end, this statement covers an 11-month period, from 30 April 2005 to 31 March 2006

employees received payments for wages and benefits in the amount of $254,364; volunteers received skills development valued at $4,950; artisan member volunteers also benefited by having to pay a lower commission for the sale of their wares ($1,100); program participants received benefits from volunteer contributions, mentorship, and donated speaker time ($91,385); the community economic development sector benefited by consultations given by the executive director of PARO valued at $35,200. In total, the amount of value added distributed is equal to the amount of value added created.

In contrast, PARO's Statement of Revenues and Expenditures shows that it spent slightly less than it received, resulting in a surplus of $1,486 (Table 9.2). This is important because it indicates that the organization is living within its means. However, this statement does not fully show the contribution that PARO is making to the surrounding community. The EVAS, by contrast, indicates that for every dollar spent on external goods and services, PARO generated expanded value added of $2.01, which is 52 per cent higher than had we used financial information only.

Table 9.2 Statement of Revenues and Expenditures for PARO for the Period Ended 31 March 2006[a]

Revenues	
Government grants	$365,711
Sales of goods and services	$74,915
Donations	$7,203
Other	$676
	$448,505
Expenditures	
Advertising and promotion	$9,423
Travel and vehicle	$11,471
Interest and bank charges	$1,253
Office supplies and expenses	$22,171
Occupancy costs	$42,507
Professional and consulting fees	$5,907
Education and training	$21,312
Wages and benefits	$254,364
Other	$78,611
	$447,019
Surplus	$1,486

Source: 2006 T3010 online at http://www.cra-arc.gc.ca.
[a] As PARO was in the process of changing its year-end, this statement covers an 11-month period, from 30 April 2005 to 31 March 2006.

DISCUSSION

Social goods and services, ones that are not given a monetary value, are often a large part of the operations of a social economy organization. Without taking these goods and services into account, there is neither a clear picture of a non-profit's performance nor the contributions made by its volunteers. The expanded value added statement is an experimental methodology to broaden the accounting for non-profits to include social indicators. The EVAS tells a different story than the financial statements alone – and to a different audience. The EVAS helps various stakeholders, particularly volunteers, to see what value they have added to an organization and what value they have received.

The strengths of the EVAS lies in its ability to take a broader look at the organization and the role of volunteers within it and to put this in a larger social-economic perspective. The challenges faced by the

EVAS are shared by other forms of alternative accounting and economics – quantifying and placing a value on goods and services that are seen as 'free.' The EVAS model attempts to integrate financial information for which there are strict methods of accounting, with non-financial or social information – and to develop a methodology that supports this.

The limitations of the EVAS are those that affect the non-profit sector as a whole: there are few resources to track free goods and services. The EVAS method attempts to place a reasonable market value on items and activities that do not pass through the market. Much more research and application will be required to refine this process. However, as the report of PARO shows, the EVAS currently captures and displays information that other forms of accounting or evaluation do not. This information can be used by the organization and its stakeholders to better understand the role and value of volunteers. Indeed, since the report was generated, the executive director of PARO has been able to demonstrate to funders and other CED organizations that PARO generates a large contribution of social value added for every dollar it receives from grants and other sources. By comparison, traditional accounting statements undertaken with non-profits like PARO portray them as the users of grants and other forms of funding, and show how they use the funds (expenditure categories) without portraying the value (both social and financial) that they add. This is a fundamental difference, as it strikes at the essence of social economy organizations – their social mission.

The EVAS is unique because it is a form of integrated social accounting. Other forms of social accounting are also important, but as noted, are supplemental to the financial statements. Although providing useful information, supplemental social accounting reports often receive secondary status (Coupland, 2006). It is also difficult with supplemental reports to judge the relative materiality of social and environmental actions with respect to financial performance. As a result, social and environmental reports published by an increasing number of corporations (especial for-profit) are frequently dismissed as 'greenwashing' or 'specious gloss' (Laufer, 2003; Owen and Swift, 2001: 5).

Other Examples to Explore

Social accounting and sustainability reports come in many different formats. Knowing how to start and what to include in an organization's first report can be daunting. The accountability standards and social accounting approaches presented in this chapter provide guidance to help organizations get started. Once you have an idea of the basic principles, it is also useful to read the reports of other social economy organizations. Several examples are presented for illustration.

SUSTAINABILITY SOLUTIONS GROUP

Sustainability Solutions Group (SSG) is a worker co-operative consulting firm that 'nurtures and embodies holistic understandings of sustainability; and works with clients and collaborators to meaningfully integrate social, ecological and economic practices in their organisations and work' (SSG, 2007: 5). Its main offices are located in Quebec, Nova Scotia, and British Columbia.

SSG's 2007 report shows how the organization is focusing on four areas: (1) towards cooperation, collaboration, and community; (2) towards healthy workplace and healthy lives; (3) towards diversity, equity, and justice; and (4) towards ecological sustainability. Within these four areas, twenty-two indicators were chosen to track and directly measure SSG's level of sustainability and progress towards strategic goals. A discussion and analysis section is presented after each area of focus, and the report ends with general and specific strategic directions for the next year.

VANCOUVER CITY SAVINGS CREDIT UNION (VANCITY)

Vancity started with twelve members and $22 in assets in 1946 and has grown to become the largest credit union in English-speaking Canada, with assets of more than $12.3 billion and fifty-seven branches located throughout British Columbia (Vancity, 2008b). Vancity has more than 2,600 employees and has repeatedly been named a top workplace in Canada. Vancity has issued social accounting reports since the early 2000s, and is a pioneer in social accounting.

One of the areas that Vancity has focused on is emissions. In 2006 it set a goal to become carbon neutral by 2010. It hired a doctoral student from the University of British Columbia to develop an emissions model compliant with the 2006 ISO standard on carbon emissions, and also created a handbook to outline its procedures and methodologies (Vancity, 2008c). As a result, Vancity found that the bulk of its emissions came from employee commuting (44%), energy use (25%), other travel (17%), and the use of paper (14%). By focusing on these areas,

Vancity has been able to reduce emissions and save significantly in energy costs. In fact, it accomplished its goal of becoming carbon neutral in 2008 – two years early. As David Suzuki remarked, 'This is no green-wash; this is the real thing' (Suzuki, 2007).

VANCOUVER OLYMPIC COMMITTEE (VANOC)

The Vancouver 2010 Olympics are organized and hosted by the non-profit organization, VANOC, that has the mission 'to touch the soul of the nation and inspire the world by creating and delivering an extraordinary Olympic and Paralympic experience with lasting legacies' (VANOC, 2008: i). Its vision is 'a stronger Canada whose spirit is raised by its passion for sport culture and sustainability' (ibid.). According to its *2006–07 Sustainability Report*, sustainability has been made a key consideration in planning and operations:

- Sustainability has been included in VANOC's mission and values.
- The board of directors has made a commitment to sustainability.
- Sustainability has been integrated into the business strategy and plans.
- Specific goals and targets are being set, and met, across the Organizing Committee.
- VANOC is monitoring its sustainability performance through risk management processes.
- Sustainability is part of employee training, compensation, and communications.
- External groups provide independent advice on VANOC's sustainability performance.
- There are internal and external checks and balances for oversight, evaluation, improvement, accountability. and assurance.
- VANOC's partners are fully engaged on a broad collaboration to achieve common goals.

VANOC's Sustainability Management and Reporting System (SMRS) provides information on environmental stewardship and impact reduction; social inclusivity and responsibility; Aboriginal participation and collaboration; economic benefits; and sport for sustainable living. Indicators in each of these areas are measured, tracked, and presented in VANOC's sustainability reports.

THE CO-OPERATIVE GROUP

In the United Kingdom, the Co-operative Group (not to be confused with the Co-operators Group in Canada) consists of nine businesses run by over 2.5 million members, of which 1.5 million are economically active. The Co-operative Group includes food stores, financial services, travel services, pharmacies, funeral care, legal services, and 'smile, the internet bank.'

The Co-operative Group issues an extensive sustainability report that can be downloaded from its website. It follows both the GRI and AA1000 guidelines. In 2006, it reported on the following co-operative, social, and environmental performance areas: governance; social responsibility; ecological sustainability; and employees and customers (Co-operative Group, 2006).

It also has an extensive sustainable development policy that guides the operations of its businesses. An example of how the Co-operative Group has implemented this policy is developing wind farms and a solar tower to provide it with renewable energy. Ninety-eight per cent of its electricity now comes from renewable energy sources.

Conclusion

As can be seen, social accounting can include a broad range of activities from formats such as the Global Reporting Initiative and the Natural Step to the expanded value added statement. Although these approaches differ, they share the common goal of broadening the framework of traditional accounting and attempting to understand the impact that an organization has on the communities to which it relates and the physical environment. Social accounting, therefore, is useful for social economy organizations as they are created to fulfil a social mission. Ignoring their social impact, as traditional accounting does, misses an essential feature of their performance story. In an age when so many demands are being made of social economy organizations, having tools that assess their accountability and their social impact is sine qua non for survival.

* * *

DISCUSSION QUESTIONS

1. Social accounting is based on stakeholder involvement in providing input and feedback. What are the benefits and potential risks of stakeholder involvement?
2. What does an expanded value added statement (EVAS) tell us about an organization that conventional accounting statements do not? How can this new information help us understand the role of social economy organizations?
3. In your view, why were the attempts of the 1970s at broadening financial statements to include social accounting items not picked up by the accounting profession? How is it different today?
4. Accounting can be seen as a driver of behaviour and thus an agent for social change. Do you agree or disagree with this statement, and why?
5. What are the pros and cons of the supplemental and integrated approaches to social accounting?
6. Outline some of the multiple accountabilities of social economy organizations.

Case for Analysis: Evergreen Brick Works

Background

Evergreen Brick Works, an innovative project in Toronto started by the national non-profit organization Evergreen, lends itself to a social accounting analysis, the exercise following this Case for Analysis. The stimulus for both Evergreen Brick Works and Evergreen came from Geoff Cape, its executive director. In the late 1980s, Cape was struck by the observation that cities were being paved over from edge to edge (Cape et al., 2007). In 1991, at the age of 25, he and two friends started a charitable organization called Evergreen to bring green spaces back into the city. Cape has been Evergreen's executive director ever since its beginning, and in 2007, won the inaugural Schwab Foundation's Canadian Social Entrepreneur of the Year Award, Canada's top social entrepreneurship honour.

Evergreen's mission is stated on its Website as: 'Evergreen is a not-for-profit organization that makes cities more livable. By deepening the connection between people and nature, and empowering Canadians to take a hands-on approach to their urban environments, Evergreen is improving the health of our cities – now and for the future' (Evergreen, 2008).

Today, Evergreen has over seventy employees, with offices in Toronto, Vancouver, and Calgary. As of 2007, it has mobilized over thirty thousand volunteers in over two hundred parks and school sites, and has overseen the planting of more than 125,000 native trees, shrubs, and wildflowers.

Core Programs

Using participatory design, hands-on planting, and the encouragement of a culture of environmental stewardship, Evergreen targets three areas through its programs: school yards, community spaces, and residential backyards.

Evergreen's school-based program is called Learning Grounds. A study of greening initiatives undertaken in one school board in Toronto found that green playgrounds make a striking positive difference in the quality of school life for students across socioeconomic variables, gender, race, class, and intellectual abilities (Dyment, 2005). Notable impacts included enhanced student learning, more positive social behaviours, promotion of environmental awareness and stewardship, and improved health. In 2008, Evergreen's Learning Grounds program was awarded a silver Canadian Environment Award in the category of environmental health (Canadian Geographic, 2008).

Evergreen's other two signature programs are called Common Grounds and Home Grounds. Common Grounds focuses on community naturalization projects that foster local stewardship and community building. Home Grounds attempts to change behaviours in homes by encouraging a lifetime adoption of organic yard and gardening care principles, biodiversity, and native habitat planting, and operates in British Columbia.

Funding

Funding for these programs comes from a variety of sources. Evergreen is a registered Canadian charity and receives support from foundation and government grants, individual donations, and corporate funding from multinational corporations like Toyota, Home Depot, Wal-Mart, and Unilever. Additionally, some of its programs earn revenue by operating on a fee-for-service basis. Evergreen adheres to the Ethical Fundraising and Financial Accountability Code of Imagine Canada.

Evergreen Brick Works

Evergreen Brick Works is Evergreen's latest and most ambitious project. It will operate as a sustainable social enterprise with two main components. The first component, the Industrial Pad, will consist of fifteen heritage buildings providing almost 200,000 square feet of space for a variety of purposes such as community events, tenant spaces, educational programming, food facilities, a plant nursery, a skating rink, and leadership training for at-risk youth. The second component is the Brick Works Park at the north of the property consisting of wetlands, wildflower meadows, and four kilometres of trails. The capital campaign to make Evergreen Brick Works a reality is $55 million, with one-half expected to come from the federal and provincial levels of government. Construction began in 2009, and LEED platinum-building guidelines will be followed.

Evergreen Brick Works is located in the Don Valley Ravine, a stretch of greenery adjoining the heavily travelled Don Valley Expressway. The Don Valley Expressway cuts north to south through the heart of east Toronto. It is the site of an abandoned heritage building complex of the former Don Valley Pressed Brick Works Company.

The idea for Evergreen Brick Works was inspired by a conversation between Geoff Cape and Bill Young of Social Capital Partners (SCP). In 2002, SCP was launching a $1 million competition to develop a social enterprise that sustains itself financially, delivers a charitable mandate, and provides youth employment. Cape returned to the Evergreen office, and after a short conversation with two other colleagues, the idea of a large-scale native plant nursery was born. After Evergreen received honourable mention in the Social Capital Partners competition (Inner City Renovation came in first), it decided to proceed with its plan.

The idea was then pitched to the City of Toronto, which had created a request for proposals for the 'Adaptive Reuse of the Heritage Structures at the Don Valley Brick Works.' After an open competition, Evergreen was selected in September 2003 to go ahead with its plan. A memorandum of understanding between the City and the Toronto and Region Conservation Authority gives Evergreen the option to lease the industrial pad at the Brick Works for $1 a year for twenty-one years once the organization has raised the necessary capital funds begin the project.

A BRIEF HISTORY OF THE ORIGINAL BRICK WORKS

In 1882, 25-year-old William Taylor, future co-owner of the Don Valley Pressed Brick Works Company, was testing clay at a site nearby to the Todmorden Mills, which was then owned and operated by his family. The clay proved to be perfectly suitable for brick-making, and Taylor and his two brothers opened the Brick Works factory at that location in 1889. The factory enjoyed great success, especially after the Great Fire of 1904 that destroyed much of the downtown core of Toronto. Indeed, the products of the Brick Works literally rebuilt most of the city. Many Toronto landmarks were also constructed with bricks from the Don Valley Brick Works, including Casa Loma, Massey Hall, the Ontario Legislature, and Hart House at the University of Toronto.

The factory operated until 1989, and was the longest operating brick works in the province. The property was then expropriated by the Toronto and Region Conservation Authority to protect its unique geological, historical, and environmental features. With thirteen habitat zones and two significant geological features, it was re-zoned by the City of Toronto as open space/parkland and has been designated as a heritage site under the Ontario Heritage Act.

OVERALL OBJECTIVES

The overall objectives of the Evergreen Brick Works are to (Sengupta et al., 2008: 18–19):

- Design and operate Evergreen as a 'zero footprint' facility
- Operate Evergreen Brick Works on an economically self-sustaining basis
- Deliver unique and innovative programs focused on motivating sustainable behavioural change
- Attract new program participants, volunteers, members, and donors to support Evergreen's mission
- Create new revenue streams to support Evergreen's programs.

One of the challenges for this project is getting people to the site without having to rely on the automobile. In June 2008, the Toronto Transit Commission provided service to the site every Saturday during the summer months. Trail maps are also available from Evergreen, which show biking and walking paths to the Brick Works.

BUSINESS OBJECTIVES

Further to the general objectives, the master plan outlines four business objectives:

1. By the second year of operation, cover 100 per cent of operating costs through office space and event rentals, conferences, parking, admissions, and other earned revenue
2. Generate over $5 million in annual revenues by the end of the first full year of operation
3. Maintain an occupancy rate of at least 90 per cent by providing unique program and rental facilities at competitive rates to suitable organizations and businesses
4. Provide a social and environmental return to the community in the form of new programs and services that improve environmental quality and promote health and wellness.

PARTNERS AND INTERVENTIONS

At the Brick Works, Evergreen is partnering with some of Canada's leading social economy organizations (Schwab, 2008). All partners are guided by the Brick Works Values Charter (Exhibit 9.1) that is tied to operating conditions and tenant leases. Some of the partners and programming are:

- Youth leadership and children's camps – providing youth programming to help develop a broad spectrum of community leaders, including:
  - Outward Bound Canada
  - YMCA of Toronto
  - Moorelands Community Services

- Arts and culture programming – programming in celebration of the art of clay and design, including:
  - Gardiner Museum of Ceramic Art
  - No. 9 Contemporary Art and the Environment

- Community food programming – offering organic and locally grown foods, including herbs and vegetables grown on-site, involving:

  - Jamie Kennedy Kitchens
  - Merchants of Green Coffee
  - Fifth Town Artisan Cheese
  - FoodShare Toronto
  - Green Belt Foundation
  - Dozens of local farmers and producers

- Health programming – lifestyle health activities that bring together alternative and traditional medicines, including:
  - University of Toronto's Centre for Effective Health
  - Bridgepoint Health

Other programming will involve the Children and Adult Discovery Centre, performance space, and skating and winter activities.

REVENUE GENERATION

The two main financial revenue generators for the Brick Works are its property management division and a Native Plant Nursery. A five-year forecast of operating revenues and expenditures from the master plan is available online at http://www.evergreen.ca. As the forecast shows, Evergreen Brick Works hopes to be self-sufficient in terms of covering operating costs by its second year of operation. There are no forecasts of social and environmental impacts.

Property Management. The Brick Works has approximately 67,000 square feet of rental space for tenants/partners and for events. Revenues from property management will come from several sources, including the following: rentals, memberships, event admissions, paid parking, and site sponsorship. Evergreen estimates that operating expenses will run at 83 per cent of gross revenues.

Plant Nursery. The Native Plant Nursery will run on 17,000 square feet of indoor and outdoor space. It consists of three interrelated elements: demonstration gardens, a retail garden centre, and a native plant nursery and propagation centre. A variety of trees, shrubs, wildflowers, grasses, heritage vegetables, and berry bushes will be available for sale at the Native Plant Nursery. The nursery will also offer at-risk youth jobs and skills training. The business plan for the retail operation forecasts a positive operating return by the fifth year of operation.

* * *

DISCUSSION QUESTIONS

1. In light of Evergreen's mission and vision, and its broader accountability as a social economy organization, outline the primary financial, social, and environmental measures of success for Evergreen Brick Works. In your response, include applicable benchmarks, indicators, and the information system required to track, measure, and report. Use the following headings to help organize your thoughts:

Goal	Why the goal is important; how it relates to sustainability	Interventions	Assumptions	Indicators

2. Develop an overall social accounting approach for either the property management division or the nursery and garden centre.

* * *

EXHIBIT 9.1 BRICK WORKS VALUES CHARTER

Who we are:

- We are a community of organizations whose mission and values celebrate the three core themes of the Brick Works – nature, culture, and community.
- We are organizations that operate in a financially, socially, and environmentally responsible manner.
- We strive for excellence in our respective fields.

Why we are here:

- We honour the history and sense of place that define the Brick Works and recognize the important role it plays promoting the conservation of Toronto's natural and cultural heritage.
- We bring together our shared values that include trust, transparency, and inclusiveness to all of our work.
- We believe that working together creates synergies that can make a more significant contribution than if we were working on our own.

Therefore, we are committed to:

- Inspiring social change by demonstrating leadership and innovation
- Making our cities more livable by reducing the impacts of our operations on the natural environment and showcasing best practices
- Working collaboratively in the spirit of the shared values that underlie the Brick Works to ensure its success and inspire its future growth
- Being accountable to our partners at the Brick Works and the broader communities that we serve.

* * *

LEARN MORE

If you want to learn more, visit these websites and other sources:

Canadian Geographic. (2008). Canadian Environment Awards: Meet the 2008 Winners! Retrieved 8 Aug. 2008 from http://www.canadiangeographic.ca/cea2008/winners.asp.

Dyment, J.E. (2005). *Gaining Ground: The Power and Potential of School Ground Greening in the Toronto District School Board.* Toronto: Evergreen. Retrieved 8 Aug. 2008 from http://www.evergreen.ca/en/lg/gaining_ground_summary.pdf.

Evergreen. (2007). Evergreen Brick Works Final Master Plan. Retrieved 6 Aug. 2008 from http://www.evergreen.ca.

Sengupta, U., Cape, G., Irvine, S., Bertrand, P., and Armstrong, A. (2008). Evergreen Brick Works: Planning for success in a triple bottom line enterprise. In J. Stoner and C. Wankel (Eds.), *Global Sustainability Initiatives: New Models and New Approaches,* 15–32. New York: Information Age Publishing.

Additional Websites

Evergreen Website. http://www.evergreen.ca

Lost River Walks Don Valley Brick Works Park Website. http://www.lostrivers.ca/BrickWorksPark.htm

Evergreen Brick Works: A Work in Progress. Social Economy Webcast, 31 Oct. 2007. http://sec.oise.utoronto.ca/english/lecture_archive.php

Video

Geoff Cape, 'Social entrepreneur of the Year' Winner 2007. Available online at http://www.youtube.com/watch?v=LuIY-HZCgcs

References

AA. (2008). A Brief Guide to Alcoholics Anonymous. Retrieved 15 June 2008 from http://www.alcoholics-anonymous.org/en_pdfs/p-42_abriefguidetoaa.pdf.

AA B.C./Yukon. (2008). About Area 79. Retrieved 15 June 2008 from http://www.bcyukonaa.org/area79/area79.html.

AA Information. (2008). A.A. Structure in US/Canada. Retrieved 15 June 2008 from http://www.alcoholics-anonymous.org.uk/geninfo/04structure.htm.

AA Online Intergroup. (2008). About Us. Retrieved 15 June 2008 from http://www.aa-intergroup.org/.

Aboriginal Canada Portal. (2004). *2003 Report on Aboriginal Community Connectivity Infrastructure.* Ottawa: Government of Canada.

Abraham, A. (2006). Financial management in the nonprofit sector: A mission-based approach to ratio analysis in membership organizations. *Journal of American Academy of Business* 9(2): 212–17.

Abt and Associates Inc. (1974). The Abt model. In D. Blake, W. Frederick, and M. Meyers (Eds.), *Evaluating the Impact of Corporate Programs,* 149–57. New York: Praeger.

AccountAbility. (1999). AA1000 Framework: Standard, Guidelines and Professional Qualification. Retrieved 26 Aug. 2008 from http://www.accountability21.net/uploadedFiles/publications/AA1000%20Framework%201999.pdf.

AccountAbility. (2005). Reinventing Accountability for the 21st Century. Retrieved 26 Aug. 2008 from http://www.accountability21.net/uploadedFiles/publications/Reinventing%20Accountability%20for%20the%2021st%20Century.pdf.

AccountAbility. (2007). Our History. Retrieved 28 July 2008 from http://www.accountability21.net/default.aspx?id=216.

ACNeilson. (2007). The ISO Survey – 2006. Retrieved 26 Aug. 2008 from http://www.iso.org/iso/survey2006.pdf.

AFL-CIO Housing Investment Trust. (2007). About Us. Retrieved 18 Jan. 2007 from http://www.aflcio-hit.com/wmspage.cfm?parm1=674.

Ake Böök, S. (1990). Observations on raising capital. *Review of International Co-operation* 83(4): 41–2.

Akingbola, K. (2002). Government funding and staffing in the nonprofit sector: A case study of the Canadian Red Cross, Toronto Region. Unpublished Master's thesis, Ontario Institute for Studies in Education, University of Toronto.

Akingbola, K. (2005). Unionization and non-profit organizations. In K.S. Devine and J. Grenier (Eds.), *Reformulating Industrial Relations in Liberal Market Economies,* 57–71. Toronto: Captus Press.

Akingbola, K. (2006). Strategic choices and change in non-profit organizations. *Strategic Change* 15: 265–81.

Al-Anon/Alateen. (2008). *What Is Al-Anon?* Retrieved 15 June 2008 from http://www.al-anon.alateen.org/about.html.

Alexander, J. (2000). Adaptive strategies of nonprofit human service organizations in an era of devolution and new public management. *Nonprofit Management and Leadership* 10(3): 287–303.

Alterna. (n.d.). Economic Development. Retrieved 25 Aug. 2008 from http://www.alterna.ca/Templates/SavingsCommunity.aspx?mid=322 andid=498.

Altruvest Charitable Services. (2008). About Us. Retrieved 20 July 2008 from http://www.altruvest.org/altruvest-main.html.

American Accounting Association (AAA). (1990). Position Statement No. One: Objectives of Education for Accountants. Retrieved 13 May 2007 from http://aaahq.org/AECC/PositionsandIssues/pos1.htm.

American Accounting Association (AAA). (1992). Position Statement No. Two: The First Course in Accounting. Retrieved 13 May 2007 from http://aaahq.org/AECC/PositionsandIssues/pos2.htm.

American Contract Bridge League (ACBL). (2008). Find a Club. Retrieved 15 June 2008 from www.acbl.org.

American Red Cross. (2005). *2005 Annual Report*. Washington, DC: Author.

Amnesty International. (2008). Facts and Figures about Amnesty International. Retrieved 15 June 2008 from www.amnesty.org.

Amnesty International Canada. (2008). Who We Are. Retrieved 14 Mar. 2008 from http://www.amnesty.org/en/region/canada.

Anderson, B.B., and Dees, J.G. (2002). Developing viable earned income strategies. In J.G. Dees, J. Emerson, and P. Economy (Eds.), *Strategic Tools for Social Entrepreneurs: Enhancing the Performance of Your Enterprising Nonprofit*. New York: Wiley.

Anderson, R.B. (2002). *Aboriginal Entrepreneurship and Business Development*. Toronto: Captus Press.

Andreoni, J. (1990). Impure altruism and donations to public goods: A theory of warm-glow giving. *Economic Journal* 100 (June): 464–77.

Arctic Co-operatives Ltd. (ACL). (2007). About Us. Retrieved 15 June 2008 from http://inuit.pail.ca/arcticco-op.htm.

Arctic Co-operatives Ltd. (ACL). (2008). Our Story. Retrieved 4 July 2008 from http://www.arcticco-op.com/about-acl-history.htm.

Arjoon, S. (2000). Virtue theory as a dynamic theory of business. *Journal of Business Ethics* 28(2): 159–78.

Armstrong, A. (2007). Personal communication.

Armstrong, R. (1998). Does the Carver Policy Model Really Work? *Front and Centre* 5(3): 13–14.

ArtSmart. (2008). About Us. Retrieved 1 July 2008 from http://www.artsmartnlac.ca/index.html.

Ashraf, N. (2008, 28 July). Personal communication.

Asmundson, P., and Foerster, S. (2001). Socially responsible investing: Better for your soul or your bottom line [Electronic version]. *Canadian Investment Review* (Winter): 1–12.

Association of Ontario Health Centres. (2006). *A Scan of the Effects of Regionalization on Community Health Centres in Selected Regions across Canada*. Toronto: Author.

Association of Polish Engineers in Canada. (2007). About Us. Retrieved 15 June 2008 from http://www.polisheng.ca/.

Associations Canada (2008). Toronto : Canadian Almanac & Directory Pub. Co.

Atkinson Charitable Foundation. (n.d.). ACF Mission Based Investment: Making Our $ Count for Social Justice. Retrieved 15 June 2008 from http://www.atkinsonfoundation.ca/about/financial.

Atlantic Canada Opportunities Agency (ACOA). (2007). Community Business Development Corporations. Retrieved 15 June 2008 from http://www.acoa.ca/e/financial/cbdc/acv2002.shtml.

Avaaz.org. (2008). About Us. Retrieved 15 June 2008 from http://www.avaaz.org/en/.

Avery, R. (2008). Changing the world from a Toronto home, $25 at a time. *Toronto Star*, 27 July, ID1, ID12.

Babcock, K. (2007). PARO Centre for Women's Enterprise: Measuring Social Impact. Retrieved 25 Aug. 2008 from http://www.ccednet-rcdec.ca/files/ccednet/PWP-11.pdf.

Badgley, R., and Wolfe, S. (1967). *Doctors' Strike: Medical Care and Conflict in Saskatchewan*. New York: Atherton Press.
Ballard. (2007). About Ballard. Retrieved 15 June 2008 from http://www.ballard.com/About_Ballard/.
Banting, K. (1990). Social housing in a divided state. In G. Fallis and A. Murray (Eds.), *Housing the Homeless and Poor,* 115–63. Toronto: University of Toronto Press.
Barber, B. (1998). *A Place for Us: How to Make Society Civil and Democracy Strong*. New York: Hill and Wang.
Barr, C., Brock, K., et al. (2006). Strengthening the Capacity of Nonprofit and Voluntary Organizations to Serve Canadians: Recommendations Based on the National Survey of Nonprofit and Voluntary Organizations. Toronto: Imagine Canada. Retrieved 25 Aug. 2008 from http://www.imaginecanada.ca/files/en/nsnvo/a_strengthening_capacity_of_organizations.pdf.
Baxter, M. (2004). Taking the first steps in environmental management. *ISO Management Systems* (July/Aug.): 13–18.
Baym, N.K. (1996). Agreements and disagreements in computer-mediated discussion. *Research on Language and Social Interaction* 29(4): 315–45.
Beaumier, G. (1998). *Regional Development in Canada*. Ottawa: Government of Canada, Economics Division.
Becker, E., and McVeigh, P. (2001). Social funds in the United States: Their history, financial performance, and social impacts. In A. Fung, T. Hebb, and J. Rogers (Eds.), *Working Capital: The Power of Labor's Pensions,* 44–66. Ithaca, NY: Cornell University Press.
Belkaoui, A. (1984). *Socio-economic Accounting*. Westport: Quorum Books.
Benet, B. (2006). The Polarity Management Model of Workplace Democracy. Unpublished doctoral dissertation, University of Toronto.
Berg, I. (1970). *Education and Jobs: The Great Training Robbery*. New York: Praeger.
Bernstein, P. (1982). Necessary elements for effective participation in decision-making. In F. Lindenfeld and J. Rothschild-Whitt (Eds.), *Workplace Democracy and Social Change,* 51–81. Boston: Horizon.
Better Business Bureau. (2008). An Overview to the Better Business Bureau. Retrieved 15 June 2008 from http://www.ccbbb.ca/about_overview.cfm.
Blackburn-Evans, A. (2003). Connecting Sick Kids to the classroom. *Edge* 4: 1.
Blue Cross Canada. (2007). About Us. Retrieved 15 June 2008 from http://www.bluecross.ca/.
Blum, F. (1968). *Work and Community: The Scott Bader Commonwealth and the Search for a New Social Order.* London: Routledge and Kegan Paul.
Boase, J., Horrigan, J., Wellman, B., and Rainie, L. (2006). The strength of

Internet ties. *PEW Internet and American Life Project*. Retrieved 13 July 2007 from http://www.pewinternet.org/pdfs/PIP_Internet_ties.pdf.

Borkman, T. (1999). *Understanding Self-Help/Mutual Aid: Experiential Learning in the Commons.* New Brunswick, NJ: Rutgers University Press.

Borzaga, C., and Defourny, J. (2001). *The Emergence of Social Enterprise.* Andover, UK: Routledge.

Bosch. (2007). Robert Bosch. Retrieved 15 June 2008 from http://www.bosch.com/assets/en/start/special/index.htm.

Bouchard, M.J., Ferraton, C., and Michaud, V. (2006). *Database on Social Economy Organizations: The Qualification Criteria.* Chaire de recherche du Canada en économie sociale, collection recherche no R-2006-3, University of Montreal.

Bozzoni, L. (1988). Local community service centres (CLSCs) in Quebec: Description, evaluation, perspectives. *Journal of Public Health Policy* 9(3): 346–75.

Brant Free Net. (2008). Free Net History. Retrieved 15 June 2008 from http://www.bfree.on.ca/index.asp?action=freeNetHistory.

Brantingham, P., and Easton, S.T. (1998). The cost of crime: Who pays and how much? [Electronic version]. *Fraser Institute Critical Issues Bulletins.* Retrieved 23 July 2006 from http://www.fraserinstitute.ca/shared/readmore.asp?sNav=pbandid=229.

Breast Cancer Action Nova Scotia (2008). About BCANS. Retrieved 23 July 2008 from http://bca.ns.ca/.

British Columbia Technology Social Venture Partners (BCTSVP). (2008). About Us. Retrieved 4 Nov. 2008 from www.bctsvp.com/about.

Broman, G., Holmberg, J., and Robèrt, K.-H. (2000). Simplicity without reduction – Thinking upstream towards the sustainable society. *Interfaces: International Journal of the Institute for Operations Research and the Management Sciences* 30 (3). Retrieved 4 Nov. 2008 from http://www.tns.org.nz/downloads/Resourses/Simplicity_without_reduction.pdf.

Brown, E. (1999). Assessing the value of volunteer activity. *Nonprofit and Voluntary Sector Quarterly* 28(1): 3–17.

Brown, W.A., and Iverson, J.O. (2004). Exploring strategy and board structure in nonprofit organizations. *Nonprofit and Voluntary Sector Quarterly* 33(3): 377–400.

Brudney, J. (1990). *Fostering Volunteer Programs in the Public Sector.* San Francisco: Jossey-Bass.

Brudney, J.L., and Murray, V. (1997). Do intentional efforts to improve boards really work? *Nonprofit Management and Leadership* 8(4): 333–48.

Brunsting, S., and Postmes, T. (2002). Social movement participation in the digital age. Predicting offline and online collective action. *Small Group Research* 33(5): 525–54.

Bruyn, S. (1977). *The Social Economy*. New York: Wiley.

Bruyn, S. (1987). *The Field of Social Investment*. Cambridge: Cambridge University Press.

Bruyn, S., and Nicolaou-Smokoviti, L. (1989). *International Issues in Social Economy: Studies in the United States and Greece*. New York: Praeger.

Bugg, G., and Dalhoff, S. (2006). *National Study of Board Governance Practices in the Non-profit and Voluntary sector in Canada*. London: Strategic Leverage Partners Inc. with Centre for Voluntary Sector Research and Development.

Bullfrog Power. (2008). Our Mission. Retrieved 15 June 2008 from http://www.bullfrogpower.com/about/mission.cfm.

Business Development Bank of Canada. (2002). BDC creates a $250,000 Aboriginal Business Development Fund with Apeetogosan (Métis) Development Inc. Retrieved 25 Aug. 2008 from http://www.bdc.ca/en/about/mediaroom/news_releases/2002/2002110601.htm.

Business Development Bank of Canada. (2006). BDC Creates New Aboriginal Business Development Fund. Retrieved 25 Aug. 2008 from http://www.bdc.ca/en/about/mediaroom/news_releases/2006/20060216.htm.

Business Development Bank of Canada. (2008). BDC Creates New Aboriginal Business Development Fund in Partnership with Nuu-chah-nulth Economic Development Corporation. Retrieved 25 Aug. 2008 from http://www.bdc.ca/en/about/mediaroom/news_releases/2008/20080202.htm.

Caisses de dépôt et placement du Québec. (2007). *Annual Report 2007*. Retrieved 25 Aug. 2008 from http://www.lacaisse.com/en/nouvelles-medias/Documents/RA2007_Rapport_annuel_EN.pdf.

Calgary Arts Development. (2008). Calgary's Juno Awards Shows Strong Economic Impact. Retrieved 30 Dec. 2008 from http://www.calgaryartsdevelopment .com/node/1413.

Calgary Association of Self Help. (2008). Calgary Mental Health Support Groups. Retrieved 20 March 2008 from http://www.calgaryselfhelp.com/programs/SupportGroups.php.

Canada Business. (2007). Fondaction: Fonds de développement de la csn pour la coopération et l'emploi. Retrieved 25 Aug. 2008 from http://entreprisescanada.gc.ca/servlet/ContentServer?cid=1130413455410andlang=endpagena me=CBSC_QC%2Fdisplayandc=Finance.

Canada Council for the Arts. (2007). History. Retrieved 20 Mar. 2008 from http://www.canadacouncil.ca/aboutus/role/.

CanadaHelps. (2008). About Us. Retrieved 15 May 2009 from http://www.canadahelps.org/InfoPages/AboutUsOverview.aspx.

Canada Mortgage and Housing Corporation (CMHC). (2005a). *2001 Census Housing Series: Issue 2 Revised: The Geography of Household Growth and Core Housing Need.* Ottawa: Author.

Canada Mortgage and Housing Corporation (CMHC). (2005b). *2001 Census Housing Series: Households Spending at Least 50% of Their Income on Shelter.* Ottawa: Author.

Canadian Alliance for Community Health Centre Associations (CAMHC). (2006). Home. Retrieved 20 Mar. 2008 from http://www.cachca.ca/english/ home/default.asp?s=1.

Canadian Alternative Investment Co-operative (CAIC). (n.d.). Who Are We? Retrieved 25 Aug. 2008 from http://www.caic.ca/.

Canadian Association of Food Banks. (2008). About the CAFB. Retrieved 20 Mar. 2008 from http://www.cafb-acba.ca/site/english/AboutCAFB.html.

Canadian Association of Mutual Insurance Companies (CAMIC). (2007). Who We Are. Retrieved 20 Mar. 2008 from http://www.camic.ca/en/whoarewe/index.html.

Canadian Association of Petroleum Producers. (2007). Climate Change. Retrieved 20 Mar. 2008 from http://www.cfib.ca/info/default_e.asp.

Canadian Association of Sexual Assault Centres. (2008). About Us. Retrieved 20 Mar. 2008 from http://www.casac.ca/english/about/about.htm.

Canadian Automobile Association (CAA). (2007). *Annual Report, 2004.* Retrieved 20 Mar. 2008 from http://www.caa.ca/pdf/2004%20caa%20annual%20report.pdf.

Canadian Business for Social Responsibility. (2008). Who We Are. Retrieved 20 Mar. 2008 from http://www.cbsr.ca/about/ourapproach.htm.

Canadian Chamber of Commerce. (2008). Canadian Chamber Profile. Retrieved 20 Mar. 2008 from http://www.chamber.ca/article.asp?id=139.

Canadian Community Economic Development Net (CCEDNet). (2007). *What Is CED?* Retrieved 20 Mar. 2008 from http://www.ccednet-rcdec.ca/en/pages/home.asp.

Canadian Community Investment Network Co-operative. (2007). Members and Allies. Retrieved 20 Mar. 2008 from http://www.communityinvestment.ca/member_list.html#circle.

Canadian Community Investment Network Co-operative (CCINC). (n.d.). Members and Allies: CAIC. Retrieved 25 Aug. 2008 from http://www.communityinvestment.ca/member_list.html#caic.

Canadian Conference of the Arts. (2007). What We Do. Retrieved 20 Mar. 2008 from http://www.ccarts.ca/en/members/members/Org.htm#w.

Canadian Co-operative Association. (2007a). Co-ops in British Columbia. Retrieved 20 Dec. 2008 from http://www.coopscanada.coop/aboutcoop/cancoopsectorprofiles/pdf/BC_co-ops_jun07.pdf.

Canadian Co-operative Association. (2007b). Co-ops in Nova Scotia. Ottawa: Author.

Canadian Co-operative Association. (2007c). News Briefs. Retrieved 30 July 2008 from http://www.coopscanada.coop/NewsLetter/NewsBriefs/archive.cfm?iid=83#c3.

Canadian Co-operative Association. (2008). Harnessing the Power of Co-operatives: New Development Initiative Responds to Federal Priorities. Retrieved 25 Aug. 2008 from http://www.coopscanada.coop/pdf/CDI/CDI_Renewal_Brochure_EN.pdf.

Canadian Council of Chief Executives. (n.d.). About CCCE. Retrieved 20 Mar. 2008 from http://www.ceocouncil.ca/en/about/about.php.

Canadian Crossroads International (CCI). (2007). *Annual Report, 2006–07.* Online at http://www.cciorg.ca/pdf_documents/CrossroadsAR0607_ENG_FINAL.pdf

Canadian Environmental Network. (2008). Mission. Retrieved 20 Mar. 2008 from http://www.cen-rce.org/eng/about_us.html.

Canadian Ethnocultural Council. (2008). About CEC. Retrieved 20 Mar. 2008 from http://www.ethnocultural.ca/cec_members.html.

Canadian Federation of Agriculture. (2007). What Is the CFA? Retrieved 20 Mar. 2008 from http://www.cfa-fca.ca/pages/index.php?main_id=2.

Canadian Federation of Independent Business. (2007). About the CFIB. Retrieved 20 Mar. 2008 from http://www.cfib.ca/info/default_e.asp.

Canadian Federation of Small Business. (2008). Mission. Retrieved 20 Mar. 2008 from http://www.cfib.ca/en/default.asp?l=E.

Canadian Health Network. (2008). CHN Network Contributors. Retrieved 20 Mar. 2008 from http://www.canadian-health-network.ca/servlet/ContentServer?cid=1042668269581andpagename=CHN-RCS/Page/ShellCHN-ResourcePageTemplateandc=Pageandlang=Enandletter=.

Canadian Institute of Chartered Accountants (CICA). (2003). *CICA Handbook.* Toronto: Author.

Canadian Institute for Health Information (CIHI). (2007). *National Health Expenditure Trends, 1975–2006.* Retrieved 20 Mar. 2008 from http://secure.cihi.ca/cihiweb/dispPage.jsp?cw_page=AR_31_E.

Canadian Institute for Health Information (CIHI). (2008). About CIHI. Retrieved 20 Mar. 2008 from http://secure.cihi.ca/cihiweb/dispPage.jsp?cw_page=profile_e.

Canadian Institute of Management. (2008). About CIM. Retrieved 20 Mar. 2008 from http://www.cim.ca/NOverview/Branches.asp.

Canadian Kennel Club. (2008). Who We Are. Retrieved 20 Mar. 2008 from http://www.ckc.ca/en/Default.aspx?tabid=75.

Canadian Labour Congress (CLC). (2007). About Us. Retrieved 20 Mar. 2008 from http://www.canadianlabour.ca/index.php/about_us.

Canadian Railroad Historical Association. (2008). The Divisions of CRHA. Retrieved 20 Mar. 2008 from http://www.exporail.org/public/en/5_achf/1_divisions.asp.

Canada Revenue Agency. (2008). Charities Directorate. Retrieved 31 July 2008 from http://www.cra-arc.gc.ca/tx/chrts/nln_lstngs/cnrg_ntrm-eng.html.

Canadian Unitarian Council. (2008). Congregations. Retrieved 20 Mar. 2008 from http://www.cuc.ca/congregations/index.htm#BC.

Canadian Wind Energy Association. (2008). About Us. Retrieved 20 Mar. 2008 from http://www.canwea.ca/about_us.cfm.

Cape, G., Irvine, S., Sengupta, U., Armstrong, A., and McBeth, L. (2007). *Evergreen at the Brick Works: Planning for Success in a Triple Bottom Line Enterprise*. Toronto: Unpublished case study.

Carmichael, I. (2005). *Pension Power*. Toronto: University of Toronto Press.

Carroll, A.B. (1979). A three dimensional conceptual model of corporate social performance. *Academy of Management Review* 4(4): 497–505.

Carroll, A.B. (1991). The pyramid of corporate social responsibility: Toward the moral management of organizational stakeholders. *Business Horizons* 34: 39–48.

Carroll, A.B. (1999). Corporate social responsibility. *Business and Society* 38(3): 268–95.

Carver, J. (2006). *Boards that Make a Difference: A New Design for Leadership in Nonprofit and Public Organizations* (3rd ed.). San Francisco: Jossey-Bass.

Carver, J., and Carver, M. (2001). *Carver's Policy Governance® Model in Nonprofit Organizations*. Retrieved 24 July 2008 from http://www.carvergovernance.com/pg-np.htm.

Carver, J., and Carver, M. (2008). *Carver Policy Governance® Model*. Retrieved 24 July 2008 from http://www.carvergovernance.com/index.html.

Centre for Community Enterprise (2007). Home. Retrieved 09 April 2008 from http://www.cedworks.com/.

Chait, R.P., Ryan, W.P., and Taylor, J. (2005). *Governance as Leadership: Reframing the Work of Nonprofit Boards*. Hoboken, NJ: Wiley.

Chantier de l'économie sociale. (2005). Social Economy and Community Economic Development in Canada: Next Steps for Public Policy. Montreal: Author.

Chantier de l'économie sociale. (2008). Mission. Retrieved 31 July 2008 from http://www.chantier.qc.ca/.

Chaves, R., and Sajardo-Moreno, A. (2004). Social economy managers: Between values and entrenchment. *Annals of Public and Cooperative Economics* 75(1): 139–61.

Cheal, D.J. 1988. *The Gift Economy.* London and New York: Routledge.

Chess Federation of Canada (2008). Chess Clubs. Retrieved 20 Mar. 2008 from http://www.chess.ca/chess_clubs.htm.

Chester, R.J., and Woofter, J.K. (2005). *Non-financial Disclosure and Strategic Planning: Sustainabiity Reporting for Good Corporate Governance.* Unpublished Master's thesis, Blekinge Institute of Technology, Sweden.

Childcare Advocacy Association of Canada. (2008). Who We Are. Retrieved 20 Mar. 2008 from http://www.ccaac.ca/aboutus/index.php.

Chinese Canadian National Council (CCNC). (2008). *CCNC Chapters.* Retrieved 20 Mar. 2008 from http://www.ccnc.ca/about.php?section=content/chapters.php.

Chinese Canadian National Council (CCNC) Toronto Chapter. (2008). *Campaigns.* Retrieved 20 Mar. 2008 from http://www.ccnctoronto.ca/links/links.html.

Chinook Community Futures Development Corporation. (2007). About Us. Retrieved 20 Mar. 2008 from http://www.biz-help.ca/contactus.htm.

CIRIEC. (2007). *The Social Economy in the European Union.* Report No. CESE/COMM/05/2005. Brussels: European Economic and Social Committee.

City of Vancouver. (2003). *2003 Year End Neighbourhood Statistics.* Retrieved 26 Aug. 2008 from http://city.vancouver.bc.ca/police/Planning/StatsNeighbourhood/2003/2003END.pdf.

Clark, C., and Ucak, H. (2006). *RISE For-profit Social Entrepreneur Report: Balancing Markets and Values.* Retrieved 23 Nov. 2008 from http://www.rise-project.org/rise-sep-report.pdf.

Clark, G.L. (2000). *Pension Fund Capitalism.* Oxford: Oxford University Press.

Clark, G.L., and Hebb, T. (2003). *Understanding Pension Fund Corporate Engagement in a Global Arena.* Oxford, Working Paper 03-01, School of Geography and the Environment, University of Oxford.

Clarkson, M. (1995). A stakeholder framework for analyzing and evaluating corporate social performance. *Academy of Management Review* 20(1): 92–117.

Cleveland, G., and Krashinsky, M. (2004). *The Quality Gap: A study of Non-profit and Commercial Child Care Centres in Canada.* Toronto: Childcare Resource and Research Unit, University of Toronto.

Cleveland, G., Forer, B., Hyatt, D., Japel, C., and Krashinsky, M. (2007). An economic perspective on the current and future role of non-profit provision of early learning and child care services in Canada. Retrieved 25 Aug.

2008 from http://childcarepolicy.net/documents/final-report-FINAL-print.pdf.

Coast Capital. (2007). Annual Report 2007. Retrieved 25 Aug. 2008 from https://www.coastcapitalsavings.com/Resources/Documents/annual reports/2007_Coast_Capital_ Savings_Annual_Report.pdf.

Collins, R. (1979). *The Credential Society: An Historical Sociology of Education and Stratification*. New York: Academic Press.

Common Ground Co-operative. (2007). About Us. Retrieved 20 Mar. 2008 from http://www.commongroundco-op.ca/home.html.

Community Foundations of Canada. (2008). *Overview: Canada's Community Foundations*. Retrieved 25 Aug. 2008 from http://www.cfc-fcc.ca/doc/CFC-2008-Fact-sheet.pdf.

Community Literacy of Ontario. (1998). *The Economic Value of Volunteers in Community Literacy Agencies in Ontario.* Barrie: Community Literacy of Ontario.

Community Literacy of Ontario. (2005). *The Literacy Volunteers: Value Added Research Report.* Barrie: Author.

Concert Properties. (2007). Corporate Overview. Retrieved 25 Aug. 2008 from http://www.concertproperties.com/management/index.html.

Concrete Works. (n.d.). About Concrete Works. Retrieved 25 Aug. 2008 from http://www.concreteworks.ca/.

Conference Board of Canada. (2008a). Awards. Retrieved 24 Feb. 2008 from www.conferenceboard.ca/GCSR/awards.

Conference Board of Canada. (2008b). Criteria. Retrieved 24 Feb. 2004 from http://www.conferenceboard.ca/GCSR/awards/criteria.htm.

Conference Board of Canada. (2008c). The Conference Board of Canada/Spencer Stuart 2008 National awards in governance. *Winners' Circle*, 18–19.

Conn, L.G., and Barr, C. (2005). Trends in Individual Donations: 1984–2003. *Research Bulletin* 12(1). Toronto: Imagine Canada.

Conseil de développement cooperative. (2008). History. Retrieved 18 Aug. 2008 from http://www.conseilcoopipe.org/Histoire.cfm?Lang=ENandCalendarID=1.

Consumers' Association of Canada (2008). About us. Retrieved 20 Mar. 2008 from http://www.consumer.ca/1480.

Consumers Council of Canada (2008). Retrieved 20 Mar. 2008 from http://www.consumerscouncil.com/.

Cook Studio Café. (2007). About Us. Retrieved 20 Mar. 2008 from http://www.foodandservice.net/cookStudioCafe.html.

Cooper, D.J. and Hopper, T. (2006). Critical theorizing in strategic management accounting research. Paper presented at the Eighth Interdisciplinary

Perspectives on Accounting Conference, Cardiff Business School, Cardiff University, 10–12 July.
Cooper D.J., and Neu, D. (1997). Accounting Interventions. Retrieved 4 July 2003 from http://les.man.ac.uk/ipa97/papers/neu14.pdf.
Cooper, G. (2000). Online Assistance for Problem Gamblers. Unpublished doctoral dissertation, University of Toronto.
Cooper, G. (2004). Exploring and understanding online assistance for problem gamblers: The pathways disclosure model: E Community. *International Journal of Mental Health and Addiction* 1(2): 32–8.
The Co-operative Group. (2006). About Us. Retrieved 26 Aug. 2008 from http://www.co-operative.coop/Master%20Brand/PDFs/Sustainability%20Report%202006.pdf.
Coopératives Forestières. (2007). History. Retrieved 20 Mar. 2008 from http://www.ccfq.qc.ca/english.htm#members.
Co-operatives Secretariat. (2006). *Co-operatives in Canada* (2003). Ottawa: Government of Canada.
Co-operatives Secretariat. (2007a). *Co-operatives in Canada* (2004). Ottawa: Government of Canada.
Co-operatives Secretariat. (2007b). *Top 50 Non-financial Co-operatives in Canada* (2005). Retrieved 20 Mar. 2008 from http://www.coop.gc.ca/index_e.php?s1=pubandpage=50coop05.
Co-operatives Secretariat. (2008). *Co-operative Development Initiative: Approved Projects*. Retrieved 25 Aug. 2008 from http://www.agr.gc.ca/rcs-src/coop/index_e.php?s1=initandpage=proj.
Co-operators Group. (2006). Our History. Retrieved 20 Mar. 2008 from http://cooperatorsjobs.employmentadvantage.com/history.html.
Co-operators Group. (2007). *Proposal to Ontario for a Program of Driver-Owned Automobile Insurance Co-operatives*. Guelph: Author.
Core Neighbourhood Youth Co-op (CNYC). (2007). About Us. Retrieved 20 Mar. 2008 from http://www.cnyc.ca/.
Côté, D., and Fairbairn, B. (n.d.). *Diagnosis of Democratic Functioning*. Ottawa: Canadian Co-operative Association / Le Conseil Canadien de la Coopération.
Coupland, C. (2006). Corporate social and environmental responsibility in web-based reports: Currency in the banking sector? *Critical Perspectives on Accounting* 17: 865–81.
Craddock, T., and Vayid, N. (2004). *The Role of Healthcare Co-operatives in Canada*. Ottawa: Co-operatives Secretariat.
Craig, J. (1993). *The nature of co-operation*. Montreal: Black Rose.
Craig, R., and Amernic, J. (2004). The deployment of accounting-related rhet-

oric in the prelude to a privatization. *Accounting, Auditing and Accountability Journal* 17(1): 41–58.

Craigslist. (2008). Craigslist Fact Sheet. Retrieved 20 Mar. 2008 from http://www.craigslist.org/about/factsheet.html.

Credit Union Central of Canada. (2007). *System Results*. Retrieved 20 Mar. 2008 from http://www.cucentral.ca/4thquarter_results_06.

CTV. (2007, 2 Feb.) Questions Surround Montreal SPCA's Fundraising. Retrieved 24 July 2008 from http://www.ctv.ca/servlet/ArticleNews/story/CTVNews/20070206/mtl_spca_070206?s_name=a ndno_ads=.

D'Aquino, T. (2007, 2 Mar.). How far are we willing to go? *National Post*. Retrieved 16 May 2009 from http://www.ceocouncil.ca/en/view/?area_id=1&document;_id=548.

Daft, R. (2007) *Organization Theory and Design*. (9th ed.). Mason, Ohio: Thomson South-Western.

Dahl, R. (1970). *After the Revolution: Authority in a Good Society*. New Haven: Yale University Press.

Daily Bread Food Bank. (2007). *Who's Hungry: 2007 Profile of Hunger in the GTA*. Toronto: Author.

Daly, H., and Cobb, J., Jr. (1994). *For the Common Good: Redirecting the Economy toward Community, the Environment and a Sustainable Future*. (2nd ed.). Boston: Beacon Press.

Dauncey, G. (2004). *Car Sharing in Vancouver*. Retrieved 25 Aug. 2008 from http://www.earthfuture.com/community/carsharevancouver.asp.

Dees, J.G. (1998). Enterprising non-profits. *Harvard Business Review* (Jan.–Feb.): 55–67.

Dees, J.G. (2001). *The Meaning of Social Entrepreneurship*. Durham: Center for the Advancement of Social Entrepreneurship at Duke University's Fuqua School of Business.

Defourny, J. (1999). *The Emergence of Social Enterprises in Europe*. Brussells: EMES European Networks.

Defourny, J., and Monzon Campos, J.L. (Eds.). (1992). *The Third Sector: Co-operative, Mutual and Nonprofit Organizations*. Brussels: CIRIEC and DeBoeck University.

Deibert, R. (2000). International plug'n play? Citizen activism, the Internet, and global public policy. *International Studies Perspectives* 1(3): 255–72.

Dembo, R., and Davidson, C. (2007). *Everything You Wanted to Know about Off-setting but Were Afraid to Ask*. Toronto: Zerofootprint.

Desjardins. (2006). *Desjardins Credit Union 2005 Annual Report*. Retrieved 25 Aug. 2008 from http://www.desjardins.com/en/dcu/a_propos/rapan706.pdf.

Desjardins. (2008). Desjardins Figures. Retrieved 25 Aug. 2008 from http://www.desjardins.com/en/a_propos/qui-nous-sommes/chiffres.jsp.

Desjardins. (n.d.). Solidarity Products. Retrieved 25 Aug. 2008 from http://www.desjardins.com/en/a_propos/profil/engagement/prets-solidaires.jsp.

Desjardins Développement International. (2007). Professional Experience. Retrieved 25 Aug. 2008 from http://www.did.qc.ca/en/pdf/publications/professional-experience-feb07.pdf.

Désrosiers, G. (1978). The introduction of a network of local community health centres: Four years of experience. *Canadian Journal of Public Health* 69 (Jan.–Feb): 7–9.

Dey, C.R. (2000). Bookkeeping and ethnography at Traidcraft plc: A review of an experiment in social accounting. *Social and Environmental Accounting Journal* 20(1): 16–18.

Dey, C.R. (2002). .Methodological issues: The use of ethnography as an active research methodology. *Accounting, Auditing and Accountability Journal* 15(1): 106–21.

Dichter, T., and Harper, M. (Eds.). (2008). *What's Wrong with Microfinance?* Rugby, Warwickshire, UK: Practical Action Publications.

Dilley, S.C., and Weygandt, J.J. (1973). Measuring social responsibility: An empirical test. *Journal of Accountancy* 136(3): 62–70.

Donkervoort, M. (2007a). Reflections on the building and sustaining of social enterprise. *Making Waves* 17(3): 20–4.

Donkervoort, M. (2007b). Inner City Renovation Inc. Retrieved 20 Feb. 2008 from http://www.enterprisingnon-profits.ca/innercity_renovations/.

Draimin, T., and Jackson, E. (2007). Social Finance: An Underdeveloped but Essential Aspect of Sustainable Investing in Canada. Retrieved 25 Aug. 2008 from http://www.socialinvestment.ca/documents/TimDraimin-Causeway-SIO-Final-070528.ppt.

Drucker, P. (1984). The new meaning of corporate social responsibility. *California Management Review* 26: 53–63.

Duboff, C. (2004). *A Scan of Community Economic Development Organizations, Rural Communities and First Nations in Manitoba and Their Participation in the New Economy.* Winnipeg: Manitoba Research Alliance.

E4C (2008). Our Partners. Retrieved 20 Mar. 2008 from http://www.eiccps.com/Partners.htm.

Earle, J. (1986). *The Italian Co-operative Movement.* London: Unwin Hyman.

Easwaramoorthy, M., Barr, C., Gumulka, G., and Hartford, L. (2006). Business support for charities and non-profits. *Research Bulletin* 12(2), 4 pp.

Ebrahim, A. (2003a). Accountability in practice: Mechanisms for NGOs. *World Development* 31(5): 813–29.

Ebrahim, A. (2003b). Making sense of accountability: Conceptual perspectives for northern and southern non-profits. *Nonprofit Management and Leadership* 14(2): 191–212.

Eddis, C. (2008). What Unitarians and Universalists Believe. Retrieved April 15, 2008 from http://www.cuc.ca/who_we_are/cucbeliefsbrochure_web.pdf.

Ekins, P. (Ed.). (1986). *The Living Economy: A New Economics in the Making.* London: Routledge and Kegan Paul.

Ekins, P., Hillman, M., and Hutchinson, R. (1992). *Wealth beyond Measure: An Atlas of the New Economics*. London: Gaia Books.

Ellerman, D. (1990). *The Democratic Worker-Owned Firm*. Boston: Harper-Collins.

Ellmen, E. (1989). *Profitable Ethical Investment*. Toronto: Lorimer.

Elson, P. (2007) A short history of voluntary sector-government relations in Canada, *Philanthropist* 21(1): 36–74.

Elson, P. (2008). History in the Making: A Historical Institutional Analysis of Voluntary Sector/Government Relations in Canada. Unpublished Ph.D. diss., University of Toronto.

Emran, M., Morshed, M., and Stiglitz, J. (2006). Microfinance and Missing Markets. Unpublished document. Retrieved 30 Dec. 2008 from https://editorialexpress.com/cgi-bin/conference/download.cgi?db_name=NAWM2007andpaper_id=427.

Enterprising Non-Profits Program. (2005). *The Canadian Social Enterprise Guide*. Vancouver: Author.

Epstein, K., and Smith, G. (2007). The ugly side of microlending. *Business-Week*. Retrieved 30 Dec. 2008 from http://www.businessweek.com/print/magazine/content/07_52/b406.

Estes, R. (1976). *Corporate Social Accounting*. New York: Wiley.

Evangeline Credit Union. (2008). Home Page. Retrieved 18 Aug. 2008 from http://www.peicreditunions.com/evangeline/about/.

Evans, R. (1997). Accounting for ethics: Traidcraft plc, U.K. In S. Zadek, P. Pruzan, and R. Evans (Eds.), *Building Corporate Accountability*, 84–101. London: Earthscan.

Everett, J., and Neu, D. (2000). Ecological modernisation and the limits of environmental accounting. *Accounting Forum* 24(1): 5–29.

Evergreen. (2007). *Master Plan*. Toronto: Author. Retrieved 15 April 2008 from http://www.evergreen.ca/en/brickworks/pdf/FINALMP.pdf.

Evergreen. (2008). About Us. Retrieved 15 May 2009 from http://www.evergreen.ca/en/about/about.html.

European Commission. (2008). Social Economy Enterprises. Retrieved 2 Nov. 2008, from http://ec.europa.eu/enterprise/entrepreneurship/coop/.

Eysenbach, G., Powell, J., Englesakis, M., Rizo, C., and Stern, A. (2004). Health related virtual communities and electronic support group: Systematic review of the effects of online peer to peer interactions. *British Medical Journal* 328(7449): 1166–71.

Fairbairn, B. (2004) Stakeholder engagement practices: Why and how? Paper presented at the Co-operative Corporate Governance Conference, Toronto, May 7.

Fairbairn, B., Ketilson, L., and Krebs, P. (1997). *Credit Unions and Community Economic Development*. Saskatoon: University of Saskatchewan.

Fallis, G. (1990). The urban housing market. In G. Fallis, and A Murray (Eds.), *Housing the Homeless and Poor,* 59–62. Toronto: University of Toronto Press.

Favreau, L. (2006). Social economy and public policy: The Quebec experience. *Horizons* 8(2): 7–15.

FCDRQ (La Fédération des coopératives de développement régional du Québec). (2007). Historique. Retrieved 15 April 2008 from http://www.fcdrq.coop/fcdrq/historique.php.

Fédération des Coopératives du Nouveau Québec. (2007). About Us. Retrieved 15 April 2008 from http://inuit.pail.ca/fcnq.htm.

FedNor. (2006). About Us. Retrieved 15 April 2008 from http://strategis.ic.gc.ca/epic/site/fednor-fednor.nsf/en/h_fn01468e.html.

Ferguson, J., Collison, D., Power, D., and Stevenson, L. (2005). What are recommended textbooks teaching students about corporate stakeholders? *British Accounting Review* 38(1): 23–46.

Ferguson, J., Collison, D., Power, D., and Stevenson, L. (2006). Accounting textbooks: Exploring the production of a cultural and political artifact. *Accounting Education* 15(3): 243–60.

Ferguson, T. (1997). Health care in cyberspace: Patients lead a revolution. *Futurist* 31(6) : 29–33.

Fiducie du Chantier. (2007). 2007 Annual Report. Retrieved 25 Aug. 2008 from http://fiducieduchantier.qc.ca/userImgs/documents/root/fiducie/RA-Fiducie-en_final.pdf.

Fiducie du Chantier. (2008). *Projects Funded 2007–2008*. Retrieved 25 Aug. 2008 from http://fiducieduchantier.qc.ca/?module=documentanduid=317.

Fiksel, J., McDaniel, J., and Mendenhall, C. (1999). Measuring progress towards sustainability principles, process and best practices. Retrieved 15 April 2008 from http://www.eco-nomics.com/images /Sustainability %20Measurement%20GIN.pdf.

Filion, P., and Bunting, T. (1990). *Affordability of Housing in Canada*. Ottawa: Statistics Canada.

Fiser, A., Clement, A., and Walmark, B. (2006). *The K-Net Development Process: A Model for First Nations Broadband Community Networks*. CRACIN Working Paper No. 12. Retrieved 15 April 2008 from http://www3.fis.utoronto.ca/research/iprp/cracin/publications/workingpapersseries.htm.

Five Winds International. (2003). Mountain Equipment Co-op's Green Building Approach. Ottawa: Author. Retrieved 18 May 2009 from http://www.fivewinds.com/publications/publications.cfm?pid=95.

Flamholtz, E. (1985). *Human Resource Accounting*. (2nd ed.). San Francisco: Jossey-Bass.

FoodShare. (2008). A Nonprofit System for Fresh-Produce Distribution. Retrieved 15 April 2008 from http://www.idrc.ca/es/ev-30607-201-1-DO_TOPIC.html.

Fowler, A. (2000). NGDOs as a moment in history: Beyond aid to social entrepreneurship or civic innovation? *Third World Quarterly* 21(4): 637–54.

Freeman, R.E. (1984). *Strategic Management: A Stakeholder Approach*. Boston: Harper Collins.

Friedman, M. (1970). Social responsibility of business is to increase its profits. *New York Times Magazine* (13 Sept.): 32–3.

Friendly, M., and Beach, J. (2005). *Early Childhood Education and Care in Canada* (6th ed.). Toronto: Childcare Resource and Research Unit, University of Toronto.

Friends of the Earth Canada. (2008). About FOE. Retrieved 15 April 2008 from http://foecanada.org/index.php?option=contentandtask=viewandid=2andItemid=25.

Friends of the Earth International. (2008). Home. Retrieved 15 April 2008 from http://www.foei.org/.

Frontier College. (2007). Frontier College History. Retrieved 15 April 2008 from http://www.frontiercollege.ca/english/aboutus/overview.htm.

Frumkin, P., and André-Clark, A. (2000). When missions, markets and politics collide: Values and strategy in the nonprofit human services. *Nonprofit and Voluntary Sector Quarterly* 29(1): 141–63.

Galabuzi, G.-E. (2001). Canada's Creeping Economic Apartheid: The Economic Segregation and Social Marginalisation of Racialised Groups. Toronto: Centre for Social Justice. Retrieved 15 April 2008 from http://www.socialjustice.org/pdfs/economicapartheid.pdf.

Galabuzi, G.-E. (2006). *Canada's Economic Apartheid: The Social Exclusion of Racialized Groups in the New Century*. Toronto: Canadian Scholars' Press.

Gaskin, K. (1999). Valuing volunteers in Europe: A comparative study of the Voluntary Investment and Value Audit (VIVA). *Voluntary Action: The Journal of Active Volunteering Research* 2(1): 35–48.

Gaskin, K., and Dobson, B. (1997). *The Economic Equation of Volunteering.* Retrieved 24 May 2002 from http://www.jrf.org.uk/knowledge/findings/socialpolicy/SP110.asp.

Gay Lea. (2008). About Us. Retrieved 29 July 2008 from http://www.gaylea.com/about/.

GayCanada. (2008). About Us. Retrieved 15 April 2008 from http://www.gaycanada.com/.

Gill, M. (2005). *Governing for Results: A Director's Guide to Good Governance.* Victoria: Trafford Publishing.

Gill, M. (2006). What type of board do you want 'yours' to be? *NonProfit Boards and Governance Review.* Retrieved 29 July 2008 from http://two.charitychannel.com/publish/templates/default.aspx?a=11686andz=24.

Girls Incorporated of York Region (GIYR). (2008). About Us. Retrieved 27 July 2008 from http://www.girlsincyork.org/about.htm.

Global Reporting Initiative (GRI). (2000). Sustainability Reporting Guidelines on Economic, Environmental, and Social Performance. Boston: Interim Secretariat, GRI. Retrieved 5 June 2002 from http://www.globalreporting.org.

Global Reporting Initiative (GRI). (2002). Introducing the 2002 Sustainability Reporting Guidelines. Retrieved 14 Feb. 2005 from http://www.globalreporting.org/guidelines/2002/gri_companion_lite.pdf.

Global Reporting Initiative (GRI). (2005). G3 Guidelines. Retrieved 14 June 2006 from http://www.grig3.org/guidelines/overview.html.

Global Reporting Initative (GRI). (2006). Sustainabilty Reporting Guidelines, version 3.0. Amsterdam: GRI. Retrieved 26 Aug. 2008 from http://www.globalreporting.org/NR/rdonlyres/2619F3AD-0166-4C7C-8FB2-D8BB3C5F801F/0/G3_GuidelinesENU.zip.

Goodwill Industries. (2007). About Us: Why Work Matters. Retrieved 15 April 2008 from http://www.goodwill.on.ca/2006_whyworkmatters.html.

Gore, A. (2006). *An Inconvenient Truth.* New York: Rodale.

Gottlieb, H. (2006). Succession Planning: The Elephant in the Room. Retrieved 19 Aug. 2008 from http:// www.help4non-profits.com/NPLibrary/NP_Bd_SuccessionPlanning_Art.htm.

Grameen Bank. (2008). A Short History. Retrieved 15 April 2008 from http://www.grameen-info.org/bank/.

Granovetter, M. (1973). The strength of weak ties. *American Journal of Sociology* 78(6): 1360–80.

Granovetter, M. (1985). Economic action and social structure: The problem of embeddedness. *American Journal of Sociology* 91(3): 481–510.

Gray, R. (1992). Accounting and environmentalism: An exploration of the challenge of gently accounting for accountability, transparency and sustainability. *Accounting, Organizations and Society* 17(5): 399–425.

Gray, R. (1998). Imagination, a bowl of petunias and social accounting. *Critical Perspectives on Accounting* 9(2): 205–16.

Gray, R. (2000). Current developments and trends in social and environmental auditing, reporting and attestation: A review and comment. *International Journal of Auditing* 4: 247–68.

Gray, R. (2002). The social accounting project and *Accounting Organizations and Society:* Privileging engagement, imaginings, new accountings and pragmatism over critique? *Accounting, Organizations and Society* 27: 687–708.

Gray, R. (2005). Taking a long view on what we now know about social and environmental accountability and reporting. *Electronic Journal of Radical Organisation Theory* 9(1). Retrieved 27 April 2007 from http://www.mngt.waikato.ac.nz/ejrot/Vol9_1/Gray.pdf.

Gray, R., Dey, C., Owen, D., Evans, R., and Zadek, S. (1997). Struggling with the praxis of social accounting: Stakeholders, accountability, audits and procedures. *Accounting, Auditing and Accountability Journal* 10(3): 325–64.

Gray, R. and Milne, M. (2004). Towards reporting on the triple bottom line: Mirages, methods and myths. In A. Henriques and J. Richardson (Eds.), *The Triple Bottom Line: Does It All Add Up?* 70-80. London: Earthscan.

Gray, R., Owen, D., and Adams, C. (1996). *Accounting and Accountability: Changes and Challenges in Corporate Social and Environmental Reporting.* London: Prentice-Hall.

Gray, R.H., Bebbington, J., and McPhail, K. (1994). Teaching ethics and the ethics of teaching: Educating for immorality and a possible case for social and environmental accounting. *Accounting Education* 3: 51–75.

Green, D. (1993). *Reinventing Civil Society: The Rediscovery of Welfare without Politics.* London: IEA Health and Welfare Unit.

Greenpeace. (2008). *History in the Making.* Retrieved 15 April 2008 from http://www.greenpeace.org/canada/en/about-greenpeace/copy-of-history-2.

Griffiths, M., and Cooper, G. (2003). Online therapy: implications for problem gamblers and clinicians. *British Journal of Guidance and Counselling* 31(1): 113–35.

GrowthWorks. (2007). Working Opportunity Fund: Annual Information Form. Retrieved 25 Aug. 2008 from http://www.growthworks.ca/files/funds/wof/AIF__FINAL__filed.pdf.

Guelph Campus Co-op (GCC). (2008a). History. Retrieved 28 July 2008 from http://www.guelphcampus.coop/page.php?id=11.

Guelph Campus Co-op (GCC). (2008b) Mission and Vision. Retrieved 28 July 2008 from http://www.guelphcampus.coop/page.php?id=5.

Gunn, A. (2003, April 5). Industrial Democracy: Are There Lessons for Quaker Businesses? John Wolstenholme Memorial Lecture. Wollaston, U.K: Scott Bader.

Gurstein, M. (2000). *Community Informatics: Enabling Communities with Information and Communications Technologies*. Hershey, PA: Idea Group Pub.

Guy, D., and Pletsch, C. (2003). *Gay Lea Foods Co-operative Limited: Choosing Leadership for the 21st Century*. Governance. Toronto: Author.

Habitat for Humanity (2008). *The History of Habitat*. Retrieved 15 April 2008 from http://www.habitat.org/how/historytext.aspx.

Haj-Assaad, L. (2008) Personal communication, 24 Feb.

Hall, H. (2006). Planning successful successions. *The Chronicle of Philanthropy*. Retrieved 19 Aug. 2008 from http://philanthropy.com/free/articles/v18/i06/06000601.htm.

Hall, J. (Ed.). (1995). *Civil Society: Theory, History, Comparison*. Cambridge: Polity Press.

Hall, M., et al. (2004). *The Capacity to Serve*. Toronto: Canadian Centre for Philanthropy. Retrieved 25 Aug. 2008 from http://non-profitscan.imaginecanada.ca/files/en/nsnvo/capacity_to_serve_english.pdf.

Hall, M., de Wit, M.L., Lasby, D., McIver, D., Evers, T., Johnson, C., et al. (2005). *Cornerstones of Community: Highlights of the National Survey of Nonprofit and Voluntary Organizations*. (Catalogue No. 61-533-XPE, Rev. Ed.). Ottawa: Statistics Canada.

Halseth, G., and Ryser, L. (2006). *Innovative Services and Voluntary Organizations*. Prince George: University of Northern British Columbia.

Handy, F., and Srinivasan, N. (2004). Improving quality while reducing costs? An economic evaluation of the net benefits of hospital volunteers. *Nonprofit and Voluntary Sector Quarterly* 33: 28–54.

Harnum, B. (2007). Personal communication, 16 March.

Harper, M. (2008). What's wrong with groups? In T. Dichter and M. Harper (Eds.), *What's Wrong with Microfinance?* 35–48. Rugby, Warwickshire, UK: Practical Action Pub.

Haween. (2007). The Somali Women and Children's Support Network. Retrieved 15 April 2008 from http://www.somaliwomenandchildren.com/programs/index.html.

Hebb, T. (2001). The challenge of labor's capital strategy. In A. Fung, T. Hebb, and J. Rogers (Eds.), *Working Capital: The Power of Labor's Pensions*, 1–12. Ithaca: Cornell University Press.

Hebb, T., and Mackenzie, D. (2001). Canadian labour-sponsored investment funds: A model for U.S. economically targeted investment. In A. Fung, T. Hebb, and J. Rogers (Eds.), *Working Capital: The Power of Labor's Pensions*, 128–57. Ithaca: Cornell University Press.

Hebb, T., Wortsman, A., Mendell, M., Neamtam, N., and Rouzier, R. (2006). *Financing Social Economy Enterprises*. Ottawa: Carleton University. Retrieved 25 Aug. 2008 from http://www.carleton.ca/ccci/files/Aug.%202006%20FINAL-%20Financing%20Social%20Economy%20Enterprises.pdf.

Hegelsen, S. (1995) *Web of Inclusion: A New Architecture for Building Great Organizations*. New York: Doubleday.

Henderson, H. (1991). *Paradigms in Progress: Life beyond Economics*. San Francisco: Berrett-Koehler.

Herzlinger, R.E. (1996). Can public trust in non-profits and government be restored? *Harvard Business Review* 74(2): 97–107.

Hewett, P. (2008). *History of the Unitarian Movement*. Retrieved 15 April 2008 from http://www.cuc.ca/who_we_are/history/history_hewett.htm.

Hines, R.D. (1988). Financial accounting: In communicating reality, we construct reality. *Accounting, Organizations and Society* 13(3): 251–61.

Hockey Canada. (2007). About Hockey Canada. Retrieved 15 April 2008 from http://www.hockeycanada.ca/6/6/9/8/index1.shtml.

Hoe, S. (1978). *The Man Who Gave His Company Away: A Biography of Ernest Bader, Founder of the Scott Bader Commonwealth*. London: Heinemann.

Home Ownership Alternatives. (2008). About Us. Retrieved 15 April 2008 from http://www.hoacorp.ca/.

Hopkins, B.R. (1987). *The Law of Tax-Exempt Organizations* (5th ed). New York: Wiley.

Hopper, T., Storey, J., and Willmott, H. (1987). Accounting for accounting: Towards the development of a dialectical view. *Accounting, Organizations and Society* 12(5): 437–56.

Hopwood, A.G. (1990). Ambiguity, knowledge and territorial claims: Some observations on the doctrine of substance over form – a review essay. *British Accounting Review* 22(1): 79–88.

Hopwood, A., Burchell, S., and Clubb, C. (1994). *Accounting: A Social and Institutional Practice*. Cambridge: Cambridge University Press.

Hospital for Sick Children. (2007). *2006–07 Annual Report*. Toronto: Author.

Hulchanski, D. (1990). Canada. In W. van Vliet (Ed.), *International Handbook of Housing Policies and Practices*, 309–13. New York: Greenwood.

Hulchanski, D. (2001). A tale of two Canadas: Homeowners getting richer, renters getting poorer. *Research Bulletin* 2. Toronto: Centre for Urban and Community Studies, University of Toronto

Hulchanski, D. (2002). *Housing Policy for Tomorrow's Cities*. Ottawa: Canadian Policy Research Networks.

Hulchanski, D. (2004). What factors influence Canada's housing policies? The intergovernmental role of Canada's housing system. In R. Young and C.

Luprecht (Eds.), *Canada: The State of the Federation in 2004,* 221–47. Montreal: McGill-Queen's University Press.

Hulchanski, D. (2005). Rethinking Canada's Housing Affordability Challenge. Discussion Paper, Centre for Urban and Community Studies, University of Toronto. Retrieved 15 April 2008 http://www.urbancentre.utoronto.ca/pdfs/elibrary/Hulchanski-Housing-Affd-pap.pdf.

Hulchanski, D. (2007). Three cities within Toronto. *Research Bulletin* 41. Toronto: Centre for Urban and Community Studies, University of Toronto. Retrieved 27 Sept. 2008 from http://www.urbancentre.utoronto.ca/pdfs/researchbulletins/CUCSRB41_Hulchanski_Three_Citie s_Toronto.pdf.

Human Resources and Social Development Canada (HRSDC). (2007). *Union Membership in Canada, 2007.* Ottawa: Strategic Policy, Analysis, and Workplace Information Directorate Labour Program, (HRSDC).

Humboldt California Foundation. (2007). Glosssary of Terms. Retrieved 4 Nov. 2008 from http://www.hafoundation.org/haf/about-us/glossary.html.

IASB (2006). Exposure Draft of Proposed Amendments to IAS 1: Presentation of Financial Statements. London: IASB. Retrieved 26 Aug. 2008 from http://www.iasb.org/NR/rdonlyres/BDD7DFE3-59D4-478B-B3AD-F18B9924ECDA/0/EDAmdmtstoIAS1.pdf .

Imagine Canada. (2005). *Canadian Directory to Foundations and Corporations* (19th ed.) Toronto: Author.

Imagine Canada. (2006a). NSNVO: Financial Challenges of Nonprofit and Voluntary Organizations. Retrieved 25 Aug. 2008 from http://www.imaginecanada.ca/files/en/nsnvo/n_financial_challenges_factsheet.pdf.

Imagine Canada. (2006b). NSNVO: The Nonprofit and Voluntary Sector in Canada Fact Sheet. Retrieved 25 Aug. 2008 from http://www.imagine canada.ca/files/en/nsnvo/sector_in_canada_factsheet.pdf.

Independent Sector. (1997). *Nonprofit Almanac: Dimensions of the Independent Sector*. San Francisco: Jossey-Bass.

Independent Sector. (2001). Giving and Volunteering in the United States: Key Findings. Retrieved 15 April 2008 from www.independentsector.org/PDFs/GV01keyfind.pdf.

Independent Sector. (2008). Volunteer Time. Retrieved 26 Aug. 2008 from http://www.independentsector.org/programs/research/volunteer_time .html.

Indian and Northern Affairs Canada. (2002). Government of Canada Invests in the Creation of the Native Venture Capital Limited Partnership of Quebec. News release 2-02140. Retrieved 25 Aug. 2008 from http://ainc-inac.com/nr/prs/m-a2002/2-02140_e.html.

Inner City Renovations. (2007). Video: Rebuilding Winnipeg's North End. Retrieved 25 Aug. 2008 from http://www.socialcapitalpartners.ca/icr_video.asp.

Institute of Corporate Directors. (2008). About Us. Retrieved 20 July 2008 from http://www.icd.ca/AM/Template.cfm?Section=About2.

Institute on Governance. (2008). Mission-Based Governance. Retrieved 24 July 2008 from http://www.iog.ca/boardgovernance/html/mod_ove_pol_mor_cri.html.

International Chamber of Commerce. (2008). What Is ICC? Retrieved 15 April 2008 from http://www.iccwbo.org/id93/index.html.

International Co-operative Alliance. (2006). *Annual Report, 2006.* Retrieved 15 April 2008 from http://www.ica.coop/publications/ar/2006annual report.pdf.

International Co-operative Alliance. (2007). Statistical Information on the Co-operative Movement. Retrieved 15 April 2008 http://guava.xeriom.net/~gmitchell/coop/statistics.html.

International Federation of Settlement and Neighborhood Centres. (2007). Who We Are. Retrieved 15 April 2008 from http://www.ifsnetwork.org /who/index.asp.

Ipsos News Centre. (2007a). Getting Real – How Do Canadians View the Environment and Energy? Retrieved 15 April 2008 from http://www.ipsos-na.com/news/pressrelease.cfm?id=3412.

Ipsos News Centre. (2007b). Nearly Four-in-Ten Canadian Adults (37%) Have Visited Online Social Networks. Retrieved 15 April 2008 from http://www.ipsos-na.com/news/pressrelease.cfm?id=3664.

ISO (2008). Discover ISO. Retrieved 15 April 2008 from http://www.iso.org/iso/about/discover-iso_the-iso-brand.htm.

Jantzi Research (2007). Jantzi Research and *Report On Business Magazine* Shed Light on CSR Performance across Five Sectors; New Research Report Finds Climate Change Starting to Impact Bottom Line. Press Release, 23 Feb.

Jensen, N. (2001). The Co-operative Auto Network Social and Environmental Report, 2000–2001. Retrieved 25 Aug. 2008 from http://www.cooperativeauto.net/pdf/report.pdf.

John Lewis Partnership. (2007). John Lewis Partnership. Retrieved 7 Feb. 2007 from http://www.johnlewispartnership.coop/Display.aspx?MasterId=6069f145-d2a7-4bb5-b076-6bd7b407b947andNavigationId=743.

Jordan, J. (1989). The multi-stakeholder concept of organization. In J. Quarter and G. Melnyk (Eds.), *Partners in Enterprise: The Worker Ownership Phenomenon,* 113–31. Montreal: Black Rose.

Just Us! (2008). Offering Document for the Just Us! Fair Trade Investment Co-operative Limited. Retrieved 25 Aug. 2008 from http://www.justuscoffee

.com/Resources/Docs/offering_document_2008_final_%20APPROVED.pdf.

Kaattari, T. (2008). Why Carver? An Overview. Retrieved 25 July 2008 from http://www.on.literacy.ca/who/carver.htm.

Kairos Canada. (2008). Ecological Justice. Retrieved 2 Dec. 2008 from http://www.kairoscanada.org/en/ecojustice/.

Karn, G.N. (1983). Money talks: A guide to establishing the true dollar value of volunteer time, Part 1. *Journal of Volunteer Administration* 1: 1–19.

Katzmarzyk, P.T., Gledhill, N., and Shephard, R.J. (2000). The economic burden of physical inactivity in Canada. *Canadian Medical Association Journal* 163(11): 1435–40.

Kaufman, T. (2007). Personal communication, 26 May.

Kealey, G. (1980) *Toronto Workers Respond to Industrial Capitalism, 1867–1892.* Toronto: University of Toronto Press.

Kealey, G., and Palmer, B. (1987). *Dreaming of What Might Be: The Knights of Labour in Ontario, 1880–1890.* Toronto: New Hogtown Press.

Keane, J. (1998). *Civil Society: Old Images, New Visions.* Stanford, CA: Stanford University Press.

Kearns, K.P. (1994). The strategic management of accountability in nonprofit organizations: An analytical framework. *Administration Review* 54(2): 185–92.

Kendall, J., and Almond, S. (1999). United Kingdom. In L. Salamon et al. (Eds.), *Global Civil Society: Dimensions of the Nonprofit Sector,* 179–200. Baltimore: Johns Hopkins University Press.

Kenyon, R. (1976). *To the Credit of the People.* Toronto: Ontario Credit Union League.

Kiva. (2007). What We Do. Retrieved 15 April 2008 from http://www.kiva.org/app.php?page=about.

Kiva. (2008). How It Works. Retrieved 27 July 2008 from http://www.kiva.org/about/how/.

Kiwanis. (2008). Kiwanis Legacy. Retrieved 15 April 2008 from http://www.kiwanis.org/WhoWeAre/KiwanisLegacy/tabid/131/Default.aspx.

Klamer, A. 2003. Gift economy. In R. Towse (Ed.), *A Handbook of Cultural Economics,* 243–47). Cheltenham, UK and Northampton, MA: Edward Elgar.

K-Net. (2008). Homepage. Retrieved 15 April 2008 from http://www.knet.ca/.

Knights of Columbus. (2008). Knights of Columbus in Canada and Around the World. Retrieved 15 April 2008 from http://www.kofc.org/un/news/releases/detail.cfm?id=4359.

Koystra, E. (2006). Community economic development provincial policy framework and lens. *Horizons* 8(2): 22–6.

Kreander, N., Beattie, V. and McPhail, K. (2006). UK Charity Ethical Investment – Policy, Practice and Disclosure. ACCA Research Report No. 97. Retrieved 25 Aug. 2008 from http://www.accaglobal.com/publicinterest/activities/research/reports/sustainable_and_transparen t/rr_097.

Kropotkin, P. (1989). *Mutual Aid: A Factor in Evolution*. Montreal: Black Rose Books.

Kuly, M., Stewart, E. and Dudley, M. (2005). *Enhancing Cultural Capital: The Arts and Community Development in Winnipeg*. Winnipeg: Institute of Urban Studies, University of Winnipeg.

La Siembra. (n.d.). Our Co-op. Retrieved 25 Aug. 2008 from http://www.lasiembra.com/en/coop_history.php.

Laidlaw, S. (2007, 16 June). All they need is someone to give them a chance. *Toronto Star*, L2

Lalonde-Graton, M. (1986). *Childcare in Quebec: An Overview*. Quebec City: Special Committee on Childcare.

Laufer, W.S. (2003). Social accountability and corporate greenwashing. *Journal of Business Ethics* 43(3): 253–61.

Laughlin, F.L., and Andringa, R.C. (2007). *Good Governance for Non-profits – Developing Principles and Policies for an Effective Board*. New York: AMACOM.

Laville, J.L., Borzaga, C., Defourny, J., Evers, A., Lewis, J., Nyssens, M., and Pestoff, V. (1999). *The Enterprises and Organizations of the Third System*. Brussels: CIRIEC.

Lavoie, J. (2008, 15 Mar.). Pandora needle site put on hold. *Times Colonist* A1.

Learning Enrichment Foundation. (2008). Home. Retrieved 7 Dec. 2008 from http://lefca.org/index.php?option=com_frontpageandItemid=1.

Lehman, G. (1999). Disclosing new worlds: A role for social and environmental accounting and auditing. *Accounting, Organizations and Society* 24: 217–41.

Lehrer, T. (1965). *That Was the Year that Was*. Retrieved 20 Feb. 2007 from http://members.aol.com/quentncree/lehrer/vonbraun.htm.

Lenzner, R., and Ebeling, A. (1997). Cited at Grassroots – GHC. Retrieved 27 July 2008 from http://ghc-grassroots.blogspot.com/2007/12/lessons-from-peter-drucker.html.

LePage, D. (2004) *Social Purchasing – Buying Locally, Helping Locally, Community Stories*. Ottawa: Caledon Institute of Social Policy.

LePage, D. (2005). How to Build a Social Purchasing Portal in Your Community. Retrieved 27 July 2008 from http://www.changemakers.net/node/10686.

LePage, D. (2006). *Coopératives de Québec*. Québec City: Direction des cooperatives.

Leung, A. (2004). The Cost of Pain and Suffering from Crime in Canada. Retrieved 23 July 2006 from http://www.justice.gc.ca/en/ps/rs/rep/2005/rr05-4/index.html.

Lewin, K. (1935). *A Dynamic Theory of Personality; Selected Papers.* New York: McGraw-Hill.

Lewis, L., Humphrey, C., and Owen, D. (1992) Accounting and the social: A pedagogic perspective. *British Accounting Review* 24(3): 219–33.

Light, P. (2006). Reshaping social entrepreneurship. *Stanford Social Innovation Review* (Fall): 45–51.

Linowes, D. (1972). An approach to socio-economic accounting. *Conference Board Record* 9(11): 58–61.

Lions Club Canada. (2008). About Us. Retrieved 27 Feb. 2007 from http://www.kiwanis.org/WhoWeAre/KiwanisLegacy/tabid/131/Default.aspx.

Litman, T. (2005). Transportation Cost Analysis Spreadsheet. Retrieved 7 June 2006, from http://www.vtpi.org/tca/tca.xls.

Livingstone, D.W. (1999). *The Education-Jobs Gap: Underemployment or Economic Democracy*? Boulder: Westview Press.

Llewellyn, S. (1994). Managing the boundary: How accounting is implicated in maintaining the organization. *Accounting, Auditing and Accountability* 7(4): 4–23.

Lodh, S.C., and Gaffikin, M.J.R. (1997). Critical studies in accounting research, rationality and Habermas: A methodological reflection. *Critical Perspectives on Accounting* 8: 433–74.

Luffman, J. (2006). Measuring housing affordability. *Perspectives on Labour and Income* 7(11): 16–25.

Mackenzie, H. (2009). Banner Year for Canada's CEOs: Record High Pay Increase. Toronto: Canadian Centre for Policy Alternatives. Retrieved 3 Jan. 2009 from http://www.policyalternatives.ca/~ASSETS/DOCUMENT/National_Office_Pubs/2008/Banner_ Year_For_CEOs.pdf

Macleod, D. (2007). *Building Character in the American Boy: The Boy Scouts, YMCA, and Their Forerunners, 1870–1920*. Madison: University of Wisconsin.

MacLeod, G. (1986). *New Age Business*. Ottawa: Canadian Council on Social Development.

MacLeod, G. (1997). *From Mondragon to America: Experiments in Community Economic Development.* Sydney, NS: UCCB Press.

MacPherson, I. (1979). *Each for All: A History of the Co-operative Movement in English-Canada: 1900–1945.* Toronto: Macmillan.

Make Poverty History. (2008). About Us. Retrieved 27 Feb. 2008 from http://www.makepovertyhistory.ca/en/about.

Makivik Corporation. (2008). Mandate. Retrieved 27 Feb. 2008 from http://www.makivik.org/eng/index.asp.

Mair, J., and Martí, I. (2006). Social entrepreneurship research: A source of explanation, prediction and delight. *Journal of World Business* 41: 36–44.

Malo, M.-C., and Vézina, M. (2004). Governance and management of collective user-based enterprises: Value-creation strategies and organizational configurations. *Annals of Public and Cooperative Economics* 75(1): 113–37.

Manley, K., Hebb, T., and Jackson, E.T. (2008). Economically targeted investing: Financial and collateral impacts. In J. Quarter, I. Carmichael, and S. Ryan (Eds.), *Pensions at Work: Socially Responsible Investment of Union-Based Pension Funds,* 207–40. Toronto: University of Toronto Press.

Mansbridge, J. (1982). Fears of conflict in face-to-face democracies. In F. Lindenfeld and J. Rothschild Whitt (Eds.), *Workplace Democracy and Social Change,* 125–37). Boston: Porter Sargent.

Martin, P. (1995). Budget Speech. Ottawa: Department of Finance Canada. Retrieved 28 Apr. 2009 from http://www.fin.gc.ca/budget95/speech/SPEECH-eng.asp.

Martin, R. (2002). The virtue matrix. *Harvard Business Review* 8(3): 69–75.

Martin, R., and Osberg, S. (2007). Social entrepreneurship: The case for definition. *Stanford Social Innovation Review.* Spring. Retrieved 20 July 2008 from http://www.ssireview.org/articles/entry/social_entrepreneurship_the_case_for_definition/.

Martin, S.A. (1985). *An Essential Grace: Funding Canada's Health Care, Education, Welfare, Religion and Culture.* Toronto: McClelland and Stewart.

Mathews, M.R. (1997). Twenty-five years of social and environmental accounting research: Is there a silver jubilee to celebrate? *Accounting, Auditing and Accountability Journal* 10(4): 481–531.

McCain, M., and Mustard, F. (1999). *Reversing the Real Brain Drain: Early Years Study.* Toronto: Ontario Children's Secretariat.

McDonough, W., and Braungart, M. (2002). *Cradle to Cradle: Remaking the Way We Make Things.* New York: North Point Press.

McDougall, B. (2007). *Results of the 2006 Feasibility Study on the For-profit Segment of the Community Sector.* Ottawa: Human Resource and Social Development Canada.

McGee, H. (1992). *Getting It Right: Regional Development in Canada.* Montreal: McGill-Queen's Press.

McMurtry, J. (1998). *Unequal Freedoms: The Global Market as an Ethical System.* Toronto: Garamond.

McMurtry, J. (1999). The lifeground, the civil commons and global development. Paper presented at the Annual Meeting of the Canadian Association for Studies in International Development (CASID), Congress of the Social Sciences and Humanities, Sherbrooke, Quebec, 7 June.

Meadows, D.H, Meadows, D.L., Randers, J., and Behrens III, W.W. (1972). *The Limits to Growth: A Report for The Club of Rome's Project on the Predicament of Mankind.* New York: Universe Books.

Media Awareness Network. (2008). Overview. Retrieved 27 Feb. 2008 from http://www.media-awareness.ca/english/corporate/about_us/index.cfm.

Melnyk, G. (1985). *The Search for Community*. Toronto: Black Rose.

Mendell, M., and Rouzier, R. (2006). Some Initiatives that Enabled the Institutionalization of Quebec's Social Economy: Civil Society's Crucial Role and the State's Essential Role. Montreal: Concordia University, Unpublished document.

Mendell, M., Lévesque, B., and Rouzier, R. (2001). New Forms of Financing Social Economy Enterprises and Organizations in Quebec. Retrieved 25 Aug. 2008 from http://www.aruc-es.uqam.ca/Portals/0/cahiers/I-03-2001.pdf.

Mendell, M., and Neamtan, N. (forthcoming). The social economy in Quebec: Towards a new political economy. In L. Mook, J. Quarter, and S. Ryan (Eds.), *Researching the Social Economy*.

Mies, M. (1986). *Patriarchy and Accumulation on a World Scale: Women in the International Division of Labour*. London: Zed Books.

Mi'kmaq Nova Scotia First Net. (2008). Latest News. Retrieved 27 Feb. 2008 from http://www.mns-firstnet.ca/index.php.

Milani, B. (2000). *Designing the Green Economy*. New York: Roman and Littlefield.

Miles, R.E., and Snow, C.C. (1978). *Organizational Strategy, Structure, and Process*. San Francisco: McGraw-Hill.

Miles, R.E., and Snow, C.C. (1984). Designing strategic human resource systems. *Organizational Dynamics* 13(1): 36–52.

Miller, H. (2005). Local youth thrilled by Queen's visit. *Around Town* 23: n.p.

Mintzberg, H. (1981). Organization design: Fashion or fit? *Harvard Business Review*, (Jan.–Feb.): 1–16.

Monahan, P., with Roth, E. (2000). *Federal Regulation of Charities: A Critical Assessment of Recent Proposals Legislative and Regulatory Reform*. Toronto: Canadian Centre for Philanthropy.

Monasterio, J., Telleria, D., and Etxebarria, I. (2007). Understanding Mondragon globalization process: Local job creation through multi-localization. Paper presented at the First CIRIEC International Conference, 22 Oct.

Mondragon Co-operative Corporation. (2007). Who We Are. Retrieved 8 Nov. 2007 from http://www.mondragon.mcc.es/ing/magnitudes/cifras.html.

Mook, L. (2007). Social and environmental accounting: The expanded value added statement. Unpublished Ph.D. diss., University of Toronto.

Mook, L., and Quarter, J. (2004). *How to Assign a Monetary Value to Volunteer Contributions*. Toronto: CCP.

Mook, L., and Sumner, J. (2010). Social accounting for sustainability in the social economy. In J.J. McMurtry (Ed.), *Living Economics: Perspectives on Canada's Social Economy*. 157–78. Toronto: Emond Montgomery.

Mook, L., Quarter, J., and Richmond, B.J. (2007). *What Counts: Social Accounting for Non-profits and Cooperatives* (2nd ed.). London: Sigel Press.

Morgan, G. (1988). Accounting as reality construction: Towards a new epistemology for accounting practice. *Accounting, Organizatons and Society* 13(5): 477–85.

Mountain Equipment Co-op (MEC). (2008a). Main 1. Retrieved 24 Feb. 2008 from www.mec.ca/Main/content_text.jsp?CONTENT%3C%3Ecnt _id=10134198673220379andFOLD ER%3C%3Efolder_id=2534374302881729 andbmUID=1203871813760.

Mountain Equipment Co-op (MEC). (2008b). Main 2. Retrieved 24 Feb. 2008 from www.mec.ca/Main/content_text.jsp?FOLDER%3C%3Efolder _id=2534374302881765andb mUID=1203888988711.

Murray, V. (2008). Personal communication, July.

Muttart Foundation. (2006). Talking about Charities. Edmonton: Author.

National Aboriginal Health Organization. (2008). Home. Retrieved 27 Feb. 2008 from http://www.naho.ca/english/chn_About.php.

National Action Committee on the Status of Women (NACSW). (2008). Entry for NACSW. *Canadian Encyclopedia*. Retrieved 27 Feb. 2008 from http://thecanadianencyclopedia.com/index.cfm?PgNm=TCEand-Params=A1ARTA0005604.

National Congress of Italian Canadians. (2008). A Brief History. Retrieved 27 Feb. 2008 from http://www.canadese.org/ncic_About_Italian_Canadi-ans.html.

National Council of Churches (2005). *The Yearbook of American and Canadian Churches*. New York: Author.

Natural Resources Canada. (2006). Energy Star Simple Savings Calculator for Volume Purchases. Retrieved 26 Aug. 2008 from http://oee.nrcan.gc.ca/energystar/english/consumers/calculators/index.cfm?text=Nandprin tview=N.

Natural Step Canada. (2006). Progress Report, 2005–2006. Retrieved 26 Aug. 2008 from http://www.naturalstep.ca/documents/TNS_AR_2005-06_004.pdf.

Nature Canada. (2008). Canadian Nature Network. Retrieved 27 Feb. 2008 from http://www.naturecanada.ca/nature_network.asp.

NDP. (2007). Regina Manifesto. Retrieved 27 Feb. 2008 from http://www.nwtndp.ca/manifesto.html.

Neighbourhoods Alive. (2007). History. Retrieved 27 Feb. 2008 from http://www.gov.mb.ca/ia/programs/neighbourhoods/faqs.html.

New Dawn Enterprises Ltd. (2006). Annual Report 2005. Sydney, NS: Author.

New Economics Foundation. (1998). Briefing Paper on Social Auditing. London: Author.

New Economics Foundation. (2008). Mission Possible: Emerging Opportunities for Mission-Connected Investment. Retrieved 25 Aug. 2008 from http://www.neweconomics.org/gen/uploads/nf5d3krg222ykpysezg2wi5529052008150616.pdf.

New Economy Development Group (NEDG). (2006a). La Siembra Co-operative Inc.: Case Study. Retrieved 25 Aug. 2008 from http://www.agr.gc.ca/rcs-src/coop/index_e.php?s1=pubandpage=case_siembra#3.4.

New Economy Development Group (NEDG). (2006b). Co-operative Auto Network: A Case Study. Retrieved 25 Aug. 2008 from http://www.agr.gc.ca/rcs-src/coop/index_e.php?s1=puband page=case_auto.

Newfoundland and Labrador Arts Council (NLAC). (2007). Awards. Retrieved 23 June 2008 from http://www.nlac.nf.ca/awards/AA2007 .shtml.

Newfoundland and Labrador Arts Council (NLAC). (2008a). Strategic Framework. Retrieved 23 June 2008 from http://www,nlac.nf.ca/resources/strategic_plan.shtml.

Newfoundland and Labrador Arts Council (NLAC). (2008b). Resources. Retrieved 1 July 2008 from http://www.nlac.nf.ca/resources/Carmelita.shtml.

New Life Mission. (2008). A Short History. Retrieved 27 Feb. 2008 from http://newlifemission.ca/index.php?option=com_contentandtask=viewandid=32andItemid=29.

Newman's Own. (2007). Home Page. Retrieved 27 Feb. 2008 from www.newmansown.com.

North American Students of Cooperation (NASCO). (2008). About Us. Retrieved 28 July 2998 from http://www.nasco.coop/node/17.

North End Community Renewal Corporation (NECRC). (2008). About NECRC. Retrieved from www.necrc.org/php/necrc.php?submenu=1&choice=1.

Oakeshott, R., and Schmid, F. (1990). *The Carl Zeisss Stiftung: Its First Hundred Years of Impersonal Ownership*. London: Job Ownership.

Obleman, J. (2008, 16 June). New co-op slated for Hall Beach. *Northern News Services*.

OECD. (2004). *Early Childhood Education and Care Policy: Canada Country Note.* Geneva: Author.

OECD. (2006). *Starting Strong: Early Childhood Education and Care.* Geneva: Author.

Office of Consumer Affairs. (2008). About Us. Retrieved 27 Feb. 2008 from http://consumerinformation.ca/app/oca/ccig/html.do?page=aboutUsandlanguage=eng.

Ontario Coalition of Better Childcare. (1989). *Discussion Paper: Fall Policy Forum*. Toronto: Author.

Ontario Literacy Coalition (OLC). (2008). Who We Are. Retrieved 24 July 2008 from http://www.on.literacy.ca/who/intro.htm.

Ontario Peer Development Initiative. (2006). Our History. Retrieved 27 Feb. 2008 from http://opdi.org/knowledge-exchange/reports.php.

Ontario Peer Development Initiative (OPDI). (2007). *Consumer/Survivor Initiatives: Impact, Outcomes and Effectiveness.* Toronto: Author.

Ontario Worker Co-op Federation (OWCF). (2008). The Process. Retrieved 26 July 2008 from http://www.ontarioworker.coop/decision_making.htm.

Options for Homes. (2008). About Options. Retrieved 27 Feb. 2008 from http://www.optionsforhomes.ca/content.php?parentID=31.

Ornstein, M. (2000). *Ethno-racial Inequality in Toronto: Analysis of the 1996 Census.* Toronto: York University, Institute for Social Science Research.

Osoyoos Indian Band. (2008). Osoyoos Indian Band Development Corporation. Retrieved 27 Feb. 2008 from http://www.oibdc.com/.

Owen, D., and Swift, T. (2001). Introduction: Social accounting, reporting and auditing: Beyond the rhetoric? *Business Ethics: A European Review* 10(1): 4–8.

Owen, R. (1969 [1813]). *A New View of Society*. Harmondsworth: Penguin.

Pan Canadian Community Futures Group. (2007). About Us. Retrieved 27 Feb. 2008 from http://www.communityfutures.ca/home/index-eng.html.

Parent, T. (2008) Pierre Barnoti Ousted as SPCE Executive Director. Retrieved 23 July 2008 from http://www.cjad.com/node/760100.

Parkinson, C., and Howorth, C. (2008). The language of social entrepreneurs. *Entrepreneurship and Regional Development* 20: 285–309.

PARO Centre for Women's Enterprise. (2008). About Us. Retrieved 27 Feb. 2008 from http://www.paro.ca/aboutparo.html/.

Part du Chef. (2007). Historique. Retrieved 27 Feb. 2008 from http://www.projetspart.ca/1_projetspart.php.

Peredo, A.M., and Chrisman, J. (2006). Toward a theory of community-based enterprise. *Academy of Management Review* 31(2): 309–28.

Peredo, A.M., and MacLean, M. (2008). Social entrepreneurship: A critical review of the concept. *Journal of World Business* 41: 56–65.

Perry, S. (1987). *Communities on the Way*. Ithaca: SUNY Press.

Perry, S. (1994). The Cape Breton Laborers Development Company: A case report. In S. Perry and M. Lewis (Eds.), *Reinventing the Local Economy: What 10 Canadian Initiatives Can Teach Us about Building Creative, Inclusive, and Sustainable Communities,* 21–9. Vernon, B.C.: Centre for Community Enterprise.

Pestoff, V.A. (1998) *Between Market and State: Social Enterprise and Civil Democracy in a Welfare Society*. Ashgate: Aldershot.

Philanthropic Foundations Canada. (2008). Foundations in Canada. Retrieved 30 Dec. 2008 from http://www.pfc.ca/cms_en/page1087.cfm.

Phillips, P. (1982). *Regional Disparities*. Toronto: Lorimer.

Plumtree, T., and Laskin, B. (2003). *From Jeans to Jackets: Navigating the Transition to More Systematic Governance in the Voluntary Sector.* Ottawa: Institute on Governance.

Pointe St-Charles. (2007). Archives populaires de Pointe-St-Charles. Retrieved 7June 2008 from http://www.museevirtuel.ca/pm.php?id=story_line andlg=Francaisandfl=0andex=297andsl=6411 andpos=1.

Polanyi, K. (1957). The economy as instituted process. In K. Polanyi, C. Arensberg, and H. Pearson (Eds.), *Trade and Market in the Early Empires,* 243–70. New York: Free Press.

Porter, J. (1965). *The Vertical Mosaic: An Analysis of Social Class and Power in Canada*. Toronto: University of Toronto Press.

Potter, B. (1904). *Co-operative Movement in Great Britain*. London: Swan Sonnenschein.

Prashad, S. (2007, 22 April,) Good green goals. *Toronto Star* A12.

Prince, M.J. (1998). Holes in the safety net, leaks in the roof: Changes in Canadian welfare policy and their implications for social housing programs. *Housing Policy Debate* 9(4): 825–48.

Prochner, L. (2000). A history of early childhood education in Canada: 1820–1966. In L. Prochner and N. Howe (Eds.), *Early Childhood Education and Care in Canada,* 11–65). Vancouver: UBC Press.

Putnam, R. (1993). *Making Democracy Work: Civic Traditions in Modern Italy.* Princeton: Princeton University Press.

Putnam, R. (1995). Bowling alone: America's declining social capital. *Journal of Democracy* 6(1): 65–78.

Putnam, R. (1996). *The Decline of Civil Society: How Come? So What?* Ottawa: John L. Manion Lecture.

Putnam, R. (2000). *Bowling Alone: The Collapse and Revival of American Community*. New York: Simon and Schuster.

Quebec Federation of Labour (QFL). (2007a). Welcome to a Different Kind of

Partnership. Retrieved 25 Aug. 2008 from http://www.fondsftq.com/internetfonds.nsf/vWebTAN/PmeAcc.

Quebec Federation of Labour (QFL). (2007b). Solidarity Fund QFL Invests a Record $665 Million in Québec Companies. Retrieved 25 Aug. 2008 from http://www.fondsftq.com/internetfonds.nsf/FMsgPopAN?openformandunid=7FA2B521BE7167 C285257378007058D0.

Quebec Federation of Labour (QFL). (2008). About the Fund. Retrieved 25 Aug. 2008 from http://www.fondsftq.com/internetfonds.nsf/VWebTAN/AprAcc.

Quarter, J. (1995). *Crossing the Line: Unionized Employees and Investment Funds*. Toronto: Lorimer.

Quarter, J. (2000). *Beyond the Bottom Line: Socially Innovative Business Owners*. Westport: Greenwood/Quorum.

Quarter, J., Carmichael, I. and Ryan, S. (2008). Socially responsible investment of pensions: Issues and debates. In J. Quarter, I. Carmichael, and S. Ryan (Eds.), *Pensions at Work: Socially Responsible Investment of Union-Based Pension Funds*, 3–41. Toronto: University of Toronto Press.

Quarter, J., Carmichael, I., and Ryan, S. (Eds.). (2008). *Pensions at Work: Socially Responsible Investment of Union-Based Pension Funds*. Toronto: University of Toronto Press.

Quarter, J., Mook, L., and Richmond, B.J. (2003). *What Counts: Social Accounting for Nonprofits and Cooperatives*. Upper Saddle River, NJ: Prentice-Hall.

Quint Development Corporation. (2007a). About Us. Retrieved 15 May 2008 from http://www.quintsaskatoon.ca/aboutquint.html.

Quint Development Corporation. (2007b). *2006 Annual Report*. Saskatoon: Author.

Rachlis, M., and Kushner, C. (1989). *Second Opinion: What's Wrong with Canada's Healthcare System and How to Fix It*. Toronto: HarperCollins.

Rao, R. (2008, 14 Dec.). Poverty's new saviour. *Business Today*. Retrieved 30 Dec. 2008 from http://businesstoday.digitaltoday.in/index.php?option =com_contentandtask=viewandissueid=44a ndid=8866andsectionid=5and Itemid=1.

RDI. (2005). *The Co-operative Movement: A Historical Overview and Relevance to Northern and Aboriginal Communities.* Working Paper #2005-1. Retrieved 15 May 2009 from http://www.brandonu.ca/RDI/Publications/Joint-CoopDevProj/A_HistoricalOverview-WorkingPaper2005-1.pdf.

Real Women of Canada. (2008). About Us. Retrieved April 7, 2008 from http://www.realwomenca.com/about.htm.

Reitz, J. (2001). *Immigrant Skill Utilization in the Canadian Labour Market: Implications for Human Capital Research*. Toronto: University of Toronto, Centre for Industrial Relations.

Richmond, B.J., and Mook, L. (2001). *Social Audit for WCRI*. Toronto, Ontario, Canada: Author.

Richmond, B.J. (1999). Counting on each other: A social audit model to assess the impact of nonprofit organizations. Unpublished Ph.D. diss., University of Toronto.

Robèrt, K.-H. (2000). Tools and concepts for sustainable development: How do they relate to a general framework for sustainable development and to each other? *Journal of Cleaner Production* 8: 243–54.

Roberts, B., and Cohen, M. (2002). Enhancing sustainable development by triple value adding to the core business of government. *Economic Development Quarterly* 16(2): 127–37.

Robinson, D., and Coward, S. (2003). *Hidden Homelessness: Your Place, Not Mine*. London: Crisis and the Countryside Agency.

Roman, R., Hayibor, S., and Agle, B.R. (1999) The relationship between social and financial performance. *Business and Society* 38(1): 109–25.

Rose, A. (1980). *Canadian Housing Policies, 1935–1980*. Toronto: Butterworths.

Rosen, M.J. (2002). Who Should Regulate Non-profits? Retrieved 22 July 2008 from http://www.afpnet.org/ka/ka-3.cfm?folder_id=1765andcontent_item_id=5663.

Roslender, R., and Dillard, J.F. (2003). Reflections on the interdisciplinary perspectives on accounting project. *Critical Perspectives on Accounting* 14(3): 325–51.

Ross, D. (1994). *How to Estimate the Economic Contribution of Volunteer Work*. Ottawa: Department of Canadian Heritage.

Rotary Club. (2008). Programs of the Rotary. Retrieved 7 April 2008 from http://www.rotary.org/en/AboutUs/RotaryInternational/Programs/Pages/ridefault.asp.

Rothschild-Whitt, J. (1982). The collective organization: An alternative to bureaucratic models. In F. Lindenfeld and J. Rothschild Whitt (Eds.), *Workplace Democracy and Social Change*, 23–49. Boston: Porter Sargent.

Royal Canadian Legion. (2008). Dominion Command. Retrieved 7 April 2008 from http://legion.ca/asp/docs/about/org_e.asp.

Ryan, S. (2005). Don't trust anyone outside your pack: Initial trust formation in an online social activist network. In M. Consalvo and M. Allen (Eds.), *AoIR Internet Research Annual 2*, 95–105. New York: Peter Lang.

Ryan, S. (2007). Trust and participation in Usenet health support communities. Paper presented at the Association of Internet Researchers, Internet Research 8.0 – Let's Play, Vancouver, 17–20 Oct.

SAAS. (2008). Certified Facilities List. Retrieved 26 Aug. 2008 from http://www.saasaccreditation.org/certfacilitieslist.htm.

Sachs, W., Loske, R., and Linz, M. (1998). *Greening the North: A Postindustrial Blueprint for Ecology and Equity.* London: Zed Books.
Sage Centre. (2008). About Us. Retrieved 7 May 2008 from http://www.sage-centre.org/about.php.
Salamon, L. (1987). Partners in public service: The scope and theory of government-nonprofit relations. In W.W. Powell (Ed.), *The Nonprofit Sector: A Research Handbook,* 99–117. New Haven: Yale University Press.
Salamon, L. (1995). *Partners in Public Service: Government-Nonprofit Relations in the Modern Welfare State.* Baltimore: Johns Hopkins University Press.
Salamon, L., and Anheier, H.K. (1997). *Defining the Nonprofit Sector: A Cross-National Analysis.* Manchester: Manchester University Press.
Salamon, L., Anheier, H., List, R., Toepler, S., Sokolowski, S.W., and Associates. (1999). *Global Civil Society: Dimensions of the Nonprofit Sector.* Baltimore: Johns Hopkins University Press.
Salvation Army. (2008). Programs and Services. Retrieved 1 June 2008 from http://www.salvationarmy.ca/services.
Saskatchewan Native Theatre Company. (2007). Performing Arts Outreach Programming. Retrieved 1 June 2008 from http://sntc.ca/Programs/Outreach.shtml.
Savers (2007). About us. Retrieved 22 April 2008 from http://www.savers.com/aboutus/aboutus.php.
Schumacher, E.F. (1973). *Small Is Beautiful.* New York: Harper and Row.
Schwab Foundation for Social Entrepreneurship. (2008). *What Is Social Entrepreneurship?* Retrieved 9 June 2008 from http://www.schwabfound.org/whatis.htm.
Science Daily. (2005). Chemical Used in Food Containers Disrupts Brain Development. Retrieved 20 July 2008 from http://www.sciencedaily.com/releases/2005/12/051203123328.htm.
Scotsburn. (2008). About Us. Retrieved 9 June 2008 from http://www.scotsburn.com/.
Scott, P., and McGhee, I. (2008). The CSR Assurance Statement Report. Retrieved 26 Aug. 2008 from http://www.corporateregister.com/pdf/AssureView.pdf.
SEED Winnipeg. (2007). The Social Purchasing Portal. Retrieved 9 June 2008 from http://www.sppwinnipeg.org/.
SEED Winnipeg. (2008). Annual Report, 2007–08. Retrieved 14 December 2008 from http://www.seedwinnipeg.ca/documents/SEEDWinnipegAnnualReport2007-2008.pdf.
Seidler, L. (1973). Dollar values in the social income statement. In A. Belkaoui, *Socio-economic accounting,* 167. Westport: Quorum Books.

Self-help Connection Clearinghouse Association. (2008). Home. Retrieved 9 June 2008 from http://www.selfhelpconnection.ca/.

Seligman, A. (1998). Between public and private: Towards a sociology of civil society. In R. Hefner (Ed.), *Democratic Civility*, 79–111. New Brunswick, NJ: Transaction.

Seventh Step. (2008). Self-help Core Groups. Retrieved 5 July 2008 from http://www.7thstep.ca/shcgroups.html.

SGRI. (2007). The GRI's Sustainability Report July 2004 – June 2007. Retrieved 26 Aug. 2008 from http://www.globalreporting.org/NR/rdonlyres/43127B6A-3816-406C-897F-AC572E0EAB2D/0/GRI_SR_20042007.pdf.

Shakya, Y., and Rankin, K. (2008). The politics of subversion in development practice: An exploration of microfinance in Nepal and Vietnam. *Journal of Development Studies* 44(8): 1214–35.

Sharpe, D. (1994). *A Portrait of Canada's Charities*. Toronto: Canadian Centre for Philanthropy.

Shiva, V. (1989). *Staying Alive: Women, Ecology and Development*. London: Zed Books.

Shragge, E., and Fontan, J.-M. (Eds.). (2000). Introduction. In E. Shragge and Fontan, J.-M. (Eds.), *Social Economy: International Debates and Perspectives*, 1–21. Montreal: Black Rose.

Shriners. (2008). Shriners of North America. Retrieved 1 Aug. 2008 from http://www.shriners.com/Shrine/.

Sick Kids Foundation. (2008). Believe. Retrieved 29 July 2008 from www.sickkidsfoundation.com/believe/caitlin.asp#.

SickKids. (2008). About HSC. Retrieved 29 July 2008 from www.sickkids.ca/AboutHSC/section.asp?s=History+and+Milestonesand-sID=11889andss=SickK ids+HistoryandssID=211 and www.sickkids.ca/AboutHSC/section.asp?s=History+and+Milestonesand-sID=11889andss=Milest onesandssID=488andsss=2001+%2D+Presen-tandsssID=495.

SickKids. (2008). Family Information. Retrieved 29 July 2008 from www.sickkids.ca/FamilyInformation/section.asp?s=EmergencyandsID=7388andss=Welcome+to +EmergencyandssID=7389.

Sierra Club. (2008). Sierra Club History. Retrieved 1 Aug. 2008 from http://www.sierraclub.org/history/timeline.asp.

Sillanpää, M. (1998). The Body Shop values report: Towards integrated stakeholder auditing. *Journal of Business Ethics* 17(13): 1443–56.

Singh, R. (2008) Personal communication, 29 July.

Skocpol, T. (1999). Advocates without members: The recent transformation of

American life. In T. Skocpol and M. Fiorina (Eds.), *Civic Engagement in American Democracy*, 461–509. Washington, DC: Brookings Institute Press.

Smith, D.H. (1997). The rest of the nonprofit sector: Grassroots associations as the dark matter ignored in the prevailing 'flat earth' maps of the sector. *Nonprofit and Voluntary Sector Quarterly* 26(2): 114–31.

Smith, S.R., and Lipsky, M. (1993). *Non-profits for Hire: The Welfare State in the Age of Contracting*. Cambridge, MA: Harvard University Press.

Social Accountability International (SAI). (n.d.). Overview of SA8000. Retrieved 26 Aug. 2008 from http://www.sa-intl.org/index.cfm?fuseaction=Page.viewPageandpageld=473.

Social Capital Partners. (n.d.). *History and Archives*. Retrieved 25 Aug. 2008 from http://www.socialcapitalpartners.ca/history_archives_concept.asp.

Social Enterprise Data Base. (2007). *SE Organizations in Canada*. Retrieved 1 Aug. 2008 from http://www.dtes.ca/embers/Enterprise%20Resource%20LIbrary%20online%20(student%20proj) /Models/ModelsCanada.htm.

Social Enterprise Fund. (n.d.) About Us. Retrieved 25 Aug. 2008 from http://socialenterprisefund.ca/about/?PHPSESSID=e5ca5753e2a2b559a24340208fa2fc2f.

Social Investment Organization (SIO). (2007). Canadian socially responsible investment review 2006: A comprehensive survey of socially responsible investment in Canada. Retrieved 25 Aug. 2008 from http://www.socialinvestment.ca/documents/SRIReview.pdf.

Social Investment Organization and Riverdale Community Development Corp. (SIO and RCDC). (2003). *A National Study of Community Investment in Canada, Final Report*. Retrieved 25 Aug. 2008 from http://www.socialinvestment.ca/Final_Community_Investment_Study_Reportff.doc.

Social Purchasing Portal (SPP). (2007a). About Us. Retrieved 1 Aug. 2008 from http://www.sppwinnipeg.org/#what.

Social Purchasing Portal (SPP). (2007b). *Social Purchasing Portal Newsletter* (Fall): 2,4.

Social Purchasing Portal (SPP). (2008). Social Purchasing Portal. Retrieved 1 Aug. 2008 from www.enterprisingnonprofits.ca/spp/.

Sousa, J. (2006). Building a Co-operative Community: The Conversion of Alexandra Park to Atkinson Housing Co-operative. Unpublished Ph.D. diss., University of Toronto.

Sousa, J., and Quarter, J. (2003). The convergence of nonmarket housing models in Canada. *Housing Policy Debate* 14(4): 559–88.

Sousa, J., and Quarter, J. (2005). Atkinson Housing Co-operative: A leading edge conversion from public housing. *Housing Studies* 20(3): 423–39.

SPCA Montréal (2008). *Give Animals a Chance.* Retrieved 24 July 2008 from http://www.spcamontreal.com/apropos1.php?lg=en.

Spear, R. (2004). Governance in democratic member-based organisations. *Annals of Public and Cooperative Economics* 75(1): 33–59.

Spear, R. (forthcoming). The social economy in Europe: Trends and challenges. In L. Mook, J. Quarter, and S. Ryan (Eds.), *Researching the Social Economy.*

Sport Canada. (2008). *Fact Sheet: Reconnecting Government with Youth.* 2003. Retrieved 1 May 2008 from http://www.pch.gc.ca/progs/sc/info-fact/youth_e.cfm.

St John Canada. (2008). History. Retrieved 1 May 2008 from http://www.sja.ca/?cid=276d79c64f9041b885e3b54f62fbccf2ContentCategoryand mainContent= 31e2d0c401fc4687b214d5cff364214dContentCategory.

Statistics Canada. (2000). *Canadian Culture in Perspective: A Statistical Overview.* Ottawa: Ministry of Industry.

Statistics Canada. (2001). *Overview: Canada still Predominantly Roman Catholic and Protestant.* Ottawa. Retrieved 12 June 2008 from http://www12.statcan.ca/english/census01/Products/Analytic/companion/rel/canada.cfm.

Statistics Canada. (2004a). Performing arts: 2003. *The Daily,* 15 Dec.

Statistics Canada. (2004b). Study: The union movement in transition. Ottawa. *The Daily,* 31 Aug.

Statistics Canada. (2005). Population by selected ethnic origins, by province and territory. (2001 Census). Retrieved 10 July 2008 from http://www40.statcan.ca/l01/cst01/demo26a.htm.

Statistics Canada. (2006a). Canada's nonprofit sector in macro-economic terms. Satellite account of Nonprofit institutions and volunteering. 13-015-XWE.

Statistics Canada. (2006b). *Women in Canada, 5th Edition: A Gender-Based Statistical Report.* Ottawa: Author.

Statistics Canada. (2006c). General Social Survey: Paid and unpaid work. *The Daily,* 19 July.

Statistics Canada. (2006d). Performing arts survey. *The Daily,* 25 July.

Statistics Canada. (2007a). *Universities and Colleges Revenue and Expenditures, by Province and Territory.* Ottawa: Author.

Statistics Canada. (2007b). Performing arts: 2005. *The Daily,* 18 April.

Status of Women. (1986). *Report of the National Task Force on Child Care.* Ottawa: Minister of Supply and Services.

Stephen Lewis Foundation. (2008). Grandmothers' campaign. *Grassroots* (Winter): 12–13.

Stoeker, R. (2005). Is community informatics good for communities? Questions confronting an emerging field. *Journal of Community Informatics* 1(3): 13–26.

Sumner, J. (2005). *Sustainability and the Civil Commons: Rural Communities in the Age of Globalization*. Toronto: University of Toronto Press.

Sustainability Solutions Group (SSG). (2007). *2007* Sustainability Assessment. Retrieved 26 Aug. 2008 from http://www.sustainabilitysolutions.ca/downloads/SSGsustainability2007.pdf.

Suzuki, D. (2007). *Vancity Video Announcement*. Retrieved 26 Aug. 2008 from https://www.vancity.com/SharedContent/video/vancity_carbon_neutral.wmv.

TakingITGlobal (2008). About Us. Retrieved 25 July 2008 from http://www.takingitglobal.org/home.html.

Taylor, M. (1978). *Health Insurance and Canadian Public Policy: The Seven Decisions that Created the Canadian Health Insurance System*. Montreal: McGill-Queen's University Press.

TD Economics Special Report. (2007). Update to the 2002 TD Special Economics Report on the Greater Toronto Area (GTA) Economy. Toronto: Author. Retrieved 8 Sept. from http://unitedwaytoronto.com/whoWeHelp/reports/pdf/2007-TD-gta-update.pdf.

Tencati, A., and Zsolnai, L. (2009). The collaborative enterprise. *Journal of Business Ethics* 85(3): 367–376.

Tetley, A. (2007). Personal communication, 25 May.

Thurow, L. (1996). *The Future of Capitalism: How Today's Economic Forces Shape Tomorrow's World*. New York: Morrow.

Tides Canada. (2006). Annual Report 2006. Accessed 25 Aug. 2008 from http://tidescanada.org/pages/ar2006/ar2006.pdf.

Tides Canada. (n.d.). Investing Responsibly. Retrieved 25 Aug. 2008 from http://tidescanada.org/about/investing-responsibly/.

Tinker, A.M., Merino, B.D., and Neimark, M.D. (1982). The normative origins of positive theories: Ideology and accounting thought. *Accounting, Organizations and Society* 7(2): 167–200.

Tinker, T. (1985). *Paper Prophets: A Social Critique of Accounting*. New York: Praeger.

Tinker, T. (2005). The withering of criticism: A review of professional, Foucauldian, ethnographic, and epistemic studies in accounting. *Accounting, Auditing and Accountability Journal* 18(1): 100–35.

TNS. (2006). The Natural Step. History. Retrieved 26 Aug. 2008 from http://www.naturalstep.ca/history.html.

Tocqueville, A. de. (1969). *Democracy in America*. Garden City: Doubleday Anchor Books.

Toronto the Better. (2008). About Us. Retrieved 25 July 2008 from http://www.torontothebetter.net/home.html.

Trainor, J., and Tremblay, J. (1992). Consumer/survivor businesses in Ontario challenging the rehabilitation model. *Canadian Journal of Community Mental Health* 11(2): 65–72.

Trainor, J., Pape, B., and Pomeroy, E. (1997). Critical challenges for Canadian mental health policy. *Canadian Review of Social Policy* 39 (Spring): 55–64.

TravelCuts. (2007). *Programmes.* Retrieved 10 July 2008 from http://www.cfs-fcee.ca/html/english/programmes/Travel_CUTS.php.

Trevisan, M. (2008, 28 July). Social networking for social change. *Globe and Mail,* B5.

Trillium Foundation. (2003). Economic Impacts of 97 Festivals and Events. Retrieved 30 Dec. 2008 from http://www.trilliumfoundation.org/User/Docs/OTF-English_downloads/files/research/festivals_ontario_overall_impact.pdf.

TSA Consultancy Ltd. (2003). Social Finance in Ireland: What It Is and Where It's Going, with Recommendations for Its Future Development. Retrieved 25 Aug. 2008 from http://www.dublinpact.ie/pdfs/social_finance.pdf.

United Church of Canada Foundation. (2001). Appendix A – Social and Environmental Screening Criteria. Retrieved 25 Aug. 2008 from http://www.unitedchurchfoundation.ca/PDFs/sri_policy.pdf.

United Church of Canada Foundation. (2008). 2007 Annual Report. Retrieved 25 Aug. 2008 from http://www.unitedchurchfoundation.ca/PDFs/UCCF_AR_2008_Web.pdf.

United Way Toronto. (2002). *Decade of Decline.* Toronto: Author.

United Way Toronto. (2004). *Poverty by Postal Code.* Toronto: Author.

United Way Toronto. (2005). *Strong Neighbourhoods: A Call to Action.* Toronto: Author.

United Way of Canada. (2008). Importance of Board Governance. Retrieved 22 July 2008 from http://www.boarddevelopment.org/importance.cfm.

United We Can Bottle Depot. (2007). About Us. Retrieved 10 July 2008 from http://newcity.ca/Pages/united_wecan.html.

University of Toronto. (2008). Student Affairs. Retrieved 10 July 2008 from http://www.sa.utoronto.ca/groups.php?waid=2andglid=21.

van Dyk, N. (1995). Financing social housing in Canada. *Housing Policy Debate* 6(4): 815–48.

Vancity. (2007). VanCity Expect Growing Interest in Socially Responsible Investing. Retrieved 10 July 2008 from http://www.cucentral.ca/Vancity.

Vancity. (2008a). Community Business Loans. Retrieved 25 Aug. 2008 from https://www.vancity.com/MyBusiness/BusinessFinancing/Community-BusinessLoan/.

Vancity. (2008b). About Us. Retrieved 26 Aug. 2008 from https://www.vancity.com/MyCommunity/AboutUs/.

Vancity. (2008c). *Greenhouse Gas Emissions Handbook,* vol. 1.1. Retrieved 26 Aug. 2008 from https://www.vancity.com/SharedContent/documents/Community/emissions_inventory.pdf.

Vancouver Food Providers' Coalition. (2008). Welcome. Retrieved 10 July 2008 from http://cln.vcn.bc.ca/welcome.

Vancouver Foundation. (n.d.). About Us. Retrieved 25 Aug. 2008 from http://www.vancouverfoundation.bc.ca/about/index.htm.

VANOC. (2008). Sustainability Report 2006–07. Retrieved 26 Aug. 2008 from http://www.vancouver2010.com/resources/PDFs/Sustainability/06_07/SustainabilityRepo rt_English.pdf.

Vartana. (n.d.) About Us. Retrieved 25 Aug. 2008 from http://www.vartana.org/aboutUs.htm.

Victoria Hospice. (2006). *Report to the Community.* Victoria: Author.

Victorian Order of Nurses (VON). (2007). *History.* Retrieved July 10, 2008 from http://www.von.ca/about_history.html.

Voluntary Sector Initiative (VSI). (2002a). *A Code of Good Practice on Funding: Building on an Accord between the Government of Canada and the Voluntary Sector.* Ottawa: Author.

Voluntary Sector Initiative (VSI). (2002b). *Code of Good Practice on Policy Dialogue: Building on an an Accord between the Government of Canada and the Voluntary Sector.* Ottawa: Author.

Waddock, S. (2000). The multiple bottom lines of corporate citizenship: Social investing, reputation, and responsibility audits. *Business and Society Review* 105(3): 323–45.

Waldie, P. (2004, 31 Mar.). Charity bank has currency. *Globe and Mail,* B1. Retrieved 25 Aug. 2008 from http://www.vartana.org/news-globeAnd-Mail.htm.

Walloon Council of the Social Market Economy. (2008). Mission. Retrieved 29 July 2008 from http://translate.google.com/translate?hl=enandsl=fr_and u=http://guide.wallonie.be/jsp/guide/pgShowGuide5.jsp%3Fpath %3Daap-CESRW-02andsa=Xandoi=translateandresnum=1andct=resultand prev=/search%3Fq%3DConseil%2BWal lon%2Bde%2Bl%25E2%2580 %2599%25C3%25A9conomie%2Bsociale%26hl%3Den%26rls% 3DGGLG,GGLG:2005-25,GGLG:en. (accessed 13 July 2008).

Waring, M. (1996). *Three Masquerades: Essays on Equality, Work and Human Rights.* Toronto: University of Toronto Press.

Waring, M. (1999). *Counting for Nothing: What Men Value and What Women Are Worth*. Toronto: University of Toronto Press.

Web Networks. (2008). About Us. Retrieved 31 July 2008 from http://services.web.ca/index.html.

Webb, S., and Webb, B. (1920). *Problems of modern industry*. New York: Longmans, Green.

Webb, S., and Webb, B. (1921). *The Consumers' Co-operative Movement*. London: Longmans, Green.

Weerwardena, J., and Mort, G.S. (2006). Investigating social entrepreneurship: A multidimensional model. *Journal of World Business* 41: 21–35.

Wei-Skillern, J., and Marciano, S. (2008) The networked nonprofit. *Stanford Social Innovation Review* 6(2): 38–43.

Wellman, B., and Gulia, M. (1999). Net surfers don't ride alone. In B. Wellman (Ed.), *Networks in the Global Village*, 331–66). Boulder: Westview.

Welton, M. (2001). *Little Mosie from the Margaree: A Biography of Moses Michael Coady*. Toronto: Thompson.

Wemindji. (2008). Economic Development. Retrieved 31 July 2008 from http://www.wemindji-nation.qc.ca/economic_development.html.

West Baffin Eskimo Co-operative. (2003). Sharing Culture. *New Sector* 54 (Feb.–Mar.): 10–11.

Wheeler, D., and Sillanpää, M. (2000). *The Stakeholder Corporation*. Southport: Pitman.

Whyte, W.F., and Whyte, K. (1988). *Making Mondragon*. Ithaca: ILR Press.

Wigle, R. (2001). *Sectoral Impacts of Kyoto Compliance*. Ottawa: Industry Canada.

Wikipedia. (2008). About Wikipedia. http://en.wikipedia.org/wiki/Wikipedia: About#Wikipedia_history.

Wilkinson, P., and Quarter, J. (1996). *Building a Community-Controlled Economy: The Evangeline Co-operative Experience*. Toronto: University of Toronto Press.

Wolfe, N. Weisbrod, B., and Bird, E. (1993). The supply of volunteer labor: The case of hospitals. *Nonprofit Management and Leadership* 4(1): 23–45.

Working Opportunity Fund. (2007). Simplified Prospectus. Retrieved 25 Aug. 2008 from http://www.growthworks.ca/files/advisors/wof/WOF_Final__Prospectus.pdf.

World Commission on Environment and Development (WCED). (1987). *Our Common Future*. New York: Oxford University Press.

World Wildlife Federation. (2008). About WWF. Retrieved 15 March 2008 from http://www.worldwildlife.org/about/.

Wyly, E.K., and Hammel, D.J. (2001). Gentrification, housing policy, and the new context of urban redevelopment. In K. Fox-Gotham (Ed.), *Critical Perspectives on Urban Redevelopment*, vol. 6, 211–76. London: Elsevier Science.

Yahoo!Groups. (2008). Directory: Health and Wellness. Retrieved 15 March 2008 from http://health.dir.groups.yahoo.com/dir/Health___Wellness/.

Yalnizyan, A. (2007). The rich and the rest of us: The changing face of the growing gap. Ottawa: Canadian Centre for Policy Alternatives. Retrieved 7 July 2008 from http://policyalternatives.ca/Reports/2007/03/ReportsStudies1565/index.cfm?pa=BB736455.

Yearbook of American and Canadian Churches. (2005). Canadian Denominations. Retrieved 7 July 2008 from http://www.electronicchurch.org/.

YMCA Canada. (2007). *Annual Report 2005.* Retrieved 7 July 2008 from http://www.ymca.ca/downloads/YMCA_Eng_AR-05.pdf.

Young, J. (1994). A divine mission: Elizabeth McMaster and the Hospital for Sick Children, 1875–92. *CBMH/BCHM* 11: 71–90.

Yunus, M. (2003). *Banker to the Poor: Micro-lending and the Battle against World Poverty*. New York: Public Affairs.

Yunus, M. (2007). *Creating a World without Poverty: Social Businesses and the Future of Capitalism*. New York: Public Affairs.

Zadek, S. (1998). Balancing performance, ethics, and accountability. *Journal of Business Ethics* 17: 1421–41.

Zarinpoush, F., and Hall, M.H. (2007). *Leadership Perspectives, Interviews with Leaders of Canada's Charities and Nonprofit Organizations*. Toronto: Imagine Canada.

Zarni. (2000). Resistance and cybercommunites: The Internet and the Free Burma Movement. In A. De Vaney, S. Gance, and Y. Ma (Eds.), *Technology and Resistance: Digital Communications and New Coalitions around the World*, 71–89. New York: Peter Lang.

Zeiss. (2007). Corporate Information. Retrieved 7 June 2008 from http://www.zeiss.de/C12567A100537AB9/allBySubject/FramedNews4.

Zerofootprint. (2008). About Us. Retrieved 14 July 2008 from http://zerofootprint.net/.

Zevi, A. (2007). The financing of cooperatives in Italy. *Annals of Public and Cooperative Economics* 61(2/3): 353–65.

Index

GOING OUT OF OUR MINDS: THE METAPHYSICS OF LIBERATION

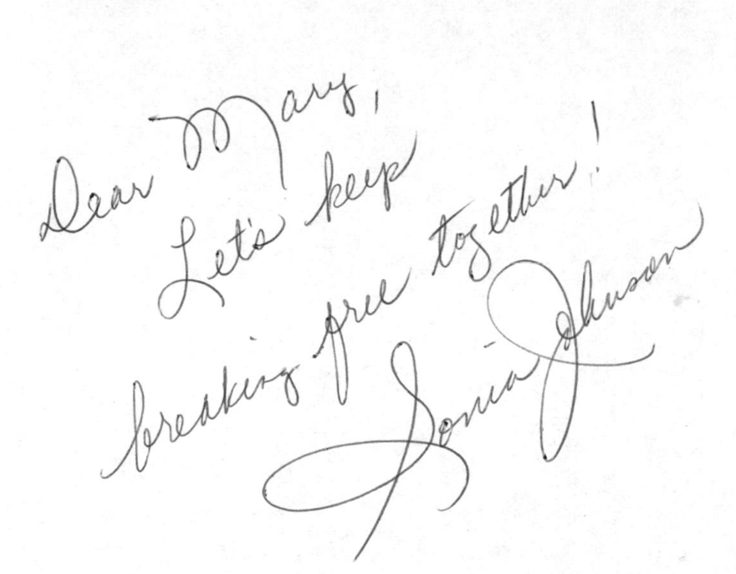